MEN AND IDEAS
History, the Middle Ages, the Renaissance

MEN AND IDEAS

History, the Middle Ages, the Renaissance

Essays by

Johan Huizinga

Translated by James S. Holmes and Hans van Marle

Princeton University Press, Princeton

Published by Princeton University Press, 41 William Street,
Princeton, New Jersey 08540
In the United Kingdom: Princeton University Press,
Guildford, Surrey
Copyright © 1959 by The Free Press, A Corporation

Introduction by Bert F. Hoselitz © Copyright 1959
by Meridian Books, Inc.

Translation © Copyright 1959 by Meridian Books, Inc.
Translated from texts in *Verzamelde Werken*
(1948-53), H. D. Tjeenk Willink & Zoon

First Princeton Paperback printing, 1984

LCC 84-42546
ISBN 0-691-00802-7
ISBN 0-691-05422-3 (pbk.)
Reprinted by arrangement with Meridian Books, Inc.

Clothbound editions of Princeton University Press books are printed
on acid-free paper, and binding materials are chosen for strength
and durability. Paperbacks, while satisfactory for personal collec-
tions, are not usually suitable for library rebinding.

Printed in the United States of America by Princeton
University Press
Princeton, New Jersey

Contents

MEN AND IDEAS

History, the Middle Ages, the Renaissance

INTRODUCTION by Bert F. Hoselitz

A look at a portrait of Johan Huizinga might lead one to think that he had been a successful Dutch lawyer or business man rather than one of the foremost innovators in history which this century has produced. His face is placid and open and has an air of ease and serenity. There is nothing intense about his features and though his expression reflects a thoughtful mind and moral force, it does not appear to be that of a man of quite uncommon creativity and imagination.

Huizinga's life was almost as commonplace as his outward appearance. He comes from a long line of steadfast Mennonite preachers. He was born on December 7, 1872, in Groningen, where his father was professor at the university. Huizinga obtained his doctor's degree there in May 1897, his studies having been mainly in the field of Indo-Aryan philology. After graduation from the university he secured a teaching position in history at a high school in Haarlem, where he remained eight years. Then he was called as professor of history to his alma mater and in 1915 he was appointed to the chair of general history and historical geography at the University of Leiden, the leading institution of higher learning in the Netherlands. He held this position until 1942, when the university was closed by the occupying authorities of Nazi Germany.

Throughout the first period of the German occupation Huizinga had maintained an intransigent attitude in favor of academic freedom and the rights of his fellow countrymen. He was therefore arrested and imprisoned in the concentration camp at St. Michielsgestel. Huizinga was then nearly seventy, suffering from poor eyesight, and as a consequence of the deprivations of German rule, from poor health in general.

9

Owing to a Swedish intervention on his behalf he was released from the concentration camp in October 1942, but he was not permitted to return to his home in Leiden. He was exiled to the small village De Steeg near Arnhem, where he produced his last works separated from his friends and pupils and deprived of his books. The last winter of the war, 1944-5, was especially hard. Holland suffered from an acute shortage of food, and De Steeg became for a time a spot in the front line. Early in 1945 Huizinga became ill, and died on February 1, without having lived to see what he had wished and worked for so intensely: the liberation of his beloved country.

The outline of Huizinga's life betrays nothing about the peculiar quality of his work or the nature of his contribution to history and social science. And even if we had included the many honors that he received in his lifetime and appended a list of his main works, they would have given only very scant indication of the flavor of his writings.

In 1933, two days before Hitler's ascent to power, Huizinga delivered a lecture in Berlin in which he discussed the position of the Netherlands as a cultural mediator between Central and Western Europe. In this lecture he tried to explain this intermediary position of Holland by its participation in two and perhaps three national cultures. Linguistically—and for a long time politically—Holland was a part of the Germanies. Its economic ties with the Hansa towns was strong, and in more recent times it formed a bridge between the industry of the Rhineland and overseas. But Holland also has close ties with France. Its membership in the Burgundian state, which was an offshoot of France, established close political ties with the French monarchy. In the sixteenth century Holland received many Huguenot refugees who settled there permanently. In the last decades of the old regime it was often visited by poets, artists, statesmen, philosophers, and scientists from France.

Holland's ties with Britain were more tenuous, but despite several wars between the two countries in the seventeenth century, Britons were prominent in Amsterdam as traders, visitors, and often residents. The Dutch were thus in an excellent position to absorb and integrate elements of several national cultures to fashion a civilization into which many of the best foreign elements—from Germany, France, Britain, and even Holland's former enemy, Spain—could find a place.

Huizinga's description of Holland's position as an intermediary forms an analogy to his own position in science. He was regarded as a historian of civilization. But his true position was that of a writer who in his own work represents a combination and integration of some of the best and most profound elements of history and social science. This is a reason why it is difficult to classify his work. It undoubtedly contains a strong ingredient derived from history. But many of his themes spill over into the realms of sociology, politics, psychology, and criticism of the arts in all their manifestations. But these various ingredients are blended into a uniform composition in which they all lose their separateness and form the seemingly indispensable parts of a well-rounded whole. Indeed, perhaps without consciously attempting it, Huizinga succeeds in mediating between a social-science and a humanistic approach, in selecting from each branch what fits best into his work, and in combining in this manner the aptest contributions each discipline has to offer.

In addition, his fine ear for language and the music of words, and his philological training, add a delicacy of expression and a new dimension of insight to his works, which make them not only unique achievements in social history but also works of art in their own right and great contributions to literature.

To be sure, in the various writings of Huizinga the particular mix of historical, sociological, and psychological elements varies. In some of his early essays on some aspects of the local history of Haarlem or Frisia, the historical element predominates. But although these essays are composed with the fullest and most exacting use of documentary materials, in the orthodox manner of historians, Huizinga betrays his meta-historical interests by the choice of his subject matter and the increasing emphasis on social interrelations. This tendency to go beyond history into the manifestations of the life of representative social groups becomes an ever growing facet of Huizinga's work, and his last major works, *In the Shadow of Tomorrow* and *Homo Ludens*, may be regarded as predominantly socio-psychological or socio-political studies drawing on a vast amount of historical erudition.

Huizinga's growing preoccupation with social and socio-psychological problems may be discerned in his successive major writings. His early studies on Dutch local history contained, as already pointed out, little besides orthodox historical materials. After his move to Groningen and even more after his appointment at Leiden, he becomes preoccupied with the social relations of the epochs he describes, with the state of mind of the persons who dominated a period and impressed upon it its character. Out of this framework grew Huizinga's most famous work, *The Waning of the Middle Ages*. But this is also the basis on which the bulk of his work of his most productive years is built. Huizinga was too well-schooled in methods of classical historiography to fail to realize that he was following an unorthodox path. He called his procedure "cultural history" and separated it, in this way, from the more conservative "general history." But more importantly, in helping to create a new discipline he had to define its central character, and in so doing he hit on a splendid simile. What the cultural historian aimed at was the creation of a portrait of an age or a society. *The Waning of the Middle Ages* may be likened to a vast canvas which, like the great altarpieces of the brothers Van Eyck, contains a prodigious variety of detail, and yet does not detract from the main central theme of the picture. They are all there in Hubert and Jan van Eyck's triptych at Ghent, the shepherds and the angels, the kings, and the philosophers, the fools and the burghers, the maidens and the clerics. And all of them are painted with a loving care for detail, with a painstaking effort to execute the most insignificant feature as carefully as the central focus of the work, the Lamb of God. Huizinga has borrowed this method from the great Flemish painters whose art dominated the period about which he wrote. In his work on the theory of cultural history Huizinga had explained that each culture develops its own expressive forms in terms of which it must be understood. And so in writing about the last flowering of Burgundian medieval civilization, he has adopted, perhaps unconsciously, the forms that resemble those of the greatest artists of that epoch.

But just as Van Eyck did not confine his art to large triptychs but also painted intimate portraits of bishops and potentates—and ordinary men and women of his time—so Huizinga found that he could interpret medieval civilization better if he supplemented his great book by a number of smaller essays. And from this feeling arose the pen portraits of some of the great figures of the Middle Ages and the

Renaissance, John of Salisbury, Joan of Arc, Abelard, Alain
de Lille, and above all, Erasmus of Rotterdam.

In the execution of these essays Huizinga became increasingly concerned with the problem of how to interpret and
evaluate critically the spirit of an age. In his work on the
outcome of medieval civilization in northwestern Europe he
had tried one approach. He was only too well aware that
Burckhardt in his *Civilization of the Renaissance in Italy*,
sixty years before *The Waning of the Middle Ages*, had
traveled a different road toward the understanding of the
spirit of an age. But whereas Burckhardt had found the
material for his study in the lives of the great, Huizinga
searched for it in the dreams and hopes, the laughter and the
tears, of the many small people of all social classes and
groups. And even in his biographies, in which perforce he
had to obtain his material from the deeds of the famous and
the wise, he tried to supply a backdrop of the everyday existence and the ordinary actions of the common people among
whom they lived.

It is perhaps no accident that the medieval personages whom
Huizinga selected for biographical treatment were almost all
prophets or poets—or a mixture of the two. Since poets and
prophets express the hopes and sentiments of their times more
freely than others, Huizinga could, by simply pursuing the
themes they develop, depict a wider vista of their culture than
if he had chosen the life histories of kings or warriors. And
since Huizinga knew that the truest expression of a culture
is found in some of the most starkly emotional utterances
of the personages who formed the intellectual elite of an age,
the lives of Abelard or Joan of Arc provide unusually apt
vehicles for a depiction of the civilization of the Middle Ages.

But Huizinga wrote essays on other than biographical subjects. In these essays the "hero" who holds the center of the
stage is not a person, but an institution, an idea, or a custom.
But the basic procedure here is the same as that which
Huizinga employs in his biographical essays. He describes
the background and environment in which an institution or
idea existed, and he traces its genesis and growth in its interaction with this background. He may select medieval chivalry
or the growth of sentiments of national consciousness in
Europe for his topic; in each case the result is an essay in
cultural history in which the special primary subject is seen

not as a thing in itself, but as an object that attains meaning and structure only by its interaction through time with the civilization of which it forms a part and in which it exists.

Huizinga's reputation as an artist in the history of culture is based primarily on his larger works, most notably on *The Waning of the Middle Ages.* But his full skill and versatility become even more apparent in his shorter essays. They are, like all of Huizinga's writings, masterpieces of integration, but by stressing sometimes individual psychological, sometimes methodological, and sometimes socio-historical factors, they provide, in their totality, the best insight into his genius.

PART I. *History*

THE TASK OF CULTURAL HISTORY •

In the theses that it requires to accompany a doctoral dissertation, Dutch law has retained a relic of an earlier era of learning. Posting and defending theses is an activity that belongs to the days of Abelard, the days of Luther. In the medieval university the thesis and the disputation were the natural media for formulating questions of scholarship. They fitted in that system as intellectual vehicles and in that sphere as spiritual forms. The medieval university was in the full sense of the word an arena, a palaestra, completely parallel to the lists of the tournaments. In it one played a serious and often dangerous game. The activities of the university, like those of knighthood, had the character either of a consecration and an initiation or of a contest, a challenge, and a conflict. Constant disputations in ceremonial forms constituted the life of the medieval university. Like the tournaments, they were one of the serious forms of social play out of which culture springs.

As techniques the thesis and the disputation answered perfectly to the structure of medieval thought and medieval

• *"De taak der cultuurgeschiedenis,"* an article based on a speech first given in 1926 to the general assembly of the Historical Association at Utrecht, and later presented as a lecture at the University of Zurich. First published in *Cultuurhistorische verkenningen* (Haarlem, 1929), 1-85. Translation from the Dutch text in *Verzamelde werken,* VII, 35-94.

17

society. Scholars fought with the weapon of syllogism. In its threefold construction it reflected, as it were, the triad of the lance, the shield, and the sword. The doctor and the bachelor, like the knight and the squire, carried noble, matched weapons. The thesis presupposes a well-defined and delimited system of thought, shared by both sides, within which every concept is precisely determined rationally—in other words, a scholastic system. It also presupposes a high degree of cultural conformity among the thinkers. There needs to be a code by means of which people understand one another. Everyone is assumed to have mastered the rules of the game and the art of sparring with formal logic. And finally, the thesis presupposes a certain degree of dogmatism, of rigidity in thinking, an absence of the awareness of a general interdependence and relativity of all our concepts and notions which is the constantly present characteristic of modern thought.

In the present day not a great deal remains of the cultural preconditions for a flourishing of the thesis. These preconditions were still maintained at the time of humanism and the Reformation, and they were even valid to some extent, though less so, in the days of the enlightened rationalism that in the Netherlands inspired the belated and rigid decree on higher education of 1815. They now no longer obtain, and as a result the thesis has become an antiquated medium, a goose quill in the hands of the typist. It retains its value as a pedagogical aid in mathematics, but for the rest its usefulness is limited to that of a convention in the academic ritual. In the nature of things it is more in place the more normative in character the discipline it serves. The less systematic a discipline is, the less use it has for the thesis. In dogmatic theology and in law it can perhaps be of good service now and then. Philology and linguistics have room for it on the fringe of their activities. The historian can easily get along without it. His conceptual world is much too fluid, his conclusions are much too loose, the configuration of his individual notions deviates too much from that of his neighbor for him to be able to catch them in the snare of a thesis or the nets of a syllogism.

Unless, perhaps, it is purely a question of criticism or methodology that is involved. There the form of the thesis, if not necessary, can nonetheless prove practical for history. One can propose a thesis regarding a question of genuineness or falsity, of priority, of derivation. Or regarding questions of the propriety or desirability of a certain method. Such questions, however, are basically not of history itself; they belong only in the forecourt of history.

The author who, after this prologue, attempts to arrange a group of reflections on cultural history under the headings of five theses must almost arouse the suspicion of vain bravura. It all seems like a new proof for the affinity of the doctor and the knight, who also liked to tread the lists with an old, rusty weapon or an unprotected arm. It is, in any case, not as a dogmatist that he enters. Or if one should prefer to justify the form that has been chosen as a hypermodern one, recognition should be given to the value of its concision and definiteness, its ability to attract attention, in brief its "headline" value.

I

The discipline of history is suffering from the defect that the issues are insufficiently formulated.

Anyone who has the habit of "keeping up" with several historical journals finds it hard to escape a feeling of discomfort now and then on glancing through the references to the flood of countless monographs, articles, and source publications that are being added to the material of history from month to month in every country. He sees the scholars of the whole world working their way further and further into the most minute details. Some letters of an insignificant diplomat in a small state here, the accounts of a pitiful monastery there—a stream of trivia. Each of these studies is a contribution to the historian's knowledge only to the extent that he is interested in the subject as a result of his own study. He hesitantly asks himself: How many minds does each of these countless, laborious products of historical thought reach? And the answer can only be: For each separate study only a few. If it were possible to collect statistics indicating how thoroughly and how widely everything printed is read and absorbed, or what the true ratio is of the labor spent on scholarly production and the intellectual consumption-value of the product as a whole, then we would often shudder. The attention devoted, expressed per page of print, the number of readers per month of research—can one imagine that the figures and graphs would be anything but appalling? If the parable of the seed fallen on stony ground gives us no consolation, then the question cannot be avoided: Is the labor expended by the machinery of scholarship not a hopeless waste of energy?

In the historical discipline, with its necessarily unsystematical character, currents in thought are constantly moving in divergent directions. Only a very few of all these studies seem to point back toward a central core of knowledge. Here the critical scholar voices his opposition, expressing the opinion that they do. Every monograph, he says, is a "preliminary study" for later integration. The material has still not been made sufficiently available, and there has still not been enough critical sifting. Before the major problems can be taken up a great deal more of the details will have to be determined. We are providing the building stones. We are the willing hewers of wood and drawers of water. But our doubts respond: you are creating an illusion of humble unselfishness for the sake of others' future profit. But when the master builder comes he will find most of the stones you have laid ready for him unusable. You are not hewing and chipping, but polishing and filing. And you are doing it because you are not strong enough for more vigorous labor.

Fortunately such an Ecclesiastes mood is not the last word of historical methodology. It is worth the trouble to visualize the actual life-process of a field of study as clearly as possible. Realists[1] that we are, it is hard for us to elude the notion that a discipline is realized somewhere in its entirety as a *Gebilde*, a "structure." Such a notion seems to prevail with regard to art, and why not with regard to scholarship as well? One can argue without exaggeration that the beauty and the essence of Gothicism are manifest in its chief products, and are realized in their entirety in the minds of quite a number of scholars, even if these have not visited every church. One involuntarily imagines something of this sort concerning the knowledge and the truth of a field of scholarship. I cannot judge to what extent such a concept would apply in a field such as physics. Perhaps it is conceivable that the knowledge of physics in its entirety can be contained in a single brain (which would not necessarily imply that that brain had a command over all the details of physics). Physics and history are natural subjects for comparison because each stands at a pole of the types of thinking obtaining in the sciences and in the humanities: the exact discipline par excellence and the inexact one par excellence. History's opposition to physics leads at once to the opinion that such a wealth of historical knowledge and understanding is in every respect inconceivable. The knowledge of history is always sheerly potential. Not only in the sense that no one knows the history of the world, or even the history of a great realm, in all its knowable details, but in the much more important sense that all historical knowledge of one and the same subject (it makes no difference whether that subject is called Leiden or Europe), has a different appearance in A's mind than in B's, even if both of them have read everything that is to be read. Even in A's head it appears different today from its appearance yesterday. Or rather it does not appear at all, it cannot take on a fixed form at any moment. It can never be more in a single mind than a memory from which images can be recalled. In actuality it exists only for the student who has identified it with what is in "the book."

To know the history of a country means in each particular instance to have so many live concepts at hand, to be so charged with knowledge of the past that one has grown conducive to new notions—that one reacts critically to them and is able to include them in one's conceptions, to assimilate them. In the person himself this situation creates the illusion that those concepts together form an "image." It can be that the conception of one aspect in the mind of one person has a higher cognitive value and even a more universal character than the concept of the whole in another's mind—one need not think in this respect of the scholar versus the schoolboy, but of two trained minds. There are wise historians among the amateurs of local history and dull gleaners of facts among the renowned professors of the universities.

This with regard to the "life" of a discipline in the individual mind. What does it mean when we think of that discipline as an objective spirit, an element in culture, when we speak not of what A or B knows, but of what "one" knows. To give an example, "one" knows nowadays that the Magna Charta was not a liberal constitution stemming from an enlightened and farseeing sense of political and civic responsibility. That is to say, the average cultured Englishman who went to school before 1900 probably does not know it yet. The average cultured foreigner knows only vaguely, if at all, what the term Magna Charta means. But in English education, thanks to the excellent way in which historical research and the teaching of history are being brought in touch with each other in recent years,[2] the more accurate view will now have replaced the traditional one. In this case, then, the subject "one" means in practice either a certain number of minds or the historical discipline considered as an entity. With that we are back to the antithesis nominalism and realism.

The metaphorical terms "scholarship recognizes," "scholarship has demonstrated," are of indispensable and vital value to us. Alongside our concept of the knowledge of the single individual we must also retain the concept of a dynamic magnitude called the discipline of history, which, despite the fact that it is nowhere and never realized in a human mind, nonetheless remains a coherent entity. Seen in this light, the amazing production working only in breadth and never in depth takes on a quite different appearance. It makes no difference whether a historical study is understood by ten thousand readers or by nine. It is quite unnecessary for each monograph to justify itself as a "preliminary study" for a later synthesis. An entity in the cosmos, it has within itself the same right to exist as every blackbird that sings and every cow that eats grass. The historical discipline is a cultural process, a function of the world, a paternal house with many mansions. Its specific subjects are innumerable, and each of them is known by only a few. But the spirit of each age determines anew a certain congruence, a harmony, a convergence in the results of research which only seem to diverge. In every intellectual period there is an actual homogeneity of historical thought, though that homogeneity is not realized in the brain of any one thinker. Manifesting itself in totally diverging knowledges of totally differing things, there is nonetheless a certain catholicity of learning, a *consensus omnium,* though one that admits an endless variety of knowledge and opinion. In every separate domain the results of diligent research aggregate into a like number of hearths of enriched learning. Not in the sense that the knowledge of details obtains its value only on the appearance of the man of synthesis who draws conclusions from it, but in the sense that the international exchange of scholarly products determines along which lines a newly defined concept of a certain historical subject shall be formed. For example, work is being done on the history of tithes in France, in Italy, in Germany, and elsewhere. A definite, accurate knowledge of the subject in general exists in reality for a few and in potentiality for everyone. What is actually meant when reference is made to "the present state of knowledge" regarding a certain subject? Let the subject be Metternich. No one knows everything contained in Heinrich von Srbik's *Metternich*, probably not even the writer himself, if knowing means retaining in one's mind or one's memory. Yet it could be said that this book, balanced by the comments of Srbik's adversaries, *represents* the momentary state of knowledge regarding the subject Metternich. From this it is immediately apparent how vague the significance of such an expression as "the state of knowledge" must necessarily remain.

If, then, one recognizes the existence of a discipline of history as an objective spirit, a form of understanding the world which exists only in the minds of countless persons taken together, and of which even the greatest scholar has, to speak in the language of the old mystics, received "only a spark," that leads to a heartening consequence. Such a recognition implies the rehabilitation of the antiquarian interest spurned disdainfully by Nietzsche as an inferior form of history. The direct, spontaneous, naïve zeal for antiquated things of earlier days which animates the dilettante of local history and the genealogist is not only a primary form of the urge to historical knowledge but also a full-bodied one. It is the impulse toward the past. A person thus impelled may want to understand only a small bit, an insignificant interrelationship out of the past, but the impulse can be just as deep and pure, just as gravid with true wisdom as in the person who wishes to encompass the heavens and the earth in his knowledge. And is not even the most humble labor enough for the pious man to serve his Lord?

Therefore it is not necessary for the researcher in details to justify the scholarly importance of his work with an appeal to its preparatory character. His true justification lies much deeper. He meets a vital need, he obeys a noble urge of the modern spirit. Whether his work yields tangible fruits for later research is, relatively, of secondary importance. In polishing one facet out of a billion he manifests the historical discipline of his day. He achieves the living contact of the mind with the old that was genuine and full of significance. Reverently handling the dead things of the past, he gradually realizes the value of small but vital truths, each of them as costly and as tender as a hothouse plant.

We seem now to have swung from an Ecclesiastes mood to a tone that is more optimistic than the negative content of our thesis would lead one to expect. So all's well with history, and every quack and historical plodder may look upon himself as a little arhat of the discipline. So it would be if everyone were wise, and if history were not a necessary of the schools as well as a necessary of life. Today every field of study is a gigantic national and international organization, quite aside from the value of the net product of its activities. And like every organization, it cannot escape the pressure of the system and the effect of the general process of mechanization, the result of our modern, perfected, all too smoothly functioning cultural media. Today the apparatus of historical study comprises not only universities with their system of seminars, examinations, and dissertations, but also academies of science, institutes and associations for the publication of source materials or the furthering of special historical studies, journals, educational publishers, congresses, committees of intellectual co-operation, and so forth. Each of these facilities wants to be and needs to be active, demands production, requires material. The new issue of the journal has to be filled, the publisher has to bring new books on the market, the publication institute has to forge ahead. The young historian must demonstrate his abilities in a dissertation and in articles, the older one must show that he is not napping. Summing all this up in its outward form as the apparatus of a discipline does no injustice to the sublimity or the fervent vitality of the aspiration impelling civilized man toward that discipline. An indomitable zest for knowledge is the foundation of all things, including the apparatus of a discipline. I am merely observing that the "business" of a discipline not only is based on the free intellectual labor of scholars; in order to make that labor possible a social vehicle is needed, one that works more impressively and compellingly the more the discipline is perfected. The mill is grinding and has to grind. What is it grinding?

The activities of the historian consist for an important part in digging up material, refining it, and preparing it for use. It is not really a process of grinding, but one of winnowing or sifting. The material of history does not lie open to the light of day. Even "tradition" is not the material itself; the material is contained in the tradition. Not only does the path from the material to knowledge seem longer and more laborious in history than in other disciplines, but there is also a toilsome path from nonknowledge to the material. For the natural sciences, insofar as they do not contain a historical element, the material is given and defined, open to observation, arrangement, and experiment. For history the material—certain events from a certain past—is not given. It no longer exists in the sense in which nature exists. In order to be able to conceive of it as existing the historian must perform a laborious amount of research and verification, sieving and sifting tradition, before he "comes to know" the raw material of his activity, the facts. To every appearance all this is no more than a preliminary function, a process of preparing and taking inventory.

Is everything, then, except the final synthesis, a "preliminary study" after all? By no means. In the historian's very research, if well done, lies the maturation of historical knowledge itself. The development of historical insight is not a process that follows upon critical treatment of the raw material, but is constantly taking place in the work of digging itself; scholarship is not realized in the individual in synthesis alone, but also in analysis. No true historical analysis is possible without the constant interpretation of meaning. In order to begin an analysis, there must already be a synthesis present in the mind. A conception of ordered coherence is an indispensable precondition even to the preliminary labor of digging and hewing.

Now herein lies the fault. Frequently the material is unearthed for which there is no demand. The accumulation of critically analyzed material which lies waiting for synthesis is filling the warehouses of scholarship. Sources are published that are not sources, but standing pools. Yet the fault is not only one regarding source publications, but also regarding monographic analyses of material. The poor student is looking for a subject on which to try his intellectual teeth, and the school tosses him a chunk of material.

Even the best and most complete tradition is in itself amorphous and mute. It only yields history once questions have been put to it. And it is not enough of a question to approach it with a general desire to know *wie es eigentlich gewesen,* how it really was. Ranke's famous phrase—misunderstood and misused, for it has been lifted out of the context in which the master used it in passing and has been interpreted as an adage—has obtained the tone of a program, which from time to time threatens to reduce it to a false slogan for sterile historical research. On hearing the question *wie es eigentlich gewesen?* one cannot help seeing someone sitting with the pieces of a vase in front of him and asking himself how it had been. But such a fitting together of pieces is only a usable image for historical activity if the following is taken into account. For the man busy with the pieces the *it* in the question "how was it?" is already determined by a certain image of the vase, even though the pieces may be mixed with others. In the same way the *es* in *wie es eigentlich gewesen,* if it is to have "meaning," must be determined beforehand by a conception of a certain historical and logical unity one is attempting to delineate more precisely. That unity can never lie in an arbitrary slice of past reality itself. The mind selects from tradition certain elements it synthesizes into a historically coherent image, which was not realized in the past as it was lived.

Herein lies the danger of unsatisfactorily formulated questions. Scholars pounce upon the material, setting out to analyze it without really knowing what they are looking for. The point of departure for sound historical research must always be the aspiration to know a specific thing well, regardless of whether that aspiration takes the form of a desire for strictly intellectual understanding or a need for spiritual contact with certain past realities. Where no clear question is put, no knowledge will give response. Where the question is vague, the answer will be at least as vague.

It is in the vagueness of the question that the fault lurks, not in the overspecialization of the subject. The endless stream of detailed studies filing past the eye, unread and undesired, sometimes gives one the longing to hold a diatribe on the limits of what is worth knowing. But it is only one's own feeling of not being able to master the whole world of history that inspires such annoyance. The frontiers are not in the material itself, but in the way it is used. The most parochial historian with a small group for whom his theme constitutes a vital question forms a full-fledged historical cult. Outside that small group his subject evokes only a very weak interest, if any. With a better treatment of his minor question the frontiers of its significance will expand to a broader circle of interested persons. On the other hand, an all too detailed treatment of a "generally important" subject can easily kill the question's significance for most people.

Anyone who is well aware of the potential character of historical knowledge will not be disturbed in his mental balance by the abundance of detailed research in itself. But he will continue to be troubled by the feeling that so much of that work, whether on large subjects or small, has become soulless, almost mechanical production. With the touchstone of history's deeper cognitive value in his hand, he will sometimes be inclined to sigh and invert the proverb: ten fools can answer more than one wise man can ask.

Cultural history is more strongly subject than political and economic history to this vagueness of its questions. The problems of political history are as a rule immediately obvious. The subjects stand out of their own accord. The state—or a part, an organ, a function of it—is unmistakably defined and understandable to all as an object for historical research; likewise, a series of events within such an entity. The same is true of economic history: a business, a form of labor, an economic relationship, are also well-defined objects for observation, though with the distinction that they demand a bit more "inside knowledge" than do political subjects in order to "appeal" to the reader.

For cultural history the situation is a bit different. The object of cultural history is culture, and this concept, modern par excellence and almost a shibboleth of our time, will always be exceedingly difficult to define. To be sure, one can put

questions of cultural history whose content and purport are
clearly defined. When did people begin to eat with forks?
How did the duel disappear from among English customs?
From the point of view of methodology these questions are
formulated more precisely and conceived more clearly than:
What is the essence of the Renaissance? But answers to them
do not produce cultural history, at least not in the deeper
sense of the word. Cultural history is distinct from political
and economic history in that it is worthy of the name only to
the extent that it concentrates on deeper, general themes. The
state and commerce exist as configurations, but also in their
details. Culture exists only as a configuration. The details of
cultural history belong to the realm of morals, customs, folklore, antiquities, and easily degenerate into curios.

This is not to say that every scholar in cultural history
constantly has to attempt to encompass the whole field. In
that, rather, there lurks another great danger, to which I
shall return later. If one likes, one can detect the natural
divisions of cultural history in church history and the history
of religion, art history, literary history, the history of philosophy, of science, of technology. For each of these the task
of studying the details is prescribed; the determination of the
objects still demands work enough. But the results of such
specialized historical studies, even if they lead to syntheses
and to explanations of significance, do not yield cultural
history. Even the history of styles and that of ideas can
hardly be called cultural history in the full sense of the word.

Only when the scholar turns to determining the patterns
of life, art, and thought taken all together can there actually
be a question of cultural history. The nature of those patterns
is not set. They obtain their form only beneath our hands.
And for this reason—that cultural history is to such a great
extent the product of the free spirit of scholars and thinkers
—greater caution is required in formulating the questions.
Every poorly formulated question throws the image out of
focus. And it sometimes seems that cultural history in its
present state is all too afflicted with out-of-focus images.

II

The concept of evolution is of little utility in the study of history, and frequently has a disturbing, obstructive influence.

"Insufficiently formulated questions?" exclaims the modern historian, full of courage. "What does it matter? Haven't we the concept of evolution and the promise of *greift nur hinein* as incentives to apply the scalpel, with the certainty of drawing the blood of history from the body of tradition, no matter where one makes an incision?"

The application of the concept of evolution seems to many scholars a stamp of scholarship, the standard seal of approval for merchandise on the intellectual market. Does not Ernst Bernheim see the validity of history as a full-bodied discipline in its concept of events as evolution? Each bit of history embodies an evolution; as soon as one has realized the temporary goal of that evolution the question has been put and the scholar is on firm ground.

It would never occur to me to deny the validity and utility of the term evolution for the humanities. The only thing I should like to argue is that the term is causing damage because it is used too slavishly and its metaphoric implications are not sufficiently understood. As undefined concept of evolution is made to serve as a panacea, and as is the case with every panacea, the cure is illusory.

Toward the end of the nineteenth century it appeared that the natural sciences, in their brilliant development, had indicated for good the norms of true scholarship, and thus they imposed their methods on modern thought as the only way toward true knowledge. Thenceforward if any intellectual activity were to lay claim to being genuine scholarship it would speedily have to train itself in a precise formulation of problems and precise methods. Had Auguste Comte not already sketched out that path? Had not some disciplines—

philology, economics, ethnology—already taken the path, and was it not to that that they owed their brilliant development? Now it was the turn of the most unsystematic of all fields of study, history, the mother of the household, to get rid of her shoddy furniture and redo her house in a modern style. Away with the rubbish of details, which were without cognitive value once they had served their purpose as experimental material for the drafting of generally applicable rules.

But as soon as history was seriously affected by such claims the *sit ut est aut non sit* sounded: "Be it as it is, or it shall not be." Almost instinctively the historians resisted the demands made on their discipline by one of their own number, Karl Lamprecht. And aid appeared from the side of philosophy. In the controversy over the essence of historical knowledge such philosophers as Wilhelm Windelband, Heinrich Rickert, and Georg Simmel, following Wilhelm Dilthey's lead, in the years between 1894 and 1905 for the first time provided the modern theory of knowledge of the humanities with a basis of its own, thus liberating it from having its norms dictated by the natural sciences. These philosophers demonstrated that historical knowledge is fundamentally different in nature and formation from knowledge in the natural sciences, that a history which no longer sought the goal of its knowledge in the specific details of the events themselves would be doomed to shrivel away completely, and that it is only begging the question to restrict the term science exclusively to a knowledge of the general expressed in concepts.

Since that struggle thirty years ago history has gone on its carefree way, undisturbed by methodological demands that it could not meet by its very nature. Essentially it has not changed; the nature of its products has remained the same. In that very constancy there is strong evidence for the necessity of its independent existence as one of the humanities. For if history had been called to become an exact and positive science, what could have prevented it from going through the process in the generation since the clarion call sounded?

To the person who today pays any attention to recent developments in the field of the theory of knowledge[1] it is clear that, at least in Germany—where these questions have been pursued most thoroughly—the viewpoint of the independence of the humanities is defended with quite a bit more conviction and further implications than when Rickert

wrote his *Grenzen der naturwissenschaftlichen Begriffsbildung.*
In fact, it appears that the attempts at a new *rapprochement*
are coming rather from the side of the natural sciences, whose
theory of exactitude has not remained unmodified in the
meantime.[2]

Even so, the fact that in the camp of the cultural philosophers there are clear concepts regarding the nature of the
humanities does not mean that the majority of historians are
aware of that fact. If one considers the term evolution in its
everyday sense, it is obvious that practical research in history
is still definitely under the strong, constant influence of natural-
scientific thought; that history is weighted down by a certain
primacy of natural science; and that the language of history
as it is spoken has a natural-scientific accent that is not its
own.

The notion of evolution as *the* means of understanding the
world has its origins rather in the field of historical thought
than in the natural sciences. The trail for it was blazed in the
French philosophy of the eighteenth century. Voltaire, Turgot,
and Condorcet were the first to view the great historical processes as gradual transition, continuous change, progress. That
view turned against the conception dominant at the time,
that historical magnitudes had to be explained as having been
instituted consciously. The idea of an efficient, gradual, unconscious development of cultural situations and phenomena
became fuller in content and deeper in meaning in the minds
of Herder, the German romanticists, and finally Hegel. In the
first half of the nineteenth century the term evolution gradually
supplanted words such as transformation, change, and progress.
It was as a rule still purely idealistic, not applied to the concrete forms of nature, but to intellectual concepts.[3] A group
of phenomena were conceived as an entity both in essence and
in meaning. The consecutive changes that one observed in the
condition of that entity were viewed in the light of the meaning that one attached to the whole. The whole became what
it had to be in keeping with that meaning, and this process
was called evolution.

The concept evolution then combined with that of organism,
in which it found its complement. Nor did the concept organism, organic, find its origin in modern natural science.[4]

It is the age-old metaphor that even in myths and fables transferred the structure of the human body to abstract things, in order to be able to grasp them. If organism is to be called a biological concept, then it is a primitive, mythological biology that is involved. The concept of the evolution of an organic entity demands a large degree of realism if it is to serve as an adequate cognitive tool. One has to have faith in the existence of the entity in which the endogenous evolution takes place. It is implicit in the metaphor that the inherent tendencies are the ones that determine a process.

Then in the second half of the nineteenth century came the great triumph of the concept of evolution in natural science. It was only in its modern biological form, as the Darwinian theory of evolution, that it took possession of the eternal throne. The concept of Darwinian evolution has fascinated whole generations, and it has permeated all our thinking. Its effect as a ready assumption is so persistent and so powerful that it almost always exerts an influence, consciously or unconsciously, whenever we attempt to consider a course of events in their interrelationship. The earlier vague, idealistic concept of evolution is now filled out by the biological aspect. It is like the echo in the Lateran: when the single tone of change, transformation, succession of stages is sounded, the chord of evolution reverberates.[5] Every situation, every relationship—in society and in nature alike—introduces itself a priori as a product of evolution. The word has become so current that it is growing shopworn. It is losing the heavy implication of its gravid imagery and becoming a vague, thoughtlessly used substitute for predetermined causation in general, without the logical content of the concept being taken into account.

And then there are the adroit, unshaken evolutionists, for whom world history, which they read cut and dried from the journal of tradition, holds no enigmas, for they have the key in their pockets to explain every difference in ages, every alternation of states and cultures. They dauntlessly place their skeleton key in the seven locks of the past. And they succeed. Beneath their hands the world process becomes the simplest matter on earth. These are the men who optimistically venture upon the history of all mankind, unfolding it in one loudly applauded pageant. How much success with the general public H. G. Wells enjoyed with his *Outline of History,* and later

Hendrik Willem Van Loon with his *Story of Mankind*. But the human past was not enough for them. In order to obtain the right perspective it had to be preceded by the history of the planet, and of life on earth. Thus they treat us to the steam bath of the condensation of the earth. Seemingly a happy thought, it is in fact a misunderstanding of the nature of historical knowledge. Geological and paleontological events are understood by another intellectual organ than history, namely by that of exact science, focused on a different sort of knowledge. The combination of the two only provides a hybrid whole that is confusing to the mind.

These are the popular works of dilettantes, it will be said, providing what the general public demands. But that would be a dangerous underestimation of the significance of the general public. A historical discipline supported only by an esoteric coterie of scholars is insecure: it must be based on the foundation of historical culture which is the possession of every cultivated person. These books testify to a dubious contemporary orientation of the general interest in history. And not only that: they help to determine the nature of that interest, also because of their unmistakable qualities. Europe's historical tradition is still offering a certain counterbalance. But in America a book like J. Harvey Robinson's *The Mind in the Making,* the work of a serious cultural historian, is considered even in the scholarly world as a significant statement of present-day knowledge, though it is based on an utterly naïve evolutionism.

Ernst Bernheim's much-used work *Lehrbuch der historischen Methode und der Geschichtsphilosophie* has undoubtedly contributed no little to the spreading of a superficial concept of evolution among the rank and file in the historical discipline. Bernheim, as every student of history knows, divides history into narrative (*referierende*), didactic (*pragmatische*), and evolutionary (*genetische*) history, according to the type of impulse toward knowledge which gives rise to a desire for it. This is not the place to argue in passing that such a division must be considered in more than one respect illogical, deceptive, and practically unusable. Wilhelm Bauer, whose briefer work [6] is now beginning to replace Bernheim for many scholars, recognizes that these three postulated forms of historical study do not succeed one another in time or surpass one another in quality. Nonetheless, he retains the system. As a tripartite ground for desiring historical knowledge it had already been seen by Leibnitz: "There are three things that we are after in history: first, the desire to learn to know singular things, then precepts useful primarily for life, and finally the origins of the present things dug up from the past, as all things are best understood from their causes." [7] This last reflects perfectly what Bernheim calls *genetische Geschichtsbetrachtung*. Now, the thought with which the savage accounts for the origin of species by means of mythology, the Greek logographers recount genealogies and the foundation of towns, and Herodotus attempts to know "for what reason they went to war" is in each case genetic. By making this concept "genetic" interchangeable with "evolutionary," Bernheim, it seems to me, makes a double mistake. He misjudges the full cognitive value of the older phases of historical study and overestimates that of modern historical thought, as if the latter were constantly maintained by a higher principle unknown in earlier times.

The important thing is to understand clearly what the term evolution covers and does not cover when it is applied to a certain historical problem. No one will deny that it can be of service for the understanding of clearly delimited phenomena. There is at least one area of history in which evolution, if tempered by mutation, would seem to rule supreme: the history of costume. In it there is indeed a sort of biological regularity which determines the development of forms, independent of the talents, the desires, or the interests of the individual or the community. The history of an institution, a commercial form, or a state agency can as a rule be comprehended without much objection under the concept of evolution. It is also useful in the history of science and that of technology, but it quickly fails one in the history of philosophy, religion, literature, and art. Yet even in the cases where it is most useful, the concept of evolution applies with a great deal more reserve than in the field where it reigns supreme: biology.

A biologist conceives of a certain organism as an autonomous object with certain inherent tendencies, an object that, reproducing itself by propagation, is in its essential structure permanent, and in the phylogenetic transformations in its organs, forms, and functions is determined by the environment in which it lives. As the result of the long duration of the phylogenetic process, the variations of these influences from outside seem to balance each other in their general similarity and repetition in such a way that the factor of environment can be considered as a constant and normal influence in accord with the internal conditions for evolution in a certain direction. This is no longer true, however, as soon as one considers a single phase of the phylogenetic process in its ontogenetic particularity (that is to say, views the biological subject historically). The sum total of all the influences from outside then manifests itself as a consecutive and varying series of larger and smaller disturbances of the organism's own condition which in fact abolish the isolated autonomy or internal coherence that one usually conceives of in any object. It is merely the methodology of biological science which prescribes that the organism must be thought of as set off from its environment, that the constant interdependence of the object and its environment is only of token importance and the object's evolution be considered as a closed causal process. The fact that no single one of the billions of influences from outside, taken by itself, is causally related to the inherent evolutionary possibilities of the organism must be neglected.

The historical phenomenon does not allow itself to be delimited conceptually from its environment in this way with impunity. If it is treated as a biological object in the way just described, it immediately takes its revenge: the methodology runs aground. It can be determined objectively what data go to make up the phenomenon "mouse." It cannot be determined objectively what historical data belong to the phenomenon Reformation and what do not. And this impossibility is not implicit in the abstract nature of the phenomenon, but in the historical view of it. This is just as true of a concrete historical individual as of a general historical concept. Luther as a specimen of the biological species man is strictly delimited, but Luther as a historical phenomenon is just as little delimited and delimitable as the Reformation. The historical object cannot be compared with the biological even in its ontogenetic aspect. And it is quite impossible for history to pass from the ontogenetic aspect of a phenomenon

to the phylogenetic. When one conceives of a historical entity-
through-the-ages, for example, the Frenchman, the idea of
that entity, only incompletely represented by any separate
object, lies in the summation of all the phenomena implicated
in it together, while the idea of the biological entity "mouse"
is realized in every mouse by itself. And when one considers
such a historical entity-through-the-ages as an "organism,"
one is already working with a poetic metaphor. There is
nothing against that from the point of view of scholarship;
in fact, scholarship cannot do without it, for language itself
thrives on such metaphors.

When one goes on to endow such a historical "organism"
with inherent tendencies that give direction to its "evolution,"
one is already knee-deep in teleology, for such an organism,
unlike a biological organism, is coherent only insofar as it
has an aim. There is nothing against that, either: history is a
way of thought which is final par excellence—a final explanation of the course of history is the only thing our minds will
allow. Yet if the touchstone of biology were applied to these
conceptions of historical "organism" and historical "evolution," the concepts would immediately prove to be distorted,
indeed forced. Have they, nonetheless, not retained enough
practical value for history that they need not be abandoned?
In the final analysis, that depends on the question to what
extent the metaphor of evolution is still applicable, still obtains.

The historical phenomenon, we have said, is in itself much
less delimitable from its environment than the biological.
Napoleon is only a historical phenomenon viewed in the world
in which he lived. One cannot think that world away from
him at all, partially isolating him as a historical organism,
in the way the organism mouse is isolated to a certain extent
in an experiment in order to study the effects of one specific
influence within a closed context. And this is just as true if
instead of Napoleon we take a general concept, the Frenchman. Every historical context always remains an open context.
No matter how many circumstances leading to Napoleon's
expedition to Russia I may sum up, the historical context I
thus recognize always remains open for the addition of new
notions as soon as my mind begins to divine them. There
are no closed historical organisms.

Nonetheless, even assuming that it is desirable to view
states and cultures as organisms in the loose sense in which

that is possible, does it make sense to speak of the evolution of inherent tendencies? Biology can to a certain extent make a distinction between the realization of inherent possibilities and the appearance of disturbing outside influences detrimental to the process of evolution. Taken strictly, even such a distinction finds its only rational basis in a teleological point of view. In historical phenomena even this defective line can never be drawn. Viewed historically, in every contact between man and man and between man and nature *everything* is an influence from outside. In every conjunction of two elements in history, in every occurrence of a fact, countless causally unrelated influences concur. The rising causal line that determined that Prince William II of Orange visit Dieren in September 1650 and the line that caused the fatal smallpox virus to be present there at just that time encounter each other only in the prime mover. Every influence from outside is a disturbance of the previous situation. The biologist, for whom this is fundamentally just as valid, is able to consider the sum total of these disturbances as one factor in the phylogenetic aspect, owing to their similarity and constancy. He considers the prevalence of certain constant conditions as essential for the existence of the organism. The historian cannot follow that path. For him every influence remains a disturbance. As a result the concept of evolution comes close to being a clincher of dubious value. Imagine a study of the evolution of Mexican or Peruvian civilization. No one will give the arrival of Cortes or Pizarro a place as a factor in that evolution: it was the catastrophe of the whole phenomenon.[8] Yet such a catastrophe is in essence only quantitatively different from the countless events which before that had determined the "evolution" of those civilizations. They in their turn, if not the catastrophe of something that had preceded them, were the strophe, the "turn." Every historical development is a result of sheer "turns," diversions at every single moment.

One can easily speak of an evolution of the political system of England, of Sweden, of the United Provinces. In each of these three states one can trace through the course of history the relation between the central authority and the aristocracy oscillating in a succession that seems almost regular. Strong rulers reinforcing the central authority were followed by minor or ineffectual successors or by a total default of the central authority, so that the aristocracy was repeatedly able to regain ground at the expense of that authority. As a result balances of power arose which one is inclined to call products of evolution. In actuality each of those changes was the result of circumstances that were accidental in regard to the so-called organism they affected.[9] It was not implicit in any tendency of English constitutional law that the Conqueror, Henry II, Edward I, and Edward III should have been able rulers each of whom was to reign fairly long, and that after each of them a period of poor government should follow because the bearer of the crown was incapable. The early deaths of Gustavus Adolphus and of Charles X Gustavus— and the regencies that resulted—were similarly external disturbances. And the early death of Stadholder William II, the childlessness of William III, the disappearance of John William Friso as candidate for the stadholdership, and the death of William IV were unrelated to the nature of the Dutch republic. Each of these genealogical facts was a disturbance from outside, and each had an important influence on the process of evolution of the state affected by it. Taken together, they even seem to suggest the concept of a certain restricted regularity, an oscillatory phenomenon that might seduce a reckless historian into formulating the rule that the evolution of a political system is determined in part by the alternation of strong and weak periods of authority to be expected with a certain regularity. He would be left holding the empty eggshell while others munch the half egg of living knowledge. The logical value of such a concept of "evolution" would be nil, and as historical knowledge such a formulation would be utterly insipid and not in the least usable.

Applied to history, then, the concept evolution in the biological sense is disturbing of a proper understanding. In its very essence it is less than completely cogent. Even if one holds one historical eye tightly shut, it remains of quite conditional and limited significance. Understood in its full metaphorical sense it is almost unusable. To realize this means to accept the indispensability of the specific facts for the explanation of any bit of history.

We shall not consider here whether, as Spengler would like, every application of a causal explanation ought to be abandoned along with the strict concept of evolution. The principle of causality is having something of a hard time of it in the theory of knowledge at the moment. The sharp restriction of its usefulness as a cognitive tool seems to be in keeping with a certain rehabilitation of the old Aristotelian and scholastic distinction of material, moving, and final causes. Be that as it may, knowing in the historical sense rarely if ever means indicating a strictly closed causality. It is always an understanding of contexts. As I argued, this context is always an open one, which is to say that it may never be represented in the metaphor of links forming a chain, but only in that of a loosely bound bundle of sticks to which new twigs can be added as long as the band around them allows it. Perhaps more suitable than a bundle of sticks might be a bunch of wild flowers. In their variety and their difference in value new notions added to the conception of a historical context are like newly found flowers in the nosegay: each one changes the appearance of the whole bouquet.

III

Our culture suffers if the writing of history for a broader public falls into the hands of the writers of an aestheticizing, emotional history that stems from a literary need, works with literary means, and aims at literary effects.

No other discipline has its portals so wide open to the general public as history. In no other discipline is the transition from the dilettante to the professional so gradual. There is nothing for which so little preliminary learning of a scholarly nature is needed as for historical understanding or historical activity. History has always been much more firmly rooted in life than in the school. There was no place for history in the scholastic system of the Middle Ages, as it developed out of that of latter-day antiquity. The seven liberal arts and the three great studies that crowned them—theology, law, and medicine—were the trunk from which most of the modern branches of study developed in a process of ramification and specialization. Not so history. Historiography springs up wherever a phase of culture has its spiritual center: in the market square, in the monastery, at court, in the commander's tent, in the anteroom, in the newspaper office. The fact that the study of history was rarely if ever associated with the liberal arts means that it was only poorly represented at the universities even after the Middle Ages, for until deep into the nineteenth century their system of education continued to be based on the medieval pattern. There are only a few academics among the renowned historians of the ages from humanism to romanticism. Hardly a single one of the great historical works of those ages is a university product. In England the figure of the statesman-historian is still of no little importance.

The nineteenth century brought a major change in the way history was studied, and consequently in the whole nature of the historical discipline. Since the end of the eighteenth century scholarship in general has become a much more integrative component of culture and society than it was. It has set itself stricter and higher requirements, requirements that can be met only by study in the nursery of learning, the university. Hence history became an academic discipline. The land that elevated it to that position, Germany, indisputably produced the largest number of important historians in the nineteenth century, and all of them were academics.

This trend toward the university did not abolish history's contact with cultural life. Names such as Ranke or Fruin are enough to prove it. It would have been a change for the worse if it had,[1] for a history that operates without vital contact with the national culture, which does not enjoy the eager interest of the cultured public, is not on the right path (unless the fault lies in the degeneration of cultural life itself). This is not to say that every piece of historical research should necessarily lead to a popular presentation. Far from it. In history, just as in every other discipline, there is work to spare for the specialist which the general reader has no need and no desire to know, work he would lack the intellectual organ for. Research, critical sifting, publication, interpretation, and synthesis remain the undisputed domain of well-trained scholarly workers. But the great image of the past which lies behind or hovers above all that work is definitely the concern of everyone. The task of functioning as an implement of culture, the implement with which culture accounts for its past, can only be fulfilled by a historical discipline that finds its sphere and its sounding-board in life in general in its own day. To be full-fledged any field of study must be accepted and supported by the culture nourishing it.

Every culture, for its part, has a certain degree of immersion in the past as a precondition for life. In every civilization there are certain concepts of earlier reality which the society sustaining that civilization takes to heart. Though such concepts assume essentially divergent forms, they do so without abrogating their common characteristic of serving as "history" for the culture that produces them. Depending on the nature of the civilization that has a need for images of its past, and the intellectual focus from which those images are created, they take on the form of myth, saga, legend, chronicle, *geste,* historical folk-song.[2] For the culture in which such forms develop, the culture they serve, they all signify to a certain extent "what really happened." They fill not only a vital need but also a need for truth. If the belief in the truth of what is recounted dies, then the productive period of the form is past, though it can prolong its life for centuries as a pastiche, or even seemingly make a comeback. Forms of consciously fictional imagination such as the pastoral poem and the romance are separated from the forms mentioned above by a deep abyss. Between the *matière de France* of the *chansons de geste* and the *matière de Bretagne* of the genuine romance, culture took a stride as great as Trivikrama, who measured heaven and earth in three steps. The less the development of the culture in which those forms are realized, the more clearly they betray their links with the cult. All of them are in their turn *morale en action.* For the culture concerned they are "history" to the extent that the picture presented answers to the form of perception natural to that culture. The myth is at all times to a much greater extent primitive scholarship than primitive literature.

Now the form of perception of modern civilization regarding the past is no longer that of the myth, but that of critical scholarship. Contemporary culture that contents itself with mythical conceptions (as it does do every day) relapses into a childish self-deceit. When we pretend to believe in historical constructions that we know are poetic license we are, at best, like the father in *Punch* playing with his son's toy train. Critical scholarship's the only form for understanding the past which is appropriate to our culture, the only form that is natural to it and is its mature product. But to supply this noble product with its full cultural value it is not enough for the specialist to know the tricks of his trade. The relation between a culture and its knowledge of history grows more satisfactory in proportion as a larger share of its cultured members is able to enjoy the refined product of its historical study.

In our culture, then, the quality of historical knowledge can be considered highest when scholarship succeeds in supplying a critically refined product of so clear a value for life that the general cultured public accepts it, desires it, and absorbs it. The more readers who request serious history, without being frightened off by strict matter-of-factness, sober narration, and pure scholarly intent, the more favorable the evidence for the soundness of that culture and for the manner in which the historian is fulfilling his calling. On the other hand, if Clio can only reach her clients by slackening somewhat the severe requirements placed upon her as the form of perception adequate to the time, then there is something wrong with both culture and scholarship.

It would be hard to maintain that the optimal situation just assumed exists in our day. It might even be asked whether the conditions for it were not better met a generation or two ago than now. The question cannot be decided with general assertions. Considered superficially, the demand for history seems greater than ever. World histories in a popular form, with emphasis on culture and art, and with many illustrations, are best-sellers. Likewise the concise handbook about any subdivision, in small format, usually a volume in a series, and often excellently compiled by the most competent authors. And then there are the memoirs, biographies, local histories, and so forth. But, on the other hand, it would seem that the chief contemporary figures in the field of historical studies in our culture are no longer the great voices their compeers were a century ago. Did a voice like Michelet's or Macaulay's not resound more clearly than any now to be heard? Or does it only seem so to us? This relative weakening in voice might in fact be caused partly by the general change in the orchestration of culture. The harmony of the written word has grown constantly more clamorous, more diffuse, more formless, more scattered, and more broken, so that the separate parts are less easy to follow. In every field the great voices are more lost in the general tone of the whole.

There is, however, still quite another circumstance that

makes it difficult for the historical discipline to fill its higher function for culture. That is the competition of literature. Literature is in itself not at all a disloyal competitor. It is, like scholarship, a cognitive form of the culture producing it. Its function is not to produce pretty poems and stories, but to make the world understandable, understandable with different means from those scholarship uses. Now, in understanding the world, today and yesterday cannot be distinguished for a single moment. Today never becomes yesterday; it is yesterday. Consequently the plastic matter of literature has always been a basically historical world of forms. In using such matter literature is not bound to the requirements of scholarship. For it the forms of that world are merely motifs. The value of the literary product lies in the representative or symbolic effect of the forms, not in a dominating preoccupation with "genuineness," with "how it really happened." Literature, therefore, prefers to create its figures from its world of forms with utter freedom, and chooses them from true "history"—that is to say, the world of the past viewed as "what really happened"—only now and then for special reasons. Literature is constantly solving the riddles of a number of cosmic or human relationships which scholarship does not, and perhaps cannot, begin to explain. Compared to the sciences of the human past and of society, the strength of literary creation lies in its unobstructed mental suppleness, its freedom of composition, its infinite suggestion. Its weakness lies in the lack of coherence between its products and in its everlasting indeterminacy.

We can with absolute certainty find the answer to the question whether someone is pursuing history or literature by testing the intellectual preoccupation from which he works. If the all-predominating need for "genuineness," the deeply sincere desire to find out how a certain thing "really happened," is lacking as such, he is not pursuing history.

Herein lies the fault of recent years, and here the discipline of history can complain about disloyal competition. The intellectual preoccupations have been confused; a hybrid product is being brought in circulation, and an attempt is made to disguise its ersatz character. It is not strictly and solely the fault of quackish men of letters, but also of the fact that the discipline of history is not supplying in sufficient quantity the sort of product our culture demands. And this in turn is not the fault of the poor professional historians. They are no longer equal to the task; the subject has become too difficult, their heads are reeling.

The material of history, not only of whole countries, but of each town, each institution, each incident, is constantly accumulating and expanding in source publications and monographic studies. Even the critical sifting it has to undergo before it can be called true historical material is itself enough to keep a host of professional historians busy. The products they bring forth are as a rule still rough ones neither intended, calculated, nor suited for direct integration into our culture. They themselves will frequently present them and excuse them as "preliminary studies," the renowned illusion we referred to earlier. If they are really only preliminary studies, then they are rushes strewn in the path of an imaginary historical Messiah who is not believed in. But we have already argued that it is not necessary to appeal to that illusion of "preliminary studies." The detailed study has a value of its own. It is no preliminary for a coming salvation; it is a cozy cult of familiar household gods, a pleasant adornment of the intellectual milieu in which one wants to live.

But culture requires more. And only too often the professional historian, surveying how much critical labor is involved in determining one single detail, and considering the infinite variety and complexity of the material, will despair of his ability to fulfill his cultural duty, shake his head, and perhaps take refuge behind the illusion that the preliminary studies necessary to treat this question properly are still completely lacking. Then he closes the door to culture and decides not to be a master builder but only a hewer of stones, and goes on chipping away.

Here the nimble hand of the dilettante willingly intervenes. He sees all the perspectives necessary for the understanding of vast complexes. The sentiment that is aroused with such dangerous ease in our intellectual life creates in him an illusion of ordered thought. The modern spirit does not require a strict formulation of logical thoughts or a clear, conscious foundation of well-defined concepts in order to be able to understand. De Tocqueville foresaw this intellectual habit with prophetic insight. "Democratic nations," he wrote—and it will be granted that to him "democratic" meant simply "modern" —"are passionately addicted to generic terms and abstract expressions because these modes of speech enlarge thought and assist the operations of the mind by enabling it to include many objects in a small compass. . . . Men living in democratic countries, then, are apt to entertain unsettled ideas, and they require loose expressions to convey them." [3] This is the classical rationalist who foresees the approach of the great derationalization of thought.

This summarizing all too readily in all too open contexts (both of them merely excesses of what history always has to do: summarizing in open contexts), is the basis for the popular histories prepared by dilettantes. Such authors are themselves not at all hybrid. Wells and Van Loon must be granted the honor of having been impelled by a serious historical preoccupation. However, there is a third factor in the process besides the despairing professional and the optimistic dilettante: the modern publisher.

The modern publisher, though he is an extremely important vehicle of culture, is a creature who is forced by his function always to squint, or if one would prefer to put it less anthropocentrically, to glare like the proverbial wild bull. He must be able to understand the spiritual aspects of the society that requires him to serve it, but also be able to evaluate the material aspects. If he ignores one of the two his product does not "catch on" and remains culturally sterile. The publisher, then, is aware of the hungry yearning for history which every culture must have. But he is also aware of the reader's decreased concentration, his addiction to amusing diversions. He knows that in the so-called democratic, standardized society it is his opportunity and his responsibility to satisfy a much broader circle of readers than cared about history in earlier periods. But he can only reach this broad circle by respecting and even currying to their cultural idiosyncracies: repugnance toward everything reminiscent of school; a strong need for emotion, color, and sentiment in their intellectual nourishment; and a preference for the personal, and subjective, and the biased. And, finally, a certain philosophic vagueness. It is not necessary for the publisher to urge the author in so many words to take all these characteristics into account. The author usually shares them himself. The more he yields to general intellectual and emotional inclinations, the more acceptable the work becomes for publication. Hence the compulsion of culture prescribes precisely for those works designed to amalgamate historical research into the general culture: no learned notes, a great deal of color, a strongly appealing point of view, and a sharp stimulation of the fantasy.

In this way there arises a hybrid product that might be called literary history, or still better historical belles-lettres, for the essence is literary, and the historical is only accessory. This present-day genre of historical belles-lettres is clearly distinguished from such older forms as the historical novel and the historical drama. The historical novel makes no pretense to being anything but literature: only its material has been taken from history. The endeavor toward a certain degree of historical accuracy can make the effect more satisfactory, but remains quite subordinate. The new form, on the other hand, pretends to be history, but with a difference: not the history of the professional historian, a much better one—

There is something wrong with the quality of this merchandise. This quality depends on the one very definite criterion that we have constantly given pride of place: the sincere need to provide as close an approximation to "truth" as research can supply. The person who unreservedly chooses the formula that history is merely *Sinngebung des Sinnlosen,* giving meaning to the meaningless, is no longer bound by such a requirement. But as long as history is considered as *Sinndeutung des Sinnvollen,* interpreting the meaning of the meaningful, the criterion obtains that nothing can be called history which does not spring from the need for a perfectly "genuine" picture of a certain past.

This forces us to make a qualitative distinction between two forms of present-day literary historical writing. The first and more respectable I should like to call the edifying historical genre. The need for truth expressed in it is sincere, but it is more aesthetic and religious than scholarly in focus. The social aspirations that led to the formation of groups of devotionalists and pietists in strongly religious ages have shifted in part from the field of religion to that of art and literature among the cultured groups in contemporary society. Any number of "pious souls" (as a psychological type) today live on a purely aesthetic diet. It is no accident that in the country of Thomas a Kempis literary criticism and art criticism so easily take on a character of literary pietism, a modern Modern Devotion (if that does not sound too much like *Cent nouvelles nouvelles*). More than one trait of the spiritual, moral, and social habits of the Brothers of the Common Life can be detected in it. The mutual adulation, the minute analysis of emotions, the limited horizon: none of them are alien to it. Edifying historical writing belongs in that sphere. It meets the vague need for a sensitive appreciation of the art and wisdom of the ages. The tone is homiletic. Overestimating the emotional content in everything it touches upon, it interprets the taut figures of history according to an unkempt generation's need for edification. It gluts itself on poorly understood and poorly understandable -isms. It knows the riddles of the soul of every saint, every wise man, every hero. It concocts tragic psychological conflicts for artists who created their greatest work while whistling a tune.

Especially in this last regard the spirit shows itself to be a child of romanticism. Permit me to digress for a moment on that extraordinary trait of our age, the pretense of vice. It is in a certain sense a modern repetition of the sentimentalism of the eighteenth century, but in a completely different form. The old sentimentalism felt itself to be intimately bound to the respect for virtue. It tended to balance passion and virtue in what was often a neck-breaking fashion. Nowadays this is no longer necessary. Passion alone, or what figures for it, is enough. In every depiction of reality in either word or image (I am here speaking of literature in general) the element of passion must be played up. Moral norms definitely may not be praised. Virtuous people assure themselves of their halo of the modern by means of a eulogy of immorality. Such a eulogy is as much a form of cultural hypocrisy as a sanctimonious display of virtue was ever able to be.

Sentimentalism and the passionate are both nurtured in the soil of the plebeian intellectual attitude that captured the fields of literature and culture in the course of the eighteenth century. If one removes the sting of disdain from the word "plebeian," the term "democratic" can be reserved for political and social fields, and the concept plebeian (including "bourgeois") can be placed in antithesis to aristocratic in the field of culture. An aristocratic culture does not advertise its emotions. In its forms of expression it is sober and reserved. Its general attitude is stoic. In order to be strong it wants to be and needs to be hard and unemotional, or at any rate to allow the expression of feelings and inclinations only in elegant forms. Ernest Seillière has repeatedly expounded these things excellently.[4]

The populace is always anti-stoic. Great waves of emotion, floods of tears, and excesses of feeling have always been breaks in the dikes of the popular soul, which then usually swept along the spirit of the upper classes. With Rousseau, "the bitter plebeian," as Faguet called him, the anti-stoic intellectual attitude triumphed for good. Its name is romanticism. With it came that immodest interest in the grimaces of love and hatred which was to find uncurbed expression in the film. The intellectual difference between the literary display of vice and the conversation of two wenches talking about a sickness in a back alley is small.

History may become democratic, but it must remain stoic. Jules Laforgue says somewhere in his letters that he cannot look upon all history as anything but one endless series of misery. But he was a poet. If the historian yielded to his sympathy with all the misery in the world he would be rendered unsuitable for his task.

Soberness, restraint, a certain skeptical reserve in investigating the deepest emotions of the heart—all of which are the duty of true historical writing—do not please the contemporary reader. At this point enters the second genre of historical belles-lettres we have in mind. The romanticized biography has in recent years become an international fashion as a genre. It frequently appears as one in a series under a general title. This indicates the role played in the phenomenon by publishing interests. There is a demand for a new sort of *Vitae,* based on a thorough knowledge of the sources and half meant as genuine history, but with the express intention that that history should be exaggerated, prepared for a market primarily literary. If the author is of a sober turn, the demand gives rise to works that exceed the bounds of history only slightly, such as André Maurois's *Disraeli.* At other times the literary is completely dominant, as in Joseph Delteil's *Jeanne d'Arc.* Emil Ludwig has become world famous in a few short years. Wilhelm Hausenstein instructs us in the conjugal secrets of Rembrandt and Saskia. And last year Dutch literature was given a remarkable specimen of the genre from the hand of Felix Timmermans: *Pieter Brueghel, zoo heb ik U uit Uw werken geroken* [literally, "Pieter Brueghel: Thus Have I Smelled You in Your Works"]. In it a well-known writer lent his name to a double novelty: the vocative book-title and olfactory historiography (though the latter had already been practiced by others before him).

More striking than all these names is the fact that the scholar most at home in French history of the fifteenth century, Pierre Champion, felt called upon, after his excellent works *Charles d'Orléans, François Villon,* and *Histoire poétique du XVe siècle,* to follow the path of romantic biography and literary effect in his *Louis XI.*

Anyone with the true historical spirit, whether he is the most academic scholar or the simplest cultured reader, reacts negatively to this whole genre, for the same reason that a connoisseur despises crusted wine. He can taste the adulteration. No literary effect in the world can compare to the pure, sober taste of history. He does not want his history dry, but he does want it *sec.* For him the first authentic historical document that comes to hand—whether a chronicle or a verdict, a deed, a letter, or a resolution—will be enough to wash away the scented taste of the hybrid genre.

The writer of historical belles-lettres will retort: But do you historians not recognize the strongly subjective element in all historical cognition—in the formulation of the question, in the selection and sifting of the material, in the interpretation and synthesis of the data ascertained? What is the difference between my work and yours, except the liveliness and the ingeniousness of the fantasy, which is also indispensable for you? The answer is that the difference lies in the intellectual preoccupation from which the work derives. Take one of the best representatives of the form I am objecting to, Guy de Pourtalès's life of Liszt, the first volume in the series of *Vie des hommes illustres.* What the author provides from the very first page is literature, not history. Everything he describes the historian will only suspect, and everything the historian would like to have described is obscured by the literary image. The utterly sincere need to understand the past as well as possible without any admixture of one's own is the only thing that can make a work history. Judgment has to rest on an absolute conviction that what is described must have been that way. And as soon as the past is converted into the language of the novel, into the form of an imaginative literary work, the sacred essence of history has been adulterated, although the author may still believe that he is writing history. In this way one abandons the form of perception natural to one's sustaining culture, and smothers in the well-meaning reader the genuine historical sense.[5]

No borders can be defined. It is a question of conscience, humility, and subservience. Goethe said to Eckermann: "When eras are on the decline, all tendencies are subjective; but on the other hand, when matters are ripening for a new epoch, all tendencies are objective. . . ." If this is true, our time must ask itself where it stands. "The retreat of historical knowledge in the last decade," is, according to Rothacker, "certainly not accidental." [6]

I can still hear the deep resonance of the words with which Ernst Troeltsch concluded an address at Leiden in the spring of 1919, speaking of the things the age needed most of all in order to regain its health. Respect, a new respect for everything that is more and higher than ourselves, he considered the most important thing. At the same time, or a little earlier, he wrote in connection with the rise of Oswald Spengler's comet on the intellectual horizon: "It would be a very serious loss if we were to abandon the critical rationalism acquired so laboriously, the philological element, empirical exactness, and careful research into causality, in order to have to acquire them later in toil and trouble, or (in case the faculty or the will for that is lacking) to perish in an initially spirited and later confused barbarism." [7]

Carlyle saw as the fundamental characteristics of his heroes their utter seriousness, their deep sincerity toward themselves and the world. Not everyone can be a hero, but everyone can strive toward a heroic sincerity.

It is up to the discipline of history to dare to compete with everything that talent, fashion, and intellectual indolence throw in the scales on the side of literature. In this the times are not favorable to the historian. It is questionable whether the structure of present-day cultural life still leaves room for a historical discipline that has precedence in the creation of culture over literary apperception of the past. Here, too, the general evolution of the dominant groups—in other words, the democratization of society—constitutes a danger. Professional scholarship can never be for more than a few: it is aristocratic. Literature (and with it popular scholarship) is for the many, must be for the many. Modern culture must be democratic if it is to be at all. The earlier situation, in which the intellectual gap between the exalted culture of the classes (within which scholarship and literature were still one) and the naïve intellectual life of the masses still corresponded to the social gap between the gentleman and the common man, can no longer exist. Yet the oppressing question with which Rostovtzeff concludes his *Social and Economic History of the Roman Empire* is still unanswered: "The ultimate problem remains like a ghost, ever present and unlaid: Is it possible to extend a higher civilization to the lower classes without debasing its standard and diluting its quality to the vanishing point? Is not every civilization bound to decay as soon as it begins to penetrate the masses?"

IV

The chief task of cultural history is the morphological understanding and description of the actual, specific course of civilizations.

1. THE HISTORICAL SENSATION. Three antitheses regarding the nature and task of historical activity will here be considered in turn. The first of them can best be expressed in the form of a question. In the intellectual activity of the historian does the element re-experiencing and intuitive understanding dominate, or that of construction and synthesis? It might seem that this question was answered in favor of the first element long ago when the theory of knowledge in the humanities was given a form of its own. Yet there is still a degree of uncertainty in the view which should be removed.

At the time when history had to be freed of the suzerainty of natural science (which considered its norms of precision the only touchstone of true scholarship and raised the demands of which Lamprecht made himself the advocate), it was, as always, necessary first of all that one knew what one was talking about. In point of fact, as so often happens, this was reflected upon only later. A clear picture of the true nature of the historian's intellectual activity was a prerequisite if scholars were to understand one another. Lamprecht demanded that all historical study should lead to the formulation of general

concepts in which the knowledge of the specific fact was
assimilated and lost all independent significance. Only then
could history be a science. It could not be worthy of the name
if it did not lead any further than to the visualization of particular events. It is clear that if those norms obtained there
had never been a historical discipline. Everything that historians had thought and written up to then had come into
existence in a quite different way. And the very claim that only
understanding and knowledge of the general led to scholarship
was an unproved proposition. Windelband and Rickert demonstrated that a knowledge of the particular not leading to any
general concepts was just as truly scholarship, and in so doing
they laid a firm foundation for the theory of knowledge in
the humanities. In their refutation of Lamprecht and his battle
cry of a concept-constructing study of history, his opponents
designed the image of the historian's intellectual activity as it
really was and as it has yielded its best products. In that image
the visualizational character of history was placed in the foreground. If I am not mistaken, in creating that image they were
thinking above all (and how could it have been otherwise?)
of the classical figure of Ranke. Ranke's spirit, as it used to
wander through all the corridors of courts and palaces, down
all the winding paths of diplomatic correspondence, in all its
intimate contact with the persons involved, weighing and
evaluating them, inspired in Lamprecht's opponents the image
of the historian. Hence it is understandable that in their conception of historical activity the emphasis came to lie on
concepts such as intuition and re-experiencing. That was the
way Ranke seemed to have worked; he had re-experienced all
those human lives, all those events in his mind.

"The historian wants to make the past real to us once more,
and he can only do that by enabling us to re-experience, to a
certain extent, the unique happenings of the past in their
individual course. . . . He will . . . always appeal to the
listener or the reader to call clearly to mind a fragment of
reality by means of his imagination." [1] Thus Rickert stated in
his renowned address *Kulturwissenschaft und Naturwissenschaft*, given in 1894. And in the same period Windelband
declared: "However intricate the conceptual activity needed
by historical criticism in assimilating tradition may be, the
ultimate aim of that criticism always remains to bring the
true form of the past from the mass of material into a live

clarity, and what it produces are images of men and men's lives in all the wealth of their specific forms, preserved in all their full, individual vitality." [2]

We shall not consider the question whether both philosophers do not here adhere to a degree of historical realism which the contemporary theory of historical knowledge would no longer be willing to take responsibility for. History cannot reproduce the troubled reality of the past, and has no desire to; it no longer even pretends to construct a pattern of the past which might be called the true one, to the exclusion of other possible configurations. Quite apart from that, a question obtrudes: How many pages of any given modern history do these words of Windelband's and Rickert's really apply to? Do they really reflect the intentions of the historian and the effect of his work on the reader? Is the historical function really a re-experiencing of a piece of reality, a visualizing of images of men and men's lives?

Let us pose the question for a moment from the point of view of an unrealized possibility. What sort of form would the image of the historian's intellectual function have obtained if not Ranke's great creations but the work of Georg Waitz had determined it? It will be said that Waitz is not a fair parallel: as a constitutional historian he had to work with historical forms that by their very nature could not be understood by means of visualization and re-experiencing. But then take a work of a general nature which, whether or not one accepts its thesis, is considered as being incontrovertibly a model of modern scholarly history. I am referring to Pirenne's *Histoire de Belgique,* especially the first two volumes. Does Pirenne depict human lives? Hardly at all. Does he describe pageants of a past reality? No. But now comes the difference. Does he call up images? Yes. Does he allow them to be re-experienced? Yes. In reading a work such as this, one does indeed repeatedly have the sense of a direct contact with the past, albeit on a purely scholarly level.

And now comes the core of the question. There is a very important element in historical understanding which might best be indicated by the term "historical sensation." One might also speak of "historical contact." "Historical imagination" says too much, and so does "historical vision," since the description as a visual conception is too restrictive. The German term *Ahnung,* "presentiment," which was already used by

Wilhelm von Humboldt in this connection, would express it
almost completely, if it were not worn a bit too threadbare in
other contexts. This not completely reduceable contact with
the past is an entry into an atmosphere, it is one of the many
forms of reaching beyond oneself, of experiencing truth, which
are given to man. It is not an aesthetic enjoyment, a religious
emotion, an awe of nature, a metaphysical recognition—and
yet it is a figure in this series. The object of the sensation is
not human figures in their individual form, not human lives
or human thoughts one thinks one can disentangle. What the
mind creates or experiences in this connection can hardly be
called an image. If and insofar as it assumes a form, it is one
that remains complex and vague: an *Ahnung* just as much
of roads and houses and fields, of sounds and colors, as of
stimulated and stimulating people. This contact with the past,
which is accompanied by an utter conviction of genuineness
and truth, can be evoked by a line from a document or a
chronicle, by a print, by a few notes of an old song. It is not an
element that the writer infuses in his work by using certain
words. It lies beyond the book of history, not in it. The reader
brings it to the writer, it is his response to the writer's call.

If it is this element in the understanding of history which is
indicated by many historians as re-experiencing, then it is the
term that is wrong. "Re-experiencing" indicates much too
definite a psychological process. One does not realize the historical sensation as a re-experiencing, but as an understanding
that is closely related to the understanding of music, or rather
of the world by means of music. Re-experiencing as a method
of cognition assumes a more or less continuous perception
constantly accompanying the labor of reading and thinking.
In reality this sensation, vision, contact, *Ahnung,* is limited to
moments of special intellectual clarity, moments of a sudden
penetration of the spirit.

This historical sensation is apparently so essential that it is
felt again and again as the true moment of historical cognition.
Inscribed on Michelet's grave are his own words: *L'histoire
c'est une résurrection.* Taine said: *L'histoire c'est à peu près
voir les hommes d'autrefois.* In their vagueness these two statements are more usable than careful definitions in the theory
of knowledge. It is the *à peu près,* the "more or less," that
matters. It is a resurrection that takes place in the sphere of

the dream, a seeing of intangible figures, a hearing of half-understood words.

Implicit in the value of the historical sensation, in its quality of a necessary of life (a quality befitting that urge toward contact with the past), is also the rehabilitation of the "antiquarian interest" that Nietzsche in his day cast aside so disdainfully. The most modest historical research, that of the genealogist and the student of heraldry, that of the local dilettante, can be exalted and ennobled by this intellectual preoccupation. Their work has its own full-fledged goal if the scholar or the reader experiences that sensation from it.

It was argued above that the function rather unhappily called re-experiencing, however important it may be, is not realized constantly, but appears only from time to time. It is merely one part of historical understanding. The comprehension of history and the writing of history are something more than merely undergoing and evoking this historical suggestion. If we continue to take as our point of departure genuine contemporary historical writing of the best quality, from the hands of its finest representatives—add to Pirenne's name those of Meinecke, Trevelyan, and a score of others—then it is obvious that the chief constituent of their effect is that they cause one not to experience moods, but to understand contexts. Anyone who analyzes a number of pages of modern historians, or just as well of Ranke or even Michelet, discovers that the intention to evoke a "re-experiencing" can be demonstrated only rarely, but that the effort to make certain forms understood occurs constantly. The true visualizational does not by any means occupy the place it has sometimes been given in opposition to the conceptual. Every work of history constructs contexts and designs forms in which past reality can be comprehended. History creates comprehensibility primarily by arranging facts meaningfully and only in a very limited sense by establishing strict causal connections. The knowledge it provides answers the questions "what?" and "how?," and only as an exception the question "why?"—though both the scholar and the reader usually have the illusion that the latter question is the one that is being answered.

2. PSYCHOLOGY OR MORPHOLOGY? Once it is agreed that the meaning of history is fathomed by the visualization of forms in which the past assembles itself in our minds, the second question that rises is this: Should not this morphology of the past, which history attempts to be and has to be, more properly be called a psychology of the past? On this point, too, the authority of Lamprecht—who believed he had demonstrated the actual task of history to be social psychology—has had a much more far-reaching and lasting influence than the later volumes of his *Deutsche Geschichte*—which were meant to provide an application of the theory—have ever had readers.

At first glance it seems quite reasonable: whoever penetrates the psychology of history's protagonists and is furthermore able to sum up the psychological life of a whole age can in that way unfold history. But it is easy to demonstrate that this is not at all true. The discipline of history, as it has developed and must develop, has never met such requirements of a historical psychology, and cannot meet them. No matter how completely I might be able to penetrate into the soul of Philip the Fair, Boniface VIII, Nogaret, and all the other participants in the drama of Anagni, and then to combine all that knowledge seen in its interrelationships, the result would by no means be the history of the tremendous event of 1300. The events themselves would thunder straight through all my psychology, which at best would reflect how the characters reacted to fate and how their impulses manifested themselves, but would be incapable of indicating as predetermined even one point in all that actually happened.

If instead of a psychological understanding of particular persons one assumes a knowledge of the soul of the masses— thus some sort of a social psychology—the result is less rather than more true historical understanding. Imagine that it is possible to describe the social psychology of the inhabitants of England in the twelfth century. In reality such a psychology seems to me not only not knowable, but actually not conceivable. What would pass for it would not yield an à Becket or a Richard, or anything of the real unfolding of England's destiny.

One can retort: But is not every attempt at psychological understanding, whether directed toward a person or a group, already morphology, the craving to grasp a form? Is the person of Thomas à Becket not a form, *forma* in the indispensable sense of the word which it had for Aristotle and Aquinas, and which our time is beginning to understand once more? When the literary historian attempts to understand a poet, is his task not one of a psychology that is also a morphology? And is that not just as true of the ordinary historian who describes a statesman?

Undoubtedly. I do not mean to deny history every psychological activity with the thesis that it is in principle morphology and not psychology. As soon as one takes a human life, a personality, or a postulated collective of many human lives as a historical form in which a fragment of the past has been realized in its actual course, the seeming contradiction disappears. Psychological understanding can be considered as one aspect of giving form to history, as long as one takes into account the fact that in historical research, quite unlike biological, phenomena are never viewed as organisms, but always as events. The organism of history, if there is one, lies outside human psychology. Pope's "The proper study of Mankind is Man" is correct from the point of view of anthropology, but from that of history it is misleading. History is not concerned with what holds man together inwardly, the psychosomatic principle of his actions, but with what binds people to one another, with relationships among people. If applied with extreme caution, the American concept "behavior," with its strongly sociological validity as the actions of people in response to the world outside, can be of use for the historian.

The dissimilarity between the historical and the psychological urge to knowledge can be demonstrated by a forceful argument from silence. If there were no such difference, history would long since have concluded a close alliance with psychology. It has not done so. Relations between the two disciplines are amicable, but not very lively. Does the student of history ever arrive at a conclusion that he first feels the need to verify with the results of psychological research? History has provided the material for the few experiments in historical psychology of the school of Gerardus Heymans, without being influenced by the results of the experiments. I may be permitted to pass over in silence the application of psychoanalytic theories to history. The possibility of a further *rapprochement* between psychology and history is suggested by Ernst Kretschmer's *Körperbau und Charakter*. There is no historian who would not read this brilliant book without adding greatly to his scholarly insight. Nonetheless his confidence in its fecundity rather gives way precisely at the point where the writer provides a few provisional examples of an application of his system on historical persons. If there is really something promising in Kretschmer's system, then I should like to detect it in its high morphological value.

History is the interpretation of the significance that the past has for us. Implicit in this character of history is that of arrangement. In order to understand a fragment of the past as reflected in his own culture, the historian must always and everywhere attempt to see the forms and functions of that fragment. History always speaks in terms of form and function, even in cases where it has not at all set itself a methodical program of morphology. The only condition is that the urge to knowledge should be genuinely historical, and that the historian is not an ass. Every historical monograph, if its problem is well defined, answers a question of historical morphology. But woe if whole schools do nothing but rashly dip the ladle into the porridge of tradition. If no definite form or function is sought the result is either an amorphous mixture of chaff and grain or else a rhetorical or romantic print.

Every event (except the very simplest fact) conceived by the faculty of historical cognition presumes an arranging of the material of the past, a combining of a number of data out of the chaos of reality into a mental image. Very often that arranging has already taken place in "ordinary life," quite apart from any historical preoccupation. In the fact that history works with the material of these spontaneous ideas lies its indissoluble link with life itself. Historical thought is merely an extension of thought in general, a proceeding further down the path that leads from the extreme nominalism of reality to the idea. The ideas that give form to the past are on hand even in the most preliminary reflections on history. For a consistent nominalist "parliament" and "world war" have no more existence than "capitalism" and "religion."

Particularly the historical forms of political life are already to be found in life itself. Political history brings its own forms: a state institution, a peace treaty, a war, a dynasty, the state itself. In this fact, which is inseparable from the paramount importance of those forms themselves, lies the fundamental character of political history. It continues to enjoy a certain primacy because it is so much the morphology of society par excellence.

Even in economic history the terms with which the historian works are much more the product of a scholarly analysis of the phenomena than are the political terms taken straight from life. This is still more the case with the terms of cultural history (unless one thinks of mores and customs and the like). The true problems of cultural history are always problems of the form, structure, and function of social phenomena. This is not to say that cultural history should be subservient to sociology. Cultural history considers phenomena in their own striking significance, while for sociology they are nothing but paradigms. The cultural historian has abandoned the design of deducing generally valid rules for the knowledge of society from phenomena. He not only sketches the contours of the forms he designs, but colors them by means of intuition and illuminates them with visionary suggestion. Quite apart from any conscious program, the great cultural historians have always been historical morphologists: seekers after the forms of life, thought, custom, knowledge, art. The more clearly they define those forms the better they succeed. A general question can only lead to a general answer. The history of the Renaissance remains a vague thing, even in Burckhardt's hands, because "Renaissance" is not a clearly comprehended form, nor can it be. Burckhardt's general thesis—itself an antithesis to the spirit of the nineteenth century and therefore understood only toward the end of that century—has in its turn had its day. But all the individual forms that he hewed and used as building stones, all his chapters about glory, ridicule and wit, domestic life, and the like, still preserve the value of that transcendent masterpiece intact. The same is true for Viollet-le-Duc, who is in general perhaps outdated, and in details sometimes perhaps inaccurate, but still always the master as a result of his unequaled feeling for forms. Hardly outdated at all is the work of a third historian contemporary with them, a historian too little known outside England, Leslie Stephen. Stephen deserves greater renown, if only to put to shame many a present-day monkey who feels he can document his own superiority by speaking scornfully of the Victorian period. Leslie Stephen's was not a constructive mind. His

English Thought in the Eighteenth Century avoids general theses and almost never leads to general conclusions. But it is precisely for that reason that his work has suffered very little at the hands of time.

It is no accident that the really significant cultural historians of the nineteenth century were almost all of them somewhat outside the stream of thought of their age. Auguste Comte had prepared the bed for that stream. But positivism was not suited to producing cultural history. Buckle is hardly read any longer, if at all. On the other hand, intellects such as Burckhardt, Viollet-le-Duc, and Leslie Stephen (for whom the autonomy of the humanities was a fact, even without a defined theory of knowledge) were able to point a way we still can follow. To understand cultural history one must recognize the spirit. The times are favorable for the cultural historian to find his confidence in his task supported. If he takes cognizance of writings such as Hans Freyer's *Theorie des objectiven Geistes,* Theodor Litt's *Wissenschaft, Bildung, Weltanschauung,* and Erich Rothacker's various studies, he will feel strengthened in the realization that with the groping methods of his discipline it is possible for him to produce true knowledge.

3. MORPHOLOGY AND MYTHOLOGY. Once one recognizes the task of history in general as that of creating a morphology of the human past, there remains an alarming question: Can cultural history, which has to create most of the names for the forms within which it views the cultural process, escape the danger of its morphology degenerating into mythology?

Oswald Spengler used the words "morphology of world history" in the subtitle to his *Decline of the West.* Perhaps in the future it will be said of Spengler, as Meinecke once said in passing of Taine, that he was among those "who have done more for scholarship by means of great errors than others by means of small truths. . . ." [3] If so, it will be because of the depth of Spengler's insight, his masterly combination of dissimilar things under a single denomination, his violent clarification of our historical thinking. It will not be because of the system he constructed. After one decade his pattern of world history stands as an uncompleted and abandoned mausoleum. The distortions, the biases, the acrobatic symmetry with which he designed it made his structure an unsuitable edifice for history from the very outset. His terms were so many shackles, his divisions so many prison cells for historical thought. However enchantingly he may have made the mosaics in his vision of Arab civilization sparkle, that vision, if carried through, would have obscured like a leaden fog every view of imperial Rome and the young West, of dying paganism, developing Christianity, and the phenomenon of Islam. The figure of Faustian man excluded any understanding of the Latin world. Spengler could not help falling short: he hated England without comprehending it, did not know America, actually did not understand either of the two strongest social institutions—religion and the state—in their tremendous significance, and had no eye for levels of culture and cultural diffusion. But the basic flaw in his work is not in the gaps in his knowledge or the limitations in his view, but in the fact that he strode recklessly down the path that leads from morphology to mythology. His anthropomorphic cultural beings passing through their youth, maturity, and senility in the imagery of all the ages have undergone the fate of every idol.

There are some scholars who, recognizing the free nature of thought in the humanities, believe that historical formalization can never be anything but the creation of myths. Only recently Theodor Litt demonstrated brilliantly in a few pages how unfounded and inadvisable such a standpoint is.[4] Contemporary man is a traitor to the spirit of his own culture if he creates myths in the knowledge that they are, or rather pretend to be, myths. Our culture's form of intellectual cognition is that of critical scholarship.

Anthropomorphism is the great enemy of the way of thought of the humanities. It is a hereditary enemy which that way of thought brings with it from life itself. All human language expresses itself anthropomorphically, in images derived from human activities, and colors everything abstract with the metaphor of sensory perception. But it is precisely the task of the humanities to be aware of the metaphorical nature of their language and to take care that the phantasm does not creep in along with the metaphor.[5]

We shall never rid ourselves completely of the old Purusha, from whose body the Vedic gods created the world, or his colleague in the Eddas, the giant Ymir. To understand a world we reach out again and again toward the conceptual tool of substituting a human being for it. History almost constantly introduces subjects of a general nature as protagonists that are basically mythologemata. Capitalism, Humanism, the Revolution, and the whole series are of this sort. It is to a certain extent unavoidable. But the more frankly the scholar recognizes the independence of the spirit, the more anxiously he should beware of the easy imagery that decks out that spirit in a masquerade costume. A cultural philosopher of significance, Karl Joël, writes: "If life wishes to attain a higher level it selects the nations and individuals suited therefor in the countries suited therefor. With the torch of Awakening the living spirit of history strides across the sleeping earth and the dreaming world of man, calling upon armies and heroes to arise for spiritual and material aims. . . . There the integrating *Weltgeist* called cultural life to a new turning and had the rupture repaired by Rome. . . ." [6] This is either allegory or rhetoric, and in either case it is dangerous.

Rothacker says: "The concept of evolution necessarily tends to bestow on a spiritual movement the character of an objective process. With such a concept the notion of a cunning of reason, that is to say the outwitting of the active subject by the objective course of evolution, is necessarily posited." [7] If the concept of evolution can be purchased in its purity only at the price of Hegel's mythical figure, is it not better to seek after other cognitive tools? Unless one prefers simply to give the name of God to this wandering *Weltgeist* or subtle Reason. In that way we would arrive at the remarkable conclusion that the concept of evolution can only be maintained on a strictly theistic basis.

But that noble conclusion is as a rule lacking when, as Spranger says, "the concept of cultural complexity is applied as if culture were an organic substance with strictly biological laws of growth, or even a mystical being like Hegel's subtle *Weltgeist*, which goes its own demonic way without regard to any living object." [8] This sentence contains extremely profound metaphysical thought,[9] but one is no longer within the bounds of the historical discipline. In every easy anthropomorphic metaphor the panorama of history's earthly contexts is rigidified. The prayer of the cultural historian ought to be: ". . . and deliver us from anthropomorphism, amen."

4. GENERAL MORPHOLOGY OR SPECIFIC MORPHOLOGY. The fault that this rigidification of thought frequently leads to lies in the fact that the scholar has staked out too large a claim for his thinking. He wants to have a view of the pattern of a vast complex and describe a general morphology without having become sufficiently familiar with the structure of its parts. The result is what De Tocqueville saw happening so clearly in the passage quoted above. A vague, indeterminate historical concept takes form, with all sorts of heterogeneous notions loosely associated in it. The whole can only be grasped and expressed by applying a striking metaphor to it. The vaster the complexes the historian wishes to fathom, the greater the danger of such hypostatizations.

Once a concept of cultural history has taken shape in this way it becomes an intellectual force and begins to dominate over our minds, which are only too willing to serve the new, consoling gods. And like every force, the concept expands, conquering territory at the cost of other concepts. The hollower the concept and the weaker the term in which it is expressed, the more that expansion of force bears the character of an inflation.

Almost all our general terms for cultural history are nowadays suffering more or less from such an inflation. The word Renaissance originally had a significance that, if not sharply delineated, was at any rate positive and historical, that is to say, factual. It served to meet an essential need, for in it an aspiration of the age resounded. Gradually the concept has been stretched out in both directions: backward into the Middle Ages and forward into the modern period. It has been applied to all sorts of terrains where related or seemingly related phenomena prevailed. "Our true Renaissance," says Herbert Cysarz, "arose in the eighteenth century. Classicism is the German High Renaissance." By transferring the term to another terrain in this way one takes away from it something of the full richness that accrued to it as long as it was restricted to the specific and unique cultural process for which it first came into use.

This is what has happened to the term Renaissance, and it is what has happened to Gothic, the Middle Ages, and baroque. There would seem to be a lively need for an intellectual medium of exchange. It sometimes seems that the modern spirit, as it outgrew dogmatism and formalism, merely obtained a new type of configuration in their place. It is the precarious privilege of the scholar in the humanities that, in the case of each form, each pattern he believes he perceives, he must decide for himself—without the support of an experiment or calculation—whether or not he is chasing a shadow.

Cultural history has for the moment more than enough to do in determining the specific forms of historical life. Its task is to determine a morphology of the particular, before it can make bold to consider the general. There is time enough for description of whole cultures around one central concept. Let us, for the time being, be pluralists above all. In cultural history so little has been done in the obvious field of defining the objectively observable and distinguishable forms of past life.

Precisely in this field there is a close interrelationship among all the humanities that can be comprehended within the concept history in the broadest sense. Each specialist works in his own field, but contact between them all is necessary. Constitutional history and the history of law investigate the most important form of all social life, the state and its institutions. Economic history describes and analyzes commercial forms; religious history, the history of technology, and sociology each do the same sort of thing in their own fields. The history of art and literary history, for a long time all too preoccupied with the determination of external genetic relations, is now seeking the way toward an understanding and a determination of delimited forms. Linguistics, since its shift from the external morphology of the *Junggrammatiker* to semantic questions—and thus to the internal morphology[10] of the expression of thought—has become more than ever an integral part of the humanities, one with which philosophy, law, and history will before long have to become better acquainted.

It might be thought that in the work of all these separate disciplines the task of cultural history is already being fully performed, that they together comprise the study of culture, and that there is no room for a separate history of culture which is not already occupied by one of the specialized disciplines. Such an opinion, however, seems to me to be incorrect.

Between history on the one hand and each of the specialized humanities (all of them by nature historical) on the other, there remains the essential difference that distinguishes history from philology. Though the extension of the concept is not usual, each of those newer disciplines—language, law, commerce, and the arts—might be called a philology in the full sense of the word. For all these specialized disciplines the problem is to understand cultural forms as such, isolated from actual events. For pure literary history the final object of study continues to be either the specific poem in its own right or the general concept of literature. For cultural history, on the other hand, the forms of the past are expressions of a spirit it attempts to understand, always viewing them in the thick of events. Cultural history directs its attention toward objects, but is continually turning back from those objects to the world in which they had a place. It goes without saying that this frontier between philology and history is constantly being crossed from both sides. That is the way of things in every peaceful society. But the frontiers retain their significance even so.

The objects of cultural history are the manifold forms and functions of civilization as they can be detected from the history of peoples and of social groups, and as they consolidate into cultural figures, motifs, themes, symbols, concepts, ideals, styles, and sentiments. Each of these can also be the object of one of the specialized humanities: the poetic theme that of literary history, style that of history of art, the concept that of historical philosophy. Even so they remain objects for general cultural history as long as they are viewed as tableaux in the great world-drama.

Comparative religion and ethnology demonstrate the significance of the myth, consecration, sacral activities, the tournament, the secret society, and the like in cultural life. Cultural history can time and again demonstrate the existence and the effect of such phenomena in the varied course of history. It makes use of those forms to understand particular events better, and in its turn thus lends confirmation and support to the schemata of the specialized disciplines. Many subjects of cultural history lie either outside the bounds of the special fields or else spread over all of them. The bucolic, for example, affects not only literature and the visual arts, but also the dance, music, social life, and political theory—

in brief, it is a cultural theme. Cultural functions such as service, honor, fidelity, obedience, imitation, resistance, and struggle for freedom are each of them subjects for sociology, if you will, but are not given conclusive treatment in the systematic study sociology makes of them unless cultural history also demonstrates their constantly varying shapes and effects in different ages and different lands.

If someone were able to write the history of vanity he would have half of cultural history at his command. Who will give us, for example, a history of pride in the seventeenth century? The seven deadly sins are seven chapters in the history of culture which are waiting for their treatment. Up to now, it would seem to me, only one of the seven has been made something of a theme in cultural history, and that because it, unlike the other six, is not immediately comprehensible to everyone, but shifts in meaning according to the culture concerned. It is *acedia,* the sin that is rendered quite unsatisfactorily as "sloth." For Petrarch it signified his *Weltschmerz.* The difficulty in properly understanding Dante's concept of *accidia* has long focused attention on this subject.[11]

Not that subjects have to be sought at all exclusively in the domain of intellectual life. How much one would like to see a history written of the garden as a cultural form, or of the road, the market, and the inn; the horse, the hound, and the falcon; the hat or the book in their cultural functions. Again and again it would become apparent that the investigations of the specialized humanities have not exhausted knowledge regarding their significance in society.

There is, then, no danger that a cultural history that paid more attention to the findings of the systematic humanities than has been done up to the present would thus surrender the territories of Clio to the much feared sociology that has already sued her once for them. Cultural history can to its own advantage still learn a great deal from the sociologists without having in the least to reduce itself to performing journeyman services to that systematic science of social forms. Close contact with the practical sociology of the Americans, the historical sociology of Marcel Mauss, and the philosophical sociology of Max Scheler, Hans Freyer, and others can only work to the advantage of cultural history. If it is threatened by dangers, then it is rather from the demiurgic allures that some present-day scholars consider their duty to follow.

Thanks to recent trends in the theory of knowledge, history is now better aware of its own worth and unassailability than it formerly was. It is precisely in its inexact character, in the fact that it can never be normative and does not have to be, that its security lies.

V

The division of history into periods, however indispensable it may be, is of secondary importance, always vague and imprecise, and always to some extent arbitrary. Colorless names derived from external and chance breaks in history are the most preferable designations for periods.

The need to have the course of events in the world divided into a sequence of periods, each with its own essence and aim, has its origin not in historiography itself but in cosmology and astrology. Concepts of time and destiny were very closely related in the old Oriental religions. In a word such as the Avestan *zerwân* (Persian *zamân*) the concepts fate, the celestial sphere, unending time, and the eternal change and movement of the world were mingled together in a single striking and meaningful complex. Time itself gave birth and was born, and affected everything that happened. Systems of cycles and aeons are not lacking in any of the advanced forms of religion.

Christian culture actually had no place for such a cosmic doctrine of aeons, any more than it had for the concept of a cyclic repetition of a similar course of events. The limited plan of Christian soteriological history did not permit such extensive periods. Hence in Christianity the concept of a succession of ages shifted from the cosmic to the historical, though with the latter focused on soteriology and the end of all things. The basis for the division into periods of world history was provided by the concept of the four world-empires, Assyria, Persia, Macedonia, and Rome, each of them succeeding and surpassing the previous one. This concept had already been developed in Hellenistic thought. It is, in fact, expressed as early as in the prophecies of Daniel, in the

vision of the four great beasts who came up out of the sea
and the image in Nebuchadnezzar's dream.[1] Parallel to this
scheme of the four world-empires was that of the six ages
of the world based on Saint Matthew.[2] As early as the fourth
century the Church Fathers Eusebius and Jerome brought
this double scheme into harmony, establishing a synchronism
of profane and biblical history. The theory of the four world-
empires reigned undisputed as the scheme for the division of
history until the sixteenth century. Throughout the Middle
Ages the fiction of the continuation of the Roman imperium
had made it possible to comprehend everything that had
happened since Christ's coming on earth and was still to
happen within the last of the four prophesied ages.

The humanists were the ones who gave the impetus to a
new conception. Their view of antiquity as a literary and
cultural ideal inspired in them the distinction that with the
fall of the Western Roman Empire a barbaric and despicable
middle age, *medium aevum,* had dawned, out of whose bad
Latin and "Gothic" art the West lifted itself only with the
revival of letters in their own day. It was only toward the
end of the seventeenth century - that the threefold division
Antiquity-Middle Ages-Modern Times penetrated from literary
usage to historiography itself. Initially it had little more than
academic significance there, but from the schoolbooks it
gradually acquired a firm place for itself. Of the three terms
actually only "antiquity" had anything more than a strictly
chronological significance.

In the eighteenth century, however, this changed. Though
the Enlightenment accented anew the negative emotional content that the term Middle Ages had already had for the
humanists, it was quickly followed by the great romantic
movement, which "discovered" another Middle Age in crusades and pious legends, ballads and Gothicism. It cannot
be said that romanticism threw overboard completely the
Enlightenment's negative estimate of the Middle Ages. Rather,
it included a shudder at the violence and cruelty of that age
as an essential and cherished element in its concept. One
could be a declared romantic and nevertheless refer from
time to time to "the terrifying Middle Ages" with their
"fanaticism" and "fables."

The field of the Middle Ages, already explored in the
seventeenth century by the industrious scholars of Saint-Maur

and their colleagues, was rediscovered by the romantics, who took possession of it as new overlords. Then they set to cultivating it with the new scholarship of the day: history, philology, art history, and so forth. But as the image of the Middle Ages became clearer and the contours of the individual phenomena sharper beneath the hands of the Grimms, Savigny, and a hundred others, doubts also arose whether the conception of the period as such was sufficiently based on the facts themselves to retain it as a historical term. Its limits had never been strictly determined. That A.D. 476 was not a break of any significance escaped no one. With regard to the period's conclusion scholars hesitated between 1453, the fall of Constantinople, and 1492, the discovery of America. Yet each of these terminal points was its own announcement of its insufficient motivation.

Then why not completely abandon the term Middle Ages (for actually it is only about it that there is disagreement)? Because the conception that has come to be attached to it can no longer be mistaken for anything else, because the term is no longer an empty, purely chronological name, but has come to imply whole complexes of valuable historical notions.

Here lies the core of the question at hand. We cannot do without the names of the periods, because they have become filled with meaning that is valuable to us, even though every attempt to motivate their validity only demonstrates the contrary. The causes for this seeming or real contradiction lie very deep. It would seem that despite the intellectualistic focus of our urge to knowledge, in this respect purely historical preoccupations can never break completely free from the cosmic sense, which demands a more profound understanding and arrangement than one of simple succession in time. And this association of historical and cosmic thought is made more complicated because the biological view of the past is imposed on it by the weight of natural scientific habits of thought.

Hence it is understandable that the studies devoted to the problem of division into periods time and again in this decade have produced the image of a great variety of opinions and attitudes and a certain instability in the point of view of each of the scholars. Most scholars recognize in principle both the shortcomings and the practical indispensability, or at least the utility, of some sort of system of division. Most of them display the tendency not to abandon the traditional system of three major periods, however imperfect it may be, but to correct it. To maintain its usability they follow one of three paths: either they shift the frontiers of the periods according to criteria they consider more precise and logical; they attempt to demonstrate that those frontiers should instead be a broad strip of no man's land; or they further delimit one of the major periods, by preference the Middle Ages, by splitting it into smaller pieces.

The undeniable continuity leading gradually from the declining culture of the Roman Empire to the culture of the new West of the Merovingians and Carolingians is the central theme of the writings of Alfons Dopsch.[3] That continuity can easily be transferred from the economic field, where Dopsch has done most of his study, to the intellectual, and to some extent even to the political. Pirenne develops the idea in his argument that the true break between antiquity and the Middle Ages ought to fall at the repulsion of the Moslem attacks on the kingdom of the Franks.[4] Ferdinand Lot, too, has come to a similar blurring of the frontiers between the ancient and the medieval world.[5]

Even more lively, and more intermingled with the question of principle, is the controversy over the transitions from the Middle Ages to the modern period. Karl Heussi, the church historian, has sharply attacked the utility of general systems of division for ecclesiastical history. Denying the possibility of general criteria, he would prefer to use the customary terms at best in a typological, not a chronological, sense.[6] Troeltsch, whose *Protestantism and Progress,* with its impressive argument, brought the question into the open on its German publication in 1906, in his last work, *Der Historismus und seine Probleme,*[7] lent his support to the profound value of division as a means of cognition, this in contrast to most other scholars. He saw in division into periods the completion and conclusion of historical thought, the structure of history. True, in the process he not only had to restrict the validity of the system to European history, as the only historical entity we are really capable of coming to know, but also had to decline to draw sharply the frontiers assumed as essential. The modern period began for him in the broadest sense in the fifteenth century, in the narrower sense in the seventeenth. It might even be questioned, in fact, whether Troeltsch did not seriously impair the value of his own thesis by recognizing *Grundgewalten*, basic forces, which lying far in the past, determine the character of the coming period. In this way the prophetic spirit of Israel, together with the Greek polis, gave life to the Middle Ages. In this way he had earlier called the Middle Ages themselves the fertile soil in which modern culture developed. These are valuable and irrefutable ideas, but what remains of the postulated periods as autonomous concepts? Von Below[8] raised his voice against both Heussi and Troeltsch with the argument that there definitely was a positive and general basis for division, though not, as Troeltsch would have it, in intellectual transformations, but in the great political transformations on which the realization of intellectual changes is dependent. It seems hardly reconcilable with this argument that Von Below nonetheless vigorously defended against Troeltsch the idea that the Reformation must be considered as the beginning of the modern period.[9]

Meanwhile, Hans Spangenberg had made a new attempt to break completely with the old tripartite division, replacing it by a differently delimited division.[10] The terms for the periods, always artificial and nothing more than makeshifts, should, he felt (in agreement with Von Below), be based on the great, decisive clashes of forces. The limits of the periods lay in crises and in conflicts threatening doom, not in enrichment of culture such as the Reformation and the voyages of discovery and exploration. Phenomena such as those mark the peaks, not the limits of periods. This thought is striking in itself, but Spangenberg's attempt at a revised division does not fit in with it at all convincingly. For him the breaks fall in the great migrations then in the thirteenth century (because of the Mongol invasions), and again in the seventeenth. It is not easy to see the logical connection between the Mongol danger and the changes in the political and social structure of Europe which led Spangenberg to distinguish the periods before and after the middle of the thirteenth century as the feudal age and the age of the "estates."

For the past three years the historical section of the Centre International de Synthèse at Paris has been working on a project designed to lead to the drafting of a "historical vocabulary intended to define rigorously the terms used by historians and to delimit as much as possible the fundamental concepts of their discipline." The plan is to do this by discussing in the sessions of the Centre each word that comes in for consideration, in order to achieve as much agreement as possible on scholarly concepts. One may question whether historical terminology can endure such a degree of definition, and also whether an approach in the form of dry symposia can promise the desired results. But it is certain that the reports of the sessions, which are published regularly as supplements to the *Revue de synthèse historique*,[11] have already contained a great deal of valuable material on a number of historical terms. In the very first session, in February 1926, the division into periods and the term Middle Ages were introduced by the Polish historian Oscar de Halecki;[12] among the persons taking part in the discussion were Nicolas Iorga, Rudolf Eisler, Henri Berr, Léon Cahen, and Lucien Febvre—enough to demonstrate how many facets of the problems under discussion were illuminated.

It is clear that there is a vital need for well-founded and defined terms of division. They are necessary to understand history in its changing phases. As we have seen, Troeltsch recognizes in division by periods the true structure of the discipline of history. But when one attempts to define precisely a term for a period it usually appears that the more the term wins in typological utility the more it loses in chronological value. The person who clings to the delimitation of chronological frontiers, viewing his period graphically as a segment of one continuous line, is acting in the same way as a person who would want to introduce the filets of a haddock into zoology. It is safer to speak of medieval culture than of the Middle Ages. A concept of medieval culture is built up out of a series of more or less harmonizing conceptions: feudalism, knighthood, monasticism, Scholasticism, and a great many others. The most important of them are concentrated round the year 1200. Spangenberg rightly feels that the great cultural achievements rather mark the middle than the beginning of a period. The frontiers of a concept Middle Ages as a period in time naturally lose themselves in antiquity on the one hand and the modern period on the other. The graphic image corresponding to a usable concept of a period is not a segment, but a number of circles of unequal size whose centers lie close together in an irregular group and whose circumferences intersect one another at a number of points, so that, viewed from a distance, the whole displays the form of a cluster.

For many scholars, however, the notion of the passage of time and of progress in a certain direction does not find sufficient expression in such a configuration.

Henri Sée rejects the principle of division by periods because it is incompatible with the concept of evolution. Only a concept of a cyclic development, he says, would admit a division corresponding to reality, but such a concept is in his opinion out of fashion, and at best applicable only to certain phases of Oriental history.[13] In fact, however, in recent years such a cyclical, or at least rhythmic, division and explanation of the process of history has been broached anew from various sides.[14]

Our age has a strong need for the concept of rhythm. Sometimes it even seems that if the concept is lacking the word is enough. Biology uses it as frequently as art criticism. It may be considered as an expression of this cultural need that in recent years the theory of generations has also been revived in history in various forms. In 1872 the French mathematician, economist, and philosopher Antoine-Auguste Cournot published a work entitled *Considérations sur la marche des idées et des événements dans les temps modernes,* in which he fitted history into a scheme of three generations of around thirty years each per century. This essay apparently eluded the attention of the German scholars completely. At any rate, when Ottokar Lorenz designed his theory of generations fourteen years later,[15] he based himself (not with complete justification) on ideas from Ranke, but not on Cournot. Lorenz's theory aroused a certain amount of sensation at the time, but found little following. Then it was completely forgotten, as appears from the following. Some five years ago Walter Vogel and Karl Joël returned to the idea almost simultaneously.[16] They both claim that they became acquainted with Lorenz's work only later. Soon afterward came the profound but extremely subjective interpretation of Wilhelm Pinder, who elevated the principle of the generation as emphatically as possible to the basis of all understanding of art history and cultural history.[17]

It seems to me that these new forms in which the theory of historical generations is proposed continue to suffer from the basic logical mistake invalidating that theory. The first generation of a series of three is always also the second and the third in two other series. But not only that. A triad of generations 1700-33, 1734-69, and 1770-1800 is proposed, by means of which a number of historical phenomena, together constituting the history of the eighteenth century, are considered in the sequence rise, maturity, and decline—or action, reaction, and synthesis. But there can just as easily be a series of generations marked by the years 1701-34, 1735-70, and 1771-1801, and so on for every year, and actually for every day. Biologically all these periods have quite the same value. The causal factor that is assumed to stamp one third of a century as a period of development and another as one of decline does not work at thirty-year intervals, but is constantly present in each of the three phases. The factor is not implicit in the human generation: the generation provides the material in which the process takes place. It is logically impossible to place the whole history of a century within the confines of a system of three generations. The theory is more valid when applied to one specific and well-defined cultural phenomenon. But even then its validity is deceptive, for the generation in itself, considered biologically, is always quite arbitrary, and can never be held responsible for an evolutionary phase of a specific historical phenomenon. In this case, as in almost every case, the junction of natural science and history appears to us to be prevented by an unbridgeable abyss.[18]

The only deliverance from the dilemma of an exact division by periods lies in the considered abandonment of every requirement of exactitude. The terms should be used, in moderation and modesty, as historical custom provides them. One should use them lightly, and not build structures on them that they cannot support. Care should be taken not to squeeze them dry, or tread them underfoot, as has been done with that of the Renaissance. One should always be aware that every term pretending to express the essence or the nature of a period is prejudicial by that very fact. One should forget, in using the terms, that Middle Ages refers to an intermediary position and Renaissance to a rebirth. One should constantly be prepared to abandon a term as soon as it seems to have lost its validity in the light of the nature of the individual details themselves.

Each term that comes into fashion for the indication of

a cultural period quickly takes on strong emotional accents, hues, and tastes. In that respect it makes no difference what sort of designation one tries to give a phenomenon. Purely arithmetical names such as Old Empire or Tang, or geographical ones such as Mycenaean, attract such emotional associations just as well as quasi-significant terms like romanticism and baroque. What a specific tone of highly unjustified and very snobbish rejection Victorian has acquired in a few short years.

Every name for a period which is taken too literally, or behind which too much is sought, disturbs the understanding. For this reason the terms that have their lack of motivation stamped on them are the terms that are most harmless in practice. Those are the national century or dynasty terms. Unless one would like to look upon a highly artificial generation theory of the centuries on the basis of our system of chronology as the true division of the past, surely no one will become the dupe of *quattrocento* and *cinquecento*, although they perform good services as a means of communication. However important the figures of Elizabeth of England, Frederick the Great, Charles XII, and Catherine II may be considered, no intelligent historian will look upon Elizabethan, *Friderizianisch, Karolinerna*, and *Yekaterinski* as organic segments of history. Hence it does not matter at all whether Elizabethan drama is allowed to continue to 1642. That is merely a bit inattentive toward the memory of James I and Charles I; it does not create a misunderstanding. True, all these terms quickly become charged conceptions, but their very names are a warning that they should be used only as tools and may not be considered as "concepts."

There is one more circumstance that ought to serve as a caution against careless use of the accepted terms for cultural periods. That is that the general, not specifically national terms of the kind have quite divergent meanings in the various European languages. German *romantisch* and French *romantique* do not mean at all the same, and "Renaissance" has quite different values in France, in Germany, and in Italy.

Nonetheless, the whole trend of contemporary historical thought forces us to bring ever more of this type of term into circulation. Though Von Wilamowitz had applied the term *Barockzeit* to Greek antiquity as early as 1881, it can be said that until about twenty years ago baroque had remained a very specific designation for certain forms of architecture and sculpture in the seventeenth century. Heinrich Wölfflin gave it life as a general concept of style in the history of art. Spengler availed himself of it. And gradually the word has become suited to indicate not only an artistic style but also a style of thought and a style of life. In this general, cultural-historical sense baroque is up to now still limited primarily to German scholarly idiom. A few years ago, when I was faced with the task of having to consider first the figure of Charles I and then immediately afterward that of Grotius, I discovered to my surprise that both of them only became understandable to me on the basis of a concept baroque as characteristic of the time.

In this way the problem of division by periods always leads our thoughts back to the quality that unites all the cultural products of an age and makes them homogeneous, the quality for which Lamprecht used the term "diapason," which Spengler's tremendous monument attempted to give form to, which Burckhardt's symphonic experiment suggested so clearly, which is always before one's eyes and is never to be grasped. We can give it a name by means of which we can more or less understand one another, but we cannot determine it. And in this indeterminateness of its supreme object the close connection between historical knowledge and life itself is revealed anew.

HISTORICAL IDEALS OF LIFE *

You have perhaps come here with the thought that there is only one possible subject for a person who has insights into world history to profess at this point in time: the historical background of the World War. If this is so, I shall disappoint you, for that is not my subject. If I summon up for a moment the winds that the war has chased through your minds, it will be in spite of myself. It is not the historian's task to speak in the storm like Demosthenes, and the clear day when he can watch nations and states drift along the stream of time like white clouds in a summer sky is now anything but near.

Even my point of departure, the example with which I wanted to introduce you to the thoughts that occupy me, I have chosen from the distant past, though there are examples enough ready at hand in the present day.

Charles the Bold, duke of Burgundy, had, like so many of his contemporaries, an unbridled craving for glory and a vast admiration for the generals of antiquity—Caesar, Hannibal, Alexander—whom he strove consciously to resemble and to imitate.[1] He had in his mind's eye an exalted

* *"Over historische levensidealen,"* inaugural lecture given as professor of history at the University of Leiden, January 27, 1915. First published Haarlem, 1915. Translation from the Dutch text in *Verzamelde werken,* IV, 411-32.

77

image of ancient grandeur, and he attempted to live in accordance with that image. In other words, Charles had a historical ideal of life.

It is about such historical life-ideals that I wish to speak: about the manner in which historical concepts may influence, and sometimes perhaps dominate, the evolution of a culture, a state, or an individual; about how such historical concepts sometimes present themselves as direct examples to be imitated, sometimes more as inspiring cultural symbols; and the way mankind, looking upward and backward to an illusory perfection in the past, attempts to advance itself by means of such an ideal, or dreams its time away in such a delusion. If I had set somewhat different, or somewhat broader, limits to my subject, I might have called it "romanticism and culture," or "renascences," or, more paradoxically, "the influence of history on history." But with such titles I should promise more than I am able to provide, and so I shall restrict myself to the title I have chosen: historical ideals—or better yet, some historical ideals—of life.

Two questions having to do with the philosophy of history present themselves forthwith. I wish to side-step them both, but I should take note of them nonetheless. The first question is this: Have I the right to look upon such historical concepts as really active factors in history, to speak of their effect as something autonomous? Are they not rather mere symptomatic phenomena on the surface, a culture's insubstantial forms of expression? It is undeniable that here, if anywhere, the position of historical materialism appears a strong one. Nothing seems more plausible than to account for such historical fancies as simply the cloak, the outward garb disguising an economic (or political) objective: arabesques of cultural history, and nothing more. Undoubtedly it is always the direction of contemporary endeavors that determines which recollections of the past will acquire value as life-ideals. It goes without saying that only those historical images in which the present can see itself reflected may become ideals or symbols. To that extent they are, in their emergence, dependent on the contemporary social or political situation. But once they are present in the mind with the value of an idea or a symbol, then (it is a concession that historical materialism itself made long ago) they continue independently, and as ideas can influence the further evolution of thoughts and situations. The socialist idea itself, in fact, provides by far the best example. If we bypass the question of the fundamental cause for the emergence of historical ideals and restrict ourselves to their role as factors in history, we shall avoid the danger of becoming entangled, at the very outset, in one of the most difficult questions in the philosophy of history.

With the aid of specific cases it is easy to demonstrate how a historical concept, as an example or a guiding principle, can very directly influence a person's or a government's conscious acts. The example of Charles the Bold is an unusually suitable one. His whole life bears the hallmark of a blind pursuit of a chimeric ideal. And the consequences for world history of the vicissitudes of that wondrous life are known all too well. Similarly his namesake and kindred spirit Charles XII of Sweden had the figure of Gustavus Adolphus in mind in his struggle for power: he attempted to make his life a conscious imitation of Gustavus's life, and hoped even to die in the same way as his hero. Louis XVI determined his attitude toward the Convention on the basis of a diligent study of the history of Charles I of England. During the preparations for the abolition of serfdom in Russia from 1857 onward, the order of the day among the Slavophiles (then still primarily a romantic literary group) was an enthusiasm for agrarian communism, which they wrongly took to be genuinely, traditionally Russian and viewed with an idyllic glorification. That sentiment determined the decision of the government to make common ownership of village lands the basis of the new agrarian system. This last example is important, because it pertains to an economic situation created as a direct result of a historical idea.[2]

The second question I had in mind is even more far-reaching. Let us again take our example as a starting point. For Charles the Bold the commanders of antiquity constituted a conscious historical ideal. But alongside them there were other historical ideals of a less defined sort which were more deeply interwoven in his whole conception of his life task: the struggle against the infidels,[3] the honor of his house, the age-old motif of vengeance against the king of France, the Anglophilia resulting from his descent in the maternal line. These were all of them historical elements in his mind which also helped to determine his actions, though he remained unaware or only half aware of their historical character. Is there, then, any basis for separating them logically from the historical ideals he was fully aware of as such? Put more generally: Does not every political and cultural concept derive its specific characteristics from its links with history; is not every action based on conclusions drawn from historical concepts? Hence, can one actually speak of special cases where historical ideals influence later history, since that situation obtains everywhere and at all times?

Indeed, I confess that, by concentrating our attention on notions whose character as separate historical concepts cannot be doubted, we are contenting ourselves with a rather arbitrary distinction.

I shall here consider as historical concepts both those based on historical research or substantiated tradition and those that are creations of mythological fancy. The historical accuracy of a concept is for the moment of no importance; the only thing that matters is whether it appeared to its advocates to be the true picture of a past reality. Not even that is utterly necessary, in fact: it is sufficient that the concept can be conceived of as living reality—even a fictional character in a romance or novel can do service in this respect as a historical concept. Hence a historical life-ideal may be defined as any concept of excellence man projects into the past. There are some such ideals that are quite general in purport, inspiring a whole cultural period, others that are valid for a state or a nation, and still others that accompany one single person's life. I shall restrict myself chiefly to the first, general type.

A survey of such ideals in their sequence over long periods of time would seem to suggest a certain line of development. In early periods of civilization they are mythical, lacking a true historical basis. They are ideals of pure happiness, very vaguely conceived and very distant. Gradually the recollection of an actual past comes to play a larger role—the historical content increases, and the ideals become more specific and closer at hand. While the ideal of perfect happiness is gazed after disconsolately, lost forever, the need arises to live in keeping with the ideal. Not only the historical quality has increased but also the ethical.

Along with general human ideals, however, there also arise specific ideals whose restricted purport render them valid only for a certain group. These are particularly national ideals.

They have survived general human ones, for while modern historical thought has removed the last glimmer of excellence from the latter, so that they have lost their naïve charm as direct examples for living, the national historical ideal is drawing more and more nourishment from history as it is studied more intensively. Nonetheless, it usually remains rather a mere symbol than an example for direct imitation. The modern world no longer seeks general historical examples of virtue and happiness, but seeks all the more historical symbols expressing national aspirations.

The oldest concept of past perfection is at the same time the most general one: it is that of the golden age as the first period of man, as it was known to the Greeks and the Indians.[4] I shall here leave out of consideration the special form that the concept assumes in the account of the earthly paradise. The vision of the golden age or *kertayugam* embraced the sum total of all vulgar and exalted pleasures, from those of the land of Cockaigne to the contemplation of God. In the forefront, however, were peace, innocence, and the absence of laws, eternal youth and longevity. For the ancients it was a historical ideal in the full sense of the word. Not only Hesiod but also Tacitus and Posidonius treated it as historical.[5]

There was, however, one thing that was not involved in the concept: the promise of return, or the stimulus to exert one's energies in an effort to restore that former bliss. On the other hand, in close connection with the idea of the golden age there also developed that of Elysium or the isles of the blessed. In both the Indian and the later Greek legend one finds the transition that the former king of the golden age— in the one case Yama, in the other Cronus—later functioned as ruler in the Elysium.[6] But while the Homeric Elysium and the Hesiodic isles of the blessed were thought of as on earth, far, far to the west, and to be reached without dying, as early as the Atharva-Veda the Indian Yama was "he who of all mortals perished first, who first departed to the other world. . . ."[7] The ideal of earthly happiness, long, long ago or far, far away, became a concept of a hereafter. It was inevitable: the ideal of absolute bliss had to cross the boundaries of life, and debouched in immortal longings.

In any period of civilization with a strong yearning for the absolute, such as the early period of Buddhism or the Christian Middle Ages, concepts of the hereafter naturally predominate emphatically over all cultural ideals. Such periods are focused on death, not on life. But no one forsakes the world and life so strictly, and the hope of immortality never can absorb an inexhaustible residue of vital energy seeking happiness and perfection on earth.

Can we not simply speak of cultural ideals in this respect? No. A belief in the perfectibility of culture was alien to the man of the Middle Ages: there was no attempt toward gradual evolution on the basis of the social situation, and the sense of constant transformation which constitutes the driving force of all present-day social and political desire did not animate him. The only medieval ideal of bliss which can be called a cultural ideal in the true sense of the word was that of world peace, Dante's ideal.

All the others were not only retrospective but also to a large extent negative. Culture denied itself by starting from the deep-rooted assumption that everything was better in earlier times, that there had to be a return to the original purity in morals and in law. A shunning of the present day, a longing to flee from hatred and misery, injustice and conflict, a turning away from earthly reality, in a word, the loosening of bonds, *moksha*—that was the fundamental link uniting the aspiration of earthly happiness and that of heavenly bliss.

The forms in which the flight from the present day can be expressed are by the nature of things limited. Cultural forms in general are very limited. In this case, where the point of departure was always an abhorrence of the hopeless variety and tumultuousness of life and the goal always simplicity and truth, quiet and peace, only a few forms could be serviceable.

Among the concepts of the past with an appeal as an ideal, it might be thought that there was one that from the very beginning would have been compellingly obvious as a lofty model for imitation: the lives of Christ and the apostles, the ideal of evangelical poverty. Yet first it was necessary for a new historical conception to develop, for a historical image of Christ, clearly seen and anguishingly experienced, to arise alongside the hieratic image, before the evangelical example could obtain practical value and effect as an ideal of life. It was not until the twelfth century that the phrase "If thou wilt be perfect, go and sell that thou hast, and give to the poor" suddenly struck home as a command. Bernard of Clairvaux caught sight of it with his vivid imagination; Peter Waldo and Francis of Assisi brought it into the world as a way of life. "What did the holy apostles teach us, and teach us still?" Saint Bernard exclaimed. "They have taught me to live." [8] It is a conscious historical ideal of life. Eleven hundred years and more, said Dante, Poverty, robbed of her first husband, was scorned and obscure, until Saint Francis came.[9] The imitation of Christ, as it arose in Saint Bernard, was a renascence, and when Thomas a Kempis, following Saint Bernard closely, announced it anew three centuries later, it was a renascence of a renascence.

The basic aspiration behind all this, the liberation from bonds, the breaking loose from attachments, could not have been expressed more purely than in the ideal of poverty. The ideal of virtue and the heavenly background completely overshadowed the ideal of happiness. Even so the latter, the promise of eathly bliss, was definitely present as well.[10] Nor was the urge to abandon home and possessions ever solely a theological impulse; it was also the age-old abandonment of culture for its own sake, a holy vagabondage in which the Poor Men of Lyons and the first followers of Francis encountered the player and the pilgrim, the wandering scholar and the ribald.

However strong the contrast may seem at first sight, there was nevertheless a close tie between the ideal of evangelical poverty and that of the pastoral life, the bucolic sentiment. It, too, signified an abandonment of culture, a yearning for simplicity and truth. But while the pastoral ideal abandoned culture for nature and pleasure, the apostolic ideal abandoned both culture and nature for virtue and the expectation of heaven. The practical effect of the two ideals was also very different. The imitation of poverty was a highly serious thing for its practitioners. No one doubts the tremendous influence of the notion on history. The imitation of the shepherd's life, on the other hand, was rarely more than a sort of party game.

It is open to doubt whether this gentle dream-image ever really influenced cultural developments.

No other single illusion has charmed humanity for so long and with such an ever fresh splendor as the illusion of the pining shepherd's pipe and surprised nymphs in rustling woods and murmuring brooks. The concept is very closely akin to that of the golden age, and constantly overlaps it: it is the golden age brought to life. To the extent that in the bucolic fantasy the idea of a long-past bliss is present (compare Horace's *Beatus ille* . . .)[11] one can speak in this case as well of a historical, that is to say a retrospective, ideal. It is only rarely that the pastoral poem becomes the victim of a confusion of real rustics with Corydon and Daphnis.

The bucolic was never really naïve and natural. In Theocritus himself it was a product of urban lassitude: a flight from culture. And even quite early the ironic tone, the awareness of the lie, can be heard now and then. The pastoral poem lived on in a series of renascences. It was a renascence when the Roman poets of Augustus' age turned bucolic, a new renascence when the late Greek pastoral romance developed, and another when the rather clumsy *beaux-esprits* at the court of Charlemagne draped themselves as Thyrsis and Damoetas and Alcuin sang of the cuckoo.[12] Later the chivalric lyric took over the bucolic motif and cultivated it in the *pastourelle*. In the fifteenth century the bucolic fantasy throve more luxuriously than ever. It set the tone at the courts of Orléans and Burgundy and in that of Lorenzo de' Medici. A king, René of Anjou, put the ideal in practice:[13]

> *J'ay un roy de Cécille*
> *Vu devenir berger,*
> *Et sa femme gentille*
> *De ce mesme mestier.*
> *Portant la pannetière,*
> *La houlette et chappeau*
> *Logeans sur la bruyère*
> *Auprès de leur trouppeau.●*

● I saw a Sicilian king / Into a shepherd turn, / And saw his gentle wife / Take up the same métier. / Carrying the shepherd's pouch, / The shepherd's crook and hat, / Dwelling upon the heath / Nearby their flock of sheep.

Then the great new pastoral play and the interminable pastoral novel came from Italy and Spain: Sannazaro, Montemayor, Tasso, Guarini, d'Urfé. A century behind the times our good Holland came to the feast with its Arcadias like a peasant schoolmaster in wooden shoes. Finally the eighteenth century brought the last and finest renascence of pastoral taste: Watteau, Boucher, and the idyls of Salomon Gessner. Then the form died out. As late as the eighteenth century literary theory sincerely viewed the pastoral poem as the most original literary genre and the most perfect expression of the natural. Then, however, the crook and the shawm and the pipes of Pan were put away as outdated properties. The form was finally outworn, but the spiritual need that had given rise to the pastoral poem continued: not only in Bernardin de Saint-Pierre's *Paul et Virginie* but also much later, down to the present day. Pan is still the most alive of the Greek gods.

Has this bucolic ideal of life, however, had any real influence on culture? Is it not mere literary history? Yet literary history is cultural history. It is of tremendous importance from the point of view of cultural history that man learned to express nature and love within the framework of the pastoral poem. And even outside the field of the possibilities for aesthetic expression the pastoral idyl exerted an influence on culture: from antiquity to Rousseau the notion of the natural state derived its strength and vitality from the concept of the golden age and the bucolic idyl.

The amazing vitality of the pastoral form also manifested itself in the ease with which the bucolic image merged with alien ideas, for example, religious ones. It was only natural that notions such as the shepherds of Bethlehem, the Good Shepherd, and even the Lamb of God came into contact with the pastoral, and the garbing of religious matter in the bucolic form was, consequently, to be found in various periods.

The reason for the great vitality of the form is undoubtedly to be found in its basically erotic character—a character that the pastoral shared with another ideal of life with which it accordingly formed intimate associations: the chivalric ideal.

With this concept we come to another ideal of life with a general human purport. It is quite different in nature from the bucolic ideal: much more substantial, much more real. And in particular it is much more genuinely a cultural ideal. The Arcadian fantasy, however important it may have been for the development of civilization, was in the final analysis an element of refined conversation and little more. It had only a limited influence on real life and the deeds of men. The notion of knighthood, on the other hand, permeated all of cultural life, inspiring political powers and military commanders. While the pastoral was born out of pure nostalgia, ideal had its basis in the firm foundation of social relationships: it emerged as the way of life of a class that was vigorously alive.

The development of the feudal system gave birth to knighthood as a class, but its origins as a way of life lie much deeper, in the sacral customs of primitive culture.[14] The three most momentous elements of chivalric life—consecration as a knight, the tournament, and the vow—stem directly from age-old sacral rites. Was it perhaps partly because of a vague awareness of those age-old origins that the chivalric ideal also took on a retrospective, or let us say a historical, character from the very outset? Even in its first development as an actual way of life, in the twelfth century, chivalry displayed the characteristics of a renascence, a conscious revival of a romantic past, whether that past was sought in antiquity, in the times of Charlemagne, or, above all, in King Arthur's circle.

Compared with the bucolic ideal, then, the chivalric ideal had in the first place more historical content. The chivalric tradition had much more of a basis in a real past and was much more open to historical specification than the vaguely described, never-changing image of happiness in the pastoral poem. A more profound difference is the following: In the concept of the golden age and the bucolic fantasy the ideal of happiness predominated over the ideal of virtue—virtue was there negative, primarily innocence, the lack of a stimulus to sin in the state of simplicity, equality, freedom, and abundance. In the chivalric ideal, on the other hand, the aspiration toward virtue outweighed that toward happiness. The calling of a knight was altruistic: protection of the oppressed, fealty to the ruler, the weal of Christendom. His life was in the service of the realm and culture. As late as the fifteenth century anachronistic minds exalted chivalry as meeting the needs of every age. This, then, is an almost pure cultural ideal.

As a result of its altruistic character, the chivalric conception of life was always closely related to religion. That relationship, in fact, was not at all subsidiary, for chivalric virtue was basically not only altruistic but also ascetic. The ascetic basis manifested itself clearly in the strange, barbaric-appearing chivalric vows to deny oneself rest or comfort until a certain heroic feat had been accomplished. These vows betray their primitive origin, for instance, in the large role played in them by hair and beard styles: one has only to think of one of the last offshoots, Lumey's vow at the outset of the Dutch struggle against Spain. Together with religious self-chastisement they had a common root that lay far outside and far before the development of Christianity. But the ascetic character of the knight was not only to be found in such vows. Bravery itself is a primitive form of asceticism: the first self-denial, the simplest self-sacrifice, the triumph over natural egotism and immediate vital interests, the elementary virtue that is born earlier and retains its value longer than any other form of asceticism.

The true knight abandons the world. Jacques de Lalaing, the exemplary knight of the fifteenth century, wanted to transfer his hereditary rights to a younger brother: "for all his desire was to use his life and to expose his body to the service of Our Lord and to remain at the borders of the marks of the infidels without ever returning from thence thereafter." [15]

It was this deep-seated trait of self-sacrifice which made it so easy for the chivalric ideal to be completely spiritualized [16]—the spiritualization that took place in the ascent from the poetry of the troubadours to Dante's *Vita nuova*. Nonetheless, that self-sacrifice was rooted in the deep erotic soil of the chivalric ideal. It cannot be brought enough to the fore that the chivalric function found its highest expression in the tournament, and that the tournament was nothing more nor less than the most elegant and most expensively adorned form of those erotic matches whose origins lie not only far outside the sphere of higher culture but also outside that of human culture in general. The essential element in both the tilt and the chivalric vow was the presence of the women under whose eyes the man shed his blood or displayed his bravery and strength. This sexual element was clearly seen and expressed throughout the Middle Ages. From it sprang the whole romanticism of chivalry: the motif of the knight who freed the maiden, of the unknown knight whose unexpected appearance and decisive courage focused all eyes on him, in short, the whole gaily colored setting and sentimental fantasy of the *pas d'armes*.

And this is also the link that binds closely together the chivalric ideal and the pastoral. The chivalric ideal brought tension into the fragile fancy with which the bucolic genre conjured up a free and undisturbed enjoyment amidst paradisiac nature; it refined and ennobled the languishing of the pastoral to the element of adventure and battle.

The direct effects of the chivalric ideal on history are easy to indicate. In the first place, the courtly love lyric and the chivalric romance, like the pastoral, played a very important part in the development of the aesthetic sense. But the chivalric ideal also exerted a constant influence on political and social relations and events. Even the scholar who believes that his task is to trace economic causes in every medieval war nevertheless has to recognize time and again the effects of the chivalric ideal both on the methods of warfare and on its results. Kings exposed themselves to the danger of the most violent battles. The best commanders were risked in pre-arranged single combats. A battle would be accepted for the sake of chivalric honor; a straight path through enemy territory would be chosen because a roundabout way was unchivalric. The success of a battle would be risked for the sake of the formal custom that the commander who passed the night on the battlefield was considered to be the victor.[17]

The chivalric ideal had an extraordinarily strong and lasting influence as a way of life. All the higher forms of bourgeois life in later times have actually been based on the imitation of the ways of life of the medieval nobility. Heroes of the third estate such as Philip van Artevelde and Jacques Cœur lived completely within the bounds of chivalric ideals and forms. Courtly life and the courtly concepts of virtue and honor served to produce the modern gentleman.

There is still one point that should be stressed in this consideration of the chivalric and the pastoral ideal. Why are both of these ideals of life to be found in a series of recurrent renascences? In this respect the situation of chivalry is no

different from that of the pastoral: the knighthood of the fourteenth century was a deliberate recreation of that of the twelfth
and thirteenth, that of the fifteenth likewise, and so forth. It
would appear that the reason for this repeated emasculation
and revitalization of the two ideals lay in the large degree
of falsity in them. The serious pretension of the chivalric ideal
to realize itself in the world was precisely what restricted it in
its impelling force. The form, so to say, constantly ran empty;
again and again a period of maximum falsification of life and
self-deceit would be followed by a reaction. An unheard-of
amount of dissimulation was needed to maintain the fiction
of the chivalric ideal in actual life. Only in the immediate
vicinity of the ruler could it be done without a blush. Around
the year 1400 the most serious and detailed preparations were
repeatedly being made for single combats between two rulers
to settle their differences, combats that no more took place
than did the crusades announced with resounding vows. The
much praised "battle of thirty against thirty," the choicest
chivalric combat, actually had a fairly mean course, according
to Froissart's own account.[18]

Those who upheld the chivalric ideal were aware of its
falsity, and it is for this reason that—almost from the very
beginning—there was a tendency for the ideal to deny itself
from time to time in irony and satire, parody and caricature.
Don Quixote was merely the last, supreme expression of that
irony: the line runs through the whole of the Middle Ages.
The renowned "vow of the heron" at the court of Edward III
of England took place amidst jesting and laughter: Jean de
Beaumont, the excellent knight of Hainault, declared cynically
that he would serve the lord from whom he could expect the
most money.[19] The bucolic ideal was safeguarded from such
constant decay much more than the chivalric ideal because
it had fewer points of contact with reality. Cervantes himself
still took the pastoral seriously.

Meanwhile, a last notion of perfection had come to occupy
the minds of men more and more, this time a historical ideal
of life in the strictest sense of the word: that of Greek and
Roman antiquity. Nothing is less accurate than the thought
that the classical ideal dawned over humanity like a sun in
fifteenth-century Italy. A glorified image of antiquity had

shone throughout the Middle Ages, only it was not discerned clearly or completely. A classical renascence was, in fact, harbored not only in Scholasticism and the study of Roman law: there were important classical elements even in the chivalric forms of life which to our way of thinking were so typically medieval. The system of courtly love was derived to no small extent from a Latin source: Ovid and Vergil signified more to medieval thought than mere storybooks.[20]

Just as little true as that the classical ideal was not reborn until the Renaissance is the notion that the medieval Christian and chivalric ideals were then supplanted. On the contrary, what we call the Renaissance is a product of classical, chivalric, and Christian aspirations, in which the classical element is the chief motive power, but not the only one.[21] Burckhardt's masterpiece has taught us to look upon ambition and a sense of honor as the two central characteristics of Renaissance man. Both of these can be explained more readily as a direct extension of chivalric honor than as a result of the revival of classical studies.[22] Not everything that glitters in the Renaissance is antiquity: the highly unclassical chivalric fantasy of the Amadis romances still reigned supreme in the minds of the sixteenth century.

The reason that the classical ideal stood out above everything else in the life of the Renaissance is that its historical content was so much richer than that of the chivalric ideal, and that it was in a much broader sense a true cultural ideal. The classical way of life was the first that could be made the object of faithful imitation down to details. Antiquity provided guidance and the finest examples for every form of expression. One's art and learning, one's epistolary style and eloquence, one's concepts of the state and military tactics, one's philosophy and faith could be imbued with or made conformable to divine antiquity, which provided a full abundance of rich nourishment for the ideal.

It was the enrichment that mattered, not the imitation. Modern culture has not derived its vitality from a determined copying of antiquity, but from a life-giving permeation by the classical spirit and form. The industrious imitator of Cicero or Brutus became just as impossible a creature as the salon shepherd or the perfect knight. Though the historical content in the concept of antiquity was larger, that does not mean that there was less falsity in its practical expression in the lives of the humanists. The ostentatious and loquacious humanist, treacherous and hollow, a peacock in his pride, soon lost his place in the eyes of his contemporaries. Rabelais can be heard chuckling at him.

As long as the world saw in Greek and Roman antiquity an objective perfection worth imitating throughout all times, and consequently attributed normative validity and absolute authority to it, in a word, as long as the Renaissance lasted, the Middle Ages actually continued. But, as is the case in every sort of education, one usually learns for good precisely the things one does not seek in books. Engrossed in antiquity as the result of an admiration for it and a desire to resurrect it, people became more and more aware of its *historical* character: seeking for what could unite, they found what divided. Via antiquity and from antiquity man learned to think historically, and once he had learned to do so he had to give up historical ideals of life with a general human significance.

The last time classicism displayed itself as a practical ideal, a directly imitative life-attitude—in the grandiose phrases of the French Revolution and the art of David—it gives the impression of an anachronism as opposed to the way in which Goethe in the same period derived purely *modern* life from antiquity.

Since that time historical cultural ideals of a general human purport have apparently passed out of the picture. Even romanticism was never completely serious in its imitation of the Middle Ages. The copying of historical forms in nineteenth-century art, like the copying of medieval architectural styles, has no significance in this respect. The plain reality of history—and the unquenchability of the desire—became too clearly conscious for modern humanity to continue to seek its salvation in the imitation of an imagined past. But the old needs continue. Culture would still like to flee from itself, the endless nostalgia for the uncultured still endures. We are perhaps too near to them to realize that, though now quite free from the old forms, the basic moods of the pastoral and of evangelical poverty continue—in anarchism, in literary naturalism, in the struggle for a reform of sexual morality.

Hence it is history itself that has banished historical ideals of life as tenuous shadows. History has taught the world to look forward in its struggle for happiness, and no longer to drug itself with retrospective dreams of life. Ideals of such general human significance that they can inspire and unite a whole society are no longer sought in the past. But at the same time other historical concepts more limited in value and more specific in content have been brought to the fore by the historicism of our day. I should like in closing to say a few words about the most important of these: national ideals of a historical sort.

National historical ideals have in common with the concepts already discussed the fact that, however accurate they may be historically, their character remains romantic. Nationalism (I am not saying patriotism) without romanticism is nonexistent. These ideals distinguish themselves from the earlier general ideals in that as a rule they do not serve as models for immediate imitation, but rather as symbols, or even as mere slogans. They are, moreover, much less ideals of happiness than of power and honor, and at best also of prosperity. And finally, their ethical value is restricted in a singular way: it is very much there for those upholding the ideal—in other words, for the group, the state, the nation in question—but it is often not recognized at all by nonmembers. Only those national ideals embodied in a genuinely human hero or in a generally admired struggle for freedom have an independent ethical value. Happy the nations that have such a chapter in their history, as does the Netherlands, or will have, as will Belgium. On the other hand, the world is unmoved when a nation appeals to Tamerlane or some other conqueror.

Like the general human ideal, the national historical ideal develops from the mythical, the vague, and the undifferentiated to the historically defined and tested. The national hero, known even to early antiquity, is of the same type everywhere: above all, a victor, an industrious servant of the true God, and sometimes also an inventor and a benefactor. Even very early in such national hero-worship conscious fabrication and political intent are at stake. Everyone knows how much the Roman Aeneas saga smells of the lamp. The same thing is true to an even greater extent of medieval national ideals. They are almost all of them hand-me-downs of the Aeneas saga transposed into the chivalric sphere. Only gradually did the nations grow aware of their true historical heroes and heroic ages. The concepts become more and more varied, ever richer and more precise in content, and history is called upon ever more emphatically as a justification for the aspirations of the present. The higher the culture, says Dietrich Schäfer, the more these historical tendencies in national life come to the fore: "The modern period is utterly permeated by these ways of thinking. The formation of the national state, which dominated the nineteenth century, drew its vitality and force from them more than from anything else." [23]

Nonetheless, the role that such historical concepts play in the life and hopes of the various nations and states does not seem to me to depend solely on the level of their culture. In this respect it is, in the first place, of great importance whether a nation has already attained its full development or is still struggling toward it. One might say that for the dissatisfied nations historical stimuli are indispensable. Hence the extraordinary place they occupy in the lives of the Balkan nations: the Greeks, Rumanians, Serbians, and Bulgarians. As a result of their hopeless ethnic confusion in a large central area all these peoples feel irredentism in its most painful form and are dominated by a strong urge toward expansion: Greater Serbia, Greater Bulgaria, Greater Greece. The Greeks, the Bulgarians, and the Serbs have each of them at some time exercised hegemony over the peninsula and held the others in subjection. But in order to form a link with that great past they all have to skip over a long period of common enslavement under the Turk. This gives something of a mythical character to their national ideals: Stephen Dushan and Czar Simeon have much of the traditional national hero about them. Among the two Slavic peoples, the strongly romantic inclination natural to the race also helps to make their historical recollections an especially active factor in their national life.

These inclinations—perhaps the romantic even more than the historical—constitute a second point determining the weight of national historical concepts. A third point is the question to what extent there is a harmony between contemporary national aspirations and the history of a nation. It is a curious phenomenon that history plays so much more prominent a role in German nationalism than in that of the

western European nations. France and England, too, are both
of them proud enough of their noble history. But they invoke
it less often. What are Vercingetorix and Boadicea to them,
compared with what Arminius means for the German consciousness? Schäfer goes on to say: "The German nation owes
a tremendous debt to the historical focus of its longings and
feelings, the recollection of its past. The 'past is our spiritual
property, one of our most valuable.' "

Without a doubt this difference is to be traced primarily to
the strongly historical inclination of the German people. As
far as France, in particular, is concerned, however, the other
point I have mentioned also plays a role. The French national
historical consciousness is obstructed in its power because of
the repeated breaks in French history. There is too much that
it has to repudiate in whole or in part. At the very outset,
French nationalism cannot yield itself wholeheartedly to
Merovingian and Carolingian greatness, because it was too
Germanic. However much glory France's kings and its great
Emperor may radiate, the French people of the republic cannot revere the Sun King, or even Napoleon, as the symbol of
the country they love with such affectionate tenderness. And
the principles of 1789 are too abstract for that function. It is
for this reason that for the French a single historical figure
(but a figure more beautiful than any other nation possesses),
Joan of Arc, has more and more tended to attract to itself
the value of a national symbol.

By way of contrast, one can see in Germany the need to
mold the whole storehouse of the national past into living
symbols of national strength which exert their influence even
far outside the circles where history is studied. Arminius,
Barbarossa, Luther and Dürer, Frederick the Great and
Blücher—all of them have a direct and vital meaning for the
German soul. The significance of Scandinavian mythology in
contemporary German culture, above all owing to Wagner,
must not be underestimated. It is singularly remarkable to
what extent Bismarck has already attained the significance of a
national symbol, even of a national hero—endowed with the
attributes of a heroic age, depicted in a medieval role, and
viewed as "the timeless ideal embodiment to our [German]
nationhood . . . ," with a place "in the Old Germanic age,
the earliest heroic age of our nationhood. . . ." [24] There is an

element of great strength, and perhaps also a danger, in this preference of German thought to orient itself toward primitive culture.

Or is it perhaps thought that, in the tremendous impetus with which we see a nation determining its will, hardly any effective value should be attributed to all these historical symbols—that they should simply be relegated to the realm of rhetoric: flowery style and colorful metaphors? The question left unanswered at the outset returns. It remains unanswered even now: the magnitude of the effects emanating from these historical concepts can never be measured. Let us admit that their influence may be infinitesimally small.

But now the other question also recurs. The historical element in national thought is not only to be found in such well-rounded concepts; it also lurks in all our notions and emotions: fatherland, renown, heroic death, honor, fidelity, duty, national interest, progress. Its effect is felt in every word and every action. The wisdom and the folly of ages speaks constantly in us. Time and again there are those to whom it seems as if history is suffocating us all.

We have spoken of the age-old impulse to abandon culture, to flee from the present day and its misery. In times such as these the impulse comes over us now and then more powerfully than ever. What will be the refuge? There are still a number of roads open. Though the past no longer proffers us the lovely dream of a peaceful perfection that may perhaps return in the future, ancient beauty and wisdom still grant sweet forgetfulness to the person who seeks it. Does the future have more to offer? We can observe this raging world from an absurd distance and say that it will take three thousand years for all the madness of the present conflict, the stupidity and the terror, the fate of states and nations, the very cultural values that now seem the highest stake to have become just as unimportant to humanity as the wars of Assyria are today. This is no consolation; that, too, is mere forgetfulness. And such resignation can also be achieved from a briefer distance: we can view all this through the eyes of those who have fallen. That is still the shortest road to liberation. The person who wants to abandon today, with its heavy burden of history, has to abandon life. But the person who wants to carry that burden and still climb upward finds a fourth road open: that of the simple act—it makes no difference whether in the trenches or in any other serious work. Giving of oneself is the end and the beginning of every philosophy of life. Liberation is to be found not in the abandonment of culture, but in the abandonment of one's own ego.

PATRIOTISM AND NATIONALISM
IN EUROPEAN HISTORY •

I

TO THE END OF THE MIDDLE AGES

In the ominous present there are two forces that, for good
or evil, are straining and convulsing the world organism like
a fever. One of them is patriotism, the will to maintain and
defend what is one's own and cherished, a will that, at present,
is everywhere and every day being put to the most severe
test, in violent combat and patient service. The other is nationalism, the powerful drive to dominate, the urge to have
one's own nation, one's own state assert itself above, over, and
at the cost of others.

Patriotism, says the fool within us all, is our virtue, and
nationalism is the vice of others. But is it necessary for an
unfavorable sense to be attached to nationalism? That question
depends on two things: one's outlook on life and the language
one speaks. For the person who professes Christianity, in

• *"Patriotisme en nationalisme in de Europeesche geschiedenis
tot het einde der negentiende eeuw,"* three lectures given February
14, 21, and 28, 1940, in an annual series under the auspices of the
University of Leiden Fund and held under the title *"Studium
Generale."* Translation from the Dutch text of the second edition,
reprinted in *Verzamelde werken*, IV, 497-554.

97

whatever form, the very definition of nationalism as a drive to dominate should imply a condemnation—assuming that the definition is correct. But that is a question of idiom, and the idiom is definitely not one and the same everywhere and every time that the word is applied. The suffix "-ism" is by no means necessarily an indication that a term is objectionable. Nor is the vocabulary regarding things national the same in every language. While Dutch makes a clear distinction between *nationaal besef* ["national awareness"], *nationaliteitsgevoel* ["sense of nationality"] and *nationaal bewustzijn* ["national consciousness"] on the one hand and *nationalisme* on the other, English uses the one word "nationalism" for all these meanings. If we wished, we might also apply the word nationalism simply as an indication that a principle of national organization dominates, or that there is an attempt to promote that sort of organization. In contrast with patriotism, however, I should like to understand nationalism as a tendency that, exceeding certain bounds, is no longer good, but evil.

To arrive at a preliminary definition of the value of our terms it is also necessary to repeat the warning, rarely superfluous, that general historical terms such as these never describe precise quantities that can be pinned down in mathematical formulas. They express what people hear, or want to hear, in them. *Verba valent usu,* which does not at all apply in an exact discipline such as physics, is a fact that must be kept constantly in mind by the historian, even when he is using a word that seems to be immediately comprehensible to everyone.

What is patriotism—a learned word for the love of one's fatherland? Is it as simple as that? I believe not. The love of his fatherland means to the Dutchman that the Netherlands is dear to him, is dearer to his heart than any other country. The word indicates a sentiment, and no more than that. In patriotism, on the other hand, it seems to me that there is also something of a conscious awareness and an aspiration: it expresses a conviction of a completely binding obligation toward the fatherland, an obligation restricted only by the supreme guiding principle of the conscience. The dividing line between patriotism and nationalism, however one may understand the latter, is in theory absolutely clear: the one is a subjective feeling, the other an objectively perceptible attitude. In the practice of the individual case the line dividing them is often very difficult to trace.

The opinion is widespread among historians and political scientists that both patriotism and national consciousness, not to mention present-day nationalism, are cultural phenomena of a recent date. The chief basis for the opinion is the fact that the words and the formulated concepts are themselves quite recent. The word "patriotism" first cropped up in the eighteenth century, and "nationalism" only in the nineteenth. In French *nationalisme* is to be found once in 1812; the oldest example of "nationalism" in English dates from 1836, and then, remarkably, with a theological significance, namely for the doctrine that certain nations have been chosen by God. Considering that "nationalism" later came to fill a larger sphere of significance in English than in Dutch (and than in French or German), the English word has carved a place for itself in the world in a single century.

The conclusion that the phenomena of patriotism and nationalism are recent because the words and concepts are recent is easily drawn, but misleading. It stems from the age-old human habit of attributing existence to things only once they have a name. On the same basis one might conclude that there were no cosmic rays in the Middle Ages. Or, to mention a more closely related parallel, on a similar basis—the lack of a name or a concept for the matter at hand—the existence of the state in medieval times has been denied. It is true that the word and the concept "state" were only brought to the fore by the Renaissance, but even though the phenomenon "state" was largely hidden behind that of the Church in the Middle Ages, medieval society made good use of the concepts *regnum* and *civitas* to express things political.

On close observation the equivalents of patriotism and nationalism prove to have been present in earlier periods, and more significantly, the only change in the two emotions in the course of time has actually been that they have become somewhat more clearly delineated. For the rest, they have remained what they always were: primitive instincts in human society.

We should here like to devote only a few words to antiquity. Actually, did not every ancient nation, and in fact does not every archaic nation in general, look upon itself as chosen to rule over others? Is such a concept not a heritage from an age-old primeval period? Intricately associated with religion, the notion consolidated itself into the unbounded pride and the vicious delusions of grandeur of the Egyptian and Babylonian kings. Here one may speak of religious nationalism in the full sense of the word. Was such religious nationalism on the part of the rulers answered by an equally deep-rooted awareness in their subjects which one might call patriotism? Undoubtedly the obsequiousness of those subjects was also very deeply anchored in devotion, adoration, and slavish servility. Was there love, attachment, and fidelity in the popular consciousness as well? Students of these ancient civilizations may decide the answer, if the sources betray it.

The picture is much clearer as soon as the gaze is turned from the ancient Near East to the Greeks. In the Hellenic world patriotism was highly developed, but there was little national consciousness. In the city-state, the polis, Hellas created an exceptionally favorable soil for a sense of the fatherland which was at the same time narrowly restricted and politically based. Greece gave us the word for fatherland, *patris*. Actually, the first time that *patris* occurs in that sense it already conveys perfectly the most essential elements of patriotic feeling. It is in Book Five of the *Iliad*, where Pandarus says to Aeneas: ". . . when I get home again, and set my eyes on my native land and my wife and my tall house. . . ." [1] Returning, seeing again—that will always be the fondest aspect of the sentiments inspired by one's native land. Above this tender awareness of one's own small bit of land there vaunted a feeling of a general community of Hellenes over against everyone non-Greek, the barbarians. Just as in other similar cases of the larger and the smaller community, that feeling did not for a moment exclude the most violent mutual enmities among Greek tribes and states. It can be called a national consciousness, but not nationalism. There was no place for nationalism in the Greek world. The remarkable spread of Hellenism throughout the Mediterranean area in the form of settlements did not take place as a sort of national expansion, for all the lasting bonds that were created between the colonies and their mother cities. Characteristic of the lack of appreciation of the national in the strict sense is the fact that in their reflections on the state neither Plato nor Aristotle devoted any comment to the national factor in its structure.

The Hellenistic kingdoms after Alexander the Great took over the Greek concepts of fatherland and nation as a matter of course, bending them to Oriental circumstances to a greater or lesser degree. Probably nowhere in ancient times does the pathos of a love for one's fatherland resound more clearly, and for us more familiarly, than in the Jewish Hellenistic form reflected in the Second Book of Maccabees. Judas Maccabeus exhorts the hosts he has gathered neither to be reconciled with the enemy nor to fear its power. He reminds them of the outrage committed against the holy places and of the way in which the Almighty God had helped them against Sennacherib and against the Galatians. "He had made them bold with these words, and ready to die for the laws and the country." [2]

Although the Latin word *patria* was no doubt modeled on the Greek *patris*, the Roman concept of the fatherland emerged pretty much independently of Greek concepts. It evolved in the heyday of the Republic in the form of genuinely national hero-worship devoted to the virtues and the glory of the state. The representatives of early Roman patriotism were so many examples of heroic courage and civic virtue: Curtius, who leaped into the abyss; Dentatus Curius, who chose his meal of turnips above the gold of the Samnites; Regulus, who kept his word to the enemy and returned to Punic captivity —in brief, the whole array of men who were to play a significant role in the political and literary education of the Europe of later times. The Roman sense of the fatherland always retained something fond and alive owing to the fact that it continued to be concentrated on the city of Rome itself, with all its sanctuaries, traditions, and symbols, even after the expansion of the realm over province after province. Moreover, there continued to be something active and forceful in it as a result of its basis in a practical political life that was well-ordered juridically and constitutionally.

Even during the centuries of the Empire the ideal of a city-state holding sway over an immense realm continued to be maintained. The Roman Empire never became a national state. It numbered many dozens of nations, in whose special dispositions the state was not interested. Hence here, too, there was no place for any true nationalism. In the long run it was inevitable that the old Latin sense of a fatherland should fade in that motley of peoples from east to west. As for terminology, in Greek *patriotes* meant simply "country-man," and was somewhat disparaging as compared with *polites*, or "citizen." It was only in the post-classical period that Latin took over the word. *Patria* had a different significance in antiquity from the one it has for us, in that it was not attached exclusively to one's native land. Cicero, who was awarded the title *pater patriae*, was able to say that everyone has two fatherlands, a natural one and a legal one (*una naturae, altera civitatis*, or *loci et iuris*). But the patriarch Aeneas had himself sought and found a new fatherland in Italy, hence when Cicero pronounced *ubicumque est bene ibi patria* ["our country is wherever we are well off"], the phrase lacked the cynical irony we easily tend to hear in it.

The Christian faith was raised above the confused contrasts of nations and kingdoms as early as the time of Saint Paul. It had no contact with questions of political allegiance or national entity, and left the state for what it was, rendering unto Caesar the things that were Caesar's. Nonetheless, the organization of the faith, the Church, required a political organization as a basis for its earthly task, and for its defenders "render unto Caesar" and "there is no power but of God" were not enough. A Christian theory of the state was indispensable. Hence Augustine constructed the tremendous edifice of his *De civitate Dei,* in which he was forced to assign to the secular state—in itself reprehensible—a dual function: that of being an emergency institution without which no human society, and no peace, was possible, and that of serving and protecting the Church for as long as this world shall last. The Roman Empire, the last of the four world-empires of Daniel's vision, would continue for a while, purified and sanctified, in the *imperator christianus*. As Augustine wrote his *De civitate* the authority of that emperor was collapsing, at least in the West, where the saint lived. It is no wonder, then, that in principle he preferred an international order in which "the kingdoms of the earth would have continued little in quantity, and peaceful in neighbourly concord. And then many kingdoms would have been in the world, as many families are now in a city." [3] Here, for the first time, the principle of independent states living together in concord is clearly formulated. Before Augustine's century had reached its end, the West would indeed number many states that sooner or later were to become Christian, although not in quite the concord that Augustine had wished for. All of them held fast, as much as possible, to the tradition of Roman imperial authority, whether they were the Ostrogoths in Italy, the Visigoths on either side of the Pyrenees, the Vandals in Africa, or the Franks in Gaul. Then from the kingdom of the Franks there suddenly sounded the clarion call of a new national awareness in which, however contradictory it may seem, the glory of Christian salvation was intermingled with the primitive pride of a barbaric tribal allegiance. I am referring to the well-known prologue to the Salic law, which, even though it may be slightly more recent than the law itself, nonetheless reflects the Merovingian situation. It speaks of "the glorious nation of the Franks" which traced its origins to God, "brave in arms, faithful in peace, wise in council," and ends with a triumphant cry:

Hail Christ, who loves the Franks. May He protect their kingdom, may He fill their leaders with the light of His grace, may He watch over their army, may He strengthen their faith, may He grant them joy and happiness! For this is the nation that with strength and bravery has shaken off the hard yoke of the Romans, and after its acceptance of Christianity has enshrined in buildings decked with gold and precious stones the bodies of the holy martyrs burnt, beheaded, and thrown to the wild beasts by the Romans.

European nationalism had started out on its path through history. The Christian West began its political evolution on a dual foundation: an ideal of a universal Christian world dominion, and a reality of as yet unsteady complexes of power, barbaric in nature and Roman in tradition. Gradually, over a period of a good six centuries, Latin Christendom arranged itself in a number of kingdoms corresponding, though still very roughly, to national lines. The neighborly concord that Augustine had set as a condition was absent, but the times were not yet ripe for major national wars. Except for occasional expeditions of conquest quite rapidly completed, violence was constant and intense, but on a small scale. Now what, in these earlier Middle Ages, was the result of the ideal of universal power above and beyond the multiplicity of separate states? It called into being both the restored imperium of Charlemagne and the supreme secular authority of the pope.

Customarily the medieval opposition of pope and emperor is viewed from the very outset in the light of the theory of the two powers as the two celestial bodies God had placed over the earth at the time of creation. This symbolism, however, was not applied to the imperium before the days of Frederick Barbarossa. The emperors from Charlemagne onward had pretended to continue the Roman Empire, but not to wield universal dominion. That ideal was first to be heard when the Hohenstaufen ruler wrote to a bishop: "One God, one pope, one emperor, are enough for the world." [4] The real power of the emperors never depended on that claim, nor on the title.

The claim of the pope to universal authority was much more one of principle than was that of the emperor, and in a certain sense it was also more effective. At first glance it seems pure hierarchical pride when Peter's successor demands the supreme right of authority over all nations and above all kings of the earth—besides the ultimate word in matters of dogma and of Church administration. Yet that demand stemmed directly from the heart of the Church's doctrine. The Holy See did not at all deny kings and princes their authority. It did, however, claim the right to judge each juridical and administrative act of the rulers in exercising that authority. The deeds of the kings continued to be subject to the power of the keys, according to the criterion of good and evil, *ratione peccati* ["for the reason of sin"]. But such a judgment of royal deeds by the criterion of religion unavoidably brought with it the criterion of justice. And hence from the time of Nicholas I in the ninth century, one finds the doctrine of papal dominion over the world formulated ever more positively, and repeatedly put into practice in deposing kings, granting lands, and bypassing existing laws.

In this great conflict between the concepts of papal and imperial dominion there was no soil for a further development of national consciousness and the sense of a fatherland. On the other hand, the concepts did not serve to impede the evolution of the national configuration of Europe. The consolidation of the states and nations of the West had gradually continued after the collapse of Carolingian power. France,

England, and Scotland, the three Scandinavian kingdoms, Aragon, Castile, and Portugal, Sicily, Hungary, and Poland had all of them taken their places as units of Latin Christianity by around 1150. The claims of the imperium, which was named after Rome and was in the hands of the Germans, were, in spite of the imperial authority, not able to prevent all those kings from demanding complete sovereignty—or in medieval terms, imperial dignity—for themselves. In exactly the same period when the struggle between the pope and the emperor for universal authority reached its height, shortly before 1200, the national organization of Europe had little by little become a fact. Saint Hildegard of Bingen betrays a remarkable insight into this fact in her visions. While the two greatest universalists of the Middle Ages, Emperor Henry VI and Pope Innocent III, were still to come, she saw the imperial aspirations to world power retreating before the national principle:

In those days the rulers of the Roman Empire shall lose the strength with which they had earlier held that empire, grown powerless in their glory. The kings and princes of the many nations that hitherto were obedient to the Roman Empire shall detach themselves from it and no longer be subject thereto. And thus shall the Roman Empire be dispersed by default. For every region and every nation shall place itself under a king, whom it shall obey.[5]

The framework within which national consciousness and a sense of fatherland were to evolve in Europe, then, was established by around 1100. How had the usage and significance of the words *patria* and *natio* developed meanwhile? The Latin terms must be taken as the points of departure, for it was in writings in Latin that the two concepts were formed. The word *patria* had not been lost with the end of the ancient period. The expression *caelestis patria*, the celestial fatherland, was of itself enough to keep the concept alive, and the word was to be found in the earthly sense in several places in the Old Testament. In that earthly sense, however, *patria* no longer had the full resonance of the ancient Roman word. It had become an administrative term without a great deal of emotional value. Such emotions did exist, as the *douce France* of the *Chanson de Roland* evinces, but they were not associated with the word *patria*. *Patria* was used to indicate a specific jurisdiction, a county or a group of several counties. It was the exact equivalent of *terra*, or in French *pays*, the word for the many regions that gave to pre-Revolutionary France so much more charming a pattern than the present-day checkerboard of departments. Hence in the twelfth and thirteenth centuries one repeatedly encounters phrases such as *tota patria congregatur*—the whole region, the entire land, is called together. A person is exiled from his *patria*.[6] Naturally there was, as a rule, a correspondence between the limits of the jurisdiction and those of the native land that one was attached to with all the fondness the *Heimat* can inspire. Here, then, is the older, more restricted sense of a fatherland, or if one prefers, a feeling for one's native soil. Only in a few cases in these centuries can the word *patria* be found used in a different way, and then probably under the influence of classical reading. Gerbert, the renowned scholar of the late tenth century who was to become Pope Sylvester II, sometimes used *patria* in a more limited sense and sometimes in a broader one, but, remarkably, neither for Aquitaine, his native land, nor for Auvergne, his *pays* in the restricted sense, and certainly not for the kingdom of France as a whole. Gerbert lent a great deal of support to transferring the French crown from the Carolingian dynasty to the house of Hugh Capet. Hence it is all the more surprising that his *patria* concept applied to the German emperors Otto II and Otto III, whom he had faithfully served. And with him that *patria* has an almost classical or modern sound. He impresses upon Otto III that he should seek his renown in "braving the greatest dangers for the fatherland, for the faith, for the welfare of his people, and for the commonweal [*rei publicae salute*]". So little, one must conclude, were the French and the Germans aware of their factual political separation around the year 1000.

The word *natio* had always remained much more current than *patria*. Actually it had changed very little in connotation since classical Latin. Closely linked with *natus* and *natura*, it vaguely indicated a larger context than *gens* or *populus*, but without there being any fixed distinction between the three terms. The Vulgate used *gentes, populos*, and *nationes* interchangeably for the nations of the Old Testament, and that biblical usage determined the significance of *natio* for the time being. It indicated a fairly indefinite interrelationship of tribe, tongue, and region, sometimes in a restricted sense, sometimes in a broader one. The Burgundians, the Bretons, the Bavarians, and the Swabians were called nations, but so were the French, the English, and the Germans. Unlike *patria, natio* did not have an administrative significance, and initially not a political one either. But little by little the various relationships of dependence and community obtaining exerted an influence on the restriction and delimitation of the concept *natio*. The glory of the kingship, the fealty to the liege lord, the protection of the bishop, the mildness of the master, created a great number of relationships of close community. Only the larger relationships of this sort could be expressed by the term *natio*. But whether the relationship was large or small the basis for the emotion embodied in *natio* was the same everywhere: the primitive in-group that felt passionately united as soon as the others, outsiders in whatever way, seemed to threaten them or to rival them. This feeling usually manifested itself as hostility and rarely as concord. The closer the contacts the fiercer the hate. It is for this reason that there were no more violent enmities than those between neighboring towns, for instance the rivalry between Genoa and Pisa, which Salimbene says in his chronicle were divided by a natural aversion such as that between men and snakes or wolves and dogs. The two noble cities, he states in his account of the naval battle of Meloria in 1284, destroyed each other out of sheer ambition, pride, and vanity "as if there were not sea enough to sail." [7] The English hated the Scots, and the Danes the Swedes, in the same way, though perhaps less violently, as did also the French of the *langue d'oïl* the Aquitanians. The form in which these emotions were expressed demonstrates their instinctive character. The eleventh-century French chronicler Radulf Gaber reproached King Robert I's queen for opening France and Burgundy to the Aquitanians, vain and frivolous folk who were as affected in their ways as in their dress: they wore their hair cropped half-long and shaved their beards like buffoons, wore improper stockings and shoes, and worst of all, they could not keep faith. Clearly their clothing was at least as irritating as their morals. This sort of thing can hardly be called political sentiment. Nor can the old, deep-seated antagonism between Romance and Germanic peoples which vaulted above all those local, regional, and national antagonisms actually be given such a label, for that antipathy was to be found even before the political division between the Romance and Germanic parts of the Carolingian empire had come about. The life of Saint Goar, written around 840 by the monk Wandalbert in the monastery of Prüm, in the Eifel, tells of a German living along the Rhine who

> with a certain national hatred [*quodam gentilicio odio*] abhorred all persons of Romance nation and language [*Romanae nationis ac linguae*] so much that he was not even willing to view the face of one of them with equanimity. Such an obtuseness born of barbaric ferocity had seized his mind that he could not look upon people of Romance language or nation passing by—even upright, noble men—without aversion.

The lasting political foundation for this great ethnic antithesis was actually only laid in the year 887. The Verdun treaty of partition in 843 had been merely a solemn repetition of the partitions that were long since traditional in the Frankish empire, perpetuating the unity of the empire in name. Only after Charles the Fat had failed in an attempt to restore that unity in actuality did the definitive partition between an East Frankish and a West Frankish realm become a fact. *Hic divisio facta est inter Teutonicos et Latinos Francos,* says the official chronicle regarding the treaty of 887: "Here was the division made between the Germanic and the Romance Franks." From that time on there was a Germany and a France. When early in the tenth century Charles the Simple met Henry, soon afterward to become king of the Germans, at Worms, the young noblemen of both retinues, *linguarum idiomate offensi* ["offended by the idiom of each others' languages"] occupied themselves, as was their custom (says the Richer chronicle), with heaping violent contumely upon each other, then drawing their swords and fighting one another to the death—a peacemaker was one of the victims.

The Crusades, far from uniting in the faith what was divided by language, descent, and allegiance, reinforced the national enmities of the peoples of Latin Christendom by bringing those peoples together again and again in martial equipment, battle array, and a more or less sanctified rivalry. Eckhart of Aura speaks of the hostility between the German and French knights in the First Crusade as an *invidia quae inter utrosque naturaliter quodammodo versatur* ["invidiousness that comes about between the two somewhat naturally"]. On the same occasion Guibert de Nogent displays Germans, Lombards, and Sicilians joined together against the French, whose pride they could not abide. Himself a Frenchman, he adds, remarkably, that the French tend to behave themselves intractably among foreigners if they are not kept well in hand.

Even this could not be called conscious nationalism. It was the primitive feeling of aversion between tribes and nations which is to be found everywhere, and is apparently unavoidable. It became something else in the twelfth century, when the first political consolidation of France and of England coincided with the acme of power of the German imperium, whose political policy took on the form of true imperialism—justified, as it were, by the imperial title itself. In 1107 the Emperor Henry V sent an illustrious embassy, headed by the archbishop of Trier and containing two other bishops and several counts, to Châlons-sur-Marne to meet the pope. The German envoys arrived in great pomp and circumstance. Especially Count Welf of Bavaria attracted attention. He was an amazingly tall and heavy-set man, says Suger of Saint-Denis, who was an eyewitness (*vir corpulentus et tota superficie longi et lati admirabilis et clamosus*), and a sword was carried before him at all times. The embassy appeared to be intended more to intimidate than negotiate (*magis ad terrendum quam ad ratiocinandum missi*), except for the archbishop, an elegant and merry man (*vir elegans et iocundus*) who spoke good French.[8] The issue was an important one: the investiture of the bishops. When views clashed, says Suger, the "headstrong envoys" (*cervicosi legati*) created a tumult, "raging with German impetuosity" (*teutonico impetu frendentes*), and threatened to settle the dispute with the sword —not there, but in Rome. Here one can see the Frenchman's picture of the German, already given shape and color. A bit later Suger uses the phrase *furor teutonicus*. It came from Lucan's *Pharsalia,* where it was applied to the Teutons of old who had frightened Rome out of its wits in Marius' day.

This is clearly a quite different sound from that of clashes between young knights on a crusade. This is a political note that unfortunately is never to fade again.

Fifty years later Frederick Barbarossa of Hohenstaufen approached the zenith of imperial power—and of the conflict between emperor and pope. The political opposition to France took on sharper forms. Among the persons attacking the emperor with the pen, one stood out far above the others: John of Salisbury. John should not be looked upon as representing a national English point of view. He was an internationally minded churchman, and as such he abhorred the emperor, the German tyrant, *teutonicus tyrannus*. In an exchange of polemics with the imperial chancellor he used the frequently quoted phrase, *Quis Teutonicos constituit iudices nationum?:*

> Who has appointed the Germans to be judges of the nations? Who has given authority to brutal and headstrong men that they should set up a prince of their own choosing over the heads of the sons of men? In truth their madness has often attempted to do this; but by God's will, it has on each occasion been overthrown and put to confusion. . . .

And he, too, lets fall the words *furor teutonicus*.[9]

It does not seem exaggerated to say that in the medieval West conscious political nationalism first appeared as a reaction to the German imperial policy of the Hohenstaufens. A century later, the final result of the emperors' long and bitter struggle against the power of the pope, the towns and princes of Germany and Italy, and the increasing authority of the French king was that, together with the proud house of Hohenstaufen, that imperial policy had succumbed. In the continuing process of organizing Europe along national lines, it was henceforth for many centuries France and England, and later also Spain, that took the lead. The national antithesis between the Romance and the Germanic nations remained what it had always been: a contrast in culture founded on the primitive basis of linguistic and ethnic differences. The contrast led to political hostility only in cases where neighbors on the two sides came into conflict with each other, such as that of the Flemish and the French, when the Leliaerts had to pronounce the difficult Dutch words *schild en vriend* ["shield and friend"] in Bruges in 1302, and when the Dutch poet Jacob van Maerlant wrote his *wat wals is, vals is* ["everything Romance is false"]. The derivatives of the

Old Teutonic word *walh* (Walloon, Valaisian, Welsh, Vlach) of course had several different meanings, depending on whether they were applied to French, Italians, or what not, just as did the derivatives of *diota* (Dutch, *diets, deutsch,* Teutonic), which could cover the whole range of Low and High German lands. The suggestive power of that antithesis *diota* and *walh* was so strong that Jan van Boendale could simply ignore all the other nations of Europe when he wrote:[10]

> *Kerstenheit es gedeelt in tween:*
> *die Walsche tonge die es een,*
> *d'andre die Dietsche al geheel.* •

There was only one place from which the national structure of Europe that had gradually developed was clearly seen: from the *curia* of the Holy See. Rome was in constant touch with all those lands and peoples, yet was above and beyond their multiplicity. Only in Rome could there actually be a question of international politics in practice, and as a result of the papacy's knowledge of affairs and widespread sources of constant information, its diplomacy was far in advance of that of the secular states. Meanwhile, the organization of administrative systems in the other countries had become more efficient by around 1300. Unity of the state had become a conscious requirement, and in France and England the administrative, judicial, and financial systems had gained enough hold to provide the basis for a vigorous national policy. And there resounded a nationalism which in its ardor and energy concedes little to modern forms, one which was at the same time based on quite real political situations and aspirations, admixed. with or disguised by Christian political ideals of a general kind. The crusades were over, that is to say, the power of the Latins in the Holy Land had been broken, but reconquest—thus the Crusade as a political concept—remained the recognized, prescribed objective of every Christian prince. Soon after 1300 Pierre Dubois, a lawyer from Normandy, wrote two political tracts, the first under the title "On the Curtailment of the Wars and Controversies of France," in which he advocated a general

• Christendom is divided in twain: / The Romance tongue it is one, / The other all the Germanic tongues.

system of peace, with sanctions, boycotts, the intervention of neutrals, and so forth; and later one entitled "On the Reconquest of the Holy Land," in which he anticipated a hegemony of France for the benefit of Christendom. He was a zealous Frenchman. The Italian, in particular, was an object of his hatred. The French, he believed, had never received their just due: France was the logical leader for the Crusade, the pope should relinquish his secular power to the French king, and it would be to the advantage of the whole world to be subject to France because the French nation used more common sense than any other.

This, then, is political nationalism in full flower. A similarly proud and drastic nationalism on the part of England inspired the first prolonged conflict between two of the great national states of Europe, the Hundred Years' War between England and France.

In both countries the national consciousness was consolidated along with the growth of the state itself, and became a clear-cut factor in political life. This was not possible in the countries where a central power and a unified state did not develop: in Germany and Italy. In Germany neither the monarchy nor the imperium was capable of functioning as an active agent toward a politically potent awareness of a general Germanic nation and state. The last great Hohenstaufen, Frederick II, had already allowed suzerainty over the German princes, lords, and towns to pass out of his hands. A live general sense of Germanness definitely continued to exist, but it broke down, either as a loyalty to a clan, a region, or a town, or as a purely dynastic feeling through the countless units into which the Holy Roman Empire gradually threatened to dissolve. Thus it lost its political character, remaining on the intuitive level of sheer sentiment for the *Heimat*.

In Italy as well, every potential principle of national political unification had fallen short. Neither the old Lombard monarchy of the iron crown, the Sicilian kingdom of the Normans and the Hohenstaufens, nor the French adventure in power politics which carried the Anjous to Naples had been the starting point for a strong administration over all Italy and a corollary sense of national unity. Papal policy had deliberately blocked such a development rather than aiding it. Venice, Genoa, Florence, Milan, and all the other larger and smaller urban signories were most violently hostile and jealous toward one another. Nonetheless, amid all the factions a general Italian national consciousness continued to grow. The designations Rome and Italy never lost the resonance of a glorious past. The classical tradition was at all times stronger there than anywhere else, and that tradition implied unity. Simultaneous with the presumptuous French nationalism of Philip IV's audacious policies, the note of an Italian patriotism and nationalism was sounded, never to fade again, for it was sounded in Dante's voice. It was in a minor key, for it lived in repression: *Ahi serva Italia, di dolore ostello* ["Thou inn of sorrow, ah, trampled Italy"]. . . . The idea of a liberated and reunited Italy became associated with the old dream of Roman universal dominion. An emperor of peace would bring to Italy the unity and tranquility that Dante cherished above all else. World dominion, *monarchia,* was the order God willed on earth. The people of Rome were destined to elect the emperor. And lo, Henry VII, the German emperor, came to fulfill his task of peace in Italy, and failed from the very outset. He died there in disillusionment, and lives forever in one of the highest spheres of Dante's *Paradiso:*[11]

> *In quel gran seggio a che tu gli occhi tieni*
> *Perla corona che già v'è su posta*
> *Prima che tu a queste nozze ceni*
> *Sedera l'alma che fia giù agosta*
> *Dell' alto Arrigi ch'a drizzare Italia*
> *Verrà in prima ch'ella sia disposta.*•

Less than thirty years after Dante's death the fiery, poetic, mystical Italian patriotism and universalism that Dante had dreamed of in his *De monarchia* was made reality, as if in a wondrous, fantastic interlude in history, by the tribune of the people, Cola di Rienzi, for half a year the liberator of Rome calling for the unity of Italy and the foundation of the universal empire, then for seven years an exile, a prisoner, and a political propagandist of a bad sort, finally to be

• On that great seat thine eyes are drawn unto / By the crown hung already over it / Ere at this wedding-feast thyself art due, / The soul, on earth imperial, shall sit / Of the high Henry, coming to enforce / Right ways on Italy, though she is yet unfit.

exalted again in Rome, this time by papal policy, and to be killed in a street riot. The ideal of popular government, the classical freedom of the senate and the people, the glory of Rome, a pride in Italy, and a sacred aspiration for universal peace have never been so strangely combined as in that small, vain, faithless man Cola di Rienzi, whose only greatness was his dream.

There were two fields outside direct political and hierarchical relationships where the peoples of Europe constantly came into contact with one another in a manner forcing them to association and understanding on the basis of mutual trust. One was trade, the other was study—that is to say, the university. For the further development of the concept of nation both were fruitful, and particularly the latter. In the important commercial centers where merchants from everywhere assembled (Bruges is for the Dutchman the most familiar type), the foreign traders united into "nations." These "nations" undoubtedly served to strengthen the sense of national cohesion, but their field of activity was generally limited to the town harboring them.

The effect of the national principle was much more intensive and general in the universities that sprang up from the twelfth century onward in Italy, Spain, France, and England, and soon found in Paris their indisputable *primus inter pares. Studium* was highly honored in the Middle Ages; sometimes it was posed as an equal member of a trinity along with *sacerdotium,* the office of the Church, and *imperium,* that of the state. Ecclesiastical authority reigned supreme in the university. Masters and scholars were clerics. The school as such was strictly international, and its instruction, in the liberal arts, theology, ecclesiastical and secular laws, and medicine, was not generally made subservient to any political or national interest. University life, however, led from the very outset to national grouping. The scholars, a turbulent mass of largely foreign, mostly poor, and always young persons, were an element of constant friction with the people among whom they were living. They often had to depend on each other for the safeguarding of their rights and their existence. What was more natural than that they should form groups according to their *natio,* either in the older, narrower sense of the region where they were born or in the broader sense of the state or realm to which they were bound by laws, language, and customs? The university became a starting point and a focal point for national organization. In Bologna, the university itself in a certain sense grew out of the combination of national student *corporationes,* each of which had before called itself *universitas.* As is known, up to that time the term *universitas* had meant nothing more than a community, a "corporation," of whatever sort. The scholars of Bologna were divided into two large groups, the Cismontanes, including the "nations" of the Lombards, Tuscans, and Romans, and the Tramontanes or Ultramontanes, in the beginning consisting of no less than fourteen different "nations."

In Paris, also, an initial grouping in numerous "nations" soon gave way to four larger ones: the French, the Picards, the Norman, and the English. Three of these thus represented regions of northern France, while the fourth, the *natio Anglica,* not only included everyone coming from the British Isles, whether he spoke English, Anglo-French, or one of the Celtic languages, but also had to accommodate Germans, Scandinavians, Poles, and what not. Here, then, there was an instability in the concept *natio* which was bound to lead to conflict in the course of time. Only in the middle of the fourteenth century was a *natio Alemanniae* split off from the *natio Angliae;* it was in turn quickly subdivided in a Low German and a High German nation.

At the English universities of Oxford and Cambridge the jealousy and the often bloody wrangling that was in many ways the distinctive element of the "nations" was, to say the least, no less evident than elsewhere. At Oxford the very statutes stipulated an official division into two "nations," strangely enough not on the basis of the differences between England, Wales, and Ireland (Scotland was not involved), but of that between northern and southern England. Wherever universities developed in the following period, for instance in the German lands, the system of "nations" was adopted. Under their procurators, chosen for a brief period from among the young masters of arts, the nations were the most unsettled part of the university. The system furthered the penetration of a national consciousness in very broad circles in every country and at the same time preserved the international character of the whole.

Ecclesiastical organization had long been on the way toward a certain process of nationalization. England, in particular, had achieved an important amount of autonomy in Church affairs as early as the thirteenth century. The popes themselves were the first to make use of the national principle, as a counterweight to the power of the college of cardinals, when the archbishops and bishops at the Council of Lyons in 1274 met by nations alongside of, and in opposition to, the cardinals. Final voting at the Council of Vienne in 1311-12 was held nation by nation. It seemed as if the Great Schism that began in 1378 would accelerate the disaggregation of the Church. Each land chose sides for the pope at Rome or the pope at Avignon. And when the Council of Pisa was finally convened in 1409 to restore the unity of the Church, the principle of the nations was indisputably master. The four nations of Italy, France, Germany, and England constituted the formal organization of the council. Dissolving without having reached a solution, the council met again five years later at Constance. There the principle of the nations gave rise to a serious controversy. The English and the Germans wanted to retain it; Cardinal d'Ailly opposed it. England refused a fifth place, after Aragon as fourth, and had its way, because King Sigismund's diplomacy led him to England's side. Several points deserve particular attention in this connection. In the first place, that the *nationes* at the council were considered to be representatives of the whole population of their country. Secondly, that the nations did not completely correspond to the existing states. Representatives from Savoy, Provence, and a large part of Lorraine voted with the French, though all those lands were still considered to be part of the Holy Roman Empire. What, then, characterized a nation as such? Language, dynastic bonds, ecclesiastical ties? The question was debated, without agreement being reached. There was, however, a dawning awareness that a difference existed between general nations and specific nations—which in turn produced new points of disagreement.[12] Men such as Cardinal d'Ailly were fully aware how dangerous for the unity of the Church the recognition of the nations as the elements of Christendom could become.

The council convening in Basel in 1431 as the last of the series allowed the authority of the nation-principle in Church affairs to lapse in its futile discussions. But at the same time the reunified papacy was busy arriving at compromises with the larger countries which confirmed the already far advanced nationalization of the Church as a fact. Gallicanism and Anglicanism were just around the corner.

Toward the end of the Middle Ages, then, the forces of patriotism and nationalism were winning more and more ground in Church and state alike, and no less so in popular life and culture.

II

FROM THE RENAISSANCE TO THE NAPOLEONIC ERA

It was not difficult to demonstrate the untenability of the notion that national antitheses were alien to the Middle Ages[1] and that national consciousness is a product of the modern period.[2] No matter how far back into the Middle Ages one looks, there is any amount of evidence of a lively sense of nationality, and even of out-and-out nationalism: feelings which stemmed directly from the soil of blood ties, love of the native land, the language community, common morals and customs, and (by no means least of all) fealty to a common prince. Initially such feelings did not have a great deal to do with the state and statecraft, and political goals and problems had little if any influence on the evolution of national ties. From the beginning there were more restricted and less restricted ties: the sense of community was of course strongest in the more restricted groups, but a broader antithesis—French versus Italian, or Germanic versus Romance —could gain the upper hand at any moment. National diversity found expression almost exclusively in the form of hostile contact. Nonetheless, such hostility was not of itself the source of major conflicts between states. It cannot be said of the prolonged war between France and England that it resulted from national differences, but it can be that in the course of that war, and as a consequence of it, the national differences grew. The only typically national struggle in the Middle Ages was that between Germans and Czechs in the Hussite wars.

Toward the end of the Middle Ages the chief national units west of the Balkans had been formed, and were more or less linked to specific political entities. The present-day nomenclature for peoples had gained currency long since: Italians, Frenchmen, Germans, Spaniards, Portuguese, Englishmen, Danes, Norwegians, Swedes, Poles, and Hungarians. Within each of those spheres there was still the greatest conceivable ethnic, linguistic, and geographical diversity. The word nation was still used primarily for the more restricted regional entities. Above the multiplicity of small and large entities vaulted an awareness of general Christian (that is to say, Latin Christian) unity, though that played a role only in ecclesiastical issues, particularly in the attempts, by then quite tainted with politics, to resume the Crusades, and in matters pertaining to the schism and the councils. Neither the imperium, which had lost its positive power, nor the papacy, which was drawn more and more into the complications of international politics, any longer exerted a unifying influence on the national configuration of Europe. The Church itself had been entangled in a process of national disintegration since the thirteenth century. The English church was in many respects already independent of Rome, and after the last of the great councils the French church was moving in the same direction. Then in the sixteenth century came the great breakaway from Rome, which in England, half of the German lands, Scotland, and the Scandinavian North ended the undisputed dominion of the old Church for good, introducing national confessions and organizations in place of it. Even Calvinism, in its essence so supranational, adapted itself to political lines in Scotland, the United Provinces, and New England.

Humanism and the Renaissance fell in a soil whose composition had been determined largely by the element of nationality. What were the reactions resulting from the contact of the national principle with the new spirit? The answer need not be sought far. What an abundance of material, what a wealth of images and examples and thoughts and formulations the enriched and now so much better comprehended classical tradition proffered to the patriotic sense and the national consciousness. In one respect, incidentally, such feelings had drawn from the fountains of antiquity even earlier, before the vigorous and purified classicism of the Renaissance set in. National pride in a number of countries had already appealed for several centuries to a descent from Troy, whether from Priam or Anchises. For every royal house boasting of a time-honored origin an impressive genealogy reaching back to the heroes of Ilium was concocted in the court literature. For the splendor of Rome, Vergil in his time had shifted the accent of hero-worship from Achilles and Agamemnon to Aeneas. Out of respect for Vergil the Christian West in its turn continued to be pro-Trojan. It is a remarkable example of the force of a literary idea.

The humanists of around 1500, with their tremendously broadened and deepened knowledge of antiquity, no longer needed the gaily colored fictions of fabulous princes for an appeal to classical glory. They had Livy, Caesar, Strabo, and Tacitus in which to find historical points of contact of more authentic value. Most of the peoples did indeed have their roots in the Roman period, hence the nobility of a nation was no longer sought in the progeny of Priam, but in Helvetians and Allobroges, and even in the Goths and the Suevi. And something more than mere pride in distant ancestors was gleaned from classical tradition. The Greek and Roman historians taught the generation of the Renaissance under-standing of what political sense and civic virtue had once meant and could again come to mean. The Roman concept *patria* regained its full resonance. The word *patria,* as we have seen, had a dual significance in medieval Latin: on the one hand, that of the kingdom of heaven, and on the other, that of the native region. In the later Middle Ages it was already being translated as "fatherland" both in Middle Dutch and in Middle High and Low German, but then ex-clusively in the religious sense. Now the word *patrie* also came into usage in French, with a fuller significance than before. Remarkably enough it there initially met with some resistence. *Qui a pays n'a que faire de patrie,* Charles Fontaine reproached Joachim du Bellay: *patrie* was a neologism, one of the *corruptions italiques.* He was right, in a sense, but the word gained a foothold.[3]

At first sight one would tend to say that humanism, in its enthusiasm to revive Rome's grandeur and Greece's glory, would have to look down upon the division of Europe in a host of nations as a barbarous deviation from the ideal. A certain cosmopolitanism as an intellectual attitude in things political was, one would think, dictated to the humanist by the ideal itself. The disintegration into nations had to seem to him an inconvenient disturbance of true civilization. And did Christian religion not point in the same direction? An internationally or supranationally uniting force would seem to derive directly from the principle of humanism.

This was indeed the point of view of the humanist whose fame was to spread furthest and last longest, Erasmus.[4] "Everyone," he writes "who is initiated in the holy heritage of the Muses which is common to all I consider my countryman [*homopatrida*]." Or elsewhere: "Toward almost all nations I am what is called blank paper. . . ."[5] He satirizes the national self-love that turns nation against nation and town against town, "so that each one considers all the others barbarians. . . ." In France they preach "that God is on the side of the French, in England and Spain that not the emperor but God is conducting the war," and so forth. This convinced antinationalism can, of course, very well go hand in hand with a sincere attachment to the land of one's birth. The word *patria* has a tender sound in Erasmus's mouth, though there is a certain hesitation in his use of the term. Sometimes it applies to Holland, *mea Hollandia,* as he continues to call it despite his repeated condemnation of the Dutch popular character. *Patriae pietas,* he writes, he rates highly. Another time he uses *patria* for all the Netherlands under the dominion of Charles V. There was as yet no definite proper name for that conglomeration of regions, either for Erasmus or for others. The political entity he, like many others of his age, called Burgundy. In the last years of his life Erasmus seems to have associated *patria* above all with Brabant, where he hoped to end his life.

This intellectual cosmopolitanism and tempered patriotic sense of Erasmus's was, however, rather the exception than the rule among humanists. However strange it may seem, for most of them the intoxicating savor of antiquity had aroused a mood of unbridled national self-exaltation, which could find just as rich nourishment as any cosmopolitanism in the spirit of the classics. The learned Guillaume Budé was gently heckled by his friend Erasmus for his national French sentiments: "Your entire devotion to your own country will be praised by many, and will be readily excused by all; although it is in my opinion more philosophical to put our relations with things and men upon such a footing, as to treat the world as the common country of us all." But like almost all of his fellow humanists, Budé remained just as sensitive as ever in regard to national honor. In his introduction to the Epistle to the Galatians Erasmus had made an allusion to the "O foolish Galatians" of the third chapter. He meant the French, Budé thought, and found it reason for serious displeasure. One could not be too careful with such things. Somewhere Erasmus had given a few examples of ironic sayings: *Scytham eruditum, negociatorem integrum, Poenum fidum, Italum bellacem.* The Italians not so militant?—the ancestors of the Black Shirts did not allow that to be said, and the result was a hard-fought paper war that caused Erasmus no end of trouble.

The extremely sensitive patriotism and nationalism of the Renaissance had a quite different tone from that of the Middle Ages. It had now attached itself firmly to certain political ideas of national unity and national interest. It spoke in learned, classical terms. It was deliberately cultivated by literature and by governments alike. It had at its disposal a well-stocked arsenal of historical examples and parallels from every past age. Among intellectuals something of a public opinion on European politics of the day was already emerging. For example, one should read Thomas More's witty fiction in his *Utopia* when he imagines himself in the council of the king of France during the most highly secret deliberations. The king is consulting with his councilors what artifices and machinations he should use to hold Milan and regain Naples, then either to conquer Venice with the French army or else to deceive it by means of a temporary alliance, and to subject all Italy and all Burgundy (that is to say the Netherlands) to France, and even more other nations whose lands he had long since invaded in his mind.[6] Apparently More really did view French politics as such an ingenious aspiration toward a national French hegemony over Europe, quite in the spirit of Machiavelli's *Prince* (written at the same time as the *Utopia*).

Now while in France, England, and Spain the national consciousness could go on developing in close connection with the strong state, with its established unity and its central administration, the situation was totally different in the German lands. The imperium had long since practically ceased to be a cohesive, let alone a uniting factor. The units to which national feelings were attached had constantly multiplied from the great power complexes such as Bavaria, Brandenburg, and Saxony, often subdivided in turn, down to the numerous, usually extremely insignificant imperial cities. A clan sense, a regional feeling, a linguistic community, and fealty to a ruler continued to dominate the German national awareness as so many loosely cohering elements. And yet above all those partial embodiments of a German consciousness there was still always a general German enthusiasm, now strongly revitalized and renewed, which made no distinction between Saxon and Swabian, between High German and Low German. This enthusiasm fed on memories of the past and ideals of the future, both newly impregnated by the knowledge of classical literature. This new German patriotism and nationalism remained one of writers and poets, and found its expression largely in the Latin of the humanists. The old designation Germania acquired a new content as an indication of the vast fatherland.

A name means a great deal for everything having to do with national consciousness. Germany had been given the name Germania by the Romans. The vernacular language had always found the designation *deutsch, diets* sufficient as an indication for the language, the country, and the people. It meant no more than "national," "native." The word found its way to Italy as *tedesco*. The French and Spaniards called the Germans *Allemands, Alemanes;* medieval Latin created the word *Teutonicus,* half from *diutisc, deutsch,* and half from classical reminiscences. The term Germania had remained alive only in ecclesiastical usage until humanism breathed new, full life into it. In that term there now resounded not only a pride in the medieval past of imperial dignity, but also a pathos over a mythical primeval period of Old Germanic heroism and innocence. Familiarity with Tacitus' *Germania* bore fruit. Erasmus made his acquaintance with this highly inflated learned patriotism when homage and praise were heaped on him by the German humanists during his first stay at Basel. For them he was the German who had surpassed Italy, and that was what they revered in him above

all. They longed fervently for him to declare openly that he
was one of them. The Rotterdamer, surprised and flattered,
at first matched their tone wholeheartedly. He wrote Wimp-
feling *Germanus Germano,* as a German to a German, that
he "will associate with him with the simple, German veracity
that is common to them." But his German friends soon went
too far. He actually felt that this tone did not become his
international convictions. And he did not want to incur the
displeasure of his French friends, who were just as fervently
national as these exuberant new friends of his. Soon he was
writing *nostra Gallia* again to Budé. With learned scruples
he asked himself whether, on the basis of ancient accounts,
his Holland should not be considered as belonging to Gaul
rather than to Germany? The more he was tugged at from
both sides, the less he was inclined to pronounce in favor
of one of the two nationalities. Hence he withdrew to his
skeptical cosmopolitanism, justified both from the classical
and Christian point of view, declaring that a difference in
country was of little importance for the scholar, and finally
even denying that, though living in Basel, he was in Germany
—a denial that at that time was certainly not warranted
either constitutionally or geographically.[7]

Since the dawn of the modern period the sense of nationality has occupied an ever larger place in more or less official
historiography, both as a factor and as a vehicle. The age of
the Renaissance had a burning interest in true historical
knowledge of one's own country and people. The desire was
for something more and better than the old chronicles had to
give. Lacking the better, the new art of printing initially
turned to the older material and published such products as
the Dutch *Divisiekroniek* and the *Grandes chroniques de
France,* compilations and extracts without any critical value,
at the same time the last phase of medieval historiography
and the first of modern. In a certain sense the publisher and
the reading public, however restricted the latter still was,
were ahead of scholarly production. Italy remained for a time
the example and the school for other countries in the new
study of history. It had had a high level of historiography
ever since the fourteenth century in Villani and his colleagues,
and its history had a much more direct link with classical

antiquity than that of France or England. A great amount
of historical knowledge and critical acumen had been developed in Italy even before 1500. As a result, the new rulers
in France and England, Louis XII and Henry VII, who
knew better than anyone else the value to the state of proper
historical study, drew historiographers from Italy. They
assigned them the task of providing an accurate and detailed
picture of the country's history to which the royal authority
could give a stamp of official validity. The Veronese who
received such a commission from the French king in 1499
called himself Paulus Aemilius; Polydore Vergil was the
humanist from Urbino who went to serve the king of England
as historiographer in 1507. Both of them produced bulky
writings in Latin: ten volumes of *De rebus gestis Francorum*
from Paulus Aemilius, incomplete at his death, twenty-six
books of *Anglicae historiae* from the other. This government-
sponsored national historiography was as a matter of course
a history under restraint, but the restraint was not all too
strict. As long as the national myth that had long since been
a pearl in the crown was respected, the compilers had every
freedom to develop their critical ingenuity. Paulus Aemilius
was able to set aside the descent from Troy as a sheer assertion, and refers neither to the dove that brought the
charisma at Clovis's baptism nor to Roland. The Tudors, with
their much more recent and less firmly established legitimacy,
kept a bit closer eye on their historiographer. Polydore
Vergil relates the fable of Brutus and the tale of King Arthur,
and alongside of them presents a critical account of England's
origins, without offering an opinion as to what he considered
to be the truth.

There can be no doubt that these standard works, in many
respects excellent, made an important contribution toward
determining and enriching the national consciousness, even
though they were read firsthand only in a small circle. The
national consciousness obtained more and more the hallmark
of an ultraloyal political doctrine and an authoritative tradition. When humanism had permeated to the level that had
neither the time nor the knowledge to read learned Latin
treatises, but nonetheless desired a new view of history for
itself, it was again the turn of the compilers in the vernacular,
a Holinshed for England, a Belleforest for France. That fate
has granted both of these longer renown than their learned

predecessors Paulus Aemilius and Polydore Vergil is not because of any higher merits, but because Shakespeare was to use them as sources. With the transition from Latin to the vernacular the critical level at once reverted to the older, outdated stage of the *Grandes chroniques* and their like. The national political purport was now placed more in the foreground than earlier. Bernard du Haillan, Charles IX's court historiographer, followed in the footsteps of Paulus Aemilius, but again inserted the national fables and legends the humanist had omitted, though he made it clear what he believed of them. What he had to satisfy was not the diligent and pure thirst for reliable knowledge which had animated the older generation of humanists, but a literary taste that demanded broad, gaily colored pageants, the taste of the readers of the *Amadis* romances, those ultraromantic hand-me-downs of the chivalric romance, the taste of noble warriors and courtly *beaux-esprits*. Hence Du Haillan had to strike the romantic and heroic note; he had to pay homage to the chivalric ideal once more, however outworn it may have become. As a result, he did not contribute to the development of historical scholarship, but he did to the evolution of the national idea of France's place among the nations.

The Renaissance, it may be said, gave to patriotism and the sense of nationality the fullness, the stability, the flourishing hue, the vitally pulsating life that are also radiated by the art that it produced, the thought that stemmed from it, and the human relationships that found form during it. Before moving on to more recent centuries I must digress here for a moment. Up to now in tracing the phenomena with which we are concerned we have made use of cases where the starting point for national development seemed quite obvious, whether it was a heartland determined by nature, a traditional ethnic and linguistic relationship, or a time-honored monarchy hallowed by tradition. However, there are also cases of the formation of nations in which the final product of a people and a state seems to us sheerly the result of a capricious coincidence of historical events. In this there is a possibility for misunderstanding. On closer observation it appears, even in the first sort of cases where the point of departure seems obvious, that the evolution was not at all as inevitable as we are inclined to see it. There are no immutably fixed processes in history.

Among the cases where the starting point of national evolution cannot be summarized in a word or two are those of the Netherlands and Switzerland. At first view natural conditions seem to have been the all-dominating factor for both of them. But that is all too cheap a simplification of the problem. The confederacies of the Alpine regions did not at all have to lead to a secession from the Holy Roman Empire; that was not in any way their aim. They were no different in nature from the leagues of towns and of classes in southern Germany in the thirteenth and fourteenth centuries. The one and the other were unions *ad hoc* to provide for the lack of effective central authority. In slightly different circumstances the Swiss leagues, like the German ones, would have lost their meaning after a short time and have disappeared again. There are few political products that have been created in as incidental and unpredictable a way as the Swiss Confederacy, first growing out of the agglomeration of Germanic cantons, with the later adherence of the Romance ones. Nothing demonstrates the elasticity of the concepts of nationality and fatherland better than the staunch community of Switzerland: three linguistic groups and yet one nation, participation in three cultural groups and yet no tendency toward disintegration, and this while the cantons as a whole do not gravitate around one cultural center, but five or six.

On the rise and development of the Dutch national consciousness I may be brief: I have spoken and written about it at various times in various contexts. Here the growth of the different regions into a single entity was no more assured by natural conditions than it was in the Swiss case. This group of low-lying tracts of land had no clear boundary either to the east or to the south. The linguistic situation tended toward duality, the economic, political, and cultural much more toward unity. Nonetheless, that unity was effected twice merely as the work of dynastic and international politics, and twice it failed. The line that divided the Republic of the United Provinces from the Spanish Netherlands was like a crack in a jug. And again the elasticity of the concept of nationality appears: two nations arose on this soil in place of one, the northern one strong in its firm ethnic homogeneity (*n'en déplaise* the Frisians) and its deep-rooted

attachment to the fortunes of the house of Orange, the south
burdened with the painful dualism of Flemish and Walloon,
but nonetheless strong as a result of its exalted achievements
in almost every cultural field and the honorable place it
acquired for itself in Europe because of the sacrifice it was
prepared to make in the Great War. In regard to Austria,
which might be called the diplomatic center of Europe for at
least two centuries, the question of nationality is more complicated than for the Netherlands, Switzerland, and Belgium.
The starting point for the evolution of Austria to unity and
power as an independent state was in this case a dynasty,
that of the Hapsburgs. The German Eastmark of the early
Middle Ages, Bavarian in ethnic origin, rapidly grew powerful among the territories of the Holy Roman Empire, first as
a margraviate, then as a duchy, and, as a result of its position
on the periphery, quite early became a very special center
of Germanic civilization. The emperorship fell to the Hapsburgs, first in passing around 1300, then for good in the
fifteenth century. They wove a chain of hereditary lands
around the Duchy of Austria; without any legal claim they
elevated themselves above all the other German princes by
means of the title of archduke,[8] and as kings of Bohemia
were the first of the electors. This whole rise of the Hapsburgs
took place within the framework of the Holy Roman Empire,
even, with a single exception, after the heritage of Burgundy
fell to them. The exception, however, was an important one:
it was wealthy Flanders, a fief of the French crown and the
most valuable piece in the Burgundian estate. It was through
Flanders that Hapsburg became a truly international power,
and from its possession came the antithesis between Hapsburg
and France which was to dominate European politics for
several centuries. Then, as if not enough material for disputes
had accumulated, came the union of Austria with Spain, and
after that the acquisition of the Hungarian crown, however
pitiably tarnished it was by the Turkish conquests. As a result,
by the middle of the sixteenth century Austria had become
the largest and most cosmopolitan power of Europe. That does
not at all mean that one could then speak of an Austrian
nation. A multitude of national and dynastic elements was
united under the splendor of an imperial title, and as yet
nothing more. In the internationality that one might justly call
the Hapsburg realm of around 1600 the German element was

no longer clearly dominant alongside of Burgundians, Dutch-men, Italians, Bohemians, Hungarians, and so forth.

The Thirty Years' War brought Hapsburg less an increase in glory than an aggravation of the chronic conflict with France. Somewhat later, nonetheless, Austria accepted a European task which it was to fulfill gloriously: resisting and driving back the Turks, whose aggressive imperialism evinced itself one last time. The European constellation was seldom as international as in 1683, when Germans and Poles together repulsed the Turks before Vienna, and soon afterward, when a French prince, Eugene of Savoy, won for the German emperor the battle that liberated Europe from the Turkish danger for all time. This vigorous policy effected what the almost unbridled expansion of Hapsburg power under Charles V had not been able to do: the Austria of Maria Theresa became a state and a fatherland that for all its ethnic variety proved susceptible to all the feelings of national attachment and loyalty. In the bosom of that "happy Austria," in imperial Vienna, German civilization attained its highest triumphs in Mozart, Haydn, Beethoven, and Schubert.

However, in its close, indissoluble ties with Germany lay the coming fate of Austria's might: the conflict with Prussia, the seclusion from the new empire, the alliance that led to 1918, the *Anschluss* of today. The tragic problem of whether to become a part of Germany or to remain independent along-side of Germany has now been temporarily solved, and the international power that held this least settled part of Europe together, however ineffectually, has yielded.

The age of Charles V, Philip II, and Elizabeth brought the phenomena of the fatherland and the nation to full growth. Both concepts were now closely linked with the notion of a powerful state and a vigorous government. Everywhere the age inclined toward absolute authority and absolute admin-istrative forms. The majesty of the crown or of the law was exalted to high heaven by the style of life of the Counter Reformation and baroque. The figure of the ruler acquired a near divine resplendence. The essence of the state and the nation seemed to find almost total expression in the august dignity of the blood royal. The policy of the sixteenth-century rulers was above all a dynastic policy. Or perhaps one could

even better speak of a crown policy, for it was not the
material interests of the dynasty as such that impelled the
ruler, but rather a national conception, an awareness of a
task, but one in which the immediate interests of the land
and its people were more or less hidden behind the splendor
of the crown. A certain understanding of the economic interests of the country definitely played a vigorous part in
shaping that policy, but it was rarely able to elevate itself
into a conscious policy of prosperity, legal order, and culture.
The common weal was clearly enough the ruler's goal in
theory. The words *res publica, salus publica* had long belonged
to the vocabulary of statecraft. Even in the Middle Ages
authors had cultivated the literary genre of the mirror for
princes, the treatise reflecting the ruler's duties and describing
his task. But the genre produced more classical flowers of
speech and Christian morality than understanding of economic
and social relations. More or less in the tradition of the
mirror for princes developed political guidebooks such as
Machiavelli's *The Prince* and the writings of Jean Bodin and
the so-called Monarchomachists. In practice, however, rulers
and statesmen continued to steer the ship of state with an
extremely primitive political compass. The calculations continued to be clumsy and shortsighted, and the means (except
perhaps for intrigue and bribery) restricted and ineffective.
With all respect for the skill of the leaders, on considering
a policy such as that of Philip II or the last Valois kings as
an intellectual accomplishment one can hardly call it much
more than bungling with factors that were neither controlled
nor understood.

In the seventeenth century the ideology, or perhaps it is
safer to say the phraseology, of patriotic awareness and national consciousness was gaily decked out in all sorts of
colors and trappings borrowed from antiquity. One need
only recall all the classical motifs in Vondel's literary terminology. Among the classical figures there was one with an
especially cherished sound, that of the *pater patriae*. This
honorary title was not only suitable for the crowned head:
the Roman spirit had created it in a republican sense, and
had wanted to grant it to Cicero. In fact the whole imagery
of Roman and Greek patriotism lent itself much better to

being applied to the few political structures still based on civic freedom and voluntary confederation than to the ostentatious majesty of established absolutism. Since the Swiss Confederacy had retired into deep shadows after the brief glory of its heroic period and Venice and Genoa had gradually grown ossified, it was primarily the young Dutch Republic that upheld the political ideal of freedom and was fully susceptible to the classical patriotic concept. The honorary name *pater patriae* was more in place there than anywhere else. If *patria* in the ancient sense was understood anywhere, then it was in the Netherlands, and if the pathos inherent in it was ever felt, then it was in the heart of those who returned to "sweet Netherland" after the endless trials and dangers of traveling and living between the tropics.

But it is not only the sounds *patria* and *pater patriae* which for the Dutch are associated with the very essence of the country's history. There is also the word "patriot," for long before the late eighteenth century was to turn that word into a violently controversial party slogan, it had resounded in the Binnenhof at The Hague in a tone that has carved itself in Dutch history like a chisel in stone, from the mouth of the servant of the state who said in his final hour: "Men, do not believe that I am a traitor; I have acted honestly and piously as a good patriot, and so shall I die."

To us, Jan van Olden Barneveldt's phrase of 1619 is enough to demonstrate the significance that the name patriot had acquired in Dutch seventeenth-century usage. The word had come in with humanism, derived from Latin, originally in the sense of countryman, compatriot. Presently it acquired that of a lover of one's fatherland as well. Kiliaen's Dutch dictionary of 1574 gives it both meanings: compatriot and *patriae amans*. At the very outset of the Dutch rebellion against Spain it becomes a factional name, usually in the combination *goede patriotten* ["good patriots"]. Patriots were set over against the pro-Spanish or proroyal faction, thus practically the same as the "sea beggars," or at any rate the adherents of the prince of Orange. It is noteworthy that *patriote* only came into general usage much later in French, though it is to be found a few times in the sixteenth century in the combination *bons patriotes*.[9] The Duc de Saint-Simon praised Vauban as a *patriote* for his endeavor to introduce reforms into the state, which led Rousseau to attribute the coining of the word to him. Others argued that it had come in from English. "Patriot" in England had indeed gradually developed the special significance of "friend of freedom." There certain groups or factions striving for reforms in the administration of the state liked to speak of themselves as patriots even in the seventeenth century. The word was sanctioned in this significance of "friend of freedom" when Lord Bolingbroke around 1738 published his polemic pamphlets attacking the policy of peace and routine pursued by Walpole's protracted ministry. *A Patriot King,* one of the pamphlets was called, and the other, *On the Spirit of Patriotism.* They constituted an appeal to the personal authority of the king and the spirit of the people against the rigidified aristocracy of parliament. It might be called true nationalism, even, if one likes, with a foretaste of fascism. But the Alcibiades figure that Bolingbroke was was not the man to influence English public opinion more than temporarily. The term patriot was quickly ridiculed and worn threadbare in England. "Patriotism is the last refuge of a scoundrel," said Doctor Johnson to Boswell. Nonetheless, it was this English usage of patriot as "friend of the people" or "friend of freedom" that now penetrated into France, finally to do service in the civic controversies of the Dutch Republic for the members of the Patriot Party with their cocked hats, Gouda pipes, and white Pomeranians.

The concept "patriot" had thus shifted from the sphere of an affectionate attachment to the fatherland to that of a political struggle for popular freedom, equality before the law, reformation of the state, social progress, and—revolution. As a result, however, the concept threatened to break loose from its original basis of the land of one's birth and to lose its original content of an instinctive inclination for one's own soil, for this ideal of freedom was no longer that of maintaining the traditional national liberties, but that of expanding human happiness and social perfection throughout the earth. A certain tension developed between the practical political concepts of the state and the nation, on one hand, and on the other, the general ideal of the love of humanity and world citizenry, the realization of which seemed to the rational and sensitive minds of the eighteenth century the future of the morrow. The nation and the fatherland seemed destined to be incorporated into the harmony and unity of the human family. How could there be place for any sort of nationalism in the optimistic picture of the future of the *philosophes?* It was possible in spite of everything, simply because the reflections of the seekers after wisdom are seldom as cogent as their systems assume. For the two leaders of social thought of the age, Montesquieu and Rousseau, the notion of concrete nations or fatherlands had not been in the forefront. Montesquieu in his *Esprit des lois* thought more in ethnological and sociological terms than in political. Rousseau expressed himself by preference in the abstractions of human social life and its political organization. Nonetheless, even in the system of the *Contrat social* the subject of the free community, the exponent of the general will, could not be anything but the given real power, the state or the people. Hence it was Rousseau who, in his *Considérations sur le gouvernement de Pologne* (1772), formulated the program for a true national policy. In it he considered the aim of law to be the creation of a nationally conscious popular soul, and that of education the maintenance of national morals and traditions in the hearts of the people.

In the spirit of the age that was hastening toward the great Revolution, two concepts strove for precedence: the vague ideal of general fraternity, tolerance, and humanity, the expectation of a peaceful society that was to find its happiness in general liberty and a life in harmony with nature, and a no less strong inclination toward everything of one's own land and one's own people. Then came the Revolution, when the mouth still called out for the universal good of virtue and love of mankind, but the mailed fist struck for the fatherland and the nation, and the heart was with the fist. The factors *patrie* and *nation* had never before had such an intense influence as in the years from 1789 to 1796. The fact merely confirms that nature constantly proves stronger than theory. Yet at the same time people constantly thought that they were acting in keeping with the theory. The National Assembly took it as its first task to formulate a Declaration of the Rights of Man and the Citizen. Observe that man comes first and the citizen second. But as soon as one sets out to formulate the rights of man, the state appears to be required as the framework for his society. Humanity could not be the vehicle of the liberty desired so ardently. Its domain was the fatherland, and its subject the people. Hence from the outset the French Revolution served pre-eminently to activate an enthusiastic patriotism and nationalism.

Strange interludes were sometimes presented on the stage of the Revolution. In 1790, the idyllic year of the Revolution when it was fancied that everything was going in the right direction and the salvation of humanity was close at hand—since mankind would almost unanimously band together in concord—there appeared in the National Assembly one day (June 19) a strange procession of Arabs, Prussians, Swiss, Swedes, Indians, Syrians, Brabanters, Liégeois, and so forth, each in his national costume, and all of them led by the fantastic baron from Cleves, Anacharsis Cloots. They came as delegates of "the human species" to request France to be allowed to take part in the festival of liberty and fraternity, in order afterward to be able to announce the coming liberation to their peoples.

Since Montesquieu it had become a doctrine that liberty was born in the forests of Tacitus' Germania, and that England's political institutions had developed from that soil of Old Germanic freedom. France, too, had accepted the doctrine. A certain pride in the Teutonic element in their ancestors was to be found in Romance nations even much earlier,[10] but now, with the prevailing romanticism, that Germanic origin became a trump card. Even De Tocqueville would still speak without hesitation of *nos pères les Germains,* and the thought went from him to his friend Gobineau. The concept found very remarkable expression during the Revolution. On April 24, 1793, the same Anacharsis Cloots appeared in the Convention to unfold his system of a universal republic. "He requested the suppression of the word 'French,' " the proceedings report, "being of the opinion that the word 'Germanic' would be perfectly suitable." [11] But the *"Marseillaise"* had already been written, enthusiasm was springing up everywhere, and the armies of the Revolution were preparing to give France its "natural boundaries" and the peoples of the world their liberty.

The natural boundaries. The more politics changes, the more it remains the same. In the aspiration for natural boundaries the militant national policy of expansion which Richelieu had conceived, and Louis XIV had continued, was revived. But the word "natural" was now laden with all the "philosophy" of the eighteenth century: Nature as the supreme force for good to which man, life, and the spirit should conform and order themselves willingly. The military expansion of the fatherland would be nothing more than obeying the command of Nature. The ideal of the general liberation of oppressed peoples also fit in perfectly with Rousseau's thought. By not basing his idea of a social contract on a specific state or nation, but designing a generally valid system, he had laid the basis for what might be called a universal nationalism, since only the national state could serve as a concrete unit of the ideal state. In this sense Rousseau's political theory found no purer expression than in the work with which Bonaparte continued what the victory of the Convention's armies had already begun: the revolutionary construction of a chain of free republics with decorative classical names — the Batavian Republic, the Helvetian, the Cisalpine, the Ligurian, and the Parthenopean (for even Neapolitan no longer sounded classical enough).

Nevertheless, there were other forces besides Rousseau's naturism and Montesquieu's sociology to nourish the idea of nation and fatherland in the eighteenth century. The concepts of national life, national character, and national customs, of folk songs, sagas, tales, and legends obtained their vivacious hue, their warmth, their pulsation not from philosophic arguments but from aesthetic perception and accurate, affectionate description. Romanticism had replaced the cool sunshine of the Enlightenment and rationalism like a summer's cloud heavy with rain and thunder. But those riches of the romantic consciousness first had to be unearthed, and for that neither the work of the philosopher nor that of the poet would have been enough if the diligent scholar had not lent support. The pioneering work in history and philology which was to give full force to the spirit of romanticism was done above all by Johann Gottfried Herder. Herder was five years older than Goethe, and died a year before Schiller. He was one of those intellects who lack great formative powers and nonetheless have a tremendously fruitful influence. He did not write any well-rounded works that are still read, but he supplied all the ingredients out of which the concepts of the nation and the fatherland have developed since his time. He filled the image of the people, as the true subject of social life and the exponent of civilization, with the thousand colorful details he found everywhere in folk songs, folk customs, and folk traditions. He is the father of everything that is now called folklore, and of comparative literature. He helped to liberate literature from the endeavor to draft an all-encompassing canon of beauty, an endeavor that had still held Voltaire captive. He sought in everything the expression of the genuine, the original, the typical. It is remarkable that Herder's insight into national character and national spirit did not begin to dawn while he was among his own German countrymen, but during his stay in Riga among the Latvians. Herder was not a person to think in political terms. He hated all statecraft of imperiousness and conquest. And he thought even less in terms of race. Is it not remarkable that the man who contributed more than anyone else to the formation of concepts such as national character, national spirit, *Volkstum,* did not adhere to the theory of an inborn and hereditary national element, but on the contrary was convinced that the environment was the decisive factor in the formation of the human mind? Nonetheless, he was to be one of the most influential promoters of the modern form of national awareness.

The eighteenth century ended with an epoch in which the problems of the nation and the fatherland were more than ever in the focal point of European life. Not, however, as a philosophical dispute or as a diplomatic exchange of competing states seeking balance, but in the turmoil of a protracted period of war. Bonaparte was busy transforming the ideal of liberty and equality of people and nations as it was adhered to by the Revolution into the needs of his lust for power and his talents as a ruler. The principles of nationality and fatherland, though still given lip service, were temporarily obscured by the unequaled successes of a ruthless imperialism. The general became consul, the consul became emperor, and the emperor drew kingdoms out of the cocked hat of earlier Europe. Paris was to be the metropolis whence all power emanated and where all culture converged. The newfangled Batavians had to forget again that they had been named Hollanders a short while before, and the Tuscans that a little earlier they were going to be rechristened Etruscans. The name of French would suffice for everyone. In the fatal dream of the empire there was absolutely no place left for the concepts of fatherland and nationality.

Until it became clear that states and nations cannot be

tossed aside and buried as easily as they can be dominated and temporarily repressed by the force of arms. The established entities of Europe regained their force of resistance, and it was the national forces—unconquered England, fanatical Spain, and rejuvenated Prussia—that were to lead Europe from Leipzig to Waterloo.

III

THE NINETEENTH CENTURY

The rulers and diplomats who assembled at Vienna in 1814 to provide exhausted Europe a new and lasting order certainly did not fail out of an excess of principles. It would, in fact, be highly unfair to label their work as a whole a failure. The treaties of the Congress of Vienna, however much there was in them that was defective, gave to Europe an era of peace that lasted for almost half a century, not counting superficial disturbances. It is an open question whether this useful result was owing to the mature wisdom of the diplomats or rather to a series of circumstances beyond their control. Perhaps precisely the fact that the Congress did not appeal all too vehemently to principles had a salutary effect. It acted as the executor of the Napoleonic empire, and nothing more. There were principles enough that could have been appealed to: cherished freedom, however understood; the unity of what naturally belongs together; the recognition of the right of each nation to independence, however realized; the necessary balance between sovereign states unable to do without or to avoid one another; and finally the citizen's right to a voice in the government of the state. It was undoubtedly fortunate that there was no opportunity to take all these points as a basis. The Congress found it hard enough to come to a satisfactory result even with a less basic, more summary procedure. One of its leading figures, Talleyrand, the representative of defeated France, did come with a principle. The principle he introduced was called legitimacy, and he had considerable success with it. It is an irony, or better a whim, of history:

legitimacy, the hereditary right of a dynasty to a throne, a concept that had been decried by the wisdom of a whole century as irrational, ridiculous, and unworthy of man, that had just been trodden underfoot by the emperor, and that now proved to be the only general principle with which any practical political result could be achieved.

There was someone else who proposed a principle in September 1814, but he had no place among the illustrious company of the Congress, and his concept hovered in dreams even more remote than liberty, nationality, constitutional government, and political unity all together. That was the Comte de Saint-Simon. On the occasion of the opening of the Congress Saint-Simon wrote a manifesto from Geneva bearing the title *De la réorganisation de la société européenne ou de la nécessité et des moyens de rassembler les peuples de l'Europe en un seul corps politique* [*On the Reorganization of European Society, or On the Necessity and the Means of Associating the Peoples of Europe in a Single Political Entity*]. He viewed Europe, then—and this is the remarkable thing —as an already existing community, a *société* that only required reorganization. It need not be said that the manifesto produced no effect.

The Congress of Vienna did what circumstances permitted and what the difficult balancing of contradictory interests allowed. It gave the tinge of restoration of legality to as many of its decisions as possible. Austria's expansion in Italy was a compensation for what it had lost in Germany, the kingdom of Poland under the rule of the Russian czar seemed to be a restoration more or less making up for the partitions, Prussia's enlargement with the Rhineland and half of Saxony served as an indemnity and a reward. In all this, national claims to independence played a role at best as a phrase. Can this be charged to the Congress of Vienna as a cardinal mistake in insight and policy? Such a judgment would be all too easy historical wisdom after the fact. The principle of nationality was no riper or more suitable than any other general abstraction to be applied as the basis for the European political community. It was to achieve consciousness as a generally recognized, passionate aspiration and animating idea only in the course of the century, and then also proved to contain dangerous consequences.

We have seen how the full awareness of a native national

character sprang from the soil of romanticism. It had become the custom to translate every intellectual need for what was intrinsic, genuine, and original into the folk idiom. The national consciousness had taken on color and form as a sense of historical tradition and as material for poetry and fiction. But if the demand of the national became more and more forcibly the slogan of the day, it was not only the current of romantic thought that was responsible but also the marked material and technological transformations in the lives of the peoples of Europe. The functions of modern social life with its increasing organization and mechanization began to operate more and more in a national context. Practically every occupation, every service, was now nationally circumscribed. Communications and commerce, education and publicity, welfare and road construction, not only occupied a much more important place than hitherto; they also took up a much greater share of individual and general energy and attention, and they did it all more or less nation by nation. Much more than before, life was approached from a national point of view. Even life-ideals had the tendency to assume a national direction. The idea of freedom no longer applied to the world or humanity, but to one's own people. The problems faced by each society were much more specific than before, whether they were political, economic, or intellectual in nature: a constitution or railways or social legislation and the betterment of all sorts of abuses. All these needs were nationally circumscribed: they applied to a land and a people as a whole.

No wonder, then, that the principle of nationality as a guiding force for all politics and statesmanship won more and more ground and that the validity and serviceability of the national principle ran the risk of being overestimated just as recklessly as it had earlier usually been neglected. There was more and more of an inclination to forget that in the long run the state is the reality of political life and the nation the ideal, the program, the slogan, the aspiration. Considered historically, the state had been primary everywhere in Europe, and the nation the product of living conditions within the limits of a certain state. The nation had formed itself only within the context of authority, even in those cases where the national unity and uniformity that have become apparent in the end result of the development seem to have been implicit as the necessary final outcome in the natural circumstances of a distant past.

From the end of the eighteenth century on, however, as the concept of the fatherland and the nation gained more and more content, color, pathos, and lifeblood, a painful disharmony necessarily developed wherever the national consciousness did not correspond to the nature of the state. If everything were in order, national sentiment, love of the fatherland, and the sense of loyalty to a state ought to be completely congruent for each people. They were not so by any means everywhere. Where such a concentric, harmonic relationship was lacking, discontents developed threatening disruption. The Europe of the Restoration was full of such discontents and potential points of disruption. The vanquishers of Napoleon—England, Austria, Prussia, and Russia—were, together with defeated France (which remained one of the leading forces in spite of the fall of her empire), the masters of the political stage as the recognized great powers. Actually, the position of being a great power implied a violation of the ideal formulated by the political theory of the eighteenth century and developed by the Revolution; in that theory there was no place for predominance of large powers over small. But in the history of two centuries of European concert and European conflict such predominance was all too familiar. Now more than ever a recognized precedence of the great powers was the inescapable consequence of the facts. This actual arrangement of Europe in large and small states did not have a great deal to do with the principle of nationality. It was based on political power and not on ethnic affinity. It was not Germany that counted as a great power, not even the newly created German Confederation, which claimed to be the embodiment of Germany's unity, but Prussia. Now Prussia itself was still far from being a homogeneous nation. It had never pretended to have risen to power as a nation. It was a state and wanted to remain so. In 1813, when Frederick William III appealed to his subjects to liberate themselves from French dominion in his *Summons to My People,* he did not address those subjects either as Prussians or as Germans, but summed up their particular names as Brandenburgers, Prussians, Silesians, Pomeranians, Lithuanians, and so forth. So little were the concepts of state and nation identified there. It is, then, no wonder that in earlier times the variety of national differences within the so vastly expanded Hapsburg territories caused no one serious worries with regard to Austria.

Alongside the great powers there were a number of smaller independent European states whose populations more or less corresponded to a like number of nationalities. These states were either based on a traditional ethnic and linguistic affinity, as in the case of the Scandinavian countries, or on a historically established political tradition of unity and cohesion, as in the case of Switzerland, and usually on a combination of the two. The political unity of the new kingdom of the Netherlands still had to be put to the test. In only a few states was the national uniformity of the population more or less complete. National discontents were fermenting almost everywhere; in the German territories, in Italy, in Ireland, and not least of all in places where peoples were still living in subjection, as in the Balkans, they had become conscious of their national character and were beginning to struggle for freedom and independence. The romantic soil in which the national consciousness had developed also produced in this period a rich flowering and ripe fruit. If ever the romantic ideas of an intellectual elite have had a direct influence on practical politics, then it was in the Greek War of Independence. All the ideals of the age were active in it: the enthusiasm for freedom, the passion for antiquity, the new admiration for the genuinely popular, and Byron's sentiment of *Weltschmerz*—and not only his sentiment, but also his courage.

Hence at the very outset of the age of the Restoration the European political system of states enlarged by one new member, Greece. Later Serbia, Rumania, and Bulgaria joined the ranks that were swelled in this century by a number of other new members. The countermovement toward the reduction of the number of states was also soon apparent in the disappearance of five states in Italy and four in Germany with the establishment of united national states. The twentieth century was also to continue along this road. Both processes, that of unification (and thus a reduction in the number of political units) and that of partitioning (and thus an increase in the number of units), are characteristic of European history since the end of the Napoleonic period. It is worth the trouble to consider this trend in two divergent directions for a moment, for the antithesis contains a problem of a general nature: that of the large and the small state.

We have learned ever since our school days to look upon two great historical events of the nineteenth century, the unification of Italy and that of Germany, a priori from the angle of progress, or if not utterly incontestable progress, that is to say, improvement, then at any rate a logical and natural necessity that silences the critical judgment. And indeed, history has spoken. No one would think of arguing with choice reasons that the results of these historical processes are regrettable. It is something else again to express doubt in general whether the absorption of smaller political and cultural units into larger ones is to be considered a blessing for the world. Our age is so inclined to prostrate itself in admiration before the quantitatively large that every word of defense for the small state is seasonable. Whoever is inclined to assume without more ado that the large state is to be preferred over the small one is the victim of a fallacy that Francis Bacon, if he were alive, might give a place among his idols of the market place, that is to say, notions that stand in the way of a clear judgment. An overestimation of the value of quantity is one of the cheapest prejudices of modern man worn muzzy by the triumphs of velocity, mechanical power, and mobility. An excellent assessment of the small state in the European thought of recent centuries was given not long ago by the Swiss historian Werner Kaegi, whose study I have made grateful use of in what follows.[1]

In the political thought of the eighteenth century, which in the nature of things took only restricted political relationships and possibilities into account, appreciation of political communities of a moderate size still reigned undisputed. Montesquieu considered the republican political form to be bound to a small territory, and the form of monarchy to a moderately large one, while despotism, based on the principle of fear, was natural to the very large realm. Small states, he taught, fall prey to large states, but large states fall prey to themselves. Montesquieu had an undeniable preference for the republic, thus for the small state: its basic principle, according to him, was virtue, while that of the monarchy was honor. He states specifically that that virtue is not the Christian virtue, but a love of the fatherland and of equality. Patriotism, then, was promoted to being a recognized foundation of the best of political forms. Rousseau, too, rejected the large state completely: the vast realm, he taught, was not a state, because the individual could no longer have any share in the conduct of affairs.

The Hellenic city-states of antiquity and the modest extent of Rome as a republic were still always looked up to as the historical embodiments of the political ideal. And when Sismondi later saw the fruitful ideal of cultural centers approximated in the gay multiplicity of the Italian town-republics or K. L. von Haller believed he could restore his monarchical conservative ideal in the patriarchal relationships of his so-called patrimonial state, it was constantly the political unit of limited dimensions that the thinkers had in mind as an optimum. Voltaire believed that true patriotic love could only exist in a territory of a restricted size: "The larger the fatherland becomes, the less one loves it, for shared love grows weaker. It is impossible to love tenderly a too-large family that one hardly knows." [2] There is a rudiment of truth in that: the core of patriotic feeling is always a close attachment to one's native soil. In the largest state of all, the United States of America, De Tocqueville found confirmation for his opinion that the smallest political association, the Roman *municipium,* the New England township, constituted the strength of a free state, thus returning in a way to a concept regarding the formation of states that Thomas Aquinas had already presented in his *De regimine principum.*

There is no denying that the old Holy Roman Empire which succumbed ingloriously in 1806 was an absurd monstrosity of a state, with its total of some eighteen hundred more or less autonomous units, and the restricted multiplicity of the new German Confederation, still with around twenty-five states, was also unsatisfactory from the point of view of practical policy and political theory alike. One tends to imagine every true, freedom-loving German as inspired from 1814 onward by the great desire for German unity to be seen in Ernst Moritz Arndt. That was by no means the case. The historian Arnold Heeren, whose German sentiments cannot be doubted, considered the possibility that Germany might be united into one state in the future as "the grave of German culture and European freedom." Nothing is more instructive in this respect than to see what place the concept fatherland held for that noble, genuine German who, as a middle-aged man, was still to demonstrate to the world what justice and freedom meant to him: Jacob Grimm. Beginning with the new year of 1830 the brothers Grimm had accepted the posts at Göttingen which they were to lose eight years later in such honorable fashion, Jacob, forty-five and already world-famous, as a professor and librarian, and Wilhelm, one year younger, as assistant librarian. In the early summer Jacob wrote a short autobiography at the request of Justi.[3] His inaugural lecture at the university followed only in November;[4] it bore the title *De desiderio patriae*, and is a typical Latin school oration for which he found inspiration by browsing in Cicero.[5] It is clear from every word in the address that under the term fatherland Grimm understood merely *Heimat* in the strictest sense, "where one has worn all the roads and paths bare ever since childhood," "where you believe you can hear voices from the graves of your forefathers encouraging and admonishing you." German, he says, speaks of "that pining love of the fatherland with the beautiful name *Heimweh*. . . ." He really did not have to confess to Lachmann that he had "secretly also meant Hesse" with his words; in his praise of the German language there is not a syllable of general German political patriotism to be heard. The restriction of his patriotic feeling is even more clearly audible in the autobiography. The fatherland that he and his brothers had learned to love from childhood was Hesse—in fact, electoral Hesse, for Darmstadt hardly shared in it. It was a close attachment: he planned to live and die in Hesse, refused a chair at Bonn in 1816, and thirteen years later allowed himself to be appointed at Göttingen only with reluctance. When he had to leave his office and the state late in 1837 as one of the "Göttingen seven" who refused to allow themselves to be absolved by the king of an oath once sworn, his heart was still with his cherished Hesse.[6]

The possibility of a unification of Italy was also called into doubt from various sides. Napoleon had not believed in it, neither did Metternich. Niebuhr and Ranke were of the same opinion, and even Gioberti, for all his being one of the founders of the *Risorgimento*, was like many other Italians of the day only able to conceive of such a unification in the form of a confederation.

But the irresistible momentum of the century was in the opposite direction. Everything in political, social, technical, and economic life was attracted toward a concentration of quantity in a sort of gravitational effect. Forces in the non-material sphere adapted themselves wonderfully well to this transformation of the material system of the world. Appreciation of the small state had to all appearances had its day. Even in the eighteenth century, in opposition to the opinions of Montesquieu and Rousseau, the large state whose essence is power and whose potential tool is violence had been praised. One of its first heralds was the German historian August Ludwig Schlözer (1735-1809). Military power, vastness of territory, and size of population determined for him the value of a state. He had no feeling for art or poetry, despised the ancient Greeks, and assigned the state no tasks other than political ones. It is often pointed out that Schlözer had spent his happiest years in Russia. In this line of the exaltation of power then came in the nineteenth century one of the first to form a front against political idealism, Johann Gustav Droysen (1808-84). In the life of the state, Droysen declared, power is just as essential as love is for the family, faith for the church, and beauty for art. In the political world the law of power obtained in the same way as the law of gravity in the physical world. However much truth there may be in that formulation, once it is accepted as a guiding principle it leads directly to the postulation of power and violence as the supreme principles of the world, even though Droysen still assumed that such power would be accumulated on a basis of justice and freedom.

The whole evolution of the nineteenth century continued to move in the direction of consolidation and expansion of large power complexes among which the chain of smaller states seemed to occupy a second-rate position, endured as long as the great powers had anything to gain from their existence and wished to abide by legality. Almost everyone came to believe in the large state. With good reason *Kleinstaaterei* had become a taunt and a mockery in Germany, which had suffered for so long from hopeless disruption and political impotence. Unfortunately there was a tendency to forget, under the influence of the general delusion of quantity, that not a single one of the great, lasting values of the world owed its existence to a great power as such, and that all the best products of wisdom, beauty, and civilization had emerged in very restricted political relationships. It must be clear to anyone at a single glance over what we know of our few thousand years of world history that this much plagued world of ours has suffered more from *Grossstaaterei* than from *Kleinstaaterei*. Perhaps, if the fundamentals of civilization remain intact and law recovers its validity, *Grossstaaterei*, too, will someday be a taunt.

The middle period of the nineteenth century was largely dominated by three great currents or movements: liberalism (understood both politically and economically), rising imperialism, and emerging socialism. To what extent were patriotism and nationalism, the aspirations forming our theme, influenced by the activity of these forces?

The word liberty had lost none of its fervent, sweeping note since the days of the French Revolution; but the ideal of freedom had taken on more positive, and in a certain sense more restricted forms. The content of the aspiration to freedom varied in each specific case. For those living under the pressure of an absolutist government it meant the citizen's right to a voice in affairs of state. For many the fulfillment of that wish seemed to find expression in the possession of a written and sworn constitution stipulating with conclusive validity how the country was to be governed. The first decade after the Restoration was full of naïve revolutions—in Naples, in Piedmont, in Spain, in Russia—that believed the goal was achieved with the proclamation of such a constitution, often drafted according to a ready-made pattern. The groups who took the lead in such movements in the name of the people usually had no mandate for their acts other than their own enthusiasm. They cannot even be called close-knit party organizations. They were no more than complots, conspiracies, hatched in the secret clubs of the *Carbonari*, in an atmosphere of oaths, daggers, and mystery. This is the romantic school of revolution-making. Not that courage and sacrifice are thereby lessened. The sentiment inspiring them can rather be called a fervent patriotism than a typical national awareness. The fatherland for which they revolted could be as large as Spain or Russia, but also as small as Naples or Piedmont.

Before long, however, this early nineteenth-century urge to liberation found embodiment in a figure in whom patriotism and nationalism were fervently combined, and who included in the ideal of liberty all the notions of intellectual and social renascence that filled the age. That figure was Giuseppe Mazzini, the apostle of Italian unity. All the idealism the nineteenth century was susceptible to came to life in Mazzini. If he remained more the theoretician than the maker of national unity, it was not because of a lack of courage or a will to act. From his youth onward he risked his life for the sake of Italy; he was twice sentenced to death, and he spent his best years in exile. He looked upon progress as a fact and a clear promise. He expected every benefit from the principle of association he borrowed from Saint-Simon; he accepted the national task as a mission, a Messianism. Everywhere he wanted to organize youth to perform the work of liberty, and founded in turn a Young Italy, a Young Switzerland, and a Young Europe. The revolution that would bring benefit everywhere, he taught, now bore the name of nationality. His ideal applied to all peoples and all states, but he looked upon the people of Italy as called first and foremost. France, he believed, had finished its role in the Revolution of 1789, and now it was the turn of ever young Italy.

Mazzini's point of departure was a purely spiritual one. God revealed himself in the progressive evolution and elevation of the nations. The individual aspirations of the past would now give way to a well-planned collectivism. Here, too, one detects the influence of Saint-Simon's ideas. The holy trinity Mazzini stipulated as the basis for the coming society were liberty, equality, and humanity. The interpreter of the divine will is the people. The only good political form is that of the republic; the rite by means of which the people fulfill their task is that of universal suffrage. Not a person but a people should be the Messiah of this new Revelation. Presently the people would arise and convene an assembly or council. From that assembly a declaration would be published in a sort of Pentecostal miracle, not this time of rights, but of principles, that is to say, the duties of man: duties of devotion, sacrifice, and solidarity. In time all other nations would adhere to the declaration. It should be remarked that the form of these ideas is highly reminiscent of those of Cola di Rienzi, though Mazzini was an incomparably nobler and purer figure than the fantastic tribune of the people of five centuries before.

An excess of intransigent idealism destined Mazzini to a fate of disappointment. His friends abandoned him, he broke with Garibaldi, and he was in constant conflict with everything adhering to socialism, which according to him was only concerned with progress in the kitchen of humanity. During the war of 1859 his influence was rather a hindrance than a help, and the result, a kingdom under the house of Savoy, left the staunch republican disappointed for good. Even so it was Mazzini who aroused the Italian people to the will to unity, who taught them to despise their petty divisions and to concentrate single-mindedly on the great task facing that nation more clearly and more imperatively than others: the establishment of the state as the well-laid framework of the nation.

Freedom as a purely political principle seemed not only to combine easily with that of nationality, but to demand recognition of nationality as an indispensable basis, for freedom needed a subject. The state had at many points failed to show itself a worthy exponent of liberty. It could not completely satisfy all the people living within its borders, either because the population lacked national homogeneity or because the administrative institutions functioned too one-sidedly. On the other hand, nationality, to which so much of the social feeling of the age had fervently attached itself, seemed the natural subject for the liberty that was longed for, precisely because there was still such a great lack of harmony between the state and liberty. The friends of freedom of the period from 1789 to 1793 had had a rather low opinion of the state. It was, they felt, good as a curb to the reckless use of liberty, but for the rest it should interfere as little as possible in the life of the community. This was the way Thomas Jefferson and his like had understood the concept of liberty and the task of democracy in the new commonwealth of the United States. That federal union was to discover rapidly enough that liberty is not served by such a disdain of the task of the state. In European countries, with their older political traditions, one was as a rule accustomed to a certain balance between authority and freedom. Political liberalism and the struggle for national independence seemed nothing more than two forms of the process of progress, which no one doubted.

The ideal of liberty had long since acquired another aspect

alongside the political: the economic. The constant expansion of economic life had focused the spirit of the age more and more on the interests of industry, trade, and agriculture. The notion of prosperity acquired an almost sacred sound for a generation concerned with utility, a generation that had gone to school to Bentham. Considered in itself, the notion of free trade had little to do with that of patriotism or nationalism. The actual situation, however, forced the ideal into the forms of the state, the country, and the nation, for the actual units of economic and commercial life were not shipping, the grain trade, mining, and the banking system, but the specific manifestations of those branches of commerce as they existed and were regulated in the various states. From the Middle Ages on, the state had almost everywhere attempted to regulate trade as much as possible to the advantage of its own treasury and its own people. Now came the new doctrine of free trade, which wanted to deny the state any interference in all this. The ideal of freedom acquired a new, purely utilitarian and material form. Nonetheless it remained the ideal. Richard Cobden was certainly no less idealistic and optimistic than Mazzini in the political field, and behind his preaching of common sense and plain morality there was undoubtedly just as much holy fervor and disinterested devotion as behind the prophetic contemplations of the Italian. And just as much illusion. The system of thought of the Manchester school was based on the assumption of a world of order and progress which, in its structure of independent and equal states, was dominated by the recognition of justice and benevolence, and thus went its way of production and exchange toward prosperity and happiness in peaceful competition. Its units of production were in theory the geographically distinct countries with their natural resources. In its production every land should restrict itself as much as possible to what it naturally produced. International free competition would create the harmony in commercial exchange that was to assure the general prosperity. Cheap goods would prove to be the solution for all social evils; they would effect the necessary social reforms and preserve the peace. Free trade, wrote Cobden, would inoculate all the nations of the world with the healthy, beneficial longing for civilization. Exports and nonintervention in the process of production would determine the policy of all future governments. England would serve the others as an example and guide along that path. The policy of the balance of power had had its time. That of colonial expansion likewise. It would be a happy day, he felt, when Britain no longer owned a foot of ground on the continent of Asia.

It was all very beautifully conceived, but there was an "if" attached to it: it would work if the world were really as virtuous as the system demanded, and if the factors in the process were indeed the geographic units of production and not the existing states, with all their uncertainty and disharmony. But not only that. Even in its purest form the system of "every man for himself and liberty for us all" embraced the recognition of a dangerous national antagonism, in fact of a law of the jungle potentially implicit in it. The theory of economic freedom concealed in itself the seeds of an unbridled expansion of capitalism, on the one hand, and on the other, those of an unavoidable imperialism of the more powerful states and nations. The preconditions required by the system were none of them met, and have never been met. The resources were divided among the producing units all too unequally. The behavior of the states was controlled only to a very small extent by international law. Moreover, they were not at all as completely governed by economic interests as befitted the systems of either Manchester or Marx. Cavour and Bismarck thought in terms and acted according to criteria quite different from those of either Cobden or Mazzini. In spite of itself the theory of free trade and the noninterference of the state in the economic field has, taken all in all, rather promoted than impeded the national, and even the nationalistic, configuration of Europe.

Meanwhile the mid-century produced a statesman who would be in the position to put the principle of independent nationalities to the proof: Napoleon III, a political adventurer who became emperor, a social and economic dreamer and theoretician who was called upon to play the main role on the stage of European practical politics. We are here concerned only with his attitude regarding the principle of nationality, and a single recollection of all too well-known facts will suffice. Was his intervention in favor of Italian unity in the last analysis much more than an unconsidered relapse to a long outdated anti-Austrian policy? In the miserable failure of his attempt at intervention in Mexico was he really more concerned with the national independence of the Mexicans than with a success for the political gallery of Europe? It will probably never be possible to probe the mind of Napoleon III, a mind that for all its undeniable talents and good intentions was shallow. However that may be, he did not add any important elements to the national development of Europe.

While the Second Empire gambled away France's chances and prestige, across the Channel Palmerston and Disraeli had gone on building on a vast power structure to which, during the second half of the nineteenth century, the two new qualifications of nationalism and imperialism fully applied. Actually, the policy of England had been nationalistic ever since the Middle Ages. We have already pointed out that English uses one and the same word for the two concepts "national awareness" and "impetus toward national preponderance." As a result of circumstances English policy became imperialistic as well from the eighteenth century on. Palmerston was still in the happy position of being able to domineer with a diplomatic warning wherever in the world one of Britain's interests seemed threatened or when he wished to poke Britain's nose into some question. It was a reckless policy for the general public, and as such aroused objections in Britain itself. Around 1878 the British themselves gave the name "jingoism" to the raucous and overweening nationalism of their countrymen. The coarsening of the national consciousness that developed in a number of countries in the last quarter of the nineteenth century is undoubtedly closely related to both the coarsening of the press and the beginning arms race that was the fatal consequence of the wars from 1864 on. In France the notion of *revanche* gave rise to a party that was the first to call itself "nationalist." The figure of Paul Déroulède, the founder of the Ligue des Patriotes and the poet of the *Chants du soldat,* already displayed various traits of the national activist of the following century. He wanted to see the parliamentary republic replaced by the plebiscitary republic, a theoretical ideal that would become a reality as a popular despotism. He was involved in the Boulanger affair and later in an outrage on the Elysée by a general: the method of the *putsch* was making strides.

In the unsavory phenomena that give an aspect of degeneration and disruption to the last five years of the century—the Dreyfus affair, the Jameson raid, and the like—nationalism, which was still seeking a formula for itself, occupied a larger place than could then be suspected. No one was able to foresee to what extremes it would lead in the new century as the impelling force of the whole life of the state and civilization. It seemed as if a quite different stream of ideas, broad and powerful, was destined before long to submerge all patriotism and nationalism and eventually to sweep it away in its irresistible current: the current of socialism. In its essence totally antinational, socialism had offered passive resistance to the forces leading imperialism and militarism throughout most of the century. Marx taught that the worker had no fatherland. When in the critical year of Marx's *Communist Manifesto* socialism was struck down so bloodily in the streets of Paris that it was no longer a direct danger to the established social order for decades, it continued to devote itself to internal organization and to philosophical and scientific development of its propaganda for the coming new day. But despite the activity of the Internationals and the appeal to the workers of the world, organization and propaganda could not escape the limitations imposed by the reality of the system of states. Social democracy was only able to develop as a complex of national party organizations. Yet the more powerful the organizations became the less one could doubt that in the hour of trial and decision socialism would remain gloriously faithful to its international calling. The hour of trial struck in August 1914, and the speed and completeness with which socialism's opposition to national policy in all the warring countries collapsed provided a dubious warning for the future. That fact illustrated how little the so-called ideologies of modern times resemble the convictions for which the martyrs of the faith once fell.

In order not to transgress the chronological limit I had set for my theme, I should like in closing to look back for a few moments more at the two phenomena patriotism and nationalism, considered in general, as we have attempted to outline them in their historical forms of expression. Would it be of any value to assay their historical and sociological factors? It has been attempted more than once.[7] In these lectures I myself have repeatedly touched on the sources from which those sentiments have derived: the sense of a father-

land I have presented as having sprung from the old idea of
the authority of kingship, already expressed in the Old Testament; national consciousness as having been promoted by the
ecclesiastical ties within which people lived, external dangers
that compelled unification, and so forth. These are all explanations that may have their value for each specific case to
which they are applied, but which actually add little that is
new to the extremely simple sense in which everyone is inclined to understand the two terms spontaneously. Both concepts constantly seem to tend toward reduction to their
simplest form, that of primitive emotions of attachment,
fealty, and group solidarity. All the variegated garbs in which
they appear in the gaily colored show of history give an impression of growth and development. But let us glance once
more at the psychological, sociological, and ethical contents
of the two conceptions.

One of the early Greek philosophers wished to reduce
everything that happens in the cosmos to an everlasting antithesis of the two principles affection and controversy. Let us
accept his point of view for a moment, in order to ask ourselves on which side the two phenomena of patriotism and
nationalism belong. It becomes clear at once that patriotism
undoubtedly belongs to the positive domain. The very word
says as much: love of the fatherland. Or is that perhaps
giving too lofty an appraisal of the concept in the course
of translating it? If the characteristic of true love is that it
gives more than it asks, then the good patriot should examine
his own sentiment. An inborn attachment to what is one's
own does not of itself deserve the name of love. If the state
is at peace and is as well governed as a human community
can be, then the citizen's loyalty to his country, his services
to it in the forms of energy, devotion, and funds, in general
coincide with his own vital interests. The fatherland repays
his loyalty by giving him safety, justice, and sometimes even
freedom. In fulfilling his patriotic duties he is not performing
an act of love. Only when the fatherland is in danger does
his giving become a sacrifice, his serving a suffering, his
loyalty a love. The world is now once more a shuddering
observer of what a true, well-considered, and firmly resolved
patriotic love can do.

We have touched a few times in passing on the qualities
of patriotism as an emotion. A great deal more might be

said, but it leads almost immediately from the historical to the lyrical. Our awareness of our own country flourishes in the sphere of recollections of childhood and nostalgia for the past. It arouses the scent of pine trees and plowed fields and sandy beaches. It feeds on symbolic values. One of these is the national anthem.

In their present form, the national anthems of most countries are fairly recent. Sometimes they have developed quite by accident; sometimes they have been fabricated on commission. The suitability of the text is of subsidiary importance —it does not matter if the text reflects a specific political situation more than a century old: the words do not have to be up-to-date, and in any case, one never knows more than a stanza or two. But the case of the Dutch national anthem is unique. In the heroic hour of the country's birth there arose a battle song, a cry for liberation. It acquired a symbolic national significance: in it spoke the founder of freedom himself. The melody, first transposed from a lighter vein to one of deeper seriousness, degenerated into a lively fanfare in the mouths of the people. The political tang that the *"Wilhelmus"* had acquired during the civic disputes of the late eighteenth century displeased the founding fathers of 1814, and the age no longer understood its tones. A competition was announced for a new national anthem, and the prize was given to Tollens's *"Wien Neêrlands bloed,"* "instead of to the much better *'Wij leven vrij'* of Brand van Cabauw," as my Dutch literature schoolbook declared. Fortunately, for otherwise perhaps the still better *"Wilhelmus"* would never have arisen from the ashes of its decline. The musical restoration of this anthem was a patriotic deed of great significance. And the text, too, was in a way rediscovered. A new generation understood with a renewed Dutch soul these words that have lost nothing of the moving force of their sober seriousness after almost four centuries, whose message will remain up to date whatever the Netherlands shall experience.

Let us now turn back to the other term, nationalism, in its contrast to patriotism. We were attempting to apply to the two concepts the old dichotomy of the cosmos as affection and controversy. Patriotism, we felt, fell indisputably in the positive sphere, that of affection. Moreover, it appears to be linked inseparably to the subjective sphere and the concrete case. It is a psychological and social attitude, an inclination, a force, a passion, but it has no form of its own once detached from a specific instance.

A national consciousness, on the other hand, can be observed, analyzed, judged, and evaluated as an objective quantity. In theory it is a conviction, in actuality to a large extent a pride. It flourishes almost entirely in the sphere of competition and opposition, hence on the side of controversy. The lives of nations together can be one of noble competition, but among the fairies standing at the cradle of nations pride, greed, hatred, and envy have never been absent. Pride transforms itself to delusion and blindness. People imagine themselves to be a master race. And so they need slaves. Where can they get them, now that the slave markets of antiquity are no longer open? They are aware of a mission, of having a calling, of being chosen for something. A divinity to charge them with a mission is hardly necessary any longer: the nation is enough to itself. Shabby illusions of the egoism of the herd, the pitiful instincts of the savage state. We tend to overestimate the ethical value of the sense of being a chosen people because we become aware of it first of all in the case of Israel, where that sense elevated itself from its primitive basis to a higher order by founding itself foursquare on the Eternal.

In order not to end in such a minor key, allow me to turn for a moment from nationalism as an attitude of competition to nationality as a mental and historical phenomenon. Every cultured and right-minded person has a particular affection for a few other nations alongside his own, nations whose land he knows and whose spirit he loves. Summon up an image of such a nation, and enjoy it. It is not necessary to revisit the countryside or go to the museums or reread the poets: in your meditations you can lump all the treasures of that foreign nation together in one view. You perceive the beauty of its art, the vigorous forms of its life, you experience the perturbations of its history, you see the enchanting panoramas of its landscapes, taste the wisdom of its words, hear the sound of its immortal music, you experience the clarity of its language, the depth of its thought, you smell the scent of its wines, you sympathize with its bravery, its vigor, its freshness, you feel all that together, stamped with the ineradicable mark of that one specific nationality that is not yours. All of this is alien to you—and tremendously precious as a wealth and a luxury in your life. Then why controversy, why envy?

I had wanted to unfold this pageant to the end of the nineteenth century, no further. Not because the twin figure I have summoned up had completed its role and left the stage by then—quite the opposite—but because I did not want to allow the violent beams of the wild floodlights of today to shoot through the evenly lighted part of the historical stage we had detected. A dash of historical perception must suffice us. We shall go home as theatergoers who have left before the play was over. We shall draw the curtain while the tragic intrigue is still becoming more involved, while the lamentations of sympathy and terror can only be heard in the distance. Let us attempt to take leave of our subject as if we were ignorant of what is to follow, let us attempt to be like those persons at the turn of the century, our own earlier selves of forty years ago, who still could imagine that in the first peace conference that had just come to a close they had seen the dawn of a glorious new age of progress and civilization.

PART II. *The Middle Ages*

JOHN OF SALISBURY:
A PRE-GOTHIC MIND •

In the spring of 1930 I brought together—from the material
for a study of the spirit of the twelfth century which I had
begun earlier and then dropped for the nonce—three personalities for a series of three lectures at the Sorbonne under
the title *"Trois esprits prégothiques."* The three were Abelard,
whose personality I attempted to approach in the intellectual
sphere, John of Salisbury, who appealed to me particularly
in the ethical sphere, and Alain de Lille, that extremely striking representative of the twelfth century, in the aesthetic
sphere. At present only the study of the last of these has been
worked out.[1]

When the occasion presented itself for me to take up the
second of the three figures once again, I had to consider the
possibility that I might have been anticipated by the brilliant
expert in the field, Clement C. J. Webb, who in the meantime
had followed his critical editions of the *Policraticus*[2] and the
Metalogicon[3] with a monograph on the author.[4] My fears
proved ungrounded. Webb provides primarily a brilliant
analysis of John's work and a chronology of his life, leaving
plenty of scope for my attempt to grasp John of Salisbury as

• *"Een praegothieke geest: Johannes van Salisbury,"* an address
given at the general assembly of the Fifteenth Netherlands Congress of Philologists on April 21, 1933, at the University of Leiden.
First published in *Tijdschrift voor Geschiedenis,* XLVIII (1933),
225-44. Translation from the Dutch text in *Verzamelde werken,*
IV, 85-103.

159

a moral type. And I approve so much of what little Webb has to say regarding John's personality and character that I may safely appeal to him in support of my view.

I shall not attempt to define what I call "pre-Gothic" in John of Salisbury by a weighty introduction on the concept "Gothic." The facts can speak for themselves.

If I were forced to characterize John of Salisbury in a single phrase, I should call him the man with the serious smile. And in the attempt to summon up his figure at the outset I cannot do better than to compare him with Abelard, to whom he was so closely akin and yet so utterly the antithesis. As I have said, to understand Abelard one naturally considers his intellect; whoever attempts to understand John finds—behind his doctrine and his knowledge—his disposition and his heart. Abelard was fundamentally a negative nature and a speaker in public; John of Salisbury, positive in everything, willingly stayed in the background all his life; he worked and acted, always serving, caring, brave, honest, and faithful.

His birth date has been set between 1115 and 1120; he was therefore a whole generation younger than Abelard. He was proud of the Roman antiquity of his birthplace, Old Sarum, or Old Salisbury, for which he was later to be named. There are good grounds for considering him of Anglo-Saxon birth.[5] Parvus appears to have been his family name or sobriquet: thus perhaps Little or Short. He called himself *homo plebeius*. Latin and French, as his written and spoken languages, must have driven his English to the background quite early.

In 1136 he went to France to hear the renowned masters, Abelard above all, at the Montagne Sainte-Geneviève in Paris, and also a series of others at Chartres. He has left us descriptions of the methods and manners of some of them. According to his own statement, he devoted twelve years to study. His career, first as a papal clerk then in the service of the archbishop of Canterbury, would thus seem to have begun around the time of the Council of Reims in 1148, which he had described so vividly. A quiet clerical life in the shadow of the cathedral was not to be his lot. Charged time after time with missions of ecclesiastical policy, he was now in

France, now in Italy. He says that he crossed the Alps ten times. His writings show vivid traces of his acquaintance with Pope Eugenius III and his friendly contact with his fellow countryman Nicholas Breakspear, Pope Adrian IV. In 1154, recommended by Bernard of Clairvaux himself, he entered the service of Archbishop Theobald, then also making repeated official trips across the sea. Thomas à Becket, archdeacon of Canterbury before he became royal chancellor, he had known long and well: he dedicated to him both his major works, the *Policraticus* and—in the same year, 1159— the *Metalogicon*. But when Thomas, after being chancellor, became archbishop in 1161 and accepted the great struggle with the King for the freedom of the Church, the King's disfavor fell on the influential servant as well as on the master. John had to leave England early in 1164—probably on order of the King with the intention of removing him from the archbishop's side—and went to France with his brother. There he found refuge at Reims with his old friend Peter of Celle, now the abbot of Saint-Rémi, and began more than six years of exile, in which the archbishop himself soon followed him. He took an active part in the attempts at reconciliation between Henry II and Thomas à Becket. When these seemed successful he preceded his master back to England. He was in the cathedral with the illustrious martyr on December 29, 1170, when the latter met his death. As so often before, he had attempted to restrain his master from unnecessary vehemence. Did he flee with the others at the moment of the violence? There does not seem to be any reason to doubt his courageous fidelity to the very end.

Then John became the great promoter of the canonization of Thomas. When in 1176 the king of France called him to Chartres, where the cathedral chapter had chosen him as bishop, he accepted that dignity in the name, as it were, of the great martyr of Canterbury, to whom a stained-glass window in the glorious Chartres cathedral was later to be dedicated. He guided his French diocese for four years, and died at Chartres on October 25, 1180, after having attended the Third Lateran Council the year before.

In summarizing his work as a writer mention should first of all be made of his magnum opus, the *Policraticus,* a guide in eight books to proper insight and the proper life for rulers and administrators. The complete title is *Policraticus sive de nugis curialium et vestigiis philosophorum.* R. L. Poole has translated the main word (which has nothing to do with Polycrates) as *The Statesman's Book.* Greek titles were the fashion, and John had a vague idea what *polis* and *kratein* meant. The work was finished in 1159 and dedicated to Thomas à Becket, then still royal chancellor. The philosophical work *Metalogicon,* the first treatise in the Christian West to be based on the entire *Organon* of Aristotle, followed in the same year. Also philosophical in nature is the poem *Entheticus,* which will be left out of consideration here.[6] The lively *Historia pontificalis,* memoirs of the papal court from 1148 to 1152, which has been preserved only in part, was first recognized as a work of John by Giesebrecht.[7] He also wrote two saints' lives, of Anselm and Thomas à Becket, with quite specific practical aims; I shall return to the latter. If the *Policraticus* is the storehouse of his comprehensive and lively knowledge, and the *Metalogicon* of his insight, the richest sources for the understanding of his personality and his mind are his letters, which he himself collected.[8]

Typical of one phase of medieval culture, John of Salisbury displays to us a figure such as is no longer to be found after the twelfth century. A whole series of personalities of that century—poets such as Hildebert of Lavardin and Marbod of Rennes, and not least of all Abelard—manifested a number of traits which strike us as early humanism. Yet when one looks more closely, these quasi-modern characteristics prove to be the vestiges of a culture and a mental attitude which were at the point of disappearing. The free spaces in which the language or the thought of such minds could spread its wings were soon to be fenced in by Scholasticism, in which form of expression was chained to the syllogism and philosophical opinion to the dogmatic formula. The world and thought had not yet been enclosed in the strict and firm system of Aquinas and Bonaventura. The shape of the world, the forms of life and the spirit, had not yet crystallized in the style of Gothicism.

Let us begin by attempting to grasp something of John's personal temperament. One is immediately struck by a cheerful nature and an optimistic tone, even under oppression. With him there is little or nothing of all the sighing and lamenting, the threatening and admonishing, that often resounds so loudly in the ecclesiastical literature of both before

and after his day. It is all resilience and energy. He responds
to a complaining letter from his friend Peter of Celle:

> But as a matter of prudence I deliberately say nothing of
> the grief and pain that your message has brought me, for
> fear lest, if I should add my own pain to that which your
> disasters have caused you, you may be overwhelmed with
> still greater anguish. . . . It is true that to remember ills
> may bring relief, but only when they are past and gone.
> Then, only then, when your valour has prevailed over your
> enemy, is it pleasant to recall that you were beaten to the
> ground. There may be pleasure too in thinking of past
> misery, but only if you are already rejoicing in your happi-
> ness.[9]

Ancient rhetorical mannerisms? But the words "steadfast-
ness," "hope," "fidelity," "confidence," constantly recur. There
is something militant in his voice. He is determined, "if grace
lead the way, to fight with my Lord of Canterbury for the
cause of God and the freedom of the Church. . . ."[10] The
expression *fixum mihi est propositum* ["I am determined"]
recurs again and again. He does not complain about his
exile: "We endure with equanimity what God places upon us,
certain that nothing can harm us if we strive after the good,
that is to say the divine law."[11] He repeatedly thanks his
friends in England for the gifts and prayers with which they
not only make his exile bearable but which also in fact bring
him honor and abundance.[12] "I am an exile, declared an
outlaw, surrendered to poverty . . . in all this I feel God
favors me, it is His gift that I gladly accept exile for the sake
of justice."[13] "He is more seriously an exile who is an exile
at home," he says another time. One begs more dauntlessly
among strangers than among one's own people. "God has
already soothed the bitterness of exile; it is easier to bear
than on the first day." He has friends and acquaintances, and
his needs are met.[14] And finally this:

> Though it is already the fourth year of my exile, and the
> third that I am an outlaw, every day I am less shocked by
> the whirlwind of fortune and less moved by disasters. . . .
> Much freer than when I was oppressed by the burden of
> earthly possessions, in a happy condition, if not to say

happy poverty, I experience the teaching of philosophy that
every soil is a fatherland for the strong. . . .[15]

Among other things he praises poverty. But how different
it will sound from the mouth of Saint Francis a half century
later! The tone is still rather classical. Philologists may be
able to tell how near this is to Seneca or some other author,
yet everyone will agree that the dignity, the spiritual power,
and the determination that are to be heard in John's writings
are no less genuine or less Christian because of the classical
model.

The life of John of Salisbury was one of work, cares, and
hardships without ceasing. For a considerable time he bore
on his shoulders the heavy burden of all ecclesiastical matters
in the whole of England.[16] There is nowhere any hint that in
doing so he ever sought his own renown, let alone his
advantage. He had nothing of the egocentricity of Abelard
or the spiritual tyranny of Saint Bernard. He always remained the zealous servant of those he knew to be above him
—Archbishop Theobald, Pope Adrian IV, Thomas à Becket
—although he often seems to us to be their superior intellectually. Perhaps there is a hint of vanity in his tendency to
present himself as the wise and sensible counselor of the
impetuous and haughty saint that Thomas à Becket was.[17]
Thomas needed such counsel. And that trace of justified self-
love is more than outweighed by his loyalty and devotion to
the militant prince of the Church and blessed martyr. John
must have been exhausted when he accepted the church of
Chartres as a new charge—and also as a haven. The choice
appears to have been specifically motivated as having been
made in honor of the martyr, whose intimate friendship John
had earned by his own merits.[18] So John himself understood
it. From that time on he styled himself, in the headings of his
letters, as "Through the favor of God and the merits of Saint
Thomas humble servant of the church of Chartres." [19] That
was his claim to glory.

He did not live to see all the splendor of the stained-glass
windows and the wealth of sculpture which was soon to
adorn his cathedral. But the window dedicated to Saint
Thomas of Canterbury[20] is also an indirect remembrance of
the faithful servant who even as a French bishop wished to
remain in the shadow of the saint.

With his feudal characteristics of an almost military stamp, John of Salisbury was of the type of churchman, by no means rare in the twelfth century, whom—in contradistinction to the forms of life of the spiritual chivalry fixed in the great orders—I should like to call "the chivalric clerk." It is as if the two great conceptions of social life which gave form to the Middle Ages, that of the knight and that of the doctor, had in some cases not yet separated themselves from each other. Abelard belonged to the type, and also Suger of Saint-Denis ("satisfyingly human and merry"), who was described by his biographer on the theme *nobiles efficit animus* ["it is the heart that makes men knights"],[21] in which one wrongly hears a heralding of the Renaissance. That chivalric trait is also to be found in the unusually attractive personality of Peter the Venerable, the abbot of Cluny, "quite surrounded by a merry graveness and a grave merriness," [22] "a princely figure." [23] Peter, it may be remembered, was the first advocate of a better knowledge of Islam; and he it was who gave refuge to the persecuted, wandering Abelard, and who after Abelard's death wrote the dignified but moving letter to Héloïse which sounds as if in the pure heart of the great monk there was a spark of understanding left for the earthly aspect of the renowned lovers' misfortune.

No one, however, embodied the type of the chivalric churchman, the noble clerk, as perfectly as Thomas à Becket himself. He intentionally avoided any overconspicuous moderation in order not to appear hypocritical. He wore expensive clothes, he put on a gay countenance, he attempted to hide the knight of Christ under the splendor of his apparel, so that vain renown should not diminish the worth of that chivalry. His table was abundantly set. The splendor of his clothing, equipment, and retinue as chancellor had given him the reputation of ostentation and pride, and for his enemies he remained proud in the glory of his ecclesiastical office and the vehemence of his struggle.

The image of Thomas which John of Salisbury summons up allows the nobleman in the saint to glitter constantly. John was much alive to the seriousness of knighthood. Playfully he called himself a knight of his friend Godwin, promised him *fidelem perseverantiam ad coronam* ["faithful perseverance to the crown"], and spoke of a knight's girdle that the latter had lent him at Sens.[24] He relates of Thomas that he had kept watch a whole night long at the altar, at Soissons, of Saint Drausius, who makes warriors invincible. These chivalric vigils are well known: Robert of Montfort, John adds, had kept vigil at the same place before his single combat with Henry of Essex.[25]

The parallelism between consecration as a priest and as a knight was highly serious for him; he speaks of *sacramentum militare* confirmed at the altar. A large share of the sixth book of the *Policraticus* is devoted to chivalric dignity.[26] It goes without saying that here the author appeals time and again to the Old Testament and to Vegetius. Not without weight is the beginning of Chapter Nine: "It makes no difference whether a soldier serves one of the faithful or an infidel, so long as he serves without impairing or violating his own faith." He is thinking in this connection of the Christian legions of Diocletian and Julian, but the expression provides for all exigencies.

Anyone who has dipped deeply into the sources of the history of ecclesiastical life, of whatever period, knows that the way of life of the churchman has always been something more than solely a religious form. Life in that group has always had an important sociological aspect as well. This is especially true of monastic life. The monastery, as a sphere of social activity, had a series of other functions in addition to developing theology and practicing asceticism. From the days of Jerome on, the cell had been a soil nourishing a noble and literate type of friendship which has strongly influenced the world as a social and intellectual force, and has found its lasting residue in the exchange of letters. It should also be remembered that, from the eleventh century on, the monasteries were also the stopping-off places of the spirit on a purely local and material level: there was a constant exchange of visits and chapter meetings, and the monasteries functioned as hostels for travelers and pilgrims.

John of Salisbury was not a monastic man. But his friends were, and where would his life as a diplomat of the Church bring him more frequently than to the monasteries? Certainly he, like Gerbert almost two hundred years before him, was one of the noblest advocates of friendship among ecclesiastics. It should be recalled that in this attitude of intimate friendship among equals they could hardly have been schooled by Cicero, whose letters were known only in part, though the thought of *de amicitia* was of course known to them. "Love (*caritas*)," says John, "which is the greatest of the virtues, I should with confidence and justification like to call nothing else but true friendship, which excels everything one can pursue on earth not only in its majesty but also in the rarity of its essence." He had devoted himself to it ever since his youth. An inclination toward others had become so much a habit with him that it even included those who did not care for him.[27] The accent of John's expressions of friendship, directed especially toward Peter of Celle, should be compared with Hugh of St. Victor's fine epistolary jewel in a few lines on the theme *charitas nunquam exidit* ["charity never faileth"],[28] or with the confessions of Suger of Saint-Denis when he writes to Bernard of Clairvaux in tones that almost make one think of the eighteenth century,[29] or with the tone of Peter of Cluny's answer to Héloïse after his visit at the Paraclete.[30]

A light, jesting note is not lacking in John's correspondence. Peter of Celle should remember that he, as an Englishman, needs plenty of wine. Otherwise he would be choked by the dryness of his loaves. He is fond of beer, too, but nonetheless he has more interest in Peter's wines. He has heard that Peter has had a press built "by means of which wine is frequently pressed for the purpose of awakening remorse in the hearts of sinners, or for the joy of devotion, the salvation of the brethren, and the profit of all that hear." [31] But it is only rarely that he writes in such a frivolous tone. Usually his letters are about books, about piety, or about his endless cares for the Church. They are always businesslike and personal at one and the same time, and they are always terse in expression. What a serious, dignified, and genuinely cordial sound have his counsels and admonitions to Thomas à Becket, whose dangerous position John recognized from the very outset. May the archbishop direct all his thoughts to God. Now was not the time to study laws and canons: "Whoever has compunction about such things? I had rather that you muse over the Psalms and read Saint Gregory's *Moralia* than philosophize scholastically. . . . God knows how seriously, how earnestly I urge this. Take it as it pleases you." [32]

The letters are predominantly in a major key. There is little or nothing of revulsion against life, of tearful lamentations about the world approaching its end, or of a constant fear of death, hell, and judgment; there are no gruesome images of terror and eternal punishment.[33] One should practice moderation in meditating on death, he writes in the *Entheticus:*[34]

> *Omnia contemnit leviter, quie se moriturum*
> *Cogitat et recolit cuncta perire brevi.*
> *Si tamen absque modo fuerit meditatio mortis,*
> *Subruat ut nimio corda pavore stupor*
> *Spesque perempta cadat variis turbata procellis,*
> *Excedit licitum mortis imago modum*
> *Excedit fines quos lex praescripsit ad usum,*
> *Et mortem veram mortis imago parit.*

A later age would not take this warning to heart. It is my impression that the work of a number of other ecclesiastical writers of the twelfth century—Hugh of St. Victor and Peter the Venerable, for example—shares in this lack of somber and threatening fantasies.

Here, from the *Policraticus,* is an expression of Christian optimism which, though based entirely on faith, nonetheless permits a full acceptance of earthly life. *Salus publica* ["public welfare"], John teaches, is *incolumitas vitae,* "the sanctity of life." It exists only where God rules the soul. The perfect life of the soul is one where God's spirit fills all its parts. "For when the understanding, in so far as it has the power and is permitted, apprehends God, who is the perfection of goodness, when inclination, uncontaminated, seeks the good it sees, and reason points the way in order that no one, attracted to good by his own healthy impulse, may stray to right or left, then the soul's life attains as it were the glory of immortality." [35]

It has been said of John of Salisbury that he had all the virtues of a humanist and none of his vices.[36] This is perhaps the best characterization. He had humanism's free and forceful spirit, its sense of the real and the detail, its catholicity

• He contemns everything lightly who believes that he / Is soon to die, and recalls that all will perish shortly. / But if the meditation of death is unrestrained, / So that hearts are stunned by an immoderate trembling / And hope, pre-empted, falls, disturbed by many storms, / The vision of death exceeds the permitted measure, / Exceeds the bounds that law prescribes to be kept, / And the vision of death gives birth to veritable death.

of knowledge and interest. His Latin is clear and muscular, his style is terse and simple: he lacks the flowery rhetoric of many of his contemporaries and the learned distortion of later writers.

John called himself *academicus*. Of course that does not mean that he was an out-and-out Platonist; that was impossible. But it indicates a dislike of hairsplitting definition of ideas having to do with religion, and a seeking of meaningful study in moderation. He wrote in the Prologue to the *Metalogicon:* "Any pretext of philosophy that does not bear fruit in the cultivation of virtue and the guidance of one's conduct is futile and false. Being an Academician in matters that are doubtful to a wise man, I cannot swear to the truth of what I say. Whether such propositions may be true or false, I am satisfied with probable certitude." [37] How he despised his old fellow students when on his return from Italy he found them on Montagne Sainte-Geneviève still busy with the same sterile dialectic questions.[38]

The way of philosophy, he says in the Prologue to the fourth book of the *Policraticus*,[39] is only accessible to those who, beyond the realm of vanity, appeal to liberty and serve the Spirit: *ubi enim Spiritus Dei, ibi libertas,* "where the Spirit of the Lord is, there is liberty." [40] It is the Spirit that speaks the truth[41] before princes and is not ashamed, and places the poor in spirit above kings.

We shall hear more of that appeal to liberty over against kings and tyrants when we come to John's theory of the state. He shows himself worthy of liberty in the wise equity and sympathy with which he does justice to both opponents, Bernard of Clairvaux and Gilbert de la Porrée, in his account of the Council of Reims,[42] and in his serious awareness of his responsibility as a historian.[43]

We may perhaps regret that he did not give his sense of intellectual liberty freer rein in one respect, that of the authority of antiquity. We should have preferred it if John of Salisbury (and so many other classicists like him) had given us more of his own times and less of the ancient figures and examples that the *Policraticus* is filled with. But it is deep awe and respectful modesty that leads him to follow antiquity. He says apologetically: "Certain things which I have not found in books I have culled from daily usage and experience as though from a sort of history of manners." [44] He it is who has handed down the renowned phrase of Bernard of Chartres, who "used to compare us to [puny] dwarfs perched on the shoulders of giants. He pointed out that we see more and farther than our predecessors, not because we have keener vision or greater height, but because we are lifted up and borne aloft on their gigantic stature." [45]

The point of view of these humanists of the twelfth century is perfectly firm and clear. In them there is nothing of the ambiguity of later scholars: all their classicism is completely subordinated to their efforts to find confirmation of the faith. They also knew what they lacked: a knowledge of the true sources. Abelard urged the study of Greek and Hebrew without being able to acquire such knowledge himself.[46] John gave his works fine-sounding Greek names that were a mystery to his readers and himself.[47] He derived *artes* from *arete* or virtue,[48] and *analytica* from *ana* and *lexis*, "equal speech." [49] But at the same time he corresponded with a certain Johannes Sarracenus, who sent him translations from the Greek together with very judicious comments on his method of translation and explanations of certain words.[50]

If his style is compared with that of the later humanists, then according to our standards everything is to the advantage of the man of the twelfth century. There are no affected turns of phrase or long and learned sentences; there is nothing bombastic. The language is concise and clear: short phrases, simple and exact terms—a lively, cogent, and compelling style, serious and yet light and filled with humor.[51] John hated exaggeration. The flatterer says *ingentes gratias* ["a thousand thanks"]. Why? *Magnas* ["many"] would have been enough.[52] He wrote to Pope Adrian: "We are aware that your holiness is much occupied. . . . Wherefore it behoves any man who approaches you to speak with brevity. Now what we have to say is brief, but is rendered longer by the emotion that it causes us." [53]

When he is writing in the name of his archbishop his style immediately takes on a tone of high and noble dignity, but even so remains concise.[54] And when he begins to describe the life of the glorious martyr, his revered master, he adorns his otherwise almost hurried style with a majestic glitter and a formal and grave pace. The opening of his *Life of Saint Thomas* is like a stained-glass window of his cathedral, bathed in sanguine red.

Again—if only John of Salisbury had had a bit less respect for the models of antiquity, and had given something more of himself and his time instead of disguising his figures in the ancient attire of Cornificius and Gnatho and Thraso and Thais.

His respect for antiquity stopped short of its paganism, and did not reach as far as the beauty of pagan art. I cannot pass over a highly curious incident John mentions in his *Historia pontificalis*.[55] The bishop of Winchester, Henry of Blois, King Stephen's brother and formerly papal legate in England, took advantage of a stay in Rome in 1152 to buy old statues there to take back to Winchester. *Idola*, says John, *subtili et laborioso magis quam studioso errore gentilium fabrefacta* ["idols, carefully made by the heathen in the error of their hands rather than their minds"]. Perhaps, he suggests, one might say that the bishop had been doing his best to deprive the Romans of their gods to prevent their restoring the ancient rites of worship, as they seemed all too ready to do, since their inborn, inveterate, and ineradicable avarice already made them idol-worshippers at heart. It is clear that the spirit of the twelfth century was no Renaissance. Nonetheless, this early Lord Elgin of Winchester apparently "saw something" in those statues.

It remains for me to say something regarding John of Salisbury's political and social ideas. His name has remained alive in broader circles not least of all because of his views regarding tyrannicide. Let us now look more closely at his chief work, the *Policraticus—The Statesman's Book*, as he intended the title to mean. (I shall disregard the subtitle for the moment.) From the fourth book on, the work is concerned with the true ruler, the government of the state, and the structure of society. In its discursive style—and also in its trappings of ancient personages and quotations and its spirit of idealistic criticism, pure humanity, and love of freedom—it is akin to the political tracts of Erasmus. But the twelfth-century author, a man of action in the service of the Church, is much more positive, much more truly a political scientist than the great humanist of three centuries later. His thought, like that of Erasmus, is more social than legalistic in its orientation. In his bitter complaint against the evils of political life in his day he speaks of the land's laws and customs as so many snares and gins of falsehood,[56] and considers the right of the chase a violation of the dignity of human nature.[57]

Time and again John fairly clutches at the terms with which the authors of antiquity—Cicero, Seneca—attempted to express what we understand by the words "society" and "civilization." *Conviventium coetus,* he says at one point,[58] literally our "community life." *Politica vita, ius humanae societatis* flows again and again from his pen: "Since one cannot even imagine how any kind of happiness could exist entirely apart from mutual association and divorced from human society, whoever assails what contributes to establish and promote rightful order in the latter [human society] (in a way the sole and unique fraternity among the children of nature), would seem to obstruct the way to beatitude for all." [59] Classical ideas, if one will, but how many writers of that day were able to apply them so clearly and precisely?

Though it should still be translated as "civility," John's concept *civilitas,* for which he found precepts in the Scriptures—a civility that does not exclude gaiety[60]—is on the very brink of the notion "civilization."

The ruler (in this, too, John follows the true trail of the philosophers) obeys the law and rules the people by its dictates, accounting himself as but their servant. He is the public power and a kind of likeness on earth of the divine majesty.[61] He can be absolved from the obligations of the law only in a very limited sense. He is the minister of the common interest and the bond servant of equity; the minister also of the priests, and inferior to them.[62] "Therefore he owes the whole of himself to God, most of himself to the country, much to his relatives and friends, very little to foreigners, but still somewhat." [63] *Minimum, nonnihil tamen:* in that phrase lies a germ of the law of nations.

In keeping with the old Aristotelian antithesis of the monarch and the tyrant, these ideas lead directly to those of resistance and rebellion. The latter are completely ecclesiastical in point of view. There is no good Christian who does not become inflamed against the enemies of the general weal. The tyrant is a public enemy. Tyranny is *crimen plus quam publicum,* worse even than high treason. It is not merely lawful to slay a tyrant, but even right and just. Whoever does not attack him sins against himself and against the whole body of the secular state.[64] John wrote all this in 1159, when Thomas à Becket was still royal chancellor. Even then he rounded sharply against English situations. About the same time he risked writing of Thomas in the *Entheticus:*[65]

Hic est, carnificum qui ius cancellat iniquum,
Quos habuit reges Anglia capta diu,
Esse putans reges, quos est perpessa tyrannos;
Plus veneratur eos, qui nocuere magis.●

That applied to earlier tyrants. For John the tyrant of the day, then and later, was Emperor Frederick Barbarossa, whom he, with his pronounced anti-German sentiments, called *Teutonicus tyrannus.* Even so, what an impression those chapters of the *Policraticus* must have made in England soon afterward, during the great conflict between the king and the archbishop.

However much he was a man of the Church, John was not at all sparing in denouncing the evil that had taken root there. His voice joined loudly in the chorus of plaintiffs against the ecclesiastical sins of the age. The churchmen, too, were guilty of tyranny.[66] The ecclesiastical judges were just as bad as the secular ones: *sicut populus sic et sacerdos* ["as is the people, so is the priest"]. Not only the deacons and archdeacons practiced evil but also bishops and even papal legates sometimes raged through the provinces under their jurisdiction as if Satan had come forth to scourge the Church.[67] Only the spirit of God could cure all this, the spirit that brings truth and freedom.[68]

Freedom from repression and the lie, from injustice and hypocrisy. With this we come to the other part of the *Policraticus,* the part referred to by the words *de nugis curialium* of the subtitle: "On the frivolities of courtiers." Or how else can *nugae* be translated here? The word is used in opposition to *de vestigiis philosophorum,*[69] and comprises everything that is beneath a serious and upright person. John finds *nugae*

● This is he who abolishes the unjust laws / Of brutes who long held England captive as its kings, / Considering as kings those it endured as tyrants; / It honors most those who have wrought most harm.

dominant everywhere, all places are filled with them: the churches, the cloisters, the princes' courts, the pontiff's palace. The cleric and the soldier, the young and the old, the rustic and the nobleman—men and women surrender themselves to it.[70] But above all the royal court cultivates it: *Curia nugaces solos amat, audit, honorat* ["The court loves, hears, and honors only frivolities"].[71]

John sees the court as quite filled with a series of bad types whom he classifies according to their natures, by way of precaution describing them under classical names. Taken all together they are *epicuraei.* The vainglorious he calls *thrasones;* they are to be found in every order. The flatterers are *gnathonici.* They become groups of imaginary moral characters such as medieval fantasy loved to create. He describes the flatterers in the strict sense, the plaintiffs, the informers, the traducers, the envious, the slanderers, the self-seeking, the corruptible, the promisers, the lip-servants, the haughty, the quarrelsome, the superstitious, the profligate, the traitors to all duties. The worldly pleasures of the nobility also fall under the concept *nugae:* hunting, gaming, music, and above all, the whole field of the detested *histriones.*[72]

If I am not wrong, this diatribe against an enemy that he describes with a great deal of nuance and close observation, deviating from the standard pattern of classifications for sins, was directed against two different quarters. In the first place John was combating the very real evils of the English monarchy in his day. In all that courtly service he saw the political evil, the thing that hardened the king in his tyranny. All the *nugaces* were in resistance to the law; they were foes of the safety of the state.[73] If only they would allow serious affairs of state to take precedence over their own diversions, at least once they had attained years of discretion.[74] He, John, had avoided being criticized by scholars and those who make a profession of philosophy, but had been utterly at a loss to evade the snapping teeth of the *curiales.*[75] Thomas, his friend and superior, was wont to complain that he had to struggle incessantly against the wild beasts of the court, *ad bestias curiae.*[76]

Yet let us keep clearly in mind the relationship between Thomas and John in the period when the latter dedicated the *Policraticus,* the *Metalogicon,* and the *Entheticus,* one after

the other, to the former. In 1158 Thomas had called all eyes
to himself with the brilliant pomp with which he went to
France to confirm the acquisition of Nantes for his royal
master.[77] Thomas was reputed to be the organizer and the
leader of Henry's expedition against Toulouse in 1159.
Thomas himself commanded a company of seven hundred
knights, the finest and best equipped of all. In single combat
he threw a French knight from his saddle. It was to Toulouse
that John sent him his handbook for the proper life of a statesman. The chancellor, he says, had followed courtly morals
only in order to be able to convert the courtiers to the proper
life.[78] That was the only reason why he tended from time to
time to participate in the display of the foolish minstrels and
to speak their language.[79] But in 1159 Thomas's faithful
admirer was uneasy in his heart. He knew the chancellor's
pride and vanity.[80]

The almost passionate closing sentences of the *Policraticus*
have a moving tone of touching admonition.[81] Do you wish to
be happy? Do you seek the support and praise of men? Do you
desire personal power, glory, and wealth? And each time he
answers with a phrase from the Psalms: All that shalt thou
find in the Lord. And then, with a direct allusion to Thomas's
much discussed love of splendor: "I am not endeavoring to
restrain you from clothing yourself gaily in gold embroidered
raiment; from feasting sumptuously every day . . . and that
I may include much within small compass, from humoring the
times and even perverse morals, upright as you personally are
in all matters; and from mocking a world which mocks its own
cajolery." And later he states: "This book is a success or
failure for you to whom it belongs. . . . What has been said
with regard to the frivolities of courtiers I have detected in
none of them, possibly in myself or in those like me; and
really I am bound by a law too narrow if I am not permitted
to criticize and improve myself and my friends."

One can plainly hear that John is not speaking as a person
who is insusceptible to the spirit he combats. As we have
already seen, he himself displayed a number of characteristics
of the chivalric and the militant. He knows that pride is not
alien to even the noblest mind, and that it is the last of all
sins to give way to true wisdom.[82] *Militia est vita hominis
super terram,* the life of man on earth is a warfare, he says

with Job. But if the prophet had had any conception of John's times he would have said "a comedy," where each, forgetting his own, plays another's role.[83] So Petronius also called it.[84] John sees the *histrio* honored everywhere. It is considered praiseworthy for men of eminence to sing and play love songs, which they call *stulticinia*, follies.[85] The *curiales* magnify the judgment of comedians and actors, and quake as groveling slaves for fear Thais or Thraso may say or think something deprecatory about them.[86] Perhaps Thomas, too, would prefer some actor to his philosopher.[87] Thomas was not to disappoint him.

What is there behind this preoccupation with the morals of the court? It becomes clear as soon as one translates the Latin terms: *histrio* is *jongleur* (minstrel), and *curialis* is *courtois* (courtly). It is no accident that the *Policraticus* was sent to those parts of southern France where *cortezia* was emerging as a new pattern of noble life, a new secular (and worldly) culture. Here, if I am not mistaken, we have a protest against the emerging courtly culture from a person who knew his own ideal of a noble Christianity drenched in classical freedom and wisdom to be more valuable than the new ethic of the *gai saber*. John of Salisbury, it goes without saying, was not able to create a concept "courtly culture." He saw his day turning to things that were alien and hostile to him. He saw the wondrous illusion of *cortezia* from its weak side, entwined with the world of place-seeking and lip-service and vanity.

If this interpretation is correct, the words *de nugis curialium* in the subtitle of *The Statesman's Book* might be translated as "*against* courtly culture." [88] And how should the rest of the title, *de vestigiis philosophorum*, then be translated? It is not difficult: "*for* an urbane Christianity." This vigorous, courageous personality, full of practical political sense, standing in the thick of life, moderate in all things (the courtly virtue of *mesura*), loyal and faithful and realistic, found unfit for the mystical even as a lad—John of Salisbury visualized the ideal of a society combining the purest of faith with the highest of civilization.[89] But even with that pure spiritual ideal he was not on the winning side. A more stringent pattern of life was to triumph and to dominate the coming centuries: that of Scholasticism, sturdily built upon formulated dogmatism and the syllogistic form; and that of mysticism, flowering in a deepened and revitalized monastic life that was to reach the people with all the means of a violent enthusiasm.

I hope that I have been able to demonstrate satisfactorily from the source material itself what I have meant in calling John of Salisbury a pre-Gothic mind.

ABELARD *

In a series of three lectures some years ago I characterized three figures of the twelfth century as "pre-Gothic minds"—without wishing to attach any excessive significance to that term. The three were Abelard, John of Salisbury, and Alain de Lille. What I attempted to approach through them was the spirit of the extraordinarily creative twelfth century, as it was reflected in Abelard's intellectual attitude, John of Salisbury's ethical attitude, and Alain de Lille's aesthetic attitude. The material on the last of the three, the poet-theologian, I developed into an extensive monograph,[1] and I presented my views on John of Salisbury, the moralist-statesman, to the 1933 Congress of Philologists.[2] The third, Abelard, the philosopher-theologian, I had up to the present kept in portfolio because I knew that my knowledge of philosophy and theology was all too deficient for me to venture to assess this much discussed figure. I can offer two excuses for the fact that I now express my insights regarding Abelard after all: in the first place, the Society for Netherlands Literature needed to find a speaker at short notice, and

* "Abaelard," a lecture given at the annual meeting of the Society for Netherlands Literature on June 12, 1935. First published in *Handelingen en levensberichten van de Maatschappij der Nederlandsche Letterkunde te Leiden*, 1934-5, pp. 66-82. Translation from the Dutch text in *Verzamelde werken*, IV, 104-22.

in the second place, my real aim is not to examine Abelard's philosophy and theology, but to attempt to define something of his place in the culture of his age. To avoid disappointment I call attention to the fact that the title of my address is "Abelard," and not "Abelard and Héloïse."

If one should want to specify in what age Western Christian civilization took on its definitive form, its configuration, one should have to decide upon the twelfth century. The twelfth century was a creative and formative age without equal. There was actually much more of an awakening, an unfolding, in the eleven hundreds than in the age to which we are wont to attach the name Renaissance. This change is like a melody that shifts to a clearer key and a livelier meter, or like the sun breaking through the clouds. Here, if anywhere, there seems to be reason to speak of a new birth. A series of new forms of mental activity and social life were developing in or around the twelfth century, forms and foundations that still serve as supports for the present day.

The tone of a new poetry rang in that age—in fact, not only one, for the courtly lyric in the vernacular tongues was preceded by the rich, flourishing, colorful, and lively scholastic poetry in Latin which is called goliard verse. There was a new epic. The *chanson de geste* had hardly acquired its strict, sober form before it passed on to the refinements of the chivalric romance. The age wove the fabric of that wondrous intellectual and social system in which chivalry was the warp and courtly manners the woof. The architecture we call Romanesque had hardly developed its incomparable gravity and sublimity before it sprouted out in the flowering forms we call Gothic. Seemingly all at once sculpture attained the noble heights one admires in the oldest portal of Chartres. The first stained-glass window sparkled.

A new form of more active social contact had developed in the towns with which the whole of the West had covered itself—both old towns flourishing anew and newly founded towns. New monastic orders sprang up: alongside the vast, ancient abbeys of Saint Benedict came the monasteries of the Carthusians and the Augustinians, the Cistercians, and the Premonstratensians. Internal agrarian expansion and the colonization of the outer fringes extended Europe. Knighthood and asceticism combined into the ideal of the sacred chivalric orders, in the East as well as in the West. Religion itself pushed toward new forms of expression: a new mysticism, that of Saint Bernard, with its flourishing and vivid expression of ecstasy at the wonders of God's grace. The schools, still few and small in the eleventh century, became the focal points of an intensive life of philosophic and dogmatic speculation and disputation. They took on the close-knit and specific form that was to be called the university and would brave the ages.

Never, it would seem to me, has the creation and formation of so many and varied cultural elements been clustered together in one age as in the twelfth century. Of course one should not cling anxiously to that hundred years: the change must not be attributed any secret cultural force in itself. The twelfth century sprang from the eleventh, which had brought the great religious movement expressed by the Truce of God, Gregory VII, and the Crusades; had seen the Normans, with their tremendous potency as state-builders, spread to England and southern Italy; and had consolidated feudalism into the system of the Western political and social organism. But in the twelfth century everything that had been budding in the West during the three hundred preceding years suddenly flowered and began to bear ripe fruit. There is, moreover, no other age of Western civilization which has been so universal, which (for all the differences in ethnic and geographical background or level of evolution) has been so little encumbered by frontiers in the exchange of material and spiritual goods.

The country that contributed more than any other to the creation and formation of the culture of that day was France. France set its stamp on medieval civilization. The French domination of the twelfth century was actually a much more glorious, and much more genuine, spectacle than that of *le grand siècle*. But the trumpet of praise did not yet sound so loudly, although Paris, which in turn was already the center of the French center of intellectual development, was considered "the tree of life planted in the earthly paradise, the torch of the house of the Lord, the source of all wisdom, the ark of the covenant, the queen of the nations, the jewel of princes." [3] When John of Salisbury returned to Paris in 1164 and saw the abundance of merchandise, the gaiety of the people, the respect for the clergy, the majesty and glory of the Church, and the busy activity of the *philosophantes*

toward whom his heart was attracted, he compared the town
to Jacob's ladder, whose top reached to heaven and was the
way for the angels to ascend and descend. And he quoted
the word of the Scriptures: "Surely the Lord is in this place;
and I knew it not." And also the poet: "Happy is he to whom
this place is given as exile." [4]

The precedence of Paris had, however, as yet by no means
dimmed the light of the smaller towns. In scholastic life
Chartres, Tours, Orléans, and Reims enjoyed older or newer
renown as well. An age of development is usually not an
age of concentration. The rise of new forms and ideas means
ferment, unrest, even confusion. The twelfth century was,
in fact, an age of great mobility, even in the physical sense.
Everyone pulled up stakes and took up the pilgrim's staff:
the pilgrims themselves, crusaders, preachers, scholars, knights
in search of service or adventure, players, craftsmen, merchants, outlaws, gypsies, migrants to eastern Europe, and not
least of all, monks. The new, lively contact with the Orient
brought materials, ideas, and customs from abroad in greater
abundance than before. The world of the West grew more
diverse and more colorful: literally through fabrics and stained
glass, and intellectually through the influx of the rich stuff of
fables and fancies and through the greater possibilities for
verbal expression.

Should this general progress of the twelfth century toward
the harmonic perfection of the thirteenth be labeled Renaissance? Or does that designation, which comes so naturally
to us, apply at least to a part of these phenomena of awakening
and development? In 1927 Charles Homer Haskins published
The Renaissance of the Twelfth Century, in which in a series
of richly documented chapters he described all the new things
of the age which grew out of a revitalized knowledge of
antiquity. There was, in the first place, the Latin poetry from
the pens of the great churchmen Hildebert of Lavardin,
Baldric of Bourgueil, and Marbod of Rennes, very classical
verse remarkably pure in language and prosody. There was
also the flourishing lyric verse named after the *vagantes* or
goliards, though it is nowadays agreed that its poets were not
by any means all of them those prodigal sons of the Church,
the wandering scholars. Then Haskins considers the revival

of Roman law and the painstaking and essential work of the translators from the Arabic and Greek, who blazed the trail for Scholasticism. Each of these phenomena he rightly calls a revival of classical civilization, which fertilized, liberated, and expanded that of the Christian West. Haskins finds in this resumption of the classical tradition the chief cause for the cultural development that led to the plenitude of the thirteenth century.

I ask myself whether Haskins has not overestimated the effect of that resumption of the classical as the source and impulse of this development. True, Aristotle and Roman law are in themselves two of the most essential cultural revivals known to history and lie at the root of a tremendous amount of later development, but they were not the basic cause, and were themselves also a consequence. The greatest moving forces, it would seem to me, are not to be found in the classicism of the schools. The emphasis Haskins places on classicism as an exercise in ingenuity for the still gaunt and rigid medieval spirit could easily cause us to lose sight of the age's own great formative and motive forces. These forces were the notion of the freedom and the supremacy of ecclesiastical authority as opposed to the secular, an idea associated with Cluny or Gregory VII, and the drive that created one great monastic order after another. Then there are feudalism, in its effects much more formative politically than disruptive; the chivalric idea, active in every sphere of life; the impulse toward the creation of brotherhoods and guilds which brought a segmentation to all of economic life; and not least of all, the idea of kingship, on the basis of which legal institutions developed and states consolidated themselves. In brief, the truly constitutive, formative, and creative principles of life in the High Middle Ages lay beyond the coterie of the school, where the flowers and fruits of antiquity were cultivated.

Varying the Scripture phrase, one might say of the relation of medieval civilization to classical tradition: antiquity was with us always. For emerging Christendom, ever since its barbarian days, classical culture had always been a wondrous and dangerous treasure trove from which one should draw with caution. The model of an inimitable civilization had never been lost sight of. Classical tradition demanded attention constantly—to be rejected, to be conformed to, or to be converted into a new significance. The classical past repeatedly arose anew. Whenever an intellectual elite sought refined and elegant expression it took recourse to a classical model, without leading to a true permeation of the dominant culture by the spirit of antiquity. For the superficial reader there is small distinction between all these poetic imitators, from Venantius Fortunatus in the sixth century, in immediate contact with antiquity itself, via Alcuin in the eighth to Marbod in the eleventh: all of them already seem like humanists. But their activity contributed only in a very small measure to the growth of the vital organism of medieval Christendom.

Around 1100 that organism had waxed to a condition of power and independence. Divided from the Christian East by the accomplished fact of the Great Schism, the Latin West manifested a new feeling of a holy unity and a holy task against the world of Islam. Strong political forms were emerging, towns reviving, and schools appearing everywhere. Ripened and strengthened, full of healthy virility, it now, so to speak, rediscovered the classical tradition for itself, and had to render an account of the significance that ever new antiquity could have for a Christianity desirous of knowledge and power. However, the relation between this inquiring century and an antiquity ever ready to reveal its secrets was new and different. It was no longer a small elite in a barbaric society which, lacking an original culture of its own, attempted to absorb the literary life of an alien past. Now antiquity was put to the stern trial it had already been put to once by Augustine in order to retain what was of genuine value in it and to reject the rest. Antiquity had taken on a new meaning and a new tone for the youthful, vigorous spirit of the twelfth century. There was a better and deeper understanding of it than before. Renaissance? I have no objection, as long as the misunderstanding that so easily clings to the term is avoided. The word "Renaissance" actually always says more than it is meant to say. What was reborn? Antiquity itself? Surely not. The classical form, then? That form was dead and would remain so. It could be filled with a new meaning, and no more nor less than that. What was born was a medieval Latin-Christian civilization stimulated by a classical element that it absorbed. Nothing was *re*born. And in fact even "born" is not a good image. It was a ripening, a coming of age.

A coming of age implies a crisis, a period of unrest, turbulence, disturbance. And that was one of the most essential traits of the twelfth century. The spirit boiled over. In every direction, whether it was one indicated by its classical model or by its own passion, it went further than prudence and temperance would admit. Not only antiquity itself was once more to prove a dangerous storehouse, but also a mode of thought trained on antiquity's lessons: the rediscovered art of the subtle distinction, which was to lead thought to unsuspected declivities. The ideal of the apostolic life, as it was activated in Arnold of Brescia and in Peter Waldo, was also to prove dangerous in its consequences before it became fruitful in Saint Francis.

Neither renewed classicism, uncurbed logicalism, nor extreme evangelism was to hold the field in the long run. In place of the unrest and confusion in thought of the twelfth century the thirteenth was to bring the systematic order and the celestial harmony in which the age of Saint Thomas was able to encompass the spirit like a diamond placed in gold setting. Scholasticism, weeding and trimming, created the strict and schematic form that was to dominate. That activity signified both progress and delimitation. The syllogism became a salutary brake for the spirit, which the discursive method would only have led into the maze of unbridled reasoning. The work of the thirteenth century was the triumph of *orthodoxia.*

The triumphant force was that of the Church. It should never be forgotten that in the Middle Ages the Church, besides being the organism of religion, was also by far the most important organism of culture, and the only one capable of holding together and fusing the elements essential to culture and society. If the orthodox minds—Saint Bernard, Saint Dominic—have exerted a stronger and more lasting influence on European culture than Peter Waldo and Arnold of Brescia, it is not necessarily because of the purity of their faith or their greater talents, but because of the fact that they worked in and through the Church, and hence influenced millions of people where the dissidents only reached thousands.

Peter Abelard began his activities in the turbulence of the early twelfth century. His name, Abaelardus, had five syllables, as the variants and the scansion of his epitaphs demonstrate:[5]

Omnia vi superans rationis et arte loquendi
Abaelardus erat . . .

Similarly:

Est satis in tumulo, Petrus hic jacet Abaelardus
Cui soli patuit scibile quidquid erat.*

Or still more clearly in another meter:[6]

Celebrem theologum vidimus Lumbardum;
Cum Yvone Helyam Petrum et Bernardum,
Quorum opobalsamum spirat os et nardum,
Et professi plurimi sunt Abaielardum.**

The surname was almost certainly first added to Peter, his given name, in school.

He was a native of Brittany. One may say, a Celt! and prepare to deduce his whole life and thought from his ethnic background. But Pallet, near Nantes, was not Brittany of the Bretons; Abelard himself says that he did not know the local language, and he has little friendly to say about the Bretons.[7] His father, moreover, was from Poitou.[8]

I shall not retell that restless, oft-told life yet another time, nor shall I attempt to give a sketch of Abelard's astonishing figure based on a full analysis. A few general traits will have to suffice. He was one of those people who throughout their lives arouse either a deep and passionate admiration or a violent hatred, one of those toward whom no one can be indifferent. He served as a stimulus by the brilliance of his mind, the sharpness of his wit, his versatility, and the extreme contrasts in his personality. Roscellinus said it well in his grimly libelous letter to Abelard:[9] it was the unprecedented novelty of his life, *vitae tuae inaudita novitas*, which brought

* Abelard, through the power of his mind and the wit of his eloquence, / Triumphed over all things . . .
This grave is full: here rests Peter Abelard, / To whom alone stood open all that was knowable.

** We have seen the famous theologian Lombard; / Most have declared Yves, Peter Helias, and Bernard, / Whose mouths breathe balsam and spikenard, / As such—and Abelard.

his contemporaries into revolt against him. The combination of a penetrating, superior intellect and a violent passion[10] made him very difficult to endure. *Odiosum me mundo reddidit logica* ["my logic has made me odious to the world"], he said rightly.[11]

He was, moreover, a sort of intellectual dandy. He loved the farfetched, and liked to surprise and irritate. There was, for instance, the bizarre name, the Paraclete, for his new convent, a name that seemed to betray a lack of respect for the first two persons of the Trinity.[12] In Abelard there was not only a deeply serious theologian and a great philosopher but also a knight, an artist, a schoolmaster, and a journalist. Some of the names of his works tend toward an Americanism *avant la lettre. Sic et non,* Yes and No, *Scito te ipsum,* Know Thyself—were they not unheard-of book titles for the twelfth century? He must have had something of Oscar Wilde about him. Even in his misfortune and his seasoned seriousness, he never forgot the glory of his early years. He spoke with poorly disguised pride of the love lyrics he had written, "which they still sing in many regions," lyrics he had playfully made for Héloïse "so sweet of tongue and voice" that they made him and his love renowned everywhere.[13] Are there perhaps poems of Abelard's among the wealth of anonymous goliard songs extant? If he was once a true poet the spark seems to have burned out in the great catastrophe, for there is little that strikes one as genuinely poetic in the rather numerous Latin poems of his later years, most of them on sacred themes.[14]

I touch only briefly on the history of his love for Héloïse. An attempt has been made to prove on stylistic and factual grounds that cannot be rejected offhand that the whole exchange of letters, including those from Héloïse, were written by Abelard on the basis of genuine letters.[15] In my opinion it does not matter a great deal: one may assume it if one wants to. Abelard did not make up the affair itself: it was known to the world in all its shocking details while the principals were still alive. And the letters must still be considered as quite authentic. Where could Abelard have discovered those profound tones of boundless feminine passion except in having experienced them with Héloïse? Was it perhaps for his own fame that he gave himself such an unheroic role in his *Historia calamitatum*? The important fact remains that a writer of the twelfth century was able to understand and express love in such deep yet violent tones and colors that after eight centuries everyone can still savor its truth and vitality.

The love of Abelard and Héloïse developed into a theme for literature and a *cause célèbre* in the history of morals so early that it has become rather difficult to avoid the traditional impression left by the affair. If I were forced to form an opinion on the value of this testimony of a truly experienced love as a document in cultural history, I should be inclined to call it the single individual testimony that we have regarding pre-courtly love.

Héloïse's emotions—for hers, not Abelard's, are the important ones—and the form in which she expresses them have nothing in common with the system of courtly love which was to impose its code on the cultured world later in the same century. The mere fact that we are here confronted with love as it was experienced by a woman is enough to place the affair outside the essentially masculine sphere of thought of the *cortezia*. Nor is it the classical expression of love, the sentiment of Ovid, or the naïve and popular emotion in a classical husk which is to be heard in the goliard song. It is a wild, dark love, a heart torn by the utterly conflicting forces of a strong faith and the most profoundly earthly passion. And in Héloïse's effusions there is something so immediate, so extravagant, that one asks oneself where there is a parallel to be found outside of Shakespeare. She would not hesitate to follow Abelard, she says, even if she saw him hastening to hell. He should not think that all is well with her in her nunnery. Not yet: she still feared more to offend him than God.[16]

In this lack of reticence, this direct passion without sentimentality, there seems to be something primitive. I should like to call such uncurbed expression un-Latin. Héloïse reminds me of the women in the Icelandic sagas. Take away the Christian element in the history of Abelard and Héloïse, the sense of sin and the belated contrition, and what remains would fit well in one of those wild tales of passion and violence which the Nordic spirit of the same time has left for us. Her name is good Germanic, Helwis or Helwidis—but so are most of the names of far and away most French men and women of that age.

Have no fear that I am going to resort to race theories.

I am not arguing that Héloïse was Germanic, as opposed to Romance, in blood and emotions. I am merely pointing out that the French world of that day was closer to its barbaric origins, and that it is good to forget for a moment the romantic accent that the name of the first great beloved of Western literature has taken on, in order to detect in it an older and deeper tone.

But what we are concerned with here is to arrive at something of an assessment of the figure of Abelard in the turbulent upsurge of intellectual life in his time. What is the meaning of those words *vitae suae inaudita novitas?* For a proper understanding of the twelfth century one must imagine a society in which books are rare, those who can read them are also rare, and those who can explain them are even rarer. Hugh of St. Victor explains the use of the word *lego* in the language of the school: *lego librum*—I read the book myself; *lego librum illi*—I explain it to someone else, I give a course on it; *lego librum ab illo*—I hear him explain it, I follow his lecture.[17] The rarity of books and the art of reading gave an extraordinary effect to the word of the master. For us, flooded as we are by the stream of words in print and on the air, the word is losing more and more of what is basically still a magic effect. In a more primeval society the word falls on a virgin soil thirsting after fecundity, it convinces and commands, it banishes and binds, in short, it effectuates. The authority of the few masters who have a command of it is extraordinarily great. Every master is more or less of a wonder. He knows, he has secrets that he will reveal to us if we propitiate him.

Where should they be found, these masters? In the schools. The schools, too, were rare in the twelfth century, and each of them was a hearth of knowledge. At a time when books are lacking or at least inaccessible to the masses, when there is no regular form of exchange for written thought, the school —provided there is a strong and general impulse to knowledge —becomes a cultural vehicle of the very first order. That was the situation in the twelfth century. However scarce the schools still were, in comparison with the previous centuries their growth was remarkable. Not much was needed for them: a hall, a lectern, and a master—that was all.

In the twelfth century, however, not only the number of schools and the number of students increased at a rapid pace, but at the same time also the direction of the urge to knowledge and the form of its activity changed. Instead of the more-or-less isolated activity of the earlier theologians and men of letters there was now, seemingly all at once, a need to dispute or come to an understanding with one another in public, a need for a contest to demonstrate to everyone the validity and superiority of an argument, a concept, or a method. The publicity of learning was seeking its entry. The lecture course and the disputation presented themselves as the outward forms, and logic as the vehicle. Logic as it was known from the classical tradition had to slake all the thirst for proof. All reason, all power of judgment seemed to be enclosed in formal logic.

Hence in the schools the search for what was substantiated philosophically began to drive the study of *grammatica*, that is to say, of letters in the broadest sense, into the background. The poetic classicism of a person like Hildebert of Lavardin was, as such, rather an elegiac farewell to the past than the annunciation of the coming time.

For a proper understanding of the philosophical flight of the twelfth century, a highly essential trait to be found in almost every phenomenon of vital cultural renewal should be pointed out. I am referring to a subject I considered in an address I gave a good two years ago,[18] and hope soon to consider in a more detailed form: the inseparability of the play element and the serious element in culture. The intellectual activity of such an age of renewal has, to a greater or lesser degree, the character of a game—a serious, weighty, even dangerous game, but nonetheless a game.

The philosophical movement of the twelfth century displays this trait of a game very clearly. The chivalric tournament and the scholastic disputation are in the truest sense two interchangeable forms of the ennobled instinct to competition of an age overflowing with a budding life force.

Abelard has been called the "troubadour among schoolmen." This is not untrue, but "the knight errant" would be even better.[19] He himself considered his work in terms of an exchange of arms. In his youth he had, in his own words, traded the arms of warfare for those of the mind, giving preference to "the armor of dialectical reasonings and to disputations above the trophies of war. . . ." [20] He trekked disputing through all the regions where the art was said to flourish. He set up "the army camp of his school" on the Montagne Sainte-Geneviève in order "to besiege" the competitor who occupied his place at Paris.[21] His opponents warned against Master Peter as one who was not a debater but a quibbler and who rather played the role of a jester than of a doctor.[22]

The great masters of dialectic earned big money. Their fame had a close resemblance to that of present-day athletic heroes. People pursued the great masters and boasted of having seen and followed them.[23] Roscellinus sketches Abelard, perhaps slanderously, as counting each evening the money his false teachings had brought in, before spending it on debauchery.[24] Abelard himself says that he began studying in order to earn money, and that he was earning a great deal. He also tells how he shifted from *physica,* that is to say, philosophy, to the explication of the Holy Scriptures as the result of a wager.[25]

The life of the schools in the twelfth century was one of competition and heated controversies, one of envy and slander, contumely and libel. What a game of quibbles and captiousness! Snares of words were set, says John of Salisbury, and nets of syllables.[26] Hugh of St. Victor describes a school where the scholars attempt to deceive each other with a thousand tricks and stratagems.[27]

It does not seem to me exaggerated to argue that there is a certain connection between the long precedence of the problem of the universals in the development of Scholasticism and the athletic-contest character of the scholastic activities of the day.

This play element of violent competition, considered as a sociological phenomenon, betrays an intellectual attitude peculiar to archaic ages. It might be called the attitude of sophism. The abilities of the rational intellect are sharpened, but the limits of its conclusiveness as proof are not clearly seen. It is precisely this somewhat primitive intellectual attitude that dragged the thinkers of the twelfth century onto dangerous inclines, and made more than one of them a dissenter, and perhaps a heretic. The skilled use of dialectic led them to a method of research for which their time, with its lack of sound and well-assimilated knowledge of natural reality, was not yet ripe. For these masters of disputation any argument was sound and conclusive if it was irrefutable in formal logic. When they applied their dialectic to the truths of religion they discovered unsuspected gaps and abysses.

It was not piety that led Abelard to theology. We have already mentioned that his comrades playfully lured him, the philosopher, toward theological problems. Once he was established in that domain, his incomparable ingenuity inspired his mind to find solutions no one had suspected before him. He came to the view of the problem of the universals which Victor Cousin has (according to some scholars not too happily) called conceptualism. As the book by J. G. Sikes illuminated anew a few years ago, it was a point of view that might be called Aristotelian realism. Abelard reached it without having access to the whole of Aristotle. It is a realism tempered by a reservation. The radical, primitive view, in which the general concepts, the universals, acquired an almost mythological nature, was resolved in an empirical definition that was not a vague middle-of-the-road point of view, but indicated a completely changed orientation of the question and a deepening of insight. A certain relativity was introduced into the problem. Abelard had understood the significance of our intellectual functions as such for the possibility of knowledge and expression of any sort. Between the hostile figures *vox* and *res* he introduced the concept, *sermo*, and abolished the question of *post* and *ante*.[28]

The formulation of so-called conceptualism did not by any means make Abelard into an iconoclast. Rather it made him a pioneer for those to follow, including Thomas Aquinas himself. His solution meant the possibility of a truce between the conflicting groups. The old, extreme nominalism was suppressed, and would appear again, in a much more subtle form, only in the fourteenth century. The indispensable realism had found an escape out of the sphere of mythology.

What should one say of Abelard's renowned *Sic et non*, which aroused such a high degree of distrust among his contemporaries and is often looked upon as the utter relativization of all morals and faith? In it Abelard placed side by side contradictory statements of the Church Fathers. He demonstrated the contradiction, and then applied the techniques of dialectical criticism to it, without arriving at a conclusion. It would seem to be a lesson in skepticism without equal. *Sic et non* contains the seeds of a whole philological method, applied to the Holy Scriptures and tradition. Every sort of doubt is raised: whether the text is corrupt, whether the writer has made a mistake, whether he is misunderstood. Abelard already knew that the circumstances must be taken into consideration; that even the Church Fathers spoke from time to time *ex opinione magis quam ex veritate* ["more on the basis of their own opinion than on that of truth"]; that the seers blessed with the gift of prophecy made a habit of it and did not always know whether they were led by divine inspiration or not. Which, he said, was very useful to help them retain their humility.[29]

Abelard explains the Gospel phrase *quaerite et invenietis* ["seek and ye shall find"] with a paraphrase: "For by doubt we come to investigation and by investigation we ascertain the truth. . . ."[30] It could have been said five centuries later by Francis Bacon. In fact, it was a phrase taken from Aristotle.

Was it really such an unprecedented modernism, that renowned *Sic et non?* Or was it rather an archaic tour de force of the agonistic instinct, an *epideixis*, a "display" such as the Greek sophists gave, a philosophical *jeu d'esprit?* To all appearances it was neither. The most recent students of Abelard's theology, Jean Cottiaux[31] and the above-mentioned J. G. Sikes, confirm that here as elsewhere Abelard (and he was not the first) was simply following in the footsteps of Aristotle when he summarized existing knowledge and left *aporiai* (perplexities) as the basis for further research.

For all that, Abelard remains the man of the nuance, of the relations with both sides, who proposes agreements and points of view and leaves ambiguities open instead of declaring in utter confidence "this is the way it is." He points out how words that, considered in isolation, seem to have quite the same meaning suddenly prove to indicate something quite different within the context of the sentence.[32] Cottiaux calls his thought "a thought that seeks, corrects, and defines itself. . . ."[33] Instead of accepting the doctrine of redemption in its literal and mystical sense, he dissolves its essence by describing the process of redemption as the arousing of a feeling of love in our souls or by explaining redemption as a divine instruction instead of a true ransom.[34] Though he himself denied having taught that sin was not situated in either work, the will, desire, or pleasure, he deprived theology of the bases of its doctrine of sin by diluting sin to a purely psychological fact.[35]

In many respects Abelard's spirit brought him remarkably close to the point of view of the later Christian humanists, and particularly of Erasmus. He already had the same reverence for the pure sources of the faith in the original languages, properly understood, though he himself did not resort to the Greek.[36] He attributed inspiration to the classical philosophers, and appears to have valued them more highly than the prophets. He was an enlightened thinker who did not attach significance either to astrologers or to the salutary effect of blessings and faith-healing. He was amused at Saint Norbert, who rebuked the people if he did not succeed in a cure by prayer.[37]

In his sequences and hymns for the virgins of the Paraclete there is a tone of optimism and teleological contentment with the world which reminds one of the eighteenth century.[38] He evinces a conscious and noble sense of the rights and the dignity of women which is rare in the ecclesiastical literature of the Middle Ages and bears a great deal of resemblance to that of Erasmus.[39] An *Introductiones parvulorum* is mentioned among his lost works.

It is clear, however, that in all this Abelard must not be considered as a harbinger of the Renaissance, but rather as a pre-Gothic thinker. His apparent modernity is itself an early spirit, an open-mindedness that had not yet experienced the strict moderation that the systematic activity of the next century was to introduce in the field of thought. He was extravagant because the field still lay open, had not yet been fenced in. The spirit of the twelfth century, says Etienne Gilson, seems to us closer to that of the Renaissance than the spirit of the thirteenth. The twelfth century was an age of preparation[40]—that is to say, preparation for the work of the thirteenth. If there seems to be something contradictory in that, then the fault lies in us: we are much too used to viewing the Renaissance as the general, final result of the evolution of the whole of the Middle Ages. To understand the twelfth century properly one must not set it beside the sixteenth, but beside the thirteenth.

Abelard, from whatever angle one views him, is precocious,

growing intellectually a bit too fast for himself. His spirit was
not ripened in the warmth of the great psychological forces
streaming through his century. His thought did not spring
from the depths of the moral crisis of his age. He was too
much a man of the intellect to have been able to point his
century the way its heart urged. And the positive content of
his learning was still too scanty for him to be able to construct
a new world of knowledge. Most of what he detected, guessed,
and suspected his wondrous intellect distilled, so to speak,
from the empty rules of dialectic by an artifice.

The great psychological forces inflaming his century are
represented by his bitter enemy Bernard of Clairvaux. These
two men who stood at the two poles of twelfth-century thought
were insufferable to one another. All the great men of the
faith went as far as Bernard, if not further, in their unanimous
agreement to abhor Abelard's misuse of the art of reasoning
and to complain against the unseasonable rationalism springing from it.

In his time Abelard and his spirit had enthusiastic admirers
and fervent advocates.[41] Few writings throw such a sharp
spotlight on the intellectual controversy of the twelfth century
as the defense of Abelard against Bernard by the scholastic
Berengarius of Poitiers, who reveals to us everything that
the age had to charge against the "mellifluous doctor." [42] In
a lively, violent, biting style filled with dramatic tension he
describes the Council of Sens, which pronounced the condemnation of Abelard. He accuses Bernard of intolerance and
hypocrisy, and adds:

"Allow Peter [that is to say, Abelard] to be a Christian
with you. And if you will, he will be Catholic with you. And
if you will not, he will be Catholic nonetheless. For God is
common to all of us . . . and not peculiar to one." [43] Again,
is it not as if we hear the accent of the Christian humanism
to come?

There was another great churchman of the day who acted
in keeping with such a call for reconciliation, the man of
whom Abelard, exhausted and pursued, sought and found a
refuge at the end of his restless life: Peter the Venerable,
the abbot of Cluny.

In the story of his life Abelard calls himself light by nature.[44] Such a light spirit is not tolerated by the heavier
spirits, in whatever age it may appear. They hated Abelard

as Luther was to hate Erasmus four centuries later. The reaction of the twelfth century to Abelard's word was in many respects similar to that of the sixteenth to Erasmus's.

Throughout the whole evolution of Christian thought one finds two intellectual types in conflict. It is the conflict of those who like to appeal to Jerome and those who base themselves on Augustine, the contrast of the two religious temperaments that manifested themselves in the two Church Fathers. Jerome was the man of urbanity, for all his asceticism and monasticism susceptible to the commodities of culture: literature, relations of intellectual sympathy, enlightened ideas, forms of feminine thought, educational needs. Augustine— well, one knows him, the man of the burning heart and absolute faith.

Abelard belonged to those on the side of Jerome. He quoted him again and again, he praised him, he sought in him the explanation of the Scriptures.[45] Erasmus, too, was later to stand on the same side.

On Augustine's side stood Bernard of Clairvaux, Hugh of St. Victor, and many another before Luther, too, was to stand there. In his own time Saint Bernard was already called "Augustine revived," and Hugh "the tongue of Augustine." Augustine's name constantly became the watchword of a conservative party, not only as a symbol of deep respect for authority and tradition but also as a symbol of the essence of faith. The words of the two Church Fathers have had a constantly shifting weight in the history of the Christian faith. Whenever there was a great religious crisis the words of Augustine outweighed those of Jerome in the scales of the ages.

THE POLITICAL AND MILITARY SIGNIFICANCE OF CHIVALRIC IDEAS IN THE LATE MIDDLE AGES •

I would be at a loss to be in your midst, and to speak at this general assembly, if I were not permitted to refer to the great honor bestowed on the University of Leiden (which I have the privilege to represent) by your invitation. It is now some months since a French scholar, in his Sorbonne dissertation, reminded us of the debt the University of Leiden owes to France. Actually we had not forgotten it; how would it be possible to forget the names of Scaliger, Doneau, Rivet, and Saumaise, who lent luster to Leiden and Holland? It is with an invocation of these memories of a long-standing spiritual kinship between France and Holland that I ask for your kind attention.

In proposing to speak to you on the political and military significance of chivalric ideas in the late Middle Ages, I make no pretense of presenting something new. I only wish to focus attention on certain well-known facts and to register a degree of reaction against present tendencies in the discipline of history.

Generally speaking, the medievalists of our day are hardly

• "La valeur politique et militaire des idées de chevalerie à la fin du moyen âge," originally a lecture given at the general assembly of the Société d'Histoire Diplomatique, June 16, 1921. First published in the Revue d'histoire diplomatique, XXXV (1921), 126-38. Translation from the French text in Verzamelde werken, III, 519-29.

favorable to chivalry. Combing the records, in which chivalry is, indeed, little mentioned, they have succeeded in presenting a picture of the Middle Ages in which economic and social points of view are so dominant that one tends at times to forget that, next to religion, chivalry was the strongest of the ideas that filled the minds and the hearts of those men of another age. We have come a long, long way from the romantics who viewed the Middle Ages above all as the era of chivalry.

Whatever chivalry may have been at the time of the Crusades, it is generally agreed today that in the fourteenth or fifteenth century it was nothing more than a rather artificial revival of things long dead, a sort of deliberate and insincere renascence of ideas drained of any real value. This romantic infatuation with the prowess of Arthurs and Lancelots is personified in King John the Good, who twice nearly compromised French independence: first by losing the battle of Poitiers and then by granting Burgundy to the bravest of his sons. In his time everyone was eager to found chivalric orders; tournaments and jousts were more the fashion than ever before; errant knights crossed Europe in fulfillment of the strangest and most extravagant vows; the romances were rewritten, and the cult of courtly love re-established.

All this one may, if one will, consider a superficial and unimportant phenomenon: a literary and sportive fashion of the nobility and nothing more.

But even if it were nothing but that it would nonetheless have been a historical fact of primary importance. For it would indicate a tendency in the spirit of the age to recreate in real life an ideal image of the past. The history of civilization is full of such desires to relive the past. And there is no more important subject of study. Is that eternal desire for a perfection that no longer exists, that never satiated need for revival, not something much more interesting than the question of knowing whether this or that man of state was a traitor or a dupe, or whether the aim of one or the other military campaign was from the outset conquest or merely diversion?

I have used the word "renascence." It should be pointed out that the links between the Renaissance proper and this revival of chivalry in the late Middle Ages are much stronger than is usually realized. The chivalric revival was, as it were, a naïve and imperfect prelude to the Renaissance. It was thought that if chivalry were resuscitated, antiquity, too, would be revived. In the mind of the fourteenth century the image of antiquity was not yet disentangled from that of the Round Table. In his poem *"Le cuer d'amours espris"* ["The Heart Enamored"] King René depicts the tombs of Lancelot and Arthur side by side with those of Caesar, Hercules, and Troilus, each adorned with its coat of arms. A coincidence of terminology helped to trace the origins of chivalry to Roman antiquity. How would it have been possible to realize that the word *miles* in Roman writings did not mean what it did in medieval Latin, that is to say, "knight," or that a Roman *eques* was not the same as a feudal knight? Romulus, as a consequence, was considered to be the founder of chivalry because he raised a band of a thousand mounted warriors. A Burgundian chronicler, Lefèvre de Saint-Rémy, wrote in praise of Henry V of England: "And he maintained the discipline of chivalry well, as did the Romans formerly."

It is manifest that the political and military history of the last centuries of the Middle Ages as described by Froissart, Monstrelet, Chastellain, and so many others reveals very little chivalry and a great deal of covetousness, cruelty, cold calculation, well-understood self-interest, and diplomatic subtlety. The reality of history seems constantly to disavow the fanciful ideal of chivalry.

And yet all those writers viewed the history of their times in the full light of their major ideal, that of chivalry. In spite of the confusion and the monotonous horror of their tales, they saw that history bathed in an atmosphere of gallantry, fidelity, and duty. They all begin by announcing their design of glorifying bravery and the knightly virtues, of reciting "noble enterprises, conquests, deeds of valor, and feats of arms" (d'Escouchy), "the great marvels and the fine feats of arms that have come to pass as a result of the great wars" (Froissart). Later on they more or less lose sight of it. Froissart, the *enfant terrible* of chivalry, recounts an endless list of betrayals and cruelties without being very much aware of the contradiction between his general views and the contents of his narrative.

All these authors are firmly convinced that the salvation of the world and the maintenance of justice alike depend on the virtues of the nobility. The times are bad; only chivalry can provide a remedy. Here is what *Le livre des faicts du mareschal Boucicaut* has to say on the subject: "Two things have, by the will of God, been established in the world, like two pillars to sustain the order of divine and human laws . . . and without which the world would be like a confused thing and without any order. . . . These two flawless pillars are Chivalry and Learning, which go very well together."

The chivalric idea tends to invade even the realm of the metaphysical. The feat of arms of the archangel Michael is glorified by Jean Molinet as "the first deed of knighthood and chivalric prowess."

The idea of chivalry constituted for these authors the sum total of general concepts with the aid of which they explained to themselves the realms of politics and history. Such a point of view was highly fantastic and shallow, no doubt. Ours is much vaster: it embraces, for example, economic and social causes. Still, this vision of a world ruled by chivalry, however superficial and mistaken it may be, was the clearest conception the secular mind of the Middle Ages could attain in the domain of political ideas. It was the formula with which man was in those days able to understand in his poor way the appalling complexity of events. What he saw about him was nothing but violence and confusion. War was usually a chronic process of isolated raids. Diplomacy was a very solemn and very verbose procedure, in which a multitude of questions of juridical detail clashed with some very general traditions and some points of honor. All the concepts we make use of in order to understand history were utterly lacking to them, and yet they, like us, felt the need to detect a pattern in it. They required a form for their political thought, and here the idea of chivalry came in. Thanks to the chivalric fiction, history was reduced for them to a grave spectacle of honor and virtue, to a noble game with edifying and heroic rules.

I will be told that all this, though of extreme interest for the history of ideas, does not constitute sufficient proof that the tradition of chivalry had any real influence on the course of political events. And that is what I set out to demonstrate. Is it, after all, rather difficult? When I called King John the Good the model of this renascence of chivalry, you will, no doubt, have recalled that his reign was disastrous to France precisely because of his chivalric prejudice. The battle of Poitiers was lost as a result of the imprudence and chivalric stubbornness he showed with regard to the tactics of the numerically inferior English army. After the escape of his son, who was serving as hostage, the king, loyal to his honor, went to England himself, leaving his country to the perils of another regency. Another deed of chivalry, a wholly admirable one: the separation of Burgundy, whatever the political calculations behind it may have been, was primarily dictated by a chivalric motive in the face of which reasons of state are reduced to nothing—it was the reward for the courage young Philip showed at Poitiers.

This example is sufficient to convince one that chivalric ideas were able to exercise a real, and most disastrous, influence on the fate of nations. It may even be said that politics and war were conceived from the chivalric point of view, whatever the diplomatic or strategic realities may have been. Every dispute between two countries presented itself to the mind as a legal case between two noble persons, as a "dispute" in the legal sense of the word. One supported one's lord in a "dispute," just as one would follow him before the judge to take oath with him. As a consequence, a battle differed only in degree from the judicial combat or the combat of knights in the lists. In his *Arbre des batailles,* Honoré Bonet places the three in the same category, though carefully distinguishing between "great general battles" and "private battles."

From this conception of war as a mere extension of the combat the idea results that the best means to settle a political difference is that of single combat between the two princes, the two parties to the "dispute." This is a curious example of a political concept which, though it was never put in practice, haunted minds for several centuries as a very serious possibility and a very practical method. Till well into the sixteenth century a number of rulers of various countries announced their intention to fight their adversary in the lists. They challenged in due form, and they prepared for the fight with great enthusiasm. But nothing more ever came of it.

This might be considered as nothing but a form of political advertisement, either to impress one's enemy or to appease the grievances of one's subjects. But I should like to believe there was something more in it, something I would call the chimerical but nonetheless sincere craving to conform to the chivalric ideal by posing before all the world as the champion of justice who does not hesitate to sacrifice himself for his people. How, otherwise, are we to explain the surprising persistence of such plans for royal duels? Richard II of England offered to fight, together with his uncles the dukes of Lancaster, York, and Gloucester, against the king of France, Charles VI, and his uncles the dukes of Anjou, Burgundy, and Berry. Louis of Orléans defied Henry IV of England. Henry V of England challenged the dauphin before marching upon Agincourt. And the Duke of Burgundy, Philip the Good, displayed an almost frenzied attachment to this mode of settling disputes. In 1425 he challenged Humphrey, Duke of Gloucester, in connection with the question of Holland. The motive, as always, was expressly formulated in the terms: "To prevent Christian bloodshed and destruction of the people, on whom my heart has compassion, [I wish] that this quarrel may be settled by my own body, without proceeding by means of war, which would entail that many noblemen and others, both of your army and of mine, would end their days pitifully."

All was in readiness for the combat: the magnificent armor and the vestments of state, the pavilions, the standards, the banners, the coats of arms for the heralds, everything richly adorned with the duke's blazons and his emblems, the flint-and-steel and the Saint Andrew's cross. Philip had gone in for a course of training, "both by abstinence from food and by taking exercise to keep him in breath." He practiced with fencing masters every day in his park of Hesdin. De Laborde lists in detail the expenses entailed in the affair, but the combat did not take place.

This did not prevent the duke, twenty years later, from wishing to decide a question touching Luxembourg by a single combat with the Duke of Saxony. And toward the close of his life he was vowing to engage in a hand-to-hand combat with the Grand Turk.

One finds this custom of challenges between sovereigns as late as the heyday of the Renaissance. Francesco Gonzaga offers to deliver Italy from Cesare Borgia by fighting the latter with sword and poniard. On two occasions Charles V himself formally proposed to the king of France to settle their differences by single combat.

Let us not attempt to determine too precisely the degree of sincerity in those fantastic, never realized projects. Without doubt they were a mixture of sincere conviction and heroic braggadocio. It should not be forgotten that in every archaic civilization the sharp line between the serious and the posed

eludes our view. In chivalric life an element of grave and
solemn play is constantly intermingled with reason and calculation. It will never be possible to understand all the aspects
of medieval politics if one neglects this play element.

I have said "play." Should it not rather be passion? Not
that I should want to say that in the political life of our times
the passions do not count. But in the Middle Ages they found
expression in distinct forms, forms almost personified, like
the allegorical figures to be seen in the tapestries. In people's
minds the passion for honor, for glory, and for revenge acquired the splendor of virtue and duty. For a fourteenth-
century prince vengeance was a political duty of the first order,
no doubt not a Christian one, but nevertheless for him one of
a sacred character. No other motive for war appealed to the
imagination so much as it did. According to the *Débat des
héraulx d'armes de France et d'Angleterre*, the "just quarrel"
obliging the king of France to conquer England found its
basis first of all in the fact that the murder of Richard II, the
husband of a French princess, had not been avenged. Only
in second place came the compensation for the "innumerable
evils" that France had suffered at the hands of the English
and the "great riches" that the conquest promised.

But we run the risk of getting off the subject, for in the
final analysis vengeance, though a point of honor pre-
eminently chivalric, has its roots in a much deeper layer of
the mind than that of chivalry.

Let us therefore return to the effects of chivalric ideas, in
the narrower sense of the term, upon the conduct of warfare.
A single example will suffice to illustrate how strategic and
tactical interests constantly clashed with chivalric prejudices.
One evening some days before the battle of Agincourt, the
king of England, riding to meet the French army, by mistake
passed by the village that the foragers of his army had
chosen for him to spend the night in. He would have had
time to go back and he would have done so if he had not
been prevented by a point of honor. The king, "as the chief
guardian of the very laudable ceremonies of honor," had just
promulgated an order according to which his knights had to
take off their coat of armor while reconnoitering, because
a knight's honor could not suffer him to retreat when ac-
coutered for battle. Now, the king himself had put on his
coat of armor, and so, having passed by the village designated,

he could not return to it. Hence he passed the night at the place he had reached and had the vanguard advance accordingly, in spite of the dangers that might have ensued from the action.

Without a doubt when an important decision was to be taken strategic prudence will have carried the day over points of honor most of the time. The customary invitations to the enemy to come to an understanding as to the choice of the battlefield—a clear indication of the similarity of a battle to a legal decision—were generally declined by the party occupying the more favorable position. Reason, however, was not always victorious. Before the battle of Nájera, or Navarrete, in which Bertrand Du Guesclin was taken prisoner, Don Enrique de Trastamara was determined to measure himself against the enemy in the open plain at any cost. He voluntarily sacrificed the advantages offered by the lay of the land, and as a result lost the battle.

It is no exaggeration to say that chivalric ideas exercised a constant influence on the conduct of warfare, causing a war's end now to be retarded and then to be precipitated, causing opportunities to be lost and profits to be neglected. They were, then, a real influence, but taken all in all a negative one.

There is, however, another side to the question which we should consider for a few moments. In referring to the system of chivalric ideas as a noble game of rules of honor and precepts of virtue, I have touched upon the point where it is possible to detect a connection between chivalry and the evolution of the law of nations. The origins of the latter lay in antiquity and in canon law, but chivalry was the ferment that made possible the development of the laws of war. The notion of a law of nations was preceded and prepared for by the chivalric ideal of a good life of honor and loyalty.

This is not a hypothesis I am advancing. The first elements of the law of nations are to be found blended with casuistic and often puerile regulations on the passage of arms and on combats in the lists. In 1352 the knight Geoffroi de Charny (who later died at Poitiers bearing the oriflamme) addressed to the king, who had just instituted his order of the Star, a treatise composed of a long list of *demandes,* that is to say, casuistic questions concerning jousts, tournaments, and war. Jousts and tournaments rank first, but the importance of questions regarding the laws of war is shown by their far greater number. It should be remembered that the order of the Star was the culmination of chivalric romanticism, founded explicitly "in the manner of the Round Table."

Better known than Geoffroi de Charny's *demandes* is a work that appeared toward the end of the fourteenth century and remained in vogue till the sixteenth: *L'arbre des batailles*, by Honoré Bonet, the prior of Selonnet in Provence. It is surprising that Ernest Nys, who has devoted so much study to the precursors of Grotius, and to Honoré Bonet in particular, has ignored the influence of chivalric ideas on the development of the law of nations. The extent to which chivalry was the guiding thought inspiring the author (for all his being an ecclesiastic) to his very remarkable ideas appears nowhere more clearly than in *L'arbre des batailles*. The problems of just and unjust war, and those of the right of spoils and of fidelity to one's given word, present themselves to the mind of Bonet as cases of chivalric conduct to be treated in special, formal detail, while questions of personal honor and the gravest questions of the law of nations are hurried over. Here are one or two examples: "Whether armor lost in battle should be made good if it has been borrowed." "Whether, if armor and horses hired for battle are lost there, they should be made good or not." It is well known that the ransoming of noble prisoners was of the utmost importance in medieval wars, and it is especially on that point that chivalric honor and the principles of international law converge. "Whether, if a man is taken while under the safe conduct of another, the latter is bound to ransom him at his own cost." "Whether, if a man has to return to prison after he has been released from it in order to visit his friends and to look after his debts and he cannot settle them, that man is required to return to prison at the risk of suffering death." Specific cases give way to questions of a general nature. "This time I want to pose the following question: to wit, by what right or what reason can one wage war against the Saracens or other unbelievers, and whether the pope has to grant pardon and indulgence for such wars." The author proves that they are not permissible, not even with the aim of converting the pagans to the faith. On the important question "whether a prince may refuse another passage through his country," we could hardly agree with the author when he proves that the king of France has the right to require passage trough Austria to war on Hungary. On the other hand we would fully agree with Bonet's answer to the question whether the king of France, if at war with England, may take prisoner "the poor English, merchants, tillers of the soil, and shepherds who tend their flocks in the fields." Bonet responds in the negative: not only do Christian morals forbid it, but also "the honor of the age." The spirit of gentleness and humanity in which the author resolves these questions goes so far as to extend the privilege of safe conduct in the enemy's country to the father of an English student wishing to visit his sick son in Paris.

L'arbre des batailles was, unfortunately, only a theoretical treatise. We know well enough that war in those times was very cruel. The fine rules and the generous exemptions enumerated by the good prior of Selonnet were all too rarely observed. Still, if a little clemency was slowly introduced into political and military practices, it was as a result rather of the sentiment of honor than of legal and moral convictions. Military duty was conceived in the first place as the honor of a knight.

Taine said: "In the middle and lower classes the chief motive of conduct is self-interest. With an aristocracy the mainspring is pride. Now, among the profound sentiments of man there is none more apt to be transformed into probity, patriotism, and conscience, for a proud man feels the need of self-respect, and to obtain it, he is led to deserve it." It would seem to me that this is the point of view from which the importance of chivalry for the history of civilization must be considered: pride assuming features of high ethical value, the pride of a knight preparing the way for clemency and law. If you wish to convince yourselves that such transitions in the realm of ideas are real, read *Le jouvencel,* the biographical romance by Jean de Bueil, the Maid of Orléans's companion in arms. Permit me to quote one passage in which the psychology of courage has found simple, touching expression.

One loves one's comrade so in war. When one sees that one's quarrel is just and one's blood is fighting well, tears rise to the eye. A sweet feeling of loyalty and pity fills the heart on seeing one's friend so valiantly exposing his body in order to do and fulfill the command of our Creator. And then one prepares to go die or live with him, and for love not to abandon him. And out of that rises such a delectation that he who has not essayed it is not man enough to say what a delight it is. Do you think that a man who does that fears death? Not at all; for he feels so strengthened, he is so elated that he does not know where he is. Truly he is afraid of nothing.

This is the spirit of chivalry which is to transform itself into patriotism. All the best elements are there: the spirit of sacrifice and the desire for justice and protection for the oppressed sprouted in the soil of chivalry. It is in the classic country of chivalry, in France, that the stirring accents of patriotic love, mingled with the sentiment of justice, are heard for the first time. One need not be a great poet to say these simple things with dignity. No author of those times has given more touching and varied expression to French patriotism than Eustache Deschamps, a rather mediocre poet. Here, for example, are the terms in which he addresses France:

> *Tu as duré et durras sanz doubtance*
> *Tant com raisons sera de toy amée,*
> *Autrement, non; fay donc à la balance*
> *Justice en toy et que bien soit gardée.*•

Chivalry would never have remained the ideal of life through the course of several centuries if it had not contained high social values. It was, in fact, in the very exaggeration of its generous and fantastic views that its strength lay. The soul of the Middle Ages, fierce and passionate, could be led only by giving much too lofty a place to the ideal toward which its aspirations should tend. Thus the Church acted, and thus also feudal thought. No one would deny that reality constantly gave the lie to such lofty illusions of a pure and noble social life. But where would we be if our thoughts never transcended the strict limits of the attainable?

• You have endured and will no doubt endure / As long as reason will be loved by you. / Not otherwise; hold then the balance / Of Justice in yourself, and let it be well kept.

BERNARD SHAW'S SAINT •
(FOR M. E. W.)

I

THE PLAY AND ITS PERFORMANCE

If there had been one miracle too few to warrant the canonization of Joan of Arc, it might have been brought forward that she has been able to wipe the grimace from Shaw's joking countenance and to force that acrobat, eternally turning somersaults about the crossbar of his ingenuity, to his knees for a moment. No one has the right to demand from the master of satiric comedy that he should refrain from every witticism and comic effect throughout a sixty-two-page Preface and a performance of three hours and a half. But, even aside from the effect of the play itself, the mere fact that this time one can read the Preface with hardly a shrug of the shoulders is proof that something unusual is happening. Shaw, in whose hands Caesar and "the man of destiny" grew small and foolish, has now experienced the power of the heroic, and whether he would or no, has written in the humble service of his incomparable subject.

The more one thinks about it, the greater the miracle

• *"Bernard Shaw's heilige,"* first published in *De Gids,* LXXXIX (1925), Part Two, 110-20, 220-32, 419-31. Translation from the Dutch text in *Verzamelde werken,* III, 530-62.

207

seems. A person with the limitations of Shaw, that man with the utterly prosaic mind (in the good sense of the word) who appears so alien to everything that seems to us to be noblest in the Middle Ages and most essential in the history of Joan of Arc—the Catholic faith, late Gothic life, the pure, clear tone of the French spirit—what will such a person make of it all?

What he has made of it is certainly a peculiar product, and there are any number of objections, from both the artistic and the historical point of view. Meanwhile, the play is traveling through the world, and it attracts people (not only because it is Shaw), moves and affects them—and uplifts them. Shaw has once more posed a problem: this time, in spite of himself, the problem of his success. There is perhaps sufficient reason to offer a historian's marginal notes on this play that everyone has seen or read, or both. For the most part these notes have to do with Shaw's conception of the historical figure of Joan of Arc, but as a result they unavoidably touch on an evaluation of the play and its performance as well.

The task that Shaw has set himself approximates the highest task the human mind has succeeded, a few times, in accomplishing: the creation of tragedy from history. Who, aside from the Greek tragedians and Shakespeare, has actually succeeded in bringing before the eye in one close-knit image, and in its most essential and exalted significance, something that once actually happened? (Or is reputed to have happened; it makes no difference whether the subject is the Seven against Thebes, sunk into the shadows of legend, or Henry VIII, dead by Shakespeare's time no longer than a good half century.) Shaw has attempted the task, completely aware of its requirements. And attempted it with material that has increased the demands, because it is historically so extraordinarily detailed, so sharply delineated, and so fully documented, and because the mere historical account is itself so chock-full of the transcendent emotions that drama attempts to arouse: the classical combination of sympathy and fear, the shuddering admiration for the hero, the being carried away by the sweep of inevitable events, the indefinable yet so clearly conscious catharsis. In *Hamlet* all the tragic element

is the work of the poet; the dramatizer of Joan of Arc may
be happy if he does no more than to allow the organ tone
of history itself to reverberate as purely as possible.

In constructing his tragedy, Shaw comprehended one important principle: that, in Hegel's phrase (it is rather a
surprise not to find it quoted in the Preface), the truly tragic
is not to be found in the conflict between right and wrong,
but in that between right and right. Joan of Arc surrounded
by nothing but cowards and rascals might be a romantic
figure, but not a dramatic one. Yet Joan as the superior being
crushed between two tremendous and necessary powers, the
Church and the interests of the State, is the very personifi-
cation of the tragic heroine. In its deeper foundations, history
is much closer to the tragic conception of the past than to
the romantic. In the historical analysis of a conflict the sense
of an awesome inevitability, of the relative justness of both
sides, always appears as the final result. The romantic emotion,
that is to say, the polarization of the pathetic, the passionate,
the personal in events, is a sentiment of a more superficial
sort.

Speaking generally, then, it was not necessary for Shaw
to do violence to history in presenting the judges as limited
but respectable persons, and Pierre Cauchon, the bishop of
Beauvais, with even a touch of greatness (whether he as a
person deserved it will be discussed below); in depicting
Dunois, the Bastard of Orléans, as a normal egoist of good
will; and in attempting to convince us of the justness, on
a lower level, of the archbishop of Reims's anxious diplomacy
and the excusability of Dauphin Charles's defeatism. In doing
so he could, with some justification, feel that he was the
mouthpiece of history. And he is no little proud of the role.
In his opinion, he has captured the historical essence of the
events. The words he puts into the mouths of his personages
Cauchon, the inquisitor Lemaître, and the Earl of Warwick
as personifications of the Church, the Inquisition, and Feudalism "are the things they actually would have said if they
had known what they were really doing. . . ." As for Saint
Joan herself, the play "contains all that need be known about
her." Does Shaw really think that we do not want to know
anything more? Does he not understand that every word she
spoke, every detail of her appearance and her actions is dear
to us? If not, then he does not know the true nature of

historical interest. But in the last analysis it is not a view
of the past which Shaw is concerned with, but the lesson that
the "case" of Joan still has to teach. "If it were only an
historical curiosity I would not waste my readers' time and
my own on it for five minutes." Here is the usual misconception of the nature and value of the historical sense: the
things of the past, as we observe them, are of themselves
nothing more than curiosities, unless a pragmatic application
to the questions of today can be deduced from them. History,
however, takes its revenge on Shaw.

It goes without saying that no blame is due the dramatist
for his deliberate abbreviation of the reality of history, for
instance, his condensation of the questioning, the sentence,
the abjuration, the relapse, and the execution into one single
scene. That he gave Warwick the place where the regent
Bedford should have stood had good grounds dramatically,
since he wished to personify the old aristocratic principle in
resistance to the emergent monarchy, and for that the noble
Warwick was more suitable than Bedford, a prince of the
blood royal. That the honor of holding the cross before Joan,
due Brother Isambard de la Pierre, is enjoyed by Martin
Ladvenu will cause a twinge of pain only to a scholar at
home with all the details of the story. For all his vagueness
I prefer the unknown Master John Tressard, the royal
secretary, who said, bitterly weeping, "we are all lost, for it
was a good and holy woman that has been burned," to
Chaplain de Stogumber, the jingo *avant la lettre* whom Shaw
has built up out of the single phrase *quidam cappellanus
Cardinalis Angliae* ["a certain chaplain of the cardinal of
England"] from the record of the rehabilitation trial. But it is
Shaw's perfect right to create such a character if it is neces-
sary for the play.

Nor do inadvertent inaccuracies affect the play's worth.
If Shaw thinks that it sounds better for the dauphin to say,
"Anne will want new dresses," we are happy to forget that
the queen's name was Marie d'Anjou, and even more so that
it was not until ten years after 1429 that the Bastard of
Orléans became Dunois. It is merely the schoolmaster in me
who cannot refrain from mentioning such trifles.

Regarding faithfulness to history, however, Shaw pretends
to much more than a painstaking accuracy in details, which
he thinks of little matter. "The ideal biographer," he says

(and that is, in a sense, what he considers himself), "must understand the Middle Ages . . . much more intimately than our Whig historians have ever understood them." The Middle Ages were a period "of which the thinking has passed out of fashion, and the circumstances no longer apply to active life. . . ." But Shaw knows them, thanks to the progress in the field of historical studies: "I write in full view of the Middle Ages, which may be said to have been rediscovered in the middle of the nineteenth century after an eclipse of about four hundred and fifty years. . . . Now there is not a breath of medieval atmosphere in Shakespeare's histories." Is there then, in *Saint Joan*? Here one's eyebrows rise automatically.

At this point we approach the almost bewildering questions raised by Shaw's play. For it is not only a question of the extent to which the play breathes a medieval atmosphere, but also of whether the presence or absence of such an atmosphere detracts from the play's dramatic effect and value. On this last point one's immediate response is a very definite Yes.

Today's general reader has his mind's eye too sharply focused on the differences in times for him to be able to endure any gross internal anachronism. Joan of Arc is too firmly anchored in French history of the fifteenth century to be able to serve as a timeless dramatic personage such as Phaedra or Alcestis. The drama of Saint Joan must transport us to the Middle Ages as we see them. Does Shaw's play do this? I should not dare say No straightaway, but even less so Yes. The archbishop of Reims strikes one as remarkably Anglican, and seems a cousin to the bishop in *Getting Married*. In the English production, which was rather over-acted compared with the Dutch, the dauphin is all too much the spoiled Eton boy. The comic element in La Hire is quite acceptable and in no sense disturbing, but the whole tone of the dialogue, the sheerly farcical effect of the page who pounds for silence with the halberd is all too Shavian to seem medieval.

Yet is it actually the lack of a sense of the time that hampers us? Is it not rather that this lack is inseparably linked with a dramatic deficiency of a much more serious sort: the lack of a high style? I do not mean literary style, of course, but dramatic style. Shaw's play would have gained nothing and would have lost a great deal if the dialogue had been filled with archaic grandiloquence and Walter Scott-like solemnity. And it is a moot question whether that would have made it more "genuinely" medieval. The fifteenth-century *novella*, Villon, and Joan herself in her answers to her judges are testimonies enough that colloquial speech in those days could be as fluent and free as our own. What we miss is something else: the transportation of our minds into a sphere where each emotion and passion has acquired a higher potential, each word affects more deeply and resonates more fully than in everyday life. There is, says Shaw, not a breath of medieval atmosphere in Shakespeare's histories. No, perhaps not, in the technically historical sense. But there is an abundance of the high dramatic style which casts a light on the difference in times without revealing it completely. For all its mannerisms, I know no historical drama that is more real and genuine than *Richard II*. It is utterly Eliza-bethan, and not at all late-fourteenth-century, but even so Shakespeare, with only his knowledge from Holinshed, came closer than any chronicler to the core of the historical character of the last Plantagenet.

Tragedy may be anything but sheerly natural and realistic. Shaw shuns the romantic like the plague: it is his perfect right to do so, but by using familiarity and humor to fumigate his work of the romantic he also banishes the heroic. To dramatize the heroic virtues of Saint Joan of Arc no less a style than the stern forms of Greek tragedy or the individual genius of Shakespeare will do.[1] And that is also the reason why, before Shaw, no one else had any better success in dramatizing the Maid.

Once one has realized, on reading *Saint Joan,* that it is too closely akin to *Man and Superman* and the rest of Shaw to be a satisfactory dramatization of its noble subject, it comes as a great surprise on seeing it to discover that the play is not only an exciting but also an affecting and elevating experience. This is undoubtedly so, in part (to leave aside the skill of the actors), because of Shaw's vivid depiction: the excellent dialogue at the court before Joan's entrance, the conversation between Warwick and Cauchon, the Inquisitor (especially in O. B. Clarence's portrayal as a blushing, debonair graybeard in the London production). Still, the high points of the play are precisely those where the author merely presents certain essential elements of the action itself: the irresistible bravery with which Joan swept away the dauphin and the court, the simplicity of the words we know she really spoke. Shaw is at his best when he sticks closest to history. "Be you Bastard of Orleans?" This is the very phrase, Dunois testified in 1455, with which Joan first greeted him. Shaw formulated as faithfully as possible from the records of the hearings themselves all Joan's answers to the judges, among them the moving reply to the query whether she thought that she was in a state of grace: "If I am not, may God bring me to it; if I am, may God keep me in it!"

It is my impression that the play achieves its deepest effect almost beyond Shaw's own activity, as if the great theme has merely passed through him to manifest itself directly in all its gripping truth and spotless purity. Even when, at the end of the extremely questionable Epilogue, the white beam of light falling on Joan sends a shudder through us, it is not Shaw's greatness that causes it, but the greatness of the saint whose servant he there was. But what more does he want than that? In the greatest ages of drama was it not best when the truth and greatness of the subject weighed more heavily than the limited abilities of the dramatist?

Related to this is the fact that such an important part of the performance's effect is a result of ordinary stage techniques. It is as though the heroic style that Shaw was not able to give to the play has to be created in despite of him, and is ensured by the basic scenic means used. This leads me to compare the performance given by the Vereenigd Tooneel [United Theater] troupe in the Netherlands with that of the company playing the piece in London, first in Haymarket and now in the Regent Theatre.[2]

From the point of view of style, one would tend to say beforehand that the theories of Eduard Verkade here applied skillfully by Wijdeveld—a sober *mise en scène,* the historical illusion reduced to a vague impression of past forms, a sharply tempered realism—are far preferable to the trappings of historical realism which are usually still sworn by in England, though in the Netherlands they have for years been looked upon as outdated and antiquated. Nevertheless, after having seen both performances I have begun to have some doubts, and Charles Ricketts's version lingers in my memory as much more forceful and impressive than Wijdeveld's. But that, it will be said, is precisely the mistake: the external trappings should not appeal so directly. Are they, then, no more than an indispensable husk, not to say a necessary evil? If that is so, there is something wrong with the theater. Now, that is certainly the case, but these notes do not pretend to provide fundamental solutions for such probing dramatic issues. Let us restrict ourselves to weighing the merits of the two types of staging in this particular case.

The advantage of a historical staging—provided it is designed as excellently as Ricketts's—seems to me to be that the shortcomings of the play, and in particular the lack of style, are obscured to some extent. A certain unity of acting, costuming, and *décor* develops, held together by a common degree of realism, or what can be taken for realism. This is true of the scene at court and of those in the tent, the cathedral, and the trial-hall, though not of the one in the castle at Vaucouleurs and the one beside the river. The more direct the appeal of the architecture or nature needs to be, the more all the objections to stage realism press their validity: in the London production the scene on the Loire is terrible, but the settings of gaily figured tapestries in the tent and at court go well with the costumes of the actors. In the Verkade production, on the other hand, there is a certain lack of harmony between the play, the costumes, and the *décors*. If the play had had Shakespeare's exalted style, which it is much in need of, a soberness in the setting would have been the prescribed thing, since every excessive effect would only damage and detract from the drama itself. But soberness clashes with the spirit of Shaw, and Ricketts's gay coloring has a salutary effect: without being discordant, it subdues that Shavian spirit a bit, distracts from it somewhat.

I have no illusions that I shall ever see the fifteenth century —or any other age—in the theater as I see it in my mind's eye, and as it is suggested to me by the slightest historical document, whether in word or in image. But I must admit that I have never seen more convincing historical staging than this work of Ricketts's. I have in mind in particular the first court entry and the tent scene. Not that I should like to defend the costuming throughout the play. Plate-iron armor, though it may be more accurate historically than the hinted-at mail used by Verkade, is too shiny and tinny, and hence always unacceptable on stage. Verkade's costuming is also quasi-historical (though only defectively so: all three of his prelates are post-Trent personages), yet by comparison to him what a fine harmony in variety Ricketts offers: the *Heures de Chantilly* come to life. Heraldic figures are used lavishly, but with how much care and consideration! I am constantly struck by the English eye for all the possibilities of the color red. We Dutch with our gray tradition must remember, before we turn up our nose at all this, that the period that for us begins with Jozef Israels started with the Pre-Raphaelites in England. Actually, the only colors we know, except for all the nuances of gray, are a great deal of green and some blue, and vistas and clouds rather than figures. The English eye, however, has been trained by an unbroken succession of masters who have tested all their aesthetic senses on the human figure clad in every shade and on its movement in gaily colored processions. I know that this decorative tendency in England gives birth to monsters every day—and yet when I see Ricketts following in the footsteps of William Morris and Rossetti and Ford Madox Brown I do not dare condemn.

It is risky to attempt to view art and its value as quite distinct from nationality. Is it not noteworthy that in the British production the two English characters, Warwick and the Chaplain, are by far the best? Or perhaps the Chaplain, whom Shaw has made too much of a caricature, is really no better than Cauchon, but Warwick is unsurpassed in his appearance as well as in other things. The care that was taken for historical accuracy is best illustrated by the fact that even his facial type has clearly been copied from the gilded bronze likeness on the earl's tomb at Warwick. Happy England, which has never known a French Revolution. For Pierre Cauchon's countenance one must be content with a seventeenth-century drawing of his tombstone, long since destroyed, at Lisieux.

The very fact that, in spite of myself, the element of historical accuracy has played a greater role in my evaluation of the performance than I had suspected, I should like to consider as evidence for the correctness of my theory that the powerful effect of the play stems from the historical theme itself. There is another argument for that point of view. Sybil Thorndike has the reputation of being England's finest tragedienne; I hope I do Nel Stants no injustice by calling her a rising young player. Nonetheless, the Dutch actress's Joan was much more to my satisfaction than her more famous English colleague's, because Nel Stants could be young, spontaneous, natural, boyish—she had the same gay, laughing face Joan's contemporaries describe. In Sybil Thorndike I was put off by an excess of dramatic art—a rapturous note in her voice and gestures, a touch of high tragedy that served as a disturbing rather than a contributing factor. I have been told that in America the choice was deliberately made to train a naïve country-girl for the part. That smacks of the film. But it does serve to confirm the fact that this drama is so subject to the gravitational pull of history that the usual dramatic requirements are distorted.

It has been remarked that though any number of writers have attempted a literary adaptation of the history of Joan of Arc, it was always without success. The work of art depicting her for all the ages to come does not exist. It will not be *Saint Joan,* no more than it is *Die Jungfrau von Orleans,* and very definitely not François Porché's *La vièrge au grand cœur,* which ran in Paris (perhaps partly as a protest against *Saint Joan*) for a while, till Shaw came, was seen, and conquered, even there.

What are the great writings one reads about Joan of Arc and her life? Michelet first of all. Then one may prefer Anatole France, the skeptic (or rather the unbeliever), or Monsignor Touchet, who devoted years of labor to bringing about Joan's canonization, or Gabriel Hanotaux, who attempted to bridge the gap between rationalists and Catholics. But it is in the books that attempt to give an accurate account of the history that the reader—including the general reader —goes searching for the Maid of Orléans. Is this not some sort of indication? Should it not be assumed that there is something in the very subject that resists literary treatment, and particularly dramatization? There are subjects, such as Troy, which find their highest expression in the epic, others that flourish only in the drama. There are also some whose character lies most intimately and indissolubly contained in the historical form itself, some in which the most sublime emotions of the tragic—the fellow suffering and the catharsis —are bound to the historical account as such. Grant Clio precedence over Melpomene now and then through the ages.

II

THE FIGURE OF JOAN OF ARC

We have reproached Shaw that his play is too much lacking in the qualities of tragic poetry to be commensurate with the sublimity of the subject, that it is too modernly prosaic to be able to take the dramatic flight that is needed—prosaic not only in form, but also in conception. The buskin is treacherous footwear; it is much more dangerous for the best of men than skis for the beginner.

And yet, I do not know whether Shaw, whom I imagine to be the most deliberate writer there is, could have given his view the poetic passion it lacks, if he had wanted to. It is, at any rate, certain that he did not want to. For it is precisely poetry, so he argues in his Preface, which has made so much mischief in regard to an accurate understanding of the figure of Joan of Arc. A twopenny-halfpenny romanticism picturing the heroine above all as a beautiful girl whose followers were all in love with her has hopelessly distorted the image of Joan. There is no other misconception that Shaw rounds on so angrily, and so justly, as this sort of cheap romanticism. But romantic sentiment is not the same thing as poetic sub-limity, and it is an open question whether he has not thrown out the baby of tragedy with the bath of romanticism.

And Shaw, in his attack on the romantic view, is, as usual, exaggerating. He would like to reason away every touch of feminine charm in Joan, at whatever price. "Not one of Joan's comrades, in village, court, or camp . . ." says Shaw, "ever claimed that she was pretty." This is not true. Jean d'Aulon, the head of her military household, called her "a beautiful and well-formed girl," and Perceval de Boulainvilliers thought her "of satisfying grace." Perhaps a few details on her appearance are appropriate here. (I repeat that this article is intended as nothing more than a series of marginal notes.)

Over against the contemporaries just mentioned, Shaw can appeal to the Lombard monk who, quite some time later, briefly described her outward appearance. He spoke of her as "short of build and with a boorish countenance." But most of his evidence is of little value. Various historians have felt uneasy with the view that Joan was short of stature. Vallet de Viriville attempted to prove the opposite. Hanotaux described her as "large and strong," thus following Quicherat, who translated the *haulte et puissante* of the extremely romanticized *Chronique de Lorraine* as *grande et forte*. Whatever her stature may have been, the Lombard monk was right about another detail: that Joan had dark hair. For so she is described in a contemporary chronicle from La Rochelle, and the fact is perhaps confirmed by a black hair embedded, apparently intentionally, in the seal of Joan's letter to the town of Riom.

One might say that there is a quite general tendency to visualize Joan as being fair-haired and preferably dressed in blue. That is the way Boutet de Monvel presents her in his fine, well-known picture book. Both Sybil Thorndike and Nel Stants portray her as fair-haired. And I imagine that a survey "Do you visualize Joan of Arc as fair or dark?" would confirm their choice by a large majority. Is this a romantic notion? Ariosto paid homage to the ideal of the fair heroine. I can imagine the antiromantic Shaw expostulating with the players to avoid every element of romantic charm in the figure. No sacrifice might be made to the ideal of fairness, and even less to contemporary fashion; as the sources specify in detail, Joan's hair should be cropped close above the ears and her temples shaven, in keeping with the fifteenth-century style. But the actors point out to Shaw that his power as an author does not reach *that* far, and go their own way.

I do not know whether Shaw's passion in supporting his desire to see a portrait of Joan in the helmeted female bust in the church of Saint-Maurice in Orléans does not, in the last analysis, betray a certain chivalric sense. His argument "If this woman be not Joan, who is she?" and his challenge to prove the negative strike one as romantic in their utter groundlessness. We have no well-substantiated authentic image of the Maid. Certainly not in the thumbnail sketch with which the greffier of the Parliament of Paris, Clément de Fauquembergue, adorned the margin of his register. (And to imagine that it would have been possible for Jan van Eyck to visit her in prison at Arras in the autumn of 1430 and draw her!)

Among the few details preserved regarding her outward

appearance, the most valuable is perhaps the phrase describing her voice. At Selles-sur-Cher, in June 1429, the brothers De Laval heard her address the ecclesiastics standing in front of the church "in a very womanly voice" as she sat on the fiery black horse she had just broken. De Boulainvilliers, too, was struck by her charming, feminine voice.

To understand her personality one would like to have something of a picture of her appearance, and though one does not need to visualize her as beautiful in the usual sense of the word, a harmony in her appearance is essential. Let us attempt to combine into a consistent picture the few scanty data preserved by her contemporaries, who were little interested in personal descriptions.

She talks little. She eats and drinks sparingly. (It is still De Boulainvilliers who is speaking, in June 1429.) She delights in beautiful horses and armor, she greatly admires armed and noble men. She avoids contact and converse with the many. "She sheds tears freely; her expression is cheerful" (*abundantia lacrimarum manat, hilarem gerit vultum*). This strange combination of strength and lightheartedness with tearful emotion and an inclination toward silence provides what is perhaps the best approach to the essence of her being.

Shaw, it seems to me, has seen the basic contours of that essence lucidly, and has portrayed them clearly. I shall not paraphrase his portrayal here; everyone has it at his disposal in the play and the Preface, and I cannot do it better justice.

"In His strength I will dare, and dare, and dare, until I die." In these words, perhaps the most moving in the play, Shaw presents the essence of Joan's personality. Actually she had given herself a name that summarizes her whole personality when she heard her voices call her *la fille au grand cuer*. *Cœur*, in this context, should be translated as "courage," and yet such a translation would not be complete, because all the other meanings of "heart" are also there as undertones. Her courage, and her confidence—these are the most immediate elements of her nature, and the ones that give the most tangible explanation of her success. A greatness that manifests itself in a superior, irresistible, and infectious bravery. What reason could there be to doubt Bertrand de Poulengy and Jean de Metz, who took her from Vaucouleurs to Chinon, when they testify that they felt incapable of resisting her will? The very fact that they took her there proves it. Anatole

France is skeptical toward the numerous testimonies in the rehabilitation trial of men who declared that they had never felt any carnal desire for her. Shaw says they were too much afraid of her to fall in love with her. One might also say that her utterly guileless concentration on one goal emanated an awe that expressed itself in a great sense of shame. A stilling of the desires in her presence is on a par with the abstention from swearing and profanity which (as the sources thoroughly document) she brought about. Whoever cannot accept the fact that an exalted personality can exert an influence on his surroundings which makes the unusual the rule will never be able to understand Joan of Arc.

The incomparably high mettle of her courage no one doubts. But there are those who question whether, aside from the great impetus emanating from her courage, her insight and military talent also played a predominant role in the deeds accomplished under her guidance: the raising of the siege of Orléans and the expedition to Reims. This is one of the most difficult problems posed by the history of Joan of Arc, and it is out of the question to go into sufficient detail on the point here. As early as the rehabilitation trial, Jean Luillier, a burgher of Orléans, gave an evasive answer to the question whether the siege was raised by means of the Maid more than the strength of the warriors. The conviction that Joan applied a natural strategic and tactical talent in deliberate calculation is based chiefly on the testimony of a comrade-in-arms, the Duke of Alençon. He praises her as being "in war . . . very expert, whether to carry a lance, to assemble an army, to order a battle, or to dispose artillery." Shaw, like Hanotaux (and Quicherat before him), tends to assume these very real talents in her. Anatole France, on the other hand, is closer to the Catholic historians on the point, though for completely different reasons. In the Catholic view the attribution of extraordinary military skill would imply a certain diminution of the supernatural nature of her mission. For France it would not tally with his thesis that Joan had been a pawn in the hands of calculating persons.

In modern military science it would certainly be unbelievable for such strategic skill to exist in a simple girl from the country. But in the uncomplicated situation of her day military talent was still largely a matter of penetrating common sense, and once one assumes the genius of her personality there seems no reason to consider impossible the presence of such a talent in Joan of Arc.

The combination of common sense and natural straight-forwardness with heroic enthusiasm gave her personality the utterly unique cast that appeals immediately to everyone. At first glance she saw everything in its true form, free of any veneer of convention. Hence the ready wit of her answers, for instance, the one to the dean of the theological faculty of Poitiers, who had asked what tongue her angel spoke. "A better than yours," she said, for Brother Seguin spoke the Limousin dialect.[1]

It is worthy of attention that Joan's conceptual world lies completely outside the conventions of her time. Anyone who knows how strongly the romanticism of chivalry dominated the culture of the fifteenth century will be amazed at the fact. She knew only the *deeds* of chivalry: pleasure in horses and arms, courage and fidelity; chivalry's gaudy concepts were alien to her. Her simple spirit did not feed on the fantasy of chivalric orders and festivities and oaths; it was not directed toward the obligatory ideal of liberating Jerusalem, but toward the one close at hand, that of liberating France. All the higher culture of her century was miles removed from her. There was no contact between her and the fashionable chivalric concepts. It is significant that even after her death literary fancy actually could find no place for her in the colorful tableau of chivalric glory. What could have been done with her? She was too real.

Also the elaborate concepts of religious life of her day were, in their details, actually alien to her. It is only when one compares Joan of Arc with other saints of the time, for instance, Saint Colette, that it becomes apparent that she lacks almost every element of mysticism, every developed sentiment of spiritual ecstasy. We find her participating in only one of the fifteenth century's many pious movements: the adoration of the name of Jesus, which she placed on her standard and had put at the head of her letters. But that is all. There is nothing to indicate that her mind was occupied by the great religious concepts of her day, the vividly colored and violently experienced awareness of the Sufferings of Our Lord, much less the shrill phantasmagoria of Death. She had no time and no place for them.

No one will ever know just how clear to Joan of Arc the

forms of her conceptual world were. That they were very simple, and very forceful and direct, is obvious. And here we come to the question of the significance of her "voices."

The history of Joan of Arc—and this is another of the precious things about her—forces us to make a strict reckoning of our own convictions. The non-Catholic can understand and enjoy the story of Saint Francis or of Saint Catherine of Siena with an admiration for the Church of the Middle Ages which, though it is inevitably roused by an unprejudiced study of history, can go much deeper than purely historical and aesthetic appreciation. The story of Joan of Arc forces one to confess at once whether or not one believes in the category of sainthood in the strict Catholic sense. The person who cannot believe that the blessed souls of certain persons once known as Catherine and Margaret manifested themselves to Joan in the substance does better not to force himself to do so. The miracle does not have to stand or fall with that.

Shaw, it seems to me, has done a service by opposing violently the idea that labeling Joan's voices a morbid symptom is enough to define their significance. But in doing so he is less original than he thinks. Quicherat, though more of a rationalist than Shaw, refused to look upon Joan as a sick person. Indeed, if every inspiration that comes to one with such commanding urgency that it is heard as a voice is to be condemned out of hand by the learned qualification of a morbid symptom, a hallucination, who would not rather stand with Joan of Arc and Socrates on the side of the mad than with the faculty of the Sorbonne on that of the sane? We know that an anomaly only becomes a sickness when it has a disturbing effect on the purpose of the organism. And Joan's voices may have had a very disturbing influence on her lower purpose of enjoying life and growing old, but it is not on such things that we should like to base our conclusion. No matter how clear the psychiatric report might be, historical judgment would retain the right not to view the voices in the first place as *ces troubles . . . hallucinations perpétuelles,* as Anatole France does, but to find in them the sign of a mind occupied completely by high impulses. History has more to do with her courage and its significance than with the physiological determination of her visions.

There is another special argument that should keep us from

viewing Joan's case too much in the pathological sphere. The gentlemen at Rouen in 1431 did their very best to lure Joan's thoughts onto the slippery terrain of demonology with their questions about whether Saint Michael was naked, what parts of the bodies of the saints she had embraced, and so forth. They succeeded not once. If there was anything really diseased in her mind, they would certainly have discovered it. A fifteenth-century inquisitor was just as skilled as a present-day Freudian in bringing the dregs of the soul into the open. Did Joan refer even once to the devil?

Also with regard to the form in which Joan conceived of her celestial advisers, Saint Michael, Saint Catherine, and Saint Margaret, it would seem to me that Shaw has gone squarely to the core of the matter. The form is bound to the conceptual world in which she lived. It was just as natural and logical for her to visualize the voices as saints and angels as it is for a modern man to borrow his terms from the concepts of physics. When Shaw has Joan say to the Archbishop, "even if they [my voices] are only the echoes of my own commonsense," he can appeal to the hearing of March 15: "Asked how she knew it was the language of angels: replies she believed it very soon; and had the will to believe."

On the question of how Joan's mind defined and explained the concepts associated with her inspirations, I should like to go a bit further than Shaw. The writers about Joan of Arc whom I have read (only a few of the countless total) present it as established fact that she associated her heavenly commands with the figures of the archangel Michael, Saint Catherine, and Saint Margaret even at the beginning of her mission. Is that so certain? She made the association in 1431, at the trial, when she was asked to describe her visions in detail. But the witnesses in the trial of rehabilitation who had heard her speak of her voices in 1429, during her glory, do not as a rule know anything of the two saints and the archangel. It is precisely in this and because of this that they seem highly reliable. If they had merely recited what everyone knew in 1456, and what everyone wanted to hear, they would un-doubtedly have mentioned Saint Michael, Saint Catherine, and Saint Margaret. It was just as natural for a person of the fifteenth century to associate a notion with a saint as for our contemporaries to use the words "mentality" and "intuition." But what do these witnesses have to say? Joan's heavenly counsel was quite without visual form, a sheer *daimonion* about which she talked with great diffidence and reticence. She speaks only of *son conseil* ["her counsel"]. When Christopher de Harcourt asked her in the presence of the dauphin whether she would "explain the manner of your counsel when it speaks to you" (*modum vestri consilii*), she blushed and replied Yes, but what she then said contains no reference to the three holy figures. And when Jean d'Aulon, one of those who were closest to her, asked her who her counsel was, she answered only: "There are three of them; one is constantly with me, the second comes and goes, and the third is the one whom the other two consult." From this it is not even clear that two of the three were female.[2]

It seems plausible to me that it was only fairly late, perhaps even only during her trial, that Joan linked her inspirations to the figures she knew best and cherished most among the saints. Even during the hearings she was very little inclined to go into detail about her visions. Asked about the great light accompanying them, she said: *passez oultre* ["pass to another question"].

Everything Joan declared regarding the spiritual state in which she heard her voices is of the utmost simplicity. It was a state of great elation, in which she would always like to be. She was filled with a feeling of knowing much more than she might or would or could express. "There is more in the books of the Lord than in yours," she said to the churchmen who examined her at Poitiers. All visionary terminology of the usual sort is utterly alien to her.

Significant is the complete skepticism she displayed toward the visions of Catherine de la Rochelle, who was able to gain access to the king as her competitor. Catherine maintained that she was visited every night by a white lady. So Joan asked to sleep with her for a night, watched until midnight and saw nothing, and then slept. When morning came she asked if the lady in white had come. Yes, while you were asleep, you could not be wakened. Then Joan slept by day and stayed awake, often asking Catherine: Will she not come? And Catherine would answer: Yes, soon!

Catherine de la Rochelle's inspirations were of a different sort from Joan's: she went through the towns with royal heralds and trumpets to summon whosoever had gold or silver or hidden treasure. That was needed to pay Joan's soldiers.

Or she would go to the Duke of Burgundy to make peace with him. But Joan advised her to go back to her husband to take care of the household and her children. And there would be no peace "except at the point of the lance."

Joan of Arc was also not a true ecstatic in that she was sometimes uncertain and doubtful. Not only of her calling but also of her fate. When she went to battle she was not at all confident that she would not be slain. Her hesitation before the battle of Montépilloy led to a defeat. Her awareness that God loved certain other living persons more than her (which she testified to at the trial, without clarfying it further) is a touching thing.

Her most human traits tend only to make her greatness more vivid. Alongside her purity, soberness, and simplicity I should not want to miss in her portrait the liking for costly clothing which is only seemingly in contrast with those qualities. "And wore very noble, well-furred habits of gold cloth and silk. . . ." She wore red by preference. An order to pay thirteen old gold crowns for two sumptuous garments made for her at Orléans in June 1429, at Charles d'Orléans's expense, has been preserved, together with the receipt.

The picture of a historical figure does not form itself in the mind on the basis of psychological definitions. It arises seemingly without any consciously logical function, like a view of something one could not see before, or could see only vaguely. It is built up out of the arbitrary and more or less circumstantial data that tradition has preserved for us. The conviction that our picture must be accurate (or let us merely say, of value) and that the tradition is reliable develops out of the feeling, usually very difficult to describe, that though the various data are disconnected in themselves, they harmonize, they fit together. The picture of Joan of Arc emerges from the sources with an unusually high degree of homogeneity and conviction. Even among scholars of quite divergent world-views, the differences in their conception of Joan of Arc are relatively small. It is as if her personality suggested itself to everyone who testified regarding her with an immediacy that forced them merely to tell the truth in all its simplicity, unobscured by the patterns of chivalric or religious forms which usually determined their expression.

To our minds all the actions and words handed down regarding Joan fit together. "The sign I have from God is to raise the siege of Orléans." "The soldiers will do battle, and God will give the victory." She carried the standard, in order not to have to kill anyone. When the women of Bourges came with rosaries for her to touch, Joan said, with a laugh toward her hostess: "Touch them yourselves. They will be quite as good with your touch as with mine." She did not like to share a bedroom with old women, and wanted only young maidens around her. Every evening at sundown she had the church bell rung for half an hour. At the peak of her happiness, shortly before the coronation at Reims, when she could not yet know that the tide was turning, came the talk on the way from Crépy-en-Valois, on August 11, 1429, while she rode between the archbishop of Reims and the Bastard of Orléans, and the populace greeted the king with glad cries of *Noël*. In the trial of rehabilitation Dunois gave testimony regarding it, testimony that was perhaps somewhat refashioned in his memory and has unfortunately been preserved only in Latin. "These are a good people!" says Joan. "I have seen none elsewhere who have shown so much joy at the coming of our noble king." And then: "Would God I might be happy enough when I shall finish my days to be buried in this soil." At which the Archbishop asked her: "Joan, in what place hope you to die?" She answered: "Wherever it may please God, I am sure neither of the time nor the place. I know no more of it than yourself. But I would it were pleasing to God, my Creator, that I might now retire, laying arms aside, and that I might serve my father and my mother, guarding their sheep[3] with my sister and my brothers, who would be greatly rejoiced to see me. . . ."

For the person who would like to take exception to the testimonies in the rehabilitation trial of 1456 as too favorable to Joan, who was then already seen in the light of a re-evaluation, the trial of 1431 presents quite the same image of unimpeachable purity. According to Brother Isambard de la Pierre and Brother Martin Ladvenu, the executioner had declared that her heart had resisted every effort to be burned. One does not have to believe it. But there is something else that is just as great a miracle, and of a more tenuous variety: all those biased persons of 1431, her judges with their dry hearts and their stiff pens, were not able to tarnish the gold of her words. Let me give only one example out of many. Asked what words she used to summon the help of her voices, she replied: "Very tender God, in honor of Thy holy passion, I pray Thee, if Thou lovest me, that Thou wilt reveal to me how I ought to answer these churchmen. I know well, as to this habit, the commandment why I took it, but I know not in what manner I ought to leave it off. Be pleased therefore to teach me. . . ."

In the testimonies of the rehabilitation trial the recollections are often fragments, rather irrelevant details reproduced by the memory with the thoughtlessness of a film image, and precisely because of that inspiring confidence. There is the talk about the carp, which Shaw makes use of, and d'Estivet's curses. There is her answer to the question whether she had ever been on the spot when Englishmen were slain: "In God's name, of course! How softly you speak!" In 1456 Thomas de Courcelles himself could recall of the sermon to Joan given by Guillaume Erard in the churchyard of Saint-Ouen only the words "the pride of this woman." He could remember but one single image of Joan's abjuration: Cauchon in conversation with some others. He stopped in the middle of a sentence, but De Courcelles no longer knew what was said. Thomas de Courcelles, in 1456 one of the lights of the Church and the University, displayed a very poor memory at the rehabilitation trial.

The picture of Joan of Arc is clear and sharply defined, but even so we cannot rigidly categorize it. Anyone who attempts to reduce it to the terms of scientific psychology will himself no doubt feel that he is violating it. That is fundamentally the case for every picture of a historical personality, but it is the more obvious the further the personality deviates from the usual norms of character and action. "The great man is unknowable," Hanotaux says rightly, and Shaw: "the superior being, being immeasurable is unbearable. . . ." For us the person of Joan of Arc, perhaps more purely than any other figure in history, lies quite utterly within the sphere of the heroic. We can seek in vain for the term summarizing her essence. "Heroine" is not satisfactory. "Genius" even less. "Saint," whether or not one understands it completely in the technical, ecclesiastical sense, is far and away the best.

III

THE OPINION OF HER AGE

"At no single moment of her existence," says Anatole France, "was Joan known in any way but through fables, and if she set the masses in movement it was as a result of the clamor of the countless legends that sprang up wherever she went, and sped on ahead of her." The first part of this statement is undoubtedly true; the second contains a serious mistake in logic. Her effect explained as a *result* of the countless legends? But then what explains the immediate emergence of those legends themselves? Wonder-workers were nothing unusual in the fifteenth century, and many of them made a fair amount of clamor, but not one aroused the amazement, the enthusiasm, and the terror that Joan of Arc immediately brought about. Nothing is more significant in this respect than the English ordinances attempting to counteract the mass desertion to the island and the refusal to be called to the colors.[1]

The way Joan of Arc's fame developed we know best from notices in Antonio Morosini's fifteenth-century chronicle, which first attracted attention in 1895. This Venetian kept a sort of diary of the news that came to Venice regarding remarkable events of the day. He recorded the news in whatever form he was able to obtain it, and so also inserted a number of letters that Pancrazio Giustiniani, a Venetian merchant at Bruges, sent to his father, Marco, in 1429 and 1430, and also letters from another Venetian in Avignon. These letters are remarkable not so much for their factual accuracy in details as for their illustration of how, in the mind of a "neutral," the image of Joan took form from day to day of her career. Giustiniani, an Italian and a merchant living in Burgundian territory, cannot be suspected of an immoderate tendency toward ready belief in the miracle of the Maid. His reports regarding Joan begin with a passing mention at the end of a detailed account of the raising of the siege of Orléans, written around the middle of May 1429: "In the past fortnight there has been much talk about all sort of prophecies found at

Paris, and other things which all together promise the dauphin great prosperity. . . . Many people made the most priceless jokes in the world about them, particularly those of a girl, a shepherdess[2] from Lorraine." Merchants in Burgundy had written him about the matter. He knows the rough outlines of her activities at Chinon. One of the persons writing him about her is reported to have said, "it is making me crazy." It all seems unbelievable, and yet. . . . In his next reference, dated July 9,[3] there is only a trace of doubt left: "These are most wondrous things if they be true, and it seems to me that they are so. . . . I believe that God's power is great. . . ." Then he finds support: in his later letters, dated November 20, 1429, and January 4, 1430, he apparently knows Jean de Gerson's cautious but understanding opinion regarding Joan (to which I shall return below) and subscribes to it: "Believe what you will of it; it is said that the Maid does all these things and a thousand wonders more, which if they be true, are done by the Lord. And it is a great wonder in our days." His last word about her he wrote on November 24, 1430: *La poncela* has been sent to the king of England at Rouen;[4] John of Luxembourg has received ten thousand crowns for her. "What will follow for her is unknown, but it is feared that they will let her die, and truly these are strange and great things."

If in Morosini's tidings we have a report of Joan's activities in a crude form, a literarily colored image also developed, even in the first months. While some people who saw her simply jotted down their impressions of the Maid, as did the brothers De Laval in a letter to their mother, others make the wondrous affair a test of their style and wit, much as a modern journalist does with athletic heroes or musicians. One of the latter was Perceval de Boulainvilliers, counselor and chamberlain of Charles VII, in a Latin letter to Filippo Maria Visconti dated June 21, 1429. Another was an unknown writer, thought to be Alain Chartier, in a similar letter to an unknown prince, a month later. Now, one might expect that the form in which such authors molded Joan's image would be inspired by the chivalric concepts that so sharply dominated the minds of the day. But that was not the case. They embroidered a humanistic and hagiographic pattern with elaborate miraculous details for purposes of adornment, and quite a bit of rhetoric, so that these most original and primary sources must, remarkably enough, be considered among the least reliable.

Two of the finest and most sensible intellects of France, whose thoughts on lofty subjects had met on another terrain long before, both devoted their last work, written shortly before their deaths, to Joan's activities. Jean de Gerson wrote his *Considerations on the Fact of the Maid* on May 14, 1429, and died two months later. Christine de Pisan, spending the days of her old age in seclusion, wrote on July 31, 1429, her *ditié* of sixty-one stanzas, the last poem known from her, a bit flat and dull, but charged with an absolute faith in the mission of the Maid. Gerson, the cautious psychologist who had earlier written a long tract on how to distinguish between true and false visions, and who feared nothing as much as that all sorts of crude and cheap superstitions would gain the upper hand, wrote with a certain reserve. He is filled with sympathy for this affair that has excited all the world. The chief arguments moving him to place confidence in the divinity of Joan's mission actually fit perfectly in Shaw's picture. The very fact that her call has been able to move the king's counselors and the commanders to attack has a great deal of weight for Gerson, and rightly so. He also counts as a sign for the genuineness of Joan's mission the fact that, despite the divine order, she and the commanders who follow her do not abandon the ways of human caution. He feels, as it were, the masterly, inspired reasonability of her idea. Even if there is much in it that is natural, he goes on to say, it can still be a miracle, for also in the ancient miracles testified to by the Scriptures, those of Deborah and Judith, "something natural was always intermingled. . . . And," Gerson carefully warns, "after the first miracle everything does not always go as people expect. Hence, even if the Maid should be disappointed in all her and our expectations—far be it from me to wish it—one may not conclude that everything that has happened has been wrought by an evil spirit, or at any rate not by God."

Where there was no sincere love for France such as Gerson's at stake, the conclusion of an ecclesiastical arbiter proved to be more hesitant. There was, for instance, that of Hendrik van Gorkum, rector of a Latin school at Cologne. This same Hendrik van Gorkum is referred to by Hugo Grotius in the Introduction to *De iure belli ac pacis* as one of his predecessors, on the basis of a tract *De iusto bello*.[5] But when in June

1429 he set side by side *Propositiones* for and against the Maid it never entered his mind that hers, too, might be referred to as a just war. His earnest objection to the genuineness of Joan's calling is that now, in the time of grace, it does not seem very probable that a spiritual mission for the advancement of a purely secular matter like the French cause against England would emanate from God. If everything was in order as regards Joan's calling, then she must be unusually holy. But that such a saintly creature should dress as a worldly warrior—how inappropriate! Judith and Esther had not done so. All of which was argued with utter logic and matter-of-factness by the good Dutchman Master Hendrik van Gorkum.

Did the archbishop of Reims, Regnault de Chartres, honestly believe even for a moment in Joan's calling? For him, the advocate of a peace by means of a *rapprochement* with the Duke of Burgundy, everything she wished to accomplish after the coronation at Reims was inopportune. As soon as she was taken prisoner by the Burgundians at Compiègne on May 23, 1430, he dropped her. He did not deny her straight out, but what he did do was worse: he cast the first stone. It was her own fault, and the reward she deserved, he wrote in a letter to the inhabitants of Reims.[6] She was unwilling to listen to advice, but did everything her own way. God had suffered the capture of the Maid because of her pride and the rich raiment she had worn, and because she had not followed His commands but her own will.

From this bit of information Shaw, in his fifth scene, worked out the figure of the Archbishop in a portrayal that is pretty much in keeping with the historical tradition. Joan's irrepressible assurance interpreted as pride and obstinacy: that was perhaps the most tragic thing in her history. Her own followers could not endure that lofty courage.

Or was it really, as Shaw would have it, crushed between the Church and the established Law that Joan met her doom as the masterly and insufferable herald of a new freedom for the individual and a new power for society? Shaw would like us to consider her trial as nothing more than the necessary defense of her age against the unknown and immeasurable danger that would destroy that age.

Undoubtedly the most exciting and most original aspect of Shaw's work is his relative rehabilitation of Joan's judges.

If this dramatic argument were used for any other subject, for Caesar or even Napoleon, we might yield readily to such a view of the matter without being bothered by historical scruples. No longer to consider the trial as an infernal design to destroy Joan, but as a well-meant, regrettable mistake— it seems so logical, so understandable, so satisfactory, so historical. The countless people throughout the world who will carry with them for years to come the image of Joan of Arc as Shaw has imprinted it in them will all have made this correction of their earlier view: Pierre Cauchon was not a bribed and dishonest judge, but a decent and relatively honorable man who spared no effort to save the Maid.

Nonetheless, I believe that in this case many people who are as a rule not interested first of all in the historical course of events, but in the imaginative powers of the artist, will ask whether Shaw's view is correct.

Several points can be granted him without further ado. The proceedings of the 1431 trial of condemnation are in many respects more reliable than those of the rehabilitation trial of 1456. Indeed, as Shaw remarks with a jeer, the judges at Rouen, who after long preparations spent more than three months on her trial proper, took an extremely serious view of their task when compared with the hasty procedures we can remember from the World War. Is this at the same time proof that they were unbiased?

Shaw traces the opinion that Cauchon served the English cause and that the trial took place under pressure to a sin of romanticism. Joan was spotless, says romantic sentiment, hence her judges must have been rascals. Shaw rightly condemns such a trivial antithesis. But what if even the most serious historical research cannot lead to any conclusion but a disqualification of the judges? True, the pressure that was exerted is frequently exaggerated. It has been claimed, without grounds, that the proceedings were forged. The trial was conducted properly. Nonetheless, while he recognizes all this, Pierre Champion, more at home than anyone else in the France of the fifteenth century, refers to it as "a masterpiece of partiality under the appearance of the most regular of procedures"; it remains "odious" to him, as it was before him to Hanotaux, to Quicherat, and to a thousand other historians.

Reading through the proceedings of the trial, one does

obtain an impression of relative gentleness, of a serious desire
to spare Joan and to save her. But Shaw, basing his opinion
on this impression, has merely become the dupe of a machina-
tion of the judges themselves. The detail and moderation of
the trial had as their basis the political intent of making
Joan's condemnation as unimpeachable as possible. Even the
unusually large number of judges, far from proving a serious
and scrupulous fairness, is suspect. They mark the trial as a
political affair, a deliberate *cause célèbre*. Cauchon said even
before the trial began "that it was intended to give her a fine
trial. . . ." During the deliberations of the judges as to
whether torture should or should not be applied, one re-
sponded in the negative, for "it might bring disrepute upon
a trial thus far so well conducted. . . ." All the expressions of
gentle admonition and sympathy with her hardened disposition
can also be explained as feigned gentleness. Shaw was perhaps
not aware that the words used on transferring a condemned
person from the ecclesiastical court to the secular arm, "with
the request to deal with her tenderly," were nothing more than
a customary formula that no one expected to lead to anything
but the bonfire.

As far as the bishop of Beauvais is concerned, Shaw could
appeal to the sources for more than one point in his picture
of Cauchon. The English accused him of being prejudiced
in favor of Joan, and he answered: "You lie: by law I must
seek the redemption of the body and the soul of this Joan.
. . ." The general accusation, both in contemporary chronicles
and in the testimonies of the rehabilitation trial, that hatred
and political intrigue had been the reasons for the acts of
1431 are not sufficient to brand Cauchon as an unjust judge,
though there is a great deal that is damning against him. Even
his antecedents in the service of England and Burgundy do
not prove that he violated his duty at Rouen. Nonetheless,
among the testimonies in 1456 there is one that it is very
difficult to reject as groundless, and which is almost enough
to condemn Cauchon and invalidate Shaw's view. It was made
in almost identical terms by Brother Isambard de la Pierre
and Brother Martin Ladvenu. When the judges had gone to
see for themselves that Joan, after her abjuration, had put
on man's dress again, and as a result were forced to adjudge
her an obstinate and relapsed heretic, the bishop of Beauvais,
on leaving the prisoner, was heard to address Warwick among

a number of Englishmen. "With laughter on his lips he said in a clear voice: 'Farewell, farewell, it is done! Have good cheer!' or similar words."

If it is hard to maintain the historicity of a well-meaning Cauchon, if many of the judges were his creatures, if a few of them did raise their voices against him, none of that indicates, on the other hand, that the whole trial was sheer wickedness and conscious bias. Though she was asked cunning questions that she could not answer, though the reasoning was formalistic and one-sided, the crucial issue—whether Joan had been able to develop her amazing power owing to divine help or demonic—was a very serious one, one that, inspected on its own merits, would have been completely dubious for any other court of that day. It is perfectly understandable that ecclesiastical judges who did not share in the enthusiasm for the cause of Charles VII catalogued Joan among a host of overwrought persons who set the world in turmoil. "If it should ever come so far that the people in their rashness would rather listen to soothsayers than to the shepherds and teachers of the Church, religion will be doomed. . . ." These words out of a letter from the University of Paris to the pope, the emperor, and the college of cardinals will be recognized as the basis for Shaw's sentences put in the mouth of Cauchon in Scene IV. It was a logical syllogism when her judges reasoned: a revelation from God always leads to obedience; Joan ran away from her parents and wears man's dress, both of which are evidence of disobedience; hence her revelation is not from God. Dogmatically it was quite correct that one might not believe in visions and inspirations "just as strongly" as one "believed that Christ was crucified. . . ." If only Joan had said "it seems to me" instead of "I know for certain," there was no man who would condemn her, Master Jehan Lohier, who was favorably inclined toward her, said to Guillaume Manchon. Visions such as hers are possible with God, Master Jehan Basset considered during the deliberations, but she did not support them with a miracle or with a proof from the Scriptures, hence they should not be believed. Again it was completely logical according to the formal rules of the faith.

Given the conceptual system of the day, an impartial modern judge would be able to endorse completely the conclusions of the 1431 deliberations. The judges reached the same decision a judge who did not believe in the cause of Joan could arrive at even today. Her visions were declared to be "certain fictions, conceived humanly or the work of the Evil One. . . ." She had "not had sufficient signs to believe therein and to know them. . . ." Jehan Beaupère, master of theology, who was inclined to consider the phenomena "to be not supernatural, but traceable, in part, to physical causes, and in part to imagination and human invention . . . ," was not so very far from explaining them as morbid symptoms. The chief distinction between the judges of 1431 and some psychologists of today is that, while the judges needed several months, the psychologists would probably have been ready with their statement within half an hour at the outside.

The method of the judges of 1431 was utterly scholarly. They are usually reviled in the historical studies (even in Champion's) because of the weight they attached to the innocent children's games of Joan's youth at Domremy, beside the spring and under the beech tree called the Fairy Tree, which they danced around and hung wreaths upon. But they are unjustly accused of cunning and antipathy in this respect. It *was* an important point for them. If it became clear from Joan's statements that there was a link between the appearance of her "voices" and the pagan customs centered around the tree, the diabolical character of her visions would be as good as proved. Whence the urge to know whether Saint Catherine and Saint Margaret had ever talked with her *beneath that tree*.

Finally there is the question of Joan's view of the Church and her refusal to submit without reserve to the judgment of the Church Militant. Again and again the judges asked her if she would leave the decision on the nature of her deeds to the Church. They attempted to explain to her the difference between the Church Triumphant and the Church Militant. But she did not understand. "I refer them to Our Lord who sent me, to Our Lady, and to all the blessed saints of Paradise," she says. "And she thought it was all one, Our Lord and the Church, and that these difficulties should not be made for her, and asked why we made difficulties when it was all one." According to the auditor of the Rota (a court of the Roman Curia who around 1454, in connection with her rehabilitation, made a close study of the twelve articles drawn from her confessions, she had sometimes understood that her judges were the Church and sometimes merely that the Church was the building where she was not allowed to go to hear mass. To the question whether she would submit, her answer in the hearings is once recorded as only to the Church on high, and later that she would submit to the Church Militant, "provided it does not command anything impossible. . . ." The ecclesiastical court of 1431 was, indeed, from its point of view on very firm ground when it counted such an attitude heavily against her. There had to be a limit to *sancta simplicitas*.

It is not in the objective value of their decision that the infamy of the judges of Rouen lies. They could justify the decision, looked upon as a matter in itself, to the feeling of their time and to their own consciences. The most august learned body of the day, the University of Paris, had done more than anyone else to help prepare the verdict, to elicit it, and to cloak it with its authority. The University of Paris should bear the burden of memory more than the judges at Rouen. Let us hope that the rector who guided the solemn assembly of the university on April 29, 1431—Pieter of Gouda, a canon of Utrecht, born at Leiden—was an insignificant chairman. The university judged logically, bitterly, and harshly; it judged from a distance, according to the facts, and did not see its victim.

Among those who did see her, the judges at Rouen, there was more than one who became somewhat aware of her greatness and her purity and was inclined toward a more favorable judgment. But the majority could see in her only "stubborn malevolence and hardness of the heart," "a sly mind tending toward evil and devoid of the grace of the Holy Ghost," without virtue and humility as they understood them. To them it was all pride and disobedience. They thought that in her they were punishing the sin of Lucifer himself.

Can the Rouen sentence rightly be looked upon as the reaction of the Church Militant to the spirit of individual religious opinion which was to shake that Church to its foundations less than a century later? In other words, is there any historical justification for Shaw's witty toying with the word "Protestantism"? I do not believe so. The concept of Protestantism is a composite concept. It assumes much more than merely Joan's naïve obstinacy against the Church Militant in her direct obsession with the glory of the Church Triumphant. The term Protestantism makes sense only with regard to persons who, after having tested the whole medieval Catholic concept of the Church, deliberately rejected it. If she had not become implicated in an ecclesiastical trial, the weak point in Joan's faith would never have become public. She does not testify against the Church of her own free will, but an ecclesiastical court forces her, on formalistic grounds, to a consistency that seems heretical. True Protestantism can only lie on the yonder side of the whole system of Scholastic theology; Joan's ignorant faith falls completely on this side of it—or outside it. Her spirit has nothing in common with those of Huss and Wycliffe. In her saintly simplicity she is just as Catholic as the (legendary) old woman who carried the bundle of faggots for Huss. Protestantism presupposes humanism, intellectual development, a modern spirit; in her faith Joan of Arc was in the full sense of the word a primitive. It would be regrettable if the non-Catholic world allowed Shaw's authority to lure it into denying the Catholic Church the glory of its most touching saint.

So much for Warwick's discovery: "I should call it Protestantism if I had to find a name for it. . . ." To a certain extent the same thing applies to Cauchon's countermove "Nationalism." But there Shaw is not alone. Many French authors before him have celebrated in Joan of Arc the birth of French patriotism. In a certain sense rightly so. The great love of France as a whole, concentrated on the king, became a conscious thing during (and because of) the protracted war against England. Long before Joan that patriotism had had its heroes and its martyrs, for example, the ship's captain from Abbeville, Ringois, who was thrown into the sea at Dover in 1360 because the demand that he swear loyalty to the king of England rebounded upon his "I am French." Eustace Deschamps had testified to it in many a poem thirty years before Alain Chartier interpreted that patriotic love. But Shaw means something more than mere love of country. The transformation that he would like to attribute to Joan is the assertion of national monarchy as opposed to feudal particularism, and that not only in France but also in England. *Tua res agitur,* Warwick believes. Now, this is completely incorrect. The national monarchy, both in France and in England, was from the very outset aware of its antithetical position toward feudalism, its superior task, and its superior right. In England the monarchy had had the upper hand in the conflict ever since the Conqueror, and repeatedly it was only as a result of crises and slumps that the aristocracy won ground temporarily. In France the monarchy was triumphing over the lords slowly but surely. The conflict had begun long before the fifteenth century—as early as with Louis VII and Philip Augustus in the twelfth. The elements of the modern state came into being in France in the thirteenth century under Saint Louis and Philip the Fair. In the fifteenth century Louis XI, in his struggle with Burgundy and the League of Public Weal, gained the ascendancy in what was merely a last dangerous crisis, and completed a structure it had taken centuries to build. Joan of Arc brought a new patriotic spirit, but not a new concept of the state. Her patriotic love, like her faith, was primitive, rather prefeudal than modern. To her—and not only to her—the cause of France was "the quarrel of the king of France." They are the king's faction, his loyal followers; he is their liege and France is his heritage, which an intruder unjustly contests. Joan's patriotism is built up out of utterly primitive notions. In this, too, she is sublime simplicity and sheer courage. As a result of those lofty qualities her conception of love and sacrifice could have a seminal influence on the modern notion of the state, but she did not create it. Shaw's "Nationalism" placed in Cauchon's mouth is nothing more than a brilliant touch of his wit.

Joan of Arc as the subject of a historical hypothesis, as Shaw would have it, an exponent of certain ways of thinking —there is something annoying in it. In her irreducible uniqueness she can be understood only by means of a sense of sympathetic admiration. She does not lend herself to being used to clarify currents and concepts of her day. Her own personality attracts all the attention as soon as one touches on her history. She is one of the few figures in history who cannot be anything but protagonists, who are never subordinate, always an end and never a means. And this—if I may end these marginal notes with a word of personal apology —is also the reason why there is hardly a reference to her in the work that I wrote some years ago on life in the fifteenth century in France and the Netherlands. It has been charged to me as an error. But it was a considered, deliberate omission. I knew that Joan of Arc would have torn the book I visualized in my mind completely out of balance. What kept me from introducing her in it was a sense of harmony—that and a vast and reverent humility.

PART III. *The Renaissance*

THE PROBLEM OF THE RENAISSANCE •

I

At the sound of the word "Renaissance" the dreamer of past beauty sees purple and gold. A festive world is bathed in mild clarity, rustling with sonorous tones. People move with grace and solemnity, untroubled by the distress of time and the beckonings of eternity. Everything is one ripe, full exuberance. The questioner says: Explain it in more detail. And the dreamer stammers: the Renaissance is altogether positive, and it is undoubtedly in the key of C major. The questioner smiles. Then the dreamer recalls the things that he has learned determine the historical phenomenon we call the Renaissance —its duration in time, its significance for the evolution of civilization, its causes, its character—and half demurring, now that the terms force themselves on him, he recites his credo. The Renaissance was the emergence of individualism, the awakening of the urge to beauty, the triumph of worldliness and *joie de vivre,* the conquest of mundane reality by the mind, the revival of a pagan zest for life, the developing consciousness of the personality in its natural relation to the world. Perhaps while he is speaking his heart has begun to beat as if he were reciting the credo of his own life. Or has he already smelled the lamp?

• "Het probleem der Renaissance," first published under the title "Renaissancestudiën, I: Het probleem," in De Gids, LXXXIV (1920), Part Four, 107-33, 231-55. Translation from the Dutch text in Verzamelde werken, IV, 231-75.

The questioner refuses to leave off. What are the names of the host of figures who pass before you if I pronounce the word Renaissance? To that every answer is different, as if we were standing on the first battlements of Babel. I see Michelangelo, irate and solitary, says one. I see Botticelli, languishing and tender, says another. Are those two Raphael and Ariosto, or Dürer and Rabelais? No, it is Ronsard, it is Hooft. There are even some who see Saint Francis in the lead, and Jan van Eyck in the midst of the procession. And there is one who says: I see a table, a bound volume, and a church tower. For he understands the word Renaissance in the narrower sense of a stylistic term instead of the broader one of a cultural concept.

The questioner smiles again, now somewhat gloatingly, and says: Your Renaissance is a Proteus. You are in disagreement about every question touching upon it: when it began, when it ended; whether classical culture was one of its causes or merely an accompanying phenomenon; whether one can separate Renaissance from humanism or not. Neither in time, extent, content, nor significance is the concept Renaissance defined. It suffers from vagueness, incompleteness, and chance, and yet is at the same time a dangerous, doctrinaire schematization. It is an almost unusable term.

Then the chorus of the dreamers pleads: Do not deprive us of the Renaissance! We cannot do without it. For us it has become the expression of an attitude to life: we want to be able to live in it and from it if we like. This word Renaissance is not your property: it is a notion of life, a rod and a staff for all mankind, not merely a technical term for historians.

So, says the questioner, not my property? Am I not the one who taught you the term? Was it not the diligent study of cultural history that developed, delineated, and determined the concept Renaissance? Though it has now fallen into the hands of a barbaric generation that denies the concept's vassalage to the discipline of history, only the historian has the right to use the term, and then in the manner it deserves: as a label used in bottling history, and nothing more.

But the questioner is not right in this. The term Renaissance is not a scholarly designation in origin. The development of the concept Renaissance is one of the clearest examples of the lack of autonomy of the historical discipline, of the relation that is at once its weakness and its glory: its indissoluble link with contemporary life. Hence the problem of the Renaissance, the question of what the Renaissance was, cannot be separated from the development of the term indicating it.[1]

The notion of a rebirth of intellectual culture, as a result of which the world revived from barrenness and decay at a certain time, is both very old and relatively new: old in its subjective value as a cultural idea, new in its quality of a scholarly concept with an objective tenor.

The age we mark with the designation Renaissance, in particular the first half of the sixteenth century, itself felt that it had been reborn into civilization, that it had returned to the pure sources of knowledge and beauty and was in possession of the unchanging norms of wisdom and art. In its direct expression, however, the sense of rebirth applied almost exclusively to literary culture, the broad field of study and poetry covered by the term *bonae literae*. Rabelais speaks of "the restoration of *bonnes lettres*" as a generally known, incontrovertible fact.[2] Some looked upon the revival as the illustrious work of princes lending their patronage to the arts and letters. In 1559 Jacques Amyot wrote to Henry II in the dedication of his translation of Plutarch (which provided so much material for Montaigne and Shakespeare): "To you will be given the praise for having gloriously crowned and completed the work founded and begun by the great King Francis, your late father, to cause *les bonnes lettres* to be reborn and to flourish in this noble realm." [3] Others recognize in the revival the spirit of their great predecessors. In the Preface to an edition of his *Adagia* Erasmus is credited as the one "who well-nigh first of all cherished the letters then being reborn [*renascentes bonas literas*], emerging from the ugly foulness of prolonged barbarity. . . ." [4]

In Italy even a century earlier writers had spoken with happy pride of the renascence of noble civilization, also specifically involving the pictorial arts in that renascence. Lorenzo Valla wrote in the foreword to his *Elegantiae Linguae latinae*—a foreword that has been called the manifesto of humanism—that he would not pass any judgment on the question of how it had happened

> that those arts that are closest to the liberal arts, to wit, painting, sculpture, and architecture, were first so long and so greatly degenerated, and almost perished with letters

themselves, and now are being reawakened and revived, and that there is such a flowering of fine artists and lettered men. Happy these, our times, in which, if we endeavor a little more, I am confident the Roman language will soon grow even more verdant than the city itself, and with it all learning will be restored. . . .[5]

The word "humanists" for the new practitioners of the rejuvenated studies had merely to be borrowed from antiquity; Cicero himself spoke of *studia humanitatis et literarum.*[6]

The Italian of around 1500 considered his time and his country in terms of a stimulus to new life after debasement and decay. Machiavelli concludes his *Dell' arte della guerra* with an admonition to the youth not to despair, ". . . because this Province seems to be altogether given, to raise up again [*risuscitare*] the things dead, as is seen by the perfection that poetry, painting, and writing is now brought unto. . . ."[7]

What was considered as the cause of the great revival? Not imitation of the Greeks and Romans as such. The sixteenth-century sense of a rebirth was too general in character and too strong in ethical and aesthetic content for the intellects of the day to pose the phenomenon to themselves as a philological question. Returning to the origins, slaking one's thirst at the pure fountains of wisdom and beauty—that was the fundamental note of the sense of rebirth. And if that sense also included the new enthusiasm for the classics and the identification of contemporary times with antiquity, it was because the classical writers themselves appeared to possess that purity and originality of knowledge, those simple norms of beauty and virtue.

The first person who clearly looked upon the event of rebirth as a historical fact that had taken place at a certain time in the past, and who at the same time derived the Italian form equivalent to the word Renaissance from the Latin *renasci,* applying it in particular to the revival in art (thus as a concept in art history), was Giorgio Vasari (1511-1574), the biographer of the painters. The word *rinascita* became for him the standard term to indicate the great fact of recent art history. He set himself the task "of writing the lives, describing the works, and setting forth the various relations of those who, when art had become extinct, first revived [*risuscitate*], and then gradually conducted her to that degree of beauty and majesty wherein we now see her."[8] Whoever had surveyed the history of art in its rise and fall "will now be able to recognize more easily the progress of her second birth [*della sua rinascita*] and of that perfection whereto she has risen again in our times." [9]

Vasari saw the highest flowering of art in Greek and Roman antiquity, followed by a long period of decay setting in as early as the time of Emperor Constantine. The Goths and Lombards had merely overthrown what was crumbling of its own accord. For ages Italy had known only "the coarse, pitiable, and harsh painting" of the Byzantine masters. Though Vasari detected a few quite early signs of a reawakening, it was only late in the thirteenth century that the great renewal came, with the two great Florentines Cimabue and Giotto. They abandoned *la vecchia maniera greca* ["the old Greek manner"], that is to say, the Byzantine tradition, which Vasari time and again called *goffa* ["coarse"] and to which he opposed *la buona maniera antica*. Cimabue was *quasi prima cagione della rinovazione dell' arte* ["perhaps the first cause of the restoration of the art of painting"], Giotto "threw open the gates of the true way to those who afterwards exalted the art to the perfection and greatness which it displays in our age. . . ." [10] That perfection in his own age Vasari saw above all in Michelangelo.

For Vasari the great restoration brought about by Cimabue and Giotto was constituted in the direct imitation of nature. To him a return to nature and a return to antiquity were almost identical. The excellence of ancient art was a result of the fact that nature itself had been its example and guide: the imitation of nature was the basic principle of art.[11] Whoever followed the ancients rediscovered nature. This is a fundamental trait in the whole concept of the Renaissance in its own time.

The significance of Vasari for the development of the concept Renaissance is, incidentally, sometimes overestimated. Vasari was not expressing anything unprecedented either in placing Cimabue and Giotto in the vanguard or in deriving the revival from a return to nature. Boccaccio already had extolled Giotto as he who had brought the art of natural painting to life once more after it had lain buried for many centuries. Leonardo da Vinci commemorated him in the same way. As early as 1489 Erasmus placed the revival of the pictorial arts some two or three hundred years before his time. According to Dürer it was generally known that painting was "resumed" or "brought to light again by the Romance nations" two hundred years earlier.[12] For him, too, a longing for true nature and a fervent desire for the art and the literature of antiquity were basically one and the same thing.

During the seventeenth century the concept of a renascence of civilization seems to have slumbered. It no longer thrust itself forward as an expression of a feeling of enthusiasm at recaptured glory. On the one hand the spirit had grown disciplined and sober, and on the other, more matter-of-fact and less emotional. People had become accustomed to the profusion of the noble, refined form, the moving, solemn word, the fullness of color and sound, the critical clarity of the intellect. All this was no longer experienced as a wonderful new triumph. "Renaissance" was no longer consciously a watchword, and there was not yet any need for it as a technical term in history.

When the concept of a birth of culture again won ground in thought it was the critical sense that availed itself of it, as a means of distinguishing historical phenomena. The dawning Enlightenment of the eighteenth century took up the term Renaissance where the generation of the sixteenth century had dropped it. But meanwhile the concept of that rebirth, no longer gravid with the live emotion of the persons who had themselves been its exponents, had become singularly academic and formal, biased, and inaccurate. In Pierre Bayle's *Dictionnaire historique et critique,* which provided the arsenal and the key for the coming Enlightenment, one already finds a conception of the Renaissance actually containing all the elements of the attitude that was to stretch out its life as the textbook point of view until late in the nineteenth century:

It is certain that most of the *beaux-esprits* and humanist savants in Italy when the humanities were flowering anew there [in other editions "when belles-lettres were beginning to be reborn"] after the fall of Constantinople were without religion. But, on the other hand, the restoration of the scholarly languages and belles-lettres had prepared the way for the Reformers—as was foreseen by the monks and their partisans, who incessantly clamored against Reuchlin, Erasmus, and the other scourges of barbarity.[13]

For Bayle, then, it was an established fact that humanism in Italy had an irreligious character, and that it had been caused by the fall of Constantinople, which is to say by the coming of Greek exiles laden with Greek knowledge. Voltaire, a few decades later, had put such a point of view far behind him. Anyone who seeks through his *Essai sur les mœurs et l'esprit des nations* (which for all its defects deserves respect as the model for modern cultural history) for the parts where Voltaire outlines the development of the arts and sciences since the late Middle Ages will be surprised by the sketchiness, the incoherence, the superficiality, the bias, the lack of penetration and sympathy with which Voltaire hastily breaks a lance with one phenomenon after another and then rushes on. But he will be equally surprised at the brilliant perception with which the author of the *Essai* detects and indicates broader contexts. It seems to me an overstatement to declare that Voltaire gave Burckhardt the inspiration for the theme of his *The Civilization of the Renaissance in Italy*,[14] but a hint toward that conception is not to be denied the *Essai*. For Voltaire, as for Burckhardt, the matrix of the Renaissance was the wealth and freedom of the towns in medieval Italy. While France was still living in misery,

it was far otherwise with the great trading cities in Italy; there the inhabitants lived with great convenience, and in opulence, and enjoyed the sweets of life. At length, wealth and liberty excited the genius, and courage of the nation.[15]

Then, in the chapter "The Sciences and the Polite Arts in the Thirteenth and Fourteenth Centuries," follows the view that has had such a long and disturbing influence: Dante, Petrarch, Boccaccio, Cimabue, and Giotto as the precursors of a later perfection:

Already had Dante the Florentine illustrated the Tuscan language with that whimsical poem entitled *Comedia*, a work famous for natural beauties, and in many parts far superior to the corrupt taste of that age, being written with as much purity as if the author had been contemporary with Ariosto and Tasso.

In Dante "but especially in Petrarch we meet with a great number of passages that resemble those fine antiques which have the beauty of antiquity, together with the freshness of modern times." It was the same with the pictorial arts as with language and poetry:

> The polite arts, which all go hand in hand, and generally decay and rise together, were emerging now in Italy from barbarism. Cimabue, without any assistance, was, in great measure, a new inventor of painting, in the thirteenth century. Giotto drew some pictures which to this day are beheld with pleasure . . . Brunelleschi began to reform the Gothic architecture.

It was the vital genius of Tuscany which was for Voltaire the creative force of the renewal.

> For all these inventions we are indebted to the Tuscans only, who by mere strength of genius revived those arts, before the little remains of Greek learning, together with that language, removed from Constantinople into Italy, after the conquest of the Ottomans. Florence was at that time a second Athens. . . . By this it appears, that it is not to the refugees of Constantinople we are indebted for the restoration of letters: those men were capable of teaching the Italians nothing more than the Greek tongue.[16]

These were new and fruitful ideas. One would expect Voltaire to follow such a beginning with a description of the *quattrocento* and the *cinquecento,* in order to demonstrate the ascendant line. He cannot have been lacking in the material for it. But there is not a trace of it in the *Essai.* The sketch of that first flowering is broken off for a long digression on the restoration of the drama. Passing mention is made of the fact that there was an uninterrupted series of poets succeeding Boccaccio "who have all passed to posterity," a series culminating in Ariosto. When he later returns to the cultural developments of the fifteenth and sixteenth centuries (in Chapter 121) one seeks in vain for an elaboration of the image of the Renaissance he had sketched so happily.

> The arts continued to flourish in Italy because the pest of religious controversy had not penetrated into that country:

and so it happened, that while they were cutting one another's throats in Germany, France, and England, for things
they did not understand; Italy, completely at rest, since the
amazing event of the plundering of Rome by the army of
Charles V, applied herself more than ever to the improvement of the liberal arts.[17]

That is all there is about the *cinquecento*. Leonardo, Raphael,
Michelangelo, Titian—not a one of them is mentioned by
name.

What was it that kept Voltaire from presenting a well-
rounded picture of Renaissance culture? He had a conception
of a clearly circumscribed period of flowering in arts and
letters gravitating around the Medici in the fifteenth and
sixteenth centuries. It was for him one of the four happy
ages in world history. "These four happy ages," he says in
his *Age of Louis XIV*, "are those wherein the arts have been
improved, and which, serving as an epocha of the grandeur
of human understanding, are an example to all posterity." [18]
The first was the age of Pericles, the second that of Caesar
and Augustus, the third that of the Medici after the fall of
Constantinople. The arrival of the Greek scholars in Florence
was here, in 1739, still seen as the cause for the revival, a
theory he was later to reject in his *Essai*. But the glory of the
third age was overshadowed by that of the *siècle de Louis
XIV*, "that age which was the most enlightened of all others."
It was that age that Voltaire extolled, even at the cost of his
own age; there lay his interest and his appreciation, and it
was this that rendered it impossible for him to visualize the
spirit and the beauty of the Renaissance.

Voltaire, then, left the image of the Renaissance behind
as an incompleted sketch, and even his own age turned to
other panoramas of the past. The further discovery of the
Renaissance would have had to be not only one of *esprit*
and critical sense such as Voltaire had but just as much or
even more one of aesthetic sympathy and emotional needs.
And in this realm of feeling and dreaming it was not the
spirit of Voltaire that reigned, but that of Rousseau. What
could the colorful variety in formal beauty of the aristocratic
culture of the Renaissance mean to persons who were only
able to hanker after the simplicity of nature and the languishing sensitivity of the heart? The murmur of oaks and the
mountain clouds of Ossian or sweet attention to the adventures

of Clarissa Harlowe's soul occupied the mind to such an extent that there was no place for an image of the Renaissance with its sunshine and sounding brass. The fantasy of romanticism turned to the Middle Ages, to seek there the opaque and somber effects of moonlight and chasing clouds that were so dear to its heart. The great transposition to the minor key of romanticism interrupted the evolution of an image of the Renaissance, and for a long time remained an obstacle to it. Only a kindred spirit could rediscover the unity of the Renaissance and explain it to mankind.

Goethe perhaps? The all-fathoming one, exalted above the contrasting pair Voltaire and Rousseau? No, not Goethe either. Goethe was familiar with the current concept of a revival of art, of course. Chevalier d'Agincourt, whom he visited in Rome, was busy, he noted, "writing the history of art from its decline to its revival." [19] From the material the Frenchman had collected for the purpose it was possible to see "how the human mind throughout the dull obscure period was very busy." Vasari could have said all this just as well. Goethe's interest and appreciation were very strongly concentrated on the sixteenth century. "At the beginning of the sixteenth century the spirit of the pictorial arts had raised itself completely out of the barbarism of the Middle Ages; it longed for freer, higher effects." [20] In one entry in his diaries he placed Raphael at the pinnacle of a pyramid [21]—which does not remove the fact that that painter seemed to him archaic in comparison with Michelangelo. When some people listed Raphael's *"Disputa"* as his best work, Goethe considered that as an indication of "the predilection that afterwards asserted itself in favour of the old school. This the quiet observer could regard as but a symptom of half and impeded talents, and in no way identify himself with it." [22] The period that Goethe saw as one of flowering in the arts does not comprise the age we call the Renaissance, but rather the last phase of the Renaissance together with the first one of baroque. In the focal point of his observation and appreciation, beside Michelangelo, were the later artists Benvenuto Cellini, Palladio, and Guido Reni. And that great flowering presented itself to Goethe only in a small degree as a historical problem. He was seeking much more the immediate, independent value of the works of art he observed.

Thus the nineteenth century dawned without the concept

of the Renaissance having been given much more content than it had had for Bayle and Voltaire. It was not yet an indication for a cultural period as such. It still served, so to speak, only as an appellation, not as a proper name; usually it was associated with a further statement of what was reborn. It was still almost on the same level with terms like "decline and fall." It did contain in itself an elation at new life, hence a definite value-judgment, but in its application it retained a fairly indifferent tone, and usually had only a limited meaning. In his *Histoire de la peinture en Italie* (1817) Stendhal used the phrase *la renaissance des arts* almost exclusively for the first quarter of the sixteenth century, which had all his enthusiasm and admiration; to him the Florentine art of the fifteenth century still embodied "the ideal beauty of the Middle Ages." Guizot, in his *Histoire générale de la civilisation en Europe* (1828), spoke of a *renaissance des lettres*, without the term having a nuance any different from the one it had had in the mouth of Voltaire, or even of Rabelais and Amyot. Sismondi transferred the concept to the field of political thought in his *Histoire de la renaissance de la liberté en Italie* (1832). We shall see later that Renaissance as a political idea was by no means new, and in fact had been one of the roots from which the whole concept of the Renaissance had developed.

According to Walter Goetz,[23] the first person who assumed that the term Renaissance without any further restriction was familiar as a specific term for a circumscribed cultural period was the Florentine Count Libri of dubious memory who, after having fled to France, in 1838 published a work entitled *Histoire des sciences mathématiques en Italie depuis la Renaissance jusqu'à la fin du XVIIième siècle*. This is not correct, however. Libri was merely following a custom that had won ground in French literary circles. Almost a decade earlier Balzac had used the word Renaissance as an autonomous cultural concept in the short novel *Le bal de Sceaux*, dated December 1829, in which it is said of one of the leading characters: "she could argue fluently on Italian or Flemish painting, on the Middle Ages or the Renaissance. . . ."

The conceptual system in which the cultural history of Europe was largely to be conceived from then on was gradually acquiring its fixed form and its full resilience: the Middle Ages and the Renaissance as an explicit antithesis, each of the two a cultural image. But before we trace the further development of the concept of the Renaissance, reference should be made to a peculiar fact for which I imagine there are parallels to be found in many other fields—that the school opinion, the condensed view of the Renaissance propagated by the textbooks, was even then lagging behind what historians understood by the term.

That school opinion may perhaps be described as follows: Toward the end of the Middle Ages (Middle Ages in the rationalistic view as representing darkness and barbarism) the arts and learning were revived, first of all in Italy, because Greeks fleeing from Constantinople brought the West once more in contact with the inspiration of the ancient Greek spirit. Or even in cases where no such predominant influence was attributed to the exiles, the revival of classical culture was viewed both as the causal element and the outward characteristic of the Renaissance. The Renaissance came because people learned how to understand the spirit of the ancients, and its essential element was the imitation of classical art and literature. Some of the textbooks also made a small place for the art of printing and the discovery of America among the causes of the general revival. I am not sure which schoolbook it was whose chapters on the modern period are said to have begun with the confident opening sentence "The rebirth of the human spirit dates from the discovery of firearms," a sentence that, well considered, is Marxism *à outrance*.

But be that as it may, the opinion then current, that the imitation of antiquity was the alpha and omega of the Renaissance, has never been more than a secondhand simplification of the views of those whose minds cherished the concept of the Renaissance and brought it to maturity. Even Voltaire, we have seen, had a much broader view of the phenomenon of revival. If any one person must be made responsible for the school opinion, it would have to be Pierre Bayle.

Now we have come to the full unfolding, beneath the hand of Jacob Burckhardt, of the concept of the Renaissance in all its rich, colorful aspects as a form of life far transcending the limits of historical study for its own sake.

It is a fact that the great Swiss scholar was inspired by a

seer whose hallucinated vision illuminated history as if with flashes of lightning: Jules Michelet. The year 1855 saw the appearance of Michelet's *Histoire de France au XVIième siècle*, the seventh volume of his *Histoire de France*, with the subtitle *Renaissance*. Michelet's attitude toward the great cultural transformation was that of the Enlightenment, as it had merged into liberalism and was reflected in his brilliant mind. What the sixteenth century had brought was, to him just as much as to the rationalists of the eighteenth century, light—light in the barbaric darkness of the Middle Ages. For him the concept of the Renaissance was merely a part of the great idea of the progress that began its triumphant course when the mind awoke from the delusion and oppression of Scholasticism and feudalism. The sixteenth century brought two great things:

The discovery of the world, the discovery of man.
The sixteenth century, in its great and legitimate extent, goes from Columbus to Copernicus, from Copernicus to Galileo, from the discovery of the earth to that of the heavens.
Man had refound himself. Before Vesalius and Servetius had revealed life to him, he had penetrated its moral mystery with Luther and Calvin, with Dumoulin and Cujas, with Rabelais, Montaigne, Shakespeare, Cervantes. He had sounded the profound bases of its nature. He had begun to settle into Justice and Reason.[24]

In other words, in the sixteenth century man became aware of his true, natural relation to the world; he learned to understand the world's properties and its significance, and came to comprehend the worth and the abilities of his own personality. Michelet lumped the Reformation and the Renaissance together as the happy dawn of the ideal of the Enlightenment. He saw the awakening as taking place in the sixteenth century, and except for Columbus and Galileo he did not mention a single Italian among the leaders in that vast process.

If, then, Burckhardt was able to borrow his view of the great cultural transformation from Michelet, it was merely to direct it toward quite different things. He applied that formula for the Renaissance, "the discovery of the world and of man," to phenomena in which Michelet had only a secondary interest, in fact, he understood the formula in a basically different way from Michelet, its creator. Michelet had proclaimed it as a watchword, and he was not the one to produce the wealth of specific images to prove his formula historically. And it would perhaps have faded like a cry in the night if Burckhardt had not chanced to hear it.

Burckhardt's combination of wisdom and depth, of the ability to synthesize on a grand scale and the patient industry of the scholar assembling and working through his material, was of the sort that is all too rare in the historical discipline. His mind was, moreover, one that, with aristocratic reserve, did not praise an opinion of the day because the day demanded it. Burckhardt was not at all caught up in banal ideas of progress, and that in itself was enough to enable him to go much deeper than Michelet. He was the first to view the Renaissance apart from any connection with Enlightenment and progress, no longer as a prelude and an annunciation of later excellence, but as a cultural ideal *sui generis*.

A phrase has been quoted from an early essay by Jacob Burckhardt in which he speaks of the "so-called Renaissance." [25] The essay dates from 1838 (he was born in Basel in 1818 and died there in 1897); that year he had visited Italy for the first time, but German and Flemish art of the Middle Ages continued to be the focus of his studies and his appreciation in the years immediately following—also after a second stay in Italy. Late in 1852 his work on the age of Constantine the Great appeared. In the next two years he visited Italy again, and in 1855 published the *Cicerone*, "a guide to the enjoyment of the works of art in Italy." Then in 1860 came *The Civilization of the Renaissance in Italy*.

Nothing demonstrates the significance of that book as clearly as the dates of its editions. The second edition appeared nine years after the first, in 1869, and the third and fourth each after eight years, 1877 and 1885. After the fifth edition of 1896 the stream began: 1897, 1899, 1901, 1904, 1908, 1913, 1919.[26] Only the following generation had become fully ripe for what Burckhardt had to offer.

The structure of this matchless example of cultural-historical synthesis is as sturdy and harmonic as any Renaissance work of art. The foundations are laid in Part I, "The State as a Work of Art," which treats of the political and social traditiors within which a more personal and more conscious attitude of the individual toward the state and toward life developed in the Italian states even in the Middle Ages. From the very outset the reader is brought into contact with the spirit of a personal definition of aims and a free determination of the course of one's life which was for Burckhardt the characteristic of the Renaissance, and which he delineates in the types of despots, *condottieri*, diplomats, courtiers, and nepotists. But at the same time the reader is provided with an indispensable survey of the political history of the period. Then Burckhardt unfolds the basic theme of his work. Part II, "The Development of the Individual," begins with the page that is almost Burckhardt's creed, and which must be cited in full.

In the character of these states, whether republics or despotisms, lies not the only but the chief reason for the early development of the Italian. To this it is due that he was the first-born among the sons of modern Europe.

In the Middle Ages both sides of human consciousness—that which was turned within as that which was turned without—lay dreaming or half awake beneath a common veil. The veil was woven of faith, illusion, and childish prepossession, through which the world and history were seen clad in strange hues. Man was conscious of himself only as a member of a race, people, party, family, or corporation—only through some general category. In Italy this veil first melted into air; an *objective* treatment and consideration of the State and of all the things of this world became possible. The *subjective* side at the same time asserted itself with corresponding emphasis; man became a spiritual *individual*, and recognized himself as such.[27]

Burckhardt traces this developing awareness of the personality in every field. The chapter "The Perfecting of the Individual" poses Leon Battista Alberti as the most complete type of the universal man who developed and controlled all his abilities consciously. Answering to this development of the individual there was also "a new sort of outward distinction—the modern form of glory." The unbridled passion for fame of Dante's subjects (and himself), the celebrity of Petrarch, the veneration of the great national heroes: all this Burckhardt views under the sign of the new concept of personality and human worth—this, and also its opposite, "modern wit and satire."

Only then comes "The Revival of Antiquity," as Part III. By this time it need hardly be said that for Burckhardt the revival of antiquity was not the causal element in the Renaissance. Nor was it to him the essential characteristic of the period. He began at once by rejecting such a point of view:

> Now that this point in our historical view of Italian civilization has been reached it is time to speak of the influence of antiquity, the "new birth" of which has been one-sidedly chosen as the name to sum up the whole period.

It was, then, neither the causal nor the essential element of the Renaissance, but nonetheless a prerequisite and vital element in its development. Classicism was indispensable as a means of expressing the newly acquired insight into life:

> The Renaissance [Burckhardt, but not the translator, puts the word between quotation marks to make it clear that he is here using it in the narrower sense of a revival of classical studies] would not have been the process of worldwide significance which it is if its elements could be so easily separated from one another.

But he immediately restricted the role of classicism in the renewal of the spirit:

> We must insist upon it, as one of the chief propositions of this book, that it was not the revival of antiquity alone, but its union with the genius of the Italian people, which achieved the conquest of the western world.[28]

Burckhardt discussed the whole influence of antiquity (to which Georg Voigt had devoted his *Wiederbelebung des klassischen Altertums oder das erste Jahrhundert des Humanismus* shortly before, in 1859, without Burckhardt's being able to use it) in a single part of his book; half of his material still remained to be dealt with. Then came "The Discovery of the World and of Man." In this part of the essay Burckhardt demonstrated what cultural history ought actually to be. He discusses the empirical tendency of the natural sciences; the discovery of the beauty of landscape; then the emergence of psychological portrayal, first of all in Dante,

Petrarch, and Boccaccio; the development of biography; the new view of national character and ethnic variety; and finally the flowering of the new ideal of beauty. Who had ever thought before of considering the significance for cultural history of social etiquette, fashion, dilettantism, festivals? The book closes with the part on "Morality and Religion." In it the conclusions of Burckhardt's view come to the fore, and the image of the "Renaissance man" is given its final touches: unbridled individualism tending toward a complete amorality; a subjective attitude toward religion—tolerant, skeptical, mocking, sometimes rejecting outright; and the paganism of the Renaissance, an admixture of ancient superstition and modern skepticism. And in the final lines of the book he praises the noble Platonism of the Florentines in Lorenzo de' Medici's circle:

> One of the most precious fruits of the knowledge of the world and of man here comes to maturity, on whose account alone the Italian Renaissance must be called the leader of modern ages.[29]

The word Renaissance had obtained its full significance. Gradually Burckhardt's thought penetrated far beyond the circles where his book was read. In the process it was, as always happens, divested of all the details giving it life and at the same time, in their irreducibility, restricting it; it was coarsened, truncated, and disjointed in the minds of those who accepted it. Burckhardt had summoned the man of the Renaissance before the face of time like one of those magnificent sinners from the *Inferno,* demonic in his unbending pride, self-satisfied and audacious, the *uomo singolare,* the "unique man." This was the only figure from his book which captured the fancy of the dilettantes. The concept of "Renaissance man" became associated with notions of impetuous acceptance and domination of life. It was imagined that Renaissance civilization as a type was to be seen in the free personality of genius, elevated above doctrines and morals, the haughty, frivolous man of pleasure who in a pagan passion for beauty seized the power to live according to his own norms. The aestheticism of the waning nineteenth century detected an echo of its own desire in that fancied picture of historical life. In the most serious cases of confusion of terms even the much loved "rebelliousness" forced its way into the picture of the Renaissance. None of this was Burckhardt's fault. The melody he had sung a later generation orchestrated *à la* Nietzsche, who, as is known, was a disciple of Burckhardt.

Meanwhile, though in many minds superficial exaggeration supplanted the rich image that had been given them, the study of art history and cultural history had not come to a standstill with Burckhardt's book. A work stemming so largely from a single conception is necessarily one-sided. The weak sides of Burckhardt's thesis could not remain hidden.

Staring into the violent sunshine of the Italian *quattrocento*, Burckhardt had only been able to see defectively what lay beyond it. The veil he saw spread over the spirit of the Middle Ages was partly caused by a flaw in his own camera. He had seen all too sharp a contrast between late medieval life in Italy and life elsewhere. That beneath the glory of the Renaissance genuinely medieval popular life continued in Italy in the same forms as in France and the Germanic countries had escaped him just as much as that the new life whose advent he hailed in Italy was also emerging in other lands where he could detect nothing but age-old repression and barbarism. He was not well enough aware of the great variety and the luxuriant life of medieval culture outside Italy. As a result he drew all too restricted spatial limits to the emerging Renaissance.

Even more open to criticism was Burckhardt's chronological delimitation of the Renaissance. He had dated around 1400 the beginning of the full flowering of individualism, which was for him the essential element of the period. Far and away the greatest share of the abundant material with which he illustrated his point of view deals with the fifteenth century and the first quarter of the sixteenth. What lay before 1400 was for him a betokening, a hopeful seed. The position he assigned to Dante and Petrarch was still that of "precursors" of the Renaissance, just as Michelet—and to a certain extent even Voltaire—had seen them. The notion of "precursors" of a trend or movement is always a dangerous metaphor in history. Dante a precursor of the Renaissance—in the same way I might with certain justification call Rembrandt a precursor of Jozef Israels, but no one would follow me. By marking someone as a precursor one lifts him out of the framework of his own time, within which he should be understood, and in doing so one distorts history.

Once he had started from the conception of detecting the Renaissance in individualism Burckhardt was forced to hail it in every phenomenon that contrasted with what was for him the dingy background of medieval civilization. The decorative art of the twelfth-century Cosmati, the Tuscan architecture of the thirteenth century, the lively, worldly, and classical twelfth-century poetry of the *Carmina burana*—all of them became proto-Renaissance. This is true not only of art but also of human character. Every man of the Middle Ages who displayed an outstanding personality fell under the beam of the great searchlight of the Renaissance.

> In far earlier times we can here and there detect a development of free personality which in Northern Europe either did not occur at all or could not display itself in the same manner [but no—the Norse sagas present a picture of free personality without equal—J. H.]. The band of audacious wrongdoers in the tenth century described to us by Luidprand, some of the contemporaries of Gregory VII, and a few of the opponents of the first Hohenstaufen, show us characters of this kind.[30]

The beginning of the line of the Renaissance, then, could be extended further back indefinitely. The consequence, already perceived by Michelet, was that every awakening of new intellectual life, of new views of life and the world in the Middle Ages, had to be seen as a dawning of the Renaissance. In doing that one had to apply the half-conscious postulate that in themselves the Middle Ages had been a dead thing, a rotten trunk (a postulate that had been an openly confessed doctrine in Michelet).

The consequence, that the Renaissance constantly had to be antedated further, was indeed drawn. The persons who have extracted the roots of the Renaissance are Emile Gebhart, Henry Thode, Louis Courajod, and Paul Sabatier. To what extent the idea of the medieval origins of the Renaissance had been prepared as early as 1877 can be seen from Walter Pater's *The Renaissance,* in which, without arguing the case explicitly, he as a matter of course ranged under the concept Renaissance everything in the Middle Ages that attracted him as spontaneous and striking—this he did, for instance, with the thirteenth-century French interlude *Aucassin et Nicolette.*

In 1879 the excellent essayist and cultural historian Emile Gebhart published his *Les origines de la Renaissance en Italie.* His conception of the nature of the Renaissance was the same as Burckhardt's: "The Renaissance in Italy was not solely a renewal of literature and arts resulting from the return of cultivated minds to classical literature and a better training for the artists who rediscovered the sense of beauty in the Greek school. It was the whole complex of Italian civilization, the proper expression of Italy's genius and moral life." [31] But what Burckhardt had only gently hinted at Gebhart accepted completely: "Actually the Italian Renaissance begins before Petrarch, for as early as in the works of the Pisan sculptors and of Giotto, as well as in the architecture of the twelfth and thirteenth centuries, the arts are renewed. . . . The origins of the Renaissance, then, are quite remote, and precede by far the scholarly culture spread by the literature of the fifteenth century." [32]

When Burckhardt's *Civilization of the Renaissance* appeared in a French translation by M. Schmitt in 1885, Gebhart posed the question somewhat more precisely.[33] The points where the Renaissance was linked to the Middle Ages are hardly visible in Burckhardt, he says; a sharper light should be focused on his book at its extremities. Gebhart himself did this with the beginning. In his *L'Italie mystique: Histoire de la Renaissance religieuse au moyen-âge* (1892), he continued to build on his *Origines,* making Joachim of Floris (the Calabrian mystic of the late twelfth century) and Francis of Assisi the points of departure for the whole intellectual movement.

This was actually no longer anything new. Also in this respect Michelet, with all too broad and violent a gesture, had scattered the seed that others saw sprouting. In the panting confession with which he introduced his volume on the Renaissance the theme was already the question why the Renaissance came three centuries too late.[34] It had repeatedly announced itself: in the twelfth century with the *chanson de geste,* Abelard, and Abbot Joachim; in the thirteenth with the *Evangelium aeternum,* the polemic pamphlet of the radical Franciscans; in the fourteenth with Dante. Actually the Middle Ages were already dead in the twelfth century,

Michelet wrote, and only the stubborn resistance to a return to nature offered by *le moyen-âge* (it is known how anthropomorphically Michelet thought) retarded the Renaissance. These ideas had become common property via Michelet, and hence it is understandable that Walter Pater easily associated the concept Renaissance with the figure of Saint Francis even before Gebhart developed the thesis on a scholarly basis.

It is no great wonder, then, that the French and the German historians, each going their own way, arrived at the same position. Henry Thode's study *Franz von Assisi und die Anfänge der Kunst der Renaissance in Italien* appeared in 1885. Thode was not so much concerned with the religious revival emanating from Francis in itself as with the influence which that revival had on the renewal of art. He considered the latter of paramount importance. The lyrical ardor and the subjective feeling of Francis, his new passion for the beauty of the world, had not only given the impulse for a profound artistic sense and the material for a new artistic imagination; socially, too, the mendicant orders provided both the motive and the impetus for the new rash of building. Thode deliberately wiped out the border between the Middle Ages and the Renaissance: "From Giotto to Raphael a uniform development takes place, based on a uniform world-view and religious conception. To want to separate Gothic art, reaching till 1400, from the Renaissance, commencing in 1400 (as is still usually done in the textbooks of art history), means to fail to recognize the organic unity comprising them both." [35] The liberation of the individual, "Who in a personal, harmonic conception of the sense of nature and religion—on the whole still within the bounds of the Catholic faith but unconsciously already venturing beyond those bounds—conquers his rights vis-à-vis the collectivity," was for Thode the intellectual content of the process. "The innermost impetus effecting such miracles is the awakening highly individual sensitivity." To what extent the picture of Francis is distorted and his influence on the development of Italian culture overrated need not be discussed at this point.

It was not Henry Thode who was the spiritual progenitor of the widespread reverence for Francis in aesthetic circles. His book remained restricted to those interested in the history of art, and it was with a certain amount of vexation that

Thode in the Preface to his second edition (1904) claimed for himself the honor of having sketched the new picture of Saint Francis long before Sabatier captivated the world with his *Vie de Saint François d'Assise* (1893).

The work of Paul Sabatier remained outside the controversy on the origins of the Renaissance, in that he, unlike Gebhart and Thode, was not concerned primarily with defining the relation of Francis to the Renaissance, but with describing the life of the inspiring saint in all its fine, lively colors and tones. The appealing but inaccurate picture that this French Protestant theologian painted in his gently poetic book was one of Francis as a subjective, lyric spirit who reconquered the beauty of the world for the fervent, passionate devotion that introduces personal emotional needs into religion; and who bowing in filial respect before the old, rigid Church that saw the danger of this new form of devotion, was to become a man of melancholy disillusionment, and almost a martyr to his own exalted goal. But these were precisely the qualities that little by little had become associated with the concept of the Renaissance: individual sensitivity, acceptance of the world and a feeling for beauty, a personal attitude toward doctrine and authority. Hence perhaps Sabatier has contributed more than anyone else to a shift in the nature and the dating of the concept Renaissance. It was now no longer primarily a growth of the mind that was conceived of in the term, but a growth of the heart: the opening of the eyes and the soul to all the excellence of the world and the individual personality. Burckhardt's thesis of individualism and the discovery of the world and man had now been carried to the extreme. The significance of the revival of classical culture for the process of the Renaissance was pushed completely into the background. That Lorenzo Valla anticipated an utterly salutary and revitalizing effect from the restoration of a pure Latinity, that Politian penned the most lively and attractive Latin verse that had been written since Horace, that Plato was revered at Florence as the new messenger of salvation—these and similar traits of the Renaissance seem to have become totally insignificant.

What had happened? The concept Renaissance, identified as it now was with individualism and a worldly spirit, had had to be stretched so far that it had completely lost its elasticity. It actually meant nothing any more. There was not a single major cultural phenomenon of the Middle Ages that did not fall under the concept Renaissance in at least one of its aspects. Gradually everything that seemed spontaneous and singular in the later Middle Ages had been lifted out of them and given a place among the origins of the Renaissance. There was no end in sight. If the opening of the eyes, the awakening of the personal, was the soul of the Renaissance, then there was no reason not to revere that other great lyric spirit, Bernard of Clairvaux, beside and above Francis as the first bearer of the crown of the Renaissance. On close examination, had there ever been any Middle Ages?

There was only one step that could still be taken: to detach the concept Renaissance completely from its basis, the revival of classical studies. In the field of art history in the strict sense that step had been taken long before by the Parisian historian of art Louis Courajod, a disciple of De la Borde. In his *Leçons professées à l'école du Louvre* (1888)—especially in the second part, on "the true origins of the Renaissance"—Courajod developed the dual thesis that the Gothic style regenerated itself quite independently by turning toward an absolute naturalism, and that it was from this regeneration that the Renaissance sprang. Neither the classical example nor Italy had any causal significance in that process such as had been attributed to them in earlier times: new forms were emerging at various points in Europe as early as the fourteenth century. In France it was primarily the Flemish masters who brought the new feeling for nature and reality. If elsewhere "individualism" had become the term used to summarize the concept of the Renaissance, for Courajod it was "realism." The bewildering, painful realism of Jan van Eyck now seemed to some scholars the most salient example of the genuine Renaissance spirit. In the trial of Courajod the Belgian art historian Fierens Gevaert devoted a study to Melchior Broederlam, Claus Sluter, and the Van Eycks and their predecessors under the title *La renaissance septentrionale* (1905).

It was a German art historian—Carl Neumann, the author of a remarkable book on Rembrandt—who formulated the total rejection of antiquity as the generative principle of the Renaissance. With Byzantine studies as his starting point, Neumann had noticed that there were suspicious resemblances between the formal virtuosity of the Italian humanists and the scholastic aridity of dying Byzantium.[36] Already fully conscious that the true origins of the true Renaissance were to be found in the development of a feeling of personality, an awareness of nature and the world, he arrived at the view that imitation of the ancients was not the fecund element of the Renaissance, but on the contrary a curbing, even a deadening element. The most typical aspect of the Renaissance in the old, limited sense, that is to say, the elegant preciosity and literary snobbism of the humanists, was nothing but Byzantinism, an alienation from the genuine, fertile spirit of the new Western culture flowering directly out of the Middle Ages, and as such it could lead only to aridity. Antiquity had diverted the true Renaissance from its course: "Now the classical examples were consciously taken as standards in life and ethics, now art was deprived of its soul in an urge toward the great, monumental airs and the noble gestures of the ancients and was removed from any real content by formal virtuosity."

Could such a complete reversal of the original concept of the Renaissance be correct? Or was Neumann's brilliantly presented thesis itself not free from a certain amount of *bel-esprit?* I shall here merely point out a few mistakes in his major premise. Even Voltaire in his time knew that the direct influence of the Byzantine exiles on the revival of higher culture cannot have been large. If some of the humanists in Rome and Florence reveal traits reminiscent of Byzantium it is not because those traits come from Byzantium. And even if Byzantium did have a certain influence on literary life, the Renaissance certainly did not acquire the example of antiquity in the pictorial arts from there. And finally, if classicism had led to mannerism and rigidity in senile Byzantium, how different its effect was in Italy, where it fell on the almost virgin soil of a ripe, fertile popular life. Canceling out the classical element in the Renaissance would definitely not serve to clarify the concept.

II

Was it not better either to stop using the term Renaissance altogether for the time being or to restore it to its original, restricted sense? It must have been clear from the oscillations of the concept that the contrast between the Middle Ages and the Renaissance, still a basic postulate, was not sufficiently defined, even if it might eventually prove to make sense. As a starting point scholars had always taken a vague conception of "medieval culture," which had to do service as the absolute antipode of the Renaissance, regardless of whether the Middle Ages were made to end a bit earlier or a bit later to accommodate the emergence of a new culture. Yet had a serious attempt actually ever been made to give a clear and positive definition of that concept medieval culture, the postulated opposite to the Renaissance? Michelet's negative view of the Middle Ages as everything static and dull and dead had long since been rejected. And the delimitation of the concept Renaissance was not only unsatisfactory on the medieval side: the relation between the Renaissance and the Reformation as cultural phenomena was also far from accurately circumscribed.

Moreover, it had been all too readily accepted that the fifteenth century and the first half of the sixteenth should count without reserve as the age of the Renaissance, at least in Italy. Had it been sufficiently investigated how many of the older, medieval elements of culture continued their life deep into and beyond the sixteenth century, even after the new spirit had gained the upper hand?

And finally, was the conclusion of the Renaissance a settled affair? Its origins had been sought diligently, but in regard to its transition to Baroque and Counter Reformation scholars were usually content with generalities amounting to the fact that Hispanization and Jesuitism brought an untimely death to the true, vital Renaissance in Italy, causing it to degenerate in mannerism, though on the other side of the Alps the Renaissance spirit was allowed to live on deep into the seventeenth century. Here, too, an account needed to be given of what it was one desired actually to understand by the term Renaissance, and what its relationship was to the intellectual currents of the seventeenth century.

In fact there was another problem looming up beyond this last one: the relationship of the Renaissance to the great Enlightenment was also eventually to demand attention. Had it been the dawn of Enlightenment? Was there a link between Renaissance and Enlightenment, or rather a contrast?

Scholars had always arbitrarily assumed that the great gap lay between the Middle Ages and the Renaissance (even though that gap had proved more and more unfindable) and that Renaissance man in his most essential traits was already representative of modern man. But the question was whether on closer inspection the great dividing lines might not prove to lie at least as clearly between Renaissance and modern culture.

No satisfactory answer has yet been given to all these questions, and to some of them hardly any have been attempted. The problem of the Renaissance has by no means been examined from all sides.

In earlier times the Renaissance and the Reformation were as a rule considered together as the dawning of a new age. That was the rationalist historical attitude. No longer aware how much it was alienated from early Protestantism, a generation of liberal rationalists believed that in the two movements it could hail the great liberation of the spirit, the dropping of the fetters from the hands and the scales from the eyes. Freedom and truth seemed the portion of both, in contrast to the delusion and the oppression of medieval theology and the medieval Church. But upon further study of details scholars could not avoid the conclusion that the content and the purport of the Renaissance and the Reformation ran parallel for but a very brief distance. Only in France did the two streams flow in the same bed at the outset: in the circle of Margaret of Navarre—the patroness of Rabelais, Clément Marot, Lefèvre d'Etaples, and Bonaventure Desperiers—Renaissance and Reformation tendencies were still undifferentiated. That harmony came to an end with the appearance of Calvin, and eventually the contrast between the new doctrine and the renovated culture would be even stronger there than in the Lutheran countries: with Ronsard and his group the French Renaissance beat a total retreat to the bosom of the Mother Church. The strict piety of the Protestants, their

puritanism and their violent urge to action, opposed to the
desire for tranquillity and the often frivolous indifference of
the humanists, made the Reformation and the Renaissance
rather contrasts than related expressions of one and the same
spirit. What perhaps divided them most was the genuinely
popular character of the Reformation movement, in contrast
to the courtly or learned and sometimes snobbish exclusivism
of the Renaissance. They were antipodes, not one entity of
modern culture blazing its trial in a dual form.

This concept of the antithetical tendencies of the Renaissance and the Reformation was further strengthened when
Ernst Troeltsch argued in a convincing essay[1] that the Reformation was not at all the dawning of modern culture; in its
nature and its purport early Protestantism was a continuation
of genuinely medieval ideals of culture, while the modern spirit
that was later to find expression in the Enlightenment and in
the ideas of tolerance and the right to a personal opinion in
matters of conscience, was prepared by the Renaissance. The
Middle Ages were indeed perpetuated in early Protestantism
as long as the starting point clung to was that medieval thought
signified an absolutely authoritative attitude of mind placing
the Church—as the living embodiment and organization of the
immediate revelation of God—squarely in the foreground and
recognizing as the only purpose of the individual and of mankind their efforts to be saved, without concerning themselves
with secular civilization as such. Early Protestantism adhered
unreservedly to compulsive doctrinary authority and shunned
worldly civilization on principle just as much as medieval
Catholicism had done. "Under these circumstances it is
obvious that Protestantism cannot be the direct representative
of the inception of the modern world. On the contrary, it
appears at present as a renewal and strengthening of the ideal
of a culture constrained by the church, a complete reaction of
medieval thought devouring the beginnings of a free, worldly
culture that had been achieved."

The Reformation, then, in sharp contrast to the trends of
the Renaissance, was almost inimical to culture: that is what
Troeltsch's surprising view amounts to. Later, yielding to the
criticism offered from many sides, he admitted that, though it
was not its primary aim, the Reformation had at many points
also created the "new soil" on which the bases of new political
and social forms were established: through the removal of half

of Europe from papal universalism, the abolition of the ecclesiastical hierarchy and the monastic system, the abrogation of ecclesiastical courts, the confiscation of Church properties and their use for political and cultural ends, and the destruction of celibacy and professional asceticism.

Here, however, we are concerned with neither the tenability of Troeltsch's thesis in itself nor the vast distinction he makes between the significance to cultural history of Calvinism and Anabaptism on the one hand and Lutheranism (which he greatly belittles) on the other, but with the consequences of his new insights for the question of the Renaissance.

If medieval culture did indeed flow on beneath the Renaissance into the Reformation, then the borderline between the Middle Ages and the Renaissance should not only be drawn vertically but also horizontally. In that case, the Renaissance was only to a small extent the beginning of a new age. This was the fact that Troeltsch, whatever the correctness of his view of Protestantism may be, illuminated more clearly than had been done before: the Renaissance did not by any means determine the culture of the sixteenth century as a whole, but only one important aspect of it. Merely to mention such names as Savonarola, Luther, Thomas Münzer, Calvin, and Loyola is enough to deny that Renaissance is synonymous with sixteenth-century culture. All these forceful personalities are very sixteenth-century and very un-Renaissance. The concept Renaissance covers but one aspect of the rich process of civilization, which was, after all, not restricted to the arts, learning, and literature. It illuminates only an elite, and even that elite perhaps only in a part of its complicated and contradictory essence. The cultural development flows on underneath the Renaissance. The Renaissance is only a very superficial phenomenon; the true, essential cultural transitions flowed directly out of the Middle Ages.[2] This, however, seems to me an exaggeration of a point of view that is in itself true. Let us again quote the wise words of Burckhardt, now with a different purport: "The Renaissance would not have been the process of world-wide significance which it is if its elements could be so easily separated from one another." Nonetheless, it cannot be denied that the Renaissance was a Sunday suit.

Or do we still have too narrow a view of the Renaissance? Do we see it too much in contrast to the vast substructure of popular culture, and do we perhaps overestimate its extravagance and hence its modern character? Burckhardt's sharp, clear image is still too indelibly printed on our retina—that image whose traits were an unbridled, free sense of personality, a pagan zest for the world, and an indifference to, a disdain for religion. It might possibly be that even the Renaissance itself was much more "medieval" than we are wont to see it. The gap dividing it from the Reformation, which seems to have become so broad, would in that way prove not to be so unbridgeable after all.

The spirit of the Renaissance is indeed much less modern than one is constantly inclined to believe. An established contrast between medieval and modern culture is that the Middle Ages set a binding authority and authoritative norms for everything intellectual—not only for religion, with philosophy and learning in its train, but for law, art, etiquette, amusement. The modern period, on the other hand, vindicates the right of the individual to determine his own way of life, his convictions, his taste. But where, then, does the Renaissance stand? Certainly not on the modern side.[3] Not only its purblind reverence for the perpetual authority and exemplary quality of the ancient stamps the Renaissance as a culture of authority; its whole spirit is extremely normative, seeking for eternally valid criteria of beauty, statesmanship, virtue, or truth. Whether one takes Dürer or Machiavelli, Ariosto or Ronsard, they all strive after impersonal, strictly circumscribed, unequivocal, and completely expressed systems of art or knowledge. None of them is aware of the unapproachable and ineffable spontaneity and contradiction of man in his deepest promptings. Doubts rise for a moment whether the individualism of the Renaissance accepted out-of-hand is such a useful hypothesis as it seems at first glance. But let us put aside such doubts for the time being.

Before the relation of the Renaissance and the Reformation could be clearly determined, a serious fault in the view of the Renaissance current at the time had to be corrected—the notion of its pagan, or at least areligious, character. Burckhardt quite definitely had a large share in developing that notion. He had devoted a great deal of attention to the paganistic peculiarities of the humanists. His strong emphasis on self-determination in matters of conscience and the predominant mundanity of Renaissance man was by itself enough to imply that a true man of the Renaissance cannot have been

genuinely Christian in his thinking. And were the writings of
the humanists, from Poggio and Valla straight down to Erasmus, not filled to overflowing with satire of every shade on
the Church and the monks, with skepticism and snobbish
superiority? Even Bayle, in his time, had been convinced that
all those fellows had "little religion." And Burckhardt could
declare that "in Italy at the Renaissance, religion (save perhaps in the form of superstition) was really alive only in the
form of art." [4]

Here new misconceptions were involved. In the first place
the custom of satirizing the Church and churchmen or haught-
ily considering oneself superior to them was not at all a theme
specific to the humanists. It had been very widespread ever
since the day of Scholasticism. Even in the thirteenth century
Averroism flourished alongside Thomas Aquinas. Even then
in the auditoria of the University of Paris and in the towns and
the courts of Italy there was a generation of parlor heretics
who prided themselves on their rejection of immortality and
were able to maintain a cautious peace with the Church. They
are the ones whom Dante condemns to hell as Epicureans.
As is known, even Giotto was suspected. Nowhere is it as
clear as here how difficult it is to draw sharp lines in cultural
history. Dante himself, who had seen the father of his friend
Guido Cavalcanti in the flaming sepulchers next to Farinata
degli Uberti, saw the master of Averroism, Siger de Brabant,
in the celestial paradise next to Thomas himself among the
lights of theology.[5]

If this could happen to Dante, then we must be on our
guard and not label the Renaissance as unchristian on the
basis of a bit of satire and frivolity. Furthermore, the impious
or impiously behaving humanists did not by any means make
up the whole of the Renaissance. If the true nature and
purport of the Renaissance were really revealed in their non-
chalance, then there would be a peculiar absurdity in the
concept of that great cultural phenomenon as a whole, for
everyone must be well aware that, for all its cross-threads
of classicism and profanity, Renaissance art was and remained
largely Christian in matter and in content, just as Christian
as medieval art before and the art of the Counter Reformation
afterwards. Whether one takes Romanesque and Gothic, the
Sienese and the Giottesque, Flemings and Quattrocentists,
Leonardo and Raphael, or Veronese and Guido Reni, on up

to high baroque, the sacred aim and the sacred subject were always the chief inspiration for art. Everyone assumes that medieval art sprang from the deepest piety. Nor does anyone doubt the severe, sincere piety of those who were newly molded in the Catholicism purified by Trent and the Jesuits. And should the art of the Renaissance proper, between the two, be largely pious pretension and pretentiousness except in the case of a few? The highest flowering of art springing from the most feeble inspiration? Would that not make the Renaissance all too incomprehensible?

One knew better, of course, as soon as one recalled the individual characters themselves, dropping for a moment the general notion of the paganism of the Renaissance. Paganism was the mask worn to acquire distinction; in the deeper layers of most personalities religious faith remained unshaken. The heroic piety of Michelangelo might serve as the symbol for the heart of the Renaissance in this as in other respects.

The pagan element of the Renaissance has been extremely overestimated. Even in humanist literature—the only domain where it ran rampant—it did not hold anything like the place it might perhaps seem to have occupied. An exaggerated light had been thrown on the pagan audacities, often not much more than fashionable swaggering; and the broad foundation of Christian conviction in the works of the humanists, none the weaker for a stoic strain, had been left in the dark. Petrarch and Boccaccio had wished to place antiquity completely in the service of the Christian faith.[6] And among later figures as well there definitely was no dichotomy, such as one might assume on the face of things, between the passion for pagan antiquity and the Christian faith.

Once the notion of the non-Christian character of the Renaissance was moderated in this way the contrast between the Renaissance and the Reformation lost much of its sharpness. And it became apparent that essentially the two cultural currents had more in common than had seemed possible, considering the great contrast in their attitudes toward life and the world. The research of the German philologist Konrad Burdach has brought remarkable things to light on this point of the common origins of the Renaissance and the Reformation from one and the same sphere of ideas. He has demonstrated that in their beginnings the Renaissance and the Reformation (including the Catholic Counter Reformation) had shared an idea, an expectation of salvation, a very old kernel of a notion of intellectual renewal. Of course, that is not at all to imply that the two phenomena were the result of that idea. No one would attempt such a one-sidedly ultra-idealistic explanation. The Renaissance and the Reformation were the product of the cultural developments of the Middle Ages in all their complexity, hence of intellectual, economic, and political factors. But it is of significance that the ideas animating the exponents of the two great movements sprang in part from a single germ.

I intentionally neglected these connections in discussing earlier how the awareness of revival, restoration, rebirth, or renewal gradually developed in the exponents of the Renaissance. It is now time to point out that the concept of a "restoration of *bonnes lettres*" which we encountered in Rabelais was merely a restriction of a much broader hope of revival which had occupied minds for centuries. The listing of Joachim of Floris as the first precursor of the Renaissance can now be given a firmer foothold in an accurately definable chain of ideas.

The origin of the whole chain of ideas lies in the New Testament notion of being born again, which itself was rooted in concepts of renewal in the Psalms and the Prophets.[7] The gospels and the epistles had acquainted the mind with ideas of renewal, rebirth, regeneration, some of them related to the effect of the sacraments, especially baptism and communion, some of them to the expectation of ultimate salvation, and some to the conversion of the living man to a state of grace.[8] The Vulgate used the terms *renasci, regeneratio, nova vita, renovari, renovatio, reformari*.

This sacramental, eschatological, and ethical concept of a spiritual renewal was given another content when, late in the twelfth century, Joachim of Floris transferred it to an expectation of a really impending transformation of the Christian world. The first state of the world, that of the Old Testament, was one of the law; the present state was one of grace, but it would soon be followed by one of a richer grace, such as was promised in the Gospel of John.[9] The first age was founded in knowledge, the second in wisdom; the third would be in perfect knowledge. The first was that of servility, the second of innocent obedience; the third would be that of freedom. There was fear in the first, and faith in the second;

there would be love in the third. Starlight illuminated the first, and dawn the second; the sun would shine over the third. The first brought nettles, the second roses; the third would bring lilies. A new leader would arise, a universal pope of the new Jerusalem who would renew Christian religion. I need not consider here to what extent Joachim's ideas were of influence on Francis of Assisi himself. It is certain that part of his followers, the Spirituals, took them up and elaborated them; it is also certain that Franciscan preaching and Franciscan poetry and mysticism spread the idea of the *renovatio vitae* among the widest circles, with the emphasis falling now more on the inward renewal of the individual person, then again more on the expectation of an actual secular event that would bring spiritual renewal. *Renovatio, reformatio* became a spiritual watchword of the thirteenth century.

It was as such that Dante took it up. His *Vita nuova* is incomprehensible except on the basis of these ideas. In the *Commedia,* however, the concept of renewal was broadened. Though still strongly under the influence of the Spirituals, it acquired a political and a cultural significance in Dante alongside its religious meaning. He who was to come would bring peace and liberate Italy. And now in a most remarkable way the Christian idea of rebirth encountered a purely classical concept of revival, that of Vergil's Fourth Eclogue:

Magnus ab integro saeclorum nascitur ordo.
Iam redit et virgo, redeunt Saturnia regna;
Iam nova progenies caelo dimittitur alto.●

Even the earliest Christian theologians had interpreted these words as a prophecy of Christ's birth, but now Dante associated them with the political renewal he so fervently desired and the aesthetic renewal he clearly detected in his day.

The symbol of the world pining for renewal and liberation was for Dante and for Petrarch lamenting Rome. The fruit-

● The great Sequence of the Ages starts afresh. Justice, the Virgin, comes back to dwell with us, and the rule of Saturn is restored. The Firstborn of the New Age is already on his way from high heaven down to earth.[10]

fulness of this symbol was that Rome could be seen in any number of roles. As the capital of Italy, subjected to the pressures of factional controversy and violence; as the center of the Church, which needed to be purified and reformed in head and body; as the setting for classical civic virtue and classical culture: "Rome, that the good world made for man's abode. . . ." [11] The basis of the image was always the thought that a return to old times would bring salvation.

And it was not long before a fervent visionary, Cola di Rienzi, transformed that obsession with ancient Rome into a basis for political action. As Burdach has demonstrated, the core of the popular tribune's notions in his strange letters consists of the concepts *renasci* and *renovari,* half in the mystical, religious sense, half in the political. Rienzi fell as a result of his own weakness, and his unseasonable work fell with him, but the symbol *Roma rinata* remained alive and filled the minds of later generations. At one time the thought of a return to ancient Roman institutions and virtues predominated in it, at another that of the restoration of pure Latinity and the noble arts, at still another the fervently desired purification of the Church and the faith. Hence renovation, revival, renascence were already the longing of an age, a nostalgia for old magnificence, even before the positive transformations in art, learning, and life later to be summarized under those terms had taken place. And as soon as minds became aware of a true renewal of things in and around them, as soon as they felt themselves the exponents of a new artistic ideal, a finer literary taste and enriched means of expression, a more critical attitude toward sacred tradition, that awareness was as a matter of course classified under the luster of the already existent ideal of revival. When the fountain began to flow the jug was already at hand.

Thus one sees the humanists on the one hand and the reformers on the other making use of concepts of restoration and rebirth which were partial applications and limitations of what was originally a very broad idea of renewal. In the circle of Zwingli the word *renascens,* applied to Christendom and the gospel, became almost a slogan.[12] "Happy we, if proper studies may be reborn through the favor of the gods," Melanchthon exclaimed. The moral and religious aspect and the aesthetic and literary aspect of the Renaissance ideal merge into one another without any clear border (and the harmless plural of Melanchthon's "gods" says volumes: not for the pagan but the Christian character of humanism).

"Now blossoms anew probity, honesty, justice, in a word, the gospel that was hidden in darkness for a long time; letters are being reborn [*renascuntur*]," a friend writes to Zwingli. "It may be hoped that some day the innocence of the ancients will be reborn, just as we witness the rebirth of their civilization," the Swiss reformer himself wrote to Beatus Rhenanus. And Erasmus, from whom these thoughts first emanated, set the three great expectations side by side in a letter to Leo X dated 1517:

> This our age,—which bids fair to be an age of gold, if ever such there was,—wherein I see, under your happy auspices and by your holy counsels, three of the chief blessings of humanity are about to be restored to her. I mean, first that truly Christian piety, which has in many ways fallen into decay, secondly, learning of the best sort [a superlative form of *bonae literae*—J. H.], hitherto partly neglected and partly corrupted, and thirdly, the public and lasting concord of Christendom, the source and parent of Piety and Erudition.[13]

For us, who look back and judge things according to results, the gap between the literary and the biblical humanists seems larger than it actually was. The idea inspiring them both bore the same hallmark, though the mind of the one was less pious than that of the other. Both of them were permeated by a nostalgia for the old, primeval purity and an aspiration to renew themselves from within. Whether their longings were directed toward primitive Christianity, the noble, well-governed Rome of the Catos and Scipios, or pure Latinity, perfect poetry, rediscovered art, it was always a longing to go backward in time: *renovatio, restitutio, restauratio.*

Assiduous study of the development of the *idea* of the Renaissance, of which I have only given a very perfunctory survey here, also has its dangers. Anyone who goes at all deeply into such studies as those of Burdach and Borinski (who hunt in even the most remote corners of classical and medieval literature for links in the great chain of the idea

of revival), will not always be able to dismiss the feeling that
with all this the problem of the Renaissance itself—the question of what it was, of what it consisted—sometimes threatens
to fade into the background. It is extremely useful, and for
a proper understanding indispensable, to know how the notion
and the sentiment of revival developed, but the important
question we must return to continues to be: What, actually,
was the cultural transformation we call the Renaissance? What
did it consist of, what was its effect?

Before these questions can be answered there is a precondition that has still not been fulfilled: a clear definition of the
opposition Middle Ages-Renaissance; and a second one that
has been fulfilled even less: a similarly clear definition of the
relation between the Renaissance and modern culture.

A description was given above of how the concept Renaissance threatened to lose all content because scholars saw
themselves required to move it further and further back into
the Middle Ages. As more and more of the most characteristic
cultural phenomena of the late Middle Ages were claimed as
germs and origins of the Renaissance, the image of medieval
culture threatened to melt and collapse like a snowman.
Eventually everything that was alive in the Middle Ages was
called Renaissance. But then what was left of the Middle Ages
themselves? Was it not possible first to determine what were
the essential properties of the true medieval spirit in all its
forms of expression—religion, thought, art, society—and then
to trace at what points the Renaissance had broken with all
that?

One approach believes that it can detect the great break
and the fundamental contrast between the Middle Ages and
the Renaissance, and that it can describe it precisely. So far
as I know it is not to be found in the scholarly literature of
the historians of culture and of art, but it is alive as a fruitful
conviction in the hearts of many present-day artists. Who
would dare to deny them a voice in such questions? If I
should have to name one person who gave life to this approach, then it would be Viollet-le-Duc, and along with him
perhaps William Morris. The approach amounts to this: the
Middle Ages were in everything the period of synthetic thought
and strong community sense. The true essence of medieval
culture was in the idea of building together. Art was aware of
its task of giving form to the loftiest ideas, not for vain delight

and personal diversion, but for the exalting expression of what affected everyone. All visual art was subordinated to architecture and was symbolic and monumental; the imitation of natural reality was never the final goal. The secret formative power of geometric proportions was still known and applied. In the Romanesque cathedral and even the early Gothic, and in the Byzantine mosaic, the genuine medieval spirit triumphed, just as it did in the intellectual accomplishments of Thomas Aquinas and the symbols of mysticism.

In this view of things the arrival of the Renaissance meant the weakening and near-loss of all these principles. In place of the co-operating community came the ambitious individual (here this point of view touches on Burckhardt's thesis). The personal realism of Giotto already signified a falling-off. An analytical art depicting reality overgrew and repressed the old and exalted synthetic, symbolic art. Even the fresco involved the elaboration of the unimportant detail, but at least it preserved its connection with architecture. The panel completely abandoned that connection: the painting became a furnishing and merchandise, a distinguished curio instead of a segment of a spiritual organism. Naturalism and individualism (which are considered as established characteristics of the Renaissance) are merely morbid symptoms in a great process of degeneration.

It would be impossible to deny that this conception, limited to the evolution of the visual arts, contains elements of a deep truth. Undoubtedly such a view of the Middle Ages is based on a recognition of the most essential element determining the culture of that period. But it curtails and simplifies the rich and heterogeneous material of history to such an extent that it is useless as an aid in understanding history. Its place is in the series of great metaphysical dualisms, valuable as props of life but unsuitable for use as scholarly distinctions. Anyone familiar with medieval history in any detail knows that it resists being summarized under the notions of collectivism and synthesis. The belief that the *chansons de geste* and the cathedrals were the products of a mysteriously, impersonally working folk-spirit is actually an inheritance from romanticism. Medievalists have abandoned it long since. Everywhere that the meager sources allow us more than a glimpse of how products of the medieval spirit came into being, individuals come to the fore, with clearly personal ambitions and thoughts. How could anyone actually ever claim individualism for the Renaissance, with figures like Abelard, Guibert de Nogent, Bertrand de Born, Chrétien de Troyes, Wolfram von Eschenbach, Villard de Honnecourt, and scores of others on the yonder side of the dividing line? To maintain the notion of a collectivist, synthetic Middle Ages in all the strict validity that the point of view demands, one would have to begin by excluding three fourths of all medieval intellectual production and restricting oneself to a very early period for which there are few sources and even less knowledge, so that the thesis would rest on an extremely negative foundation. Even the social and economic structure of medieval life does not offer as much support as one might think, for there, too, recent research has pointed out a number of individualistic traits where earlier nothing but collectivism was seen.[14]

The rejection of such a rigorous, clear-cut division between the Middle Ages and the Renaissance also affects Lamprecht's once sensational *Kulturzeitalter,* in so far as the periods under discussion are concerned. When Lamprecht elevated the Middle Ages to "the typical age" as opposed to the individualistic age that succeeded it, he actually had merely taken Burckhardt's individualism as the basic characteristic of the Renaissance and considered everything contradictory to it as characteristic for the preceding cultural period. Medieval man, in contrast to his descendant of the Renaissance, supposedly had an eye only for the typical, the general traits uniting all things, and not for the specific that leads the mind to react to each thing in its particularity. Lamprecht believed that he could describe the whole of medieval intellectual life with that single concept of "typicalness," which was actually nothing more than the reverse of individualism.

Lamprecht's thesis has had its day, and this is not the place to dispute it in detail; so far as I know, no one uses the designation "the typical age" any more. Everyone has come to see that it will not do to deny the Middle Ages every trace of individualism.

True, it will be said; but that does not alter the fact that the Renaissance was the age of individualism par excellence, that the individual has never made himself the basis of his personal thoughts and actions more than he did then. Even if the notion of the collectivist, synthetic character of the Middle

Ages is not valid in such a strict sense as was thought, individualism remains the basic characteristic and the essence of the Renaissance.

A protest must also be entered against this belief. It is wrong to follow Burckhardt in considering individualism as the all-dominating, fundamental trait of the Renaissance. It is at best one trait out of many, crossed by completely contradictory traits. Only unwarranted generalization has been able to elevate individualism into the one principle explaining the Renaissance.

To prove this thesis, or to make it acceptable, may remain the subject of later studies, if one admits for the time being the validity of the point that one must in any case begin by abandoning a single formula to explain the whole of the Renaissance. The scholar must open his eyes wide to the gay multiplicity and even contrariety of the forms in which the Renaissance found expression. And as long as individualism appears to have been just as much a dominating factor in history long before and long after the Renaissance, one would do better to declare it taboo.

Again: the concept Renaissance is not defined, neither in its limits in time nor in the nature and essence of the phenomena constituting it. The terms to define it cannot be borrowed from the history of the Renaissance itself. The poles must be placed wider apart. Over against the Middle Ages one must set modern culture. It must be asked: What are the characteristics of the culture which may be called medieval? What are the basic traits in which modern culture deviates from medieval? Between the two lies the Renaissance. It is often called a period of transition, but nonetheless it is involuntarily placed too much on the modern side. We almost inevitably run ahead of time in our historical judgments. We are so sensitive to the relationships we discern between the past and what has since developed and is familiar to us that we nearly always overestimate the emerging elements of a culture. We have to be corrected time and again by the sources themselves, which display the period as much more primitive, burdened much more than we had expected with accumulated tradition.

The Renaissance was a turning of the tide. The image for the transition from the Middle Ages to modern times is (and how could it help but be?) not that of one revolution of a great wheel, but that of a long succession of waves rolling onto a beach, each of them breaking at a different point and a different moment. Everywhere the lines between the old and the new are different; each cultural form, each thought turns at its own time, and the transformation is never that of the whole complex of civilization.

To define the Renaissance in its relation between the Middle Ages and modern culture will, consequently, be a work for many scholars. Here, where I am only concerned with the present state of the problem, I may restrict myself to a cursory sketch of the lines that such research should follow, especially outside the fields of art and letters in the strict sense.[15]

When according to our customary (and indispensable) periodization the modern period began, none of the great medieval forms of thought had died out. In both the old faith and the new (and in everything connected with them, thus also in the Renaissance with its storehouse of religious material), the symbolic, sacramental way of thinking (which does not inquire first of all what is the natural causal relationship of things, but their significance in God's plan for the world) maintained itself. Two basic qualities of medieval thought, formalism and anthropomorphism, faded only very slowly. Machiavelli was just as strict a formalist as Gregory VII.

The search for truth and the acquisition of knowledge had meant to the medieval mind the substantiation by logical proof of given, independent truths, whether those truths lay open to the light of day or were obscured for the time being because the old, genuine sources had been forgotten. The whole truth regarding each thing could be expressed in a few logical formulas, and the revelation was somewhere to be found— in the Scriptures, in antiquity. This was how the Middle Ages conceived of the urge to truth and knowledge. For the modern mind it was to be to estimate, develop, and define truths as yet unexpressed, each of them in turn raising new questions. Inductive research, the view of nature and the world as a secret to be unraveled—that is the modern thinker's approach to his task. But did this change in spirit come with the Renaissance? Definitely not. Leonardo da Vinci may himself have been a representative of the modern method of searching for truth, but the Renaissance as a whole was still inclined toward the old attitude, believing in authority. The turning point did not come until Descartes.

Copernicus brought the concept of an unlimited universe. But that is not to say that the geocentric and anthropocentric view gave way at once in the sixteenth century. The Renaissance placed the earth and man at the pivot of the universe with an emphasis that was different from that of the medieval world-view, but that was no less strong. In fact, the most anthropocentric notion of all, the teleological view of creation as a wise system for the edification and benefit of man, did not flourish until the eighteenth century. Or is it by nature impossible for us to give up placing the earth and man at the center of things?

The boundary in time between medieval rejection of the world and its acceptance by the more recent periods of thought is just as diffuse. It is so easy to imagine that the Middle Ages as a whole professed a *contemptus mundi,* and that with the coming of the Renaissance the full orchestra suddenly struck up a jubilant arrangement of the theme *iuvat vivere,* it is a joy to be alive. But the truth is so different. In the first place, medieval Christian thought never rejected the world in its beauty and its pleasures as completely as is usually assumed. In a thousand ways enjoyment of the world was given a lawful place in the life pleasing to God. And an optimistic, aesthetic view of the world began to break through the old negation even in the intellects representing Scholasticism at its height: in Thomas Aquinas, in Dante. True, on this point it is the Renaissance that sings the paean of the great, new delight in the world, with the voices of Pico, Rabelais, and scores of others. But did those voices dominate their age? Certainly they did not drown out the voices of Luther, Calvin, and Loyola. And is it so certain that their paean was the voice of the Renaissance as a whole? Or was the basic tone of most representatives of the Renaissance not much graver than we imagine? The victory (was it a Pyrrhic victory?) of basic optimism came, again, only with the eighteenth century. The two forms in which optimistic thought found embodiment, the concept of progress and that of evolution, were neither of them Renaissance forms. Also in this it is not at all possible to place the Renaissance on one level with modern culture.

A whole complex of views regarding the attitude of the

individual toward life and society which are fairly basic to
modern culture was alien to the Middle Ages. The goal of a
personal life-work as an end in itself, the endeavor to give
expression to one's life and personality by consciously developing all the abilities and potentialities one has; the awareness of personal independence and the fatal delusion of a
right to earthly happiness; and allied to that, responsibility
toward society, the notion of a personal task of helping to
protect and preserve it or change and improve it, the urge
to reform, the desire for social justice, and in pathological
cases the basic and permanent complaint against society whatever the prevailing system may be, expressing itself as a
feeling of being wronged or as one of superiority to society—
all these emotions medieval man either did not know at all
or knew only in the garb of religious duty and religious
morality.

What did the Renaissance know of them? No more than
the germs. Renaissance man, it is true, had something of
a sense of personal independence and personal aims, though
not by any means as strong and as general a sense as Burckhardt attributed to him. But the whole altruistic element of
this cluster of ideas, the sense of social responsibility, was
largely lacking. Socially the Renaissance was extraordinarily
sterile and immobile, and in this respect marked rather a
stagnation than a revival as compared with the Middle Ages
and their religiously based social awareness.

One of the most important and fundamental changes between medieval and modern culture is the shift in the concepts of class, service, and respect, and to some extent their
decay. These changes are so complicated that it is out of the
question even to delineate them here. I can merely point
briefly to two generally known results of that process in order
to demonstrate that also in this field the Renaissance is in
no sense to be placed on the same level with modern culture.
The great process of abstraction which, instead of continuing
to view the contrast between high and low in degree as a
result of difference in power and wealth, transferred it to the
ethical and intellectual domain, had actually already set in
in the thirteenth century. The troubadours in their courtly
lyrics had developed the concept of a nobility of the heart.
Then came appreciation—highly theoretical appreciation—
of the simple and diligent peasant life nourished by the images

of the pastoral poem. The Renaissance inherited all these notions from the Middle Ages and furbished them in classical colors. Ideals of life that had earlier been separate were now coalesced: together, the courtly and learned nobleman, the erudite monk who knew how to behave in the world, and the wealthy burgher with his appreciation of learning and art provided the type of the humanist, at home in every court, acquainted with all learning and theology, suited (or imagining himself to be suited) for every city or state office. But this does not mean at all that the earlier independent forms of life ceased to exist. The medieval ideal of knighthood, the old chivalric code and everything that went with it, was not only retained undiluted, but was filled with new fervor by Ariosto, Tasso, and the Amadis romances. The class concept, however much more rich in nuance, remained what it had been in the Middle Ages, both in its coarser and its finer forms, long after the Renaissance.

Very closely allied to the class concept is the concept of service. Modern culture has developed the idea that it is beneath human dignity to serve anyone or anything—truly to serve in humility and obedience—except God and the commonweal. The Middle Ages knew true service and true fealty of man to man (but always seen as a reflection of the service of God), as the heart of Oriental peoples still knows service—if, at any rate, Western propaganda has not yet eradicated that sense. What was the attitude of the Renaissance in this respect? Outwardly completely on the medieval side. The man of the Renaissance, usually dependent on the favor of the court or a Maecenas, served sedulously and zealously, with all the strings of his lyre and all the sparks of his wit— but not with his heart. Medieval fealty had fled from it all. Behold how Erasmus, writing to his friend Battus, denies their patroness, the lady of Borselen, at the same time that he sends her epistles filled with the most flattering glorification, or how Ariosto, though praised as one of the most sincere and independent minds of his time, exalts the repulsive Ippolito, Cardinal d'Este to high heaven in the *Orlando furioso* while he heckles him in satires not intended for the public. Here, if anywhere, is a field where the Renaissance displays the unresolved contradictions of an intellectual turning of the tide.

At first glance the break between the Renaissance and the

Middle Ages in the products of the visual arts and literature seems complete. One can detect a ripeness and fullness that the earlier ages missed, a plethora of color, an ease of expression, a magnificence, a grandeur, which all together give a feeling of the modern, the no longer primitive. But on closer inspection all this, whether one would prefer to rate it higher or lower than the tautness and the reserve of the earlier arts, has only to do with the quality of art and not its fundamentals. There the continuity was much greater than is usually assumed. None of the great imaginative forms upon which medieval art and literature in their highest flowering had thrived actually died out with the Renaissance. In literature chivalric romanticism maintained itself until deep into the seventeenth century. Both literature and the visual arts continued to cultivate the pastoral as a favorite form for expressing sentiment as late as the eighteenth century. Allegory did not retire from the field in either the visual arts or in literature, though the Renaissance pruned and chastened it a bit, and fitted it out a little more tastefully and elegantly. The mythological apparatus of imagination, on the other hand, was in the process of emerging long before the Renaissance and continued to be honored, together with allegory, long after the period had come to an end.

In brief, if the question is so posed that the important thing is to give the Renaissance its proper place between medieval and modern culture, then there is still a hoard of unsolved or insufficiently defined questions. The Renaissance cannot be considered as a pure contrast to medieval culture, nor even as a frontier territory between medieval and modern times. Among the basic lines dividing the older and the more modern intellectual culture of the peoples of the West there are some that run between the Middle Ages and the Renaissance, others between the Renaissance and the seventeenth century, still others straight through the heart of the Renaissance, and more than one as early as through the thirteenth century or as late as through the eighteenth.

The picture displayed by the Renaissance is one of transformation and hesitation, one of transition and of intermixture of cultural elements. Anyone seeking in it a total unity of spirit capable of being stated in a simple formula will never be able to understand it in all its expressions. Above all, one must be prepared to accept it in its complexity, its heterogeneity, and its contradictions, and to apply a pluralistic approach to the questions it poses. Whoever casts out a single schema as a net to capture this Proteus will only catch himself in the meshes. It is a vain ambition to want to describe *the* man of the Renaissance. The numerous types offered by that rich period are divided by other characteristics much more basically than any individualism can unite them. It is on each of the separate qualities of Renaissance society that research should be focused. Burckhardt provided a brilliant introduction to this method when he caught sight of the passion for fame of the Renaissance, and its ridicule and wit. It would be pleasing to see the bravery, the vanity, and the sincerity of the Renaissance treated in the same way, and its feeling for style, its pride, its enthusiasm, its critical sense. And all of it by scholars with open minds such as Burckhardt's was, without the ponderous better-than-thou attitude that for us northern Europeans so often stands in the way of an understanding of the Renaissance. For this should always be kept clearly in sight: the Renaissance was one of the triumphs of the Romance spirit. Whoever wants to understand it must be susceptible to the Romance combination of stoic seriousness and a clearly focused will (occupied with quite other things than the "full expression of the personality") with light, happy gaiety; rich, broad good-nature; and naïve irresponsibility. He must be able to give up seeking everywhere for the soul in order to experience a violent, direct interest in things for their own sake. He must be able to enjoy the essence of things *in their form beautiful*. Behind a countenance by Holbein or Anthony More he must be able to suspect the laughter of Rabelais.

RENAISSANCE AND REALISM •

If we would still be content with Burckhardt's formula for
the understanding of the Renaissance, the interrelationship of
the two concepts "Renaissance" and "realism" would be a
cut-and-dried affair. It still seems to be so for many people.
If one understands by realism the need and the skill to ap-
proximate the natural reality of things as closely as possible
in word or image, and if the Renaissance means the discovery
of the world and of man, the rise of a personal, direct view
and conception of reality, it would seem to follow that realism
can only be a corollary to the Renaissance. Man becomes
aware of his natural relationship to the world around him
and acquires the ability to express that relationship plainly
and clearly. Realism in the sense of an endeavor to be true
to nature, to reproduce natural proportions precisely, becomes
an inseparable attribute and hallmark of the Renaissance.

Burckhardt has long since joined the masters who are exalted above the antithesis of right and wrong: one no longer
asks what the opinions of such men were, but what their spirit

• *"Renaissance en realisme,"* text based on an address given at
London in 1920, and in a completely revised version, at Basel,
Bern, Zurich, and Freiburg im Breisgau in 1926. First published in
this form in *Cultuurhistorische verkenningen* (Haarlem, 1929), 86-
116 Translation from the Dutch text in *Verzamelde werken,* IV,
276-97.

was. In many respects cultural history today has the task of breaking away from Burckhardt, without that breaking away at all injuring his greatness or reducing the debt we owe him. For quite some time the concept of the Renaissance has not appeared to be so simple as it seemed to Burckhardt. It has started to crumble around all its edges. Each attempt to define it rebounds on its lack of delimitation and its relative arbitrariness. The safest thing remains to use it in the conventional sense as an indication of the flowering of European intellectual culture which, culminating shortly after 1500, had its starting point and center in Italy, whence it radiated outward and shone with new luster in France, Spain, the High and Low Germanies, and England. It is not absolutely necessary to determine the nature and the essence of that cultural flowering in order to survey and sense the phenomenon and its variegated harmony.

Realism has seemed so inseparable from individualism, and individualism so much the chief characteristic of the Renaissance, that there has been a tendency to detect the promise of the Renaissance everywhere in the Middle Ages where realistic forms of composition asserted themselves. Burckhardt himself discussed the goliard poetry of the twelfth century in that spirit. Courajod labeled the art of Sluter and the Van Eycks as Renaissance, and has found a hearing straight down to the present day. In this way the concept of realism was simply substituted for that of Renaissance, and it was forgotten to ask whether the phenomena thus designated really reflected the tone of the Renaissance in the original sense of the word. However it is interpreted, the term Renaissance remains a historical idea that one can understand as one wants to. The concept of realism, in the modern aesthetic sense in which we are using it here, can be traced and described much more objectively, in order to arrive at a definition of its relation to the Renaissance.

The current significance of the word realism is most clearly to be seen from a few examples where it is applicable and a few antitheses in which it is used. We call the Egyptian village bailiff, Dutch painting of the seventeenth century, and Flaubert's novels realistic. Realism is considered the opposite of idealism,[1] romanticism, stylization. In most cases it seems interchangeable with naturalism, though in common parlance specific distinctions are made between the two. The imitation of an outward or inward reality seems to be the aspiration leading to realistic composition.

If one traces the occurrence of realistic forms in cultural history, however, it quickly becomes apparent that realism is definitely not a general attitude of mind dominating whole periods alternately with its antipodes. Rather it displays itself as a fairly subsidiary cultural growth that springs up now here and now there, often quite unexpectedly, to disappear again just as unexpectedly. Realistic composition in literature and in the pictorial arts does not run at all parallel, nor does it within the various pictorial arts themselves. An age can produce realistic works of art without its spirit being markedly realistic. One and the same age or style can exalt the sheerest idealism as a principle of form and yet alongside works of art manifesting that principle also produce works that are utterly true to nature. Egyptian civilization was always realistic to the extreme if one understands the word in the Scholastic sense—that is to say, focused on the general, the idea, the symbol. Its art testifies to this fact. It does not depict personalities or events, but types or ideas.[2] Yet this same art also provides those countless examples of an ennobled naturalism the average art-lover usually obtains the most vivacious enjoyment from as "Egyptian." A realistic work of art tells us nothing regarding the mind of its creator. He reproduced the natural appearance of specific things because he had a gift to depict in that way, or because he could not do anything else, or because he had it in his hands. Realism in art cannot even be explained as the technical result of long training, for it is also to be found at the beginning of all art history in the caves of the Paleolithic age. And to cause us to doubt the concept of realism completely, at the point of its highest perfection it inexorably swings over to its antipode: the word is no longer applicable to the sculptures on the Bamberg cathedral.

On tracing realistic composition in literature one detects another dichotomy of the notion. Our starting point was realism as an aesthetic concept, but in literature it also manifests an ethical aspect. The endeavor to be true to nature in depicting a given material can spring from an irresistible desire to copy, to imitate a fragment of reality, whether in plastic form, color, line, word, or tone. But it can also spring from a need to see and depict life, man, and the world as they really are, and no better, stripped of all the trappings of an ideal or conventional form, without illusions. In the latter case realism has a strong ethical, or perhaps better pragmatic, content. This ethical realism belongs in literature. When the pictorial arts profess to it, for example in the late medieval depiction of the corpse, or in Hogarth or Steinlen, it is, it would seem, usually because of a literary preoccupation. At any rate, the pictorial arts do not as a rule moralize when they are realistic.

Examples of this ethical realism can be found, for example, in the ascetic literature of ancient India and of Christendom. The descriptions of the superficiality of physical beauty intended to arouse revulsion and disgust, the oft-repeated theme of the tracts *De contemptu mundi*, are frequently based on Saint John Chrysostom, even to the very wording. Closely related to the penitential sermon and the ascetic tract in its end and its means is the satire. Its realism is also of the ethical sort. There is another close link between the satire and the folk tale, but in the latter the ethical aspect has become negative: the folk tale does not admonish to virtue and lament vice, but relates successful "tricks." The realism of the French fabliau of the thirteenth century can already be called pragmatic and no longer ethical—unless one wants to interpret it as a conscious denial of the contemporary ideal of courtly life. Was it indeed a jeering No to the artificial and exaggerated attitudes of *courtoisie*, an attempt to tear off the mask of the whole of higher culture, to give the lie to the dream of earthly perfection, and in passing to revile the priests and monks as well? In that case we should here have realism as a protest, an expression of a sharp reaction against convention, against the very style of the age. But it seems to me a little exaggerated to see all this in the fabliaux.

It goes without saying that where the intention is ethical the realistic effect is nonetheless still dependent on aesthetic means. The satire, the moral sermon, and the folk tale would have an insipid taste if their realism were exhausted in their purport.

Realism as a purely aesthetic factor requires further differentiation. Its effect is always that of truth to nature, but that can be of various sorts, and achieved in various ways.

It can be based on a single significant trait of the image, or on the illusion of a complete and accurate imitation of visual reality. The artist can have meant it as an effect and have used it as a conscious expedient, or it can have been an unintentional and even unconscious product of his creative powers.

An effect of reality can be achieved by detailed imitation or by suggestive emphasis on a few significant traits of the object. The former always happens consciously and intentionally, the latter can be either spontaneous or by design. It makes no difference whether the reality depicted answers to the environment in which the person who made it or the person who enjoys it lives, or even whether the event really took place in the way it is portrayed. Flaubert is just as realistic in *Salammbô* as in *Madame Bovary*. The antithesis between imitative realism and suggestive realism is not absolute: as things are, the first type must of necessity also be selective. The very interpretation of our sensory perceptions by our own minds works selectively, and every mental image of an object is based on selection.

If a name must be given to these two forms of realistic composition, one might speak of analytic, descriptive, or illustrative realism over against emphatic or evocative realism. Illustrative and emphatic seem to me to express the antithesis most satisfactorily. It is already implicit in the two words that illustrative realism belongs more to the visual arts and emphatic to the literary.

Actually, emphatic realism must be considered as old as language and art themselves. Every word, every image serves to express a proportion considered as real, and works by means of suggestive selection. What can be indicated as emphatic realism in the history of art and literature, then, is nothing more than the series of peaks of a number of curves. The great similarity of the realistic effect in widely separated ages and areas, whether in the visual arts or in literature, is characteristic and at the same time quite understandable. In the Old Icelandic saga and in early Arab tradition what is of importance is to record accurately the memory of specific events that are still clearly visualized and are considered important. It is not the national character or the level of civilization which determines closely related forms of expression, but a similar intellectual aim.

The inhabitants of Medina hurriedly dig a ditch under the guidance of Mohammed to protect themselves against an attack of the Koreish. One witness reports:[3]

> I saw the Moslems digging, the ditch was a fathom wide; the boys carried basketloads of earth on their heads and emptied them in piles near the place where Mohammed stood. When that was done they brought stones in the baskets and piled them there as well; stones were the chief weapon to ward off the enemy. . . . Mohammed helped to carry earth; the men made doggerel rhymes while they worked, and if one of them got stuck they laughed at him. . . .

A second relates:

> I saw the Prophet covered with earth and dust from digging; he was given ground barley with a gravy of rancid butter, and ate it saying: O God, the true bread is that of the life hereafter. . . . We *banu salâma* improvised verses while we were digging; but Mohammed, who had no other objections to it, since it was not meant badly, forbade it to me and Hassan, because we were all too much the others' superiors. . . . No man in a fine red tunic has ever seemed handsomer to me than the half-naked Prophet then. He was unusually white, his thick hair hung to his shoulders; I watched him carrying earth on his back till the dust obscured my view. . . . I saw Mohammed digging and the dust lying on his back and in the folds of his belly.

Here, by way of comparison, is a passage from the saga of Egil Skallagrímsson. Egil has won a battle for the English King Athelstan, but his brother Thórólfr has been killed. At the royal court Egil is told to take his place in the seat of honor facing the king.

> Egil sat him down there, and shot down his shield before his feet. He had helm on head, and laid his sword across his knees, and whiles he drew it halfway, and whiles he slammed it back into the scabbard. He sat upright, but his head was much bent. Egil was great of face, broad of forehead, with great eye-brows: the nose not long, but marvellous thick: that place wide and long where the moustachios

grow: the chin wonderfully broad, and so all about the jaw: thick-necked and great-shouldered beyond the measure of other men: hard-looking and grim-like whensoever he was wroth. He was of goodly growth and taller than any man else: his hair wolf-grey and close of growth, and become early bald.

Now while he sat as is afore-writ, he kept a-twitching now one now another of his eye-brows down toward the cheek, and the other up toward the hair-roots. Egil was black-eyed and his eye-brows joined in the middle. Nought would he drink though drink were borne to him, but twitched his eye-brows, now one now the other, down and up.

King Athelstane sat in the high seat. He laid his sword too across his knees: and when they had sat so for a while, then drew the King his sword from its scabbard and took a gold ring from his arm, great and good, and drew it over the sword's point: stood up and went upon the floor and reached it over the fire to Egil. Egil stood up and drew his sword and went upon the floor. He stuck the sword in the bend of the ring and drew it to him: went back to his place. The King sat him down in his high-seat. But when Egil sat him down, he drew the ring on to his arm, and then went his eye-brows into their right line. Laid he down his sword and helm, and took the beast's horn that was borne to him, and drank it off.[4]

This last example particularly gives an excellent indication of how little literary realism, here already developing from the emphatic to the illustrative, needs to be the product of a cultivated evolution of literature. And both examples are suitable to demonstrate all the more clearly that up to around 1200 the medieval literature of Western Europe provides nothing that is comparable from the point of view of forceful literary realism. The reason for this should not be sought in a lack of ability in that direction among the Germanic and Romance peoples, but in the fact that the rhetorical classical tradition completely dominated literature, whether the subject was sacred or secular. Both a place in literature and a literary detachment were lacking for a plastic prose such as this. What there was of realistic description was usually in imitation of classical models. But as a rule it remains schoolish and restricted: it does not attain the level of direct examples offered by the Hadith and sagas.

Realistic observation and depiction can deal with the human figure; with movements, forms, and colors; with the spoken word; and with the environment as a whole. As medieval culture developed, realism began to appear here and there, not at all as a conscious artistic technique, but as a random trait, and rather in depicting speech and gestures than appearances, let alone environment. One must always be on the alert to see whether Suetonius or another classical author is not being imitated. Yet it is quite wrong to detect in every realistic trait the approach of the Renaissance. The classical example remained more an obstacle than an encouragement for true realistic expression. Nor was the system of the courtly love lyric favorable to it: the nature motifs in the opening of a poem have little significance in this connection. The romance gave more inducement to realistic expression, though without allowing it to become dominant.

Then suddenly Dante provided an emphatic realism that was so tremendously piercing, so alive, and so visionary that his work supplies the very criterion with which to measure the concept of literary realism. In his godlike work he delineates and brings to life figure and gesture, movement, conversation, and landscape alike. Dante, like all truly great men, seems rather to upset our theories than to confirm them. Unless it is that he demonstrates that realistic composition as such has nothing to do with the Renaissance in the usual sense of the word. One can, if one likes, see a certain connection between many things in Dante and the Renaissance, but not in the absolute clarity of his view, which no one has equaled, or the pithy pointedness of his words.

The term realism is of little use in the art of sculpture. It would seem as if the most supreme realism and the most absolute idealization cancel one another out as soon as sculpture reaches a certain level. There is no place for the qualification realism between archaic stylization and picturesque naturalism—or rather it can be applied, but it does not hold any essential implications.[5] There is a perfection that links the sculpture of the Bamberg cathedral to Donatello, and Donatello to Sluter, but that perfection lies in something else than the faithful reproduction of natural reality. One can detect realistic effects, and can say, for example, that the statues of Naumburg are more realistic than those of Bamberg, but the distinction is of little importance. In sculptural realism the emphasis is on the "-ism"; it is a phenomenon of exaggeration or degeneration. Its appearance is not by any means always at the end of a period. Immediately after Nicola Pisano, and before Andrea's clear harmony, came Giovanni with his excessive movement, confused composition, and distorted grimace. Ghiberti, already, went astray in his vistas and bas-reliefs while the sculpture of the *quattrocento* was only entering on its heyday.

In painting, on the other hand, the term emphatic realism is excellently applicable to Giotto. And with him the close link between realism and Renaissance seems to announce itself quite emphatically. Giotto, the man of the utterly expressive gesture who, as Burckhardt put it, "detected the most significant aspects of every action," has always been called the father of later realism, and it was precisely because of that realism that Boccaccio already labeled him the renewer of art. With Giotto, he taught, art refound the path to nature and truth. Boccaccio's opinion established the tradition, and the later writers Leonardo da Vinci, Erasmus, and Vasari also began the revival with Giotto.[6] It would seem impossible to separate Giotto and his realism from the beginnings of the Renaissance. The link posited between the Renaissance and realism seems to find its proof in him.

It should not be forgotten, however, that our whole conception of the Renaissance is actually built upon the foundations laid by Boccaccio and Vasari. In that conception the accuracy of Boccaccio's opinion is still taken as a more or less axiomatic starting point, at least by Burckhardt. Does what we now know of the cultural development of the later Middle Ages still really harmonize with the postulated principle that Giotto, by being a realist, was the founder of the Renaissance?

This essay does not at all pretend to solve that question completely. It is no more than an attempt to trace whether realism, which denotes a form, is really indissolubly linked with the Renaissance, which denotes a spirit. If it were so linked, every expression of realism to be detected in the art and literature of the later Middle Ages would be sufficient to declare the spirit producing it as one representative of the Renaissance. And this was the consequence that the concept of the Renaissance seemed to force one to accept. It was in this way that scholars came to look upon the art of the Van Eycks as Renaissance art. But if that was done, then the same had to be done with the literary art of Froissart and Chastellain, contemporaries and countrymen of Broederlam and Jan van Eyck, and just as much realists as they. In this respect literary products offer one criterion more than the visual arts: they make it possible for us to appraise the spirit as well as the form. The Van Eycks were utter realists as far as form is concerned, but we know as good as nothing about their spirit. Everything that modern, aestheticizing art criticism concludes from their works regarding their spirit is fantasy and paraphrase. Froissart, too, is a realist: he seeks truth to nature in lively dialogue, simple and direct observation, and the sphere of ordinary human intercourse in which he places his figures. But who would consider Froissart as belonging to the spirit of the Renaissance without realizing that by doing so he was distorting the concept hopelessly?

Chastellain, the pompous court chronicler of the Burgundians, was a master of striking realistic effects: a gesture, a light effect, the weather, an altercation, a landscape. I have given examples of it elsewhere.[7] His description of Philip the Good, too long to be quoted here,[8] is a model of forceful, telling, and sober portraiture, in which the style vibrates like a steel spring, as if to suggest the steel figure of the duke all the more clearly. Now, Chastellain constantly did his best to be modern, after his fashion, that is to say, classical, rhetorical, and grandiloquent. One can distinguish two stylistic forms: the heavily laden festive style that has unjustly cost him prestige in French literary history, and his luscious Flemish realism (though expressed in French). It is undoubtedly the former that links him to the Renaissance. He attempted to find the new form, but did not yet feel anything of the new spirit. His spirit was medieval, and it was from that spirit that his realism stemmed. It did not flourish in him as a fruit or a flower of the Renaissance, but rather the contrary. If there is any artist who can serve to demonstrate that the Renaissance and realism were not correlatives, then it is Chastellain.

Aesthetic realism found expression at a number of points throughout the Middle Ages, quite independently of the Renaissance. When it was consciously realized it was experienced as something new, an increase in artistic skill and expressive ability.

Scholasticism had instilled in the medieval spirit a belief in realistic composition as an authoritative directive. Aristotle himself had said: *hè technè mimeitai tèn phusin—ars imitatur naturam in quantum potest*. But that does not at all simply imply a praise of aesthetic realism. In the first place, *technè* or *ars* is not at all art in the modern sense, but in the much broader and deeper sense, which had not died out even in the eighteenth century, comprising everything made or given shape by man. In connection with it *mimeitai* or *imitatur* meant not only "copies" but also "follows." The principle of imitation, interpreted in this way, pointed beyond Nature to God. Dante had Vergil say:[9]

> *Filosofia, mi disse, a chi la intende,*
> *Nota non pure in una sola parte,*
> *Come Natura lo suo corso prende*
> *Dal divino intelletto e da sua arte;*
> *E se tu ben la tua Fisica note,*
> *Tu troverai non dopo molte carte,*
> *Che l'arte vostra quella, quanto puote,*
> *Segue, come il maestro fa il discente,*
> *Si che vostr' arte a Dio quasi è nipote.•*

The theory of *ars imitatur naturam*, then, implied much more than the praise of artistic realism, though that also was contained in it. For both the practicing artist and the naïve connoisseur of art the phrase corresponded all too well to the natural urge to imitation, which must be deep-seated in human nature. Saint Thomas Aquinas says that "it is natural to man to be pleased with representations," [10] and by placing "imitation" under the concept "representation" in the full, pregnant sense which that word had for medieval thought, he suddenly gave to aesthetic realism itself a much deeper note.

It is, then, in every way understandable that for a long

• "Philosophy, to him who will attend," / Said he, "in divers places hath discerned / How Nature her example and her end / From Divine Intellect and its art hath learned. / And to thy Physics if good heed thou pay, / Thou wilt find, after but few pages turned, / That your art follows her, far as it may, / As scholar his master, so that your art is / Of the Godhead the grandchild, so to say."

time the only excellence art criticism was able to detect in works of art was a successful imitation of nature. Even the anecdotes handed down from antiquity regarding Zeuxis' deceptive artistry testify to that appreciation. Dante also professed that artistic ideal in describing the marble reliefs on the terraces and banks of the Mount of Purgatory.[11] Boccaccio said that Giotto

> had a spirit of so great excellency, as there was not any particular thing in Nature, the Mother and Work-mistress of all, by continual motion of the heavens; but he by his pen and pencil could perfectly portrait; shaping them all so truly alike and resemblable, that they were taken for the real matters indeed; and whether they were present or no, there was hardly any possibility of their distinguishing. So that many times it happened, that by the variable devices he made, the visible sense of men became deceived, in crediting those things to be natural, which were but merely painted.[12]

Villani expressed the same appreciation.[13] A century later the Genoese Bartolomeo Fazio praised the art of the Van Eycks in rapt phrases, just as naïvely surprised at their utter truth to nature: hair that surpassed real hair, the sunbeam falling through a chink, a reflection, the drops of sweat on a body, the painstakingly detailed landscapes in the background.

Another century later Castiglione, in *The Courtier*,[14] considered the controversy whether painting or sculpture ranked higher among the visual arts. For him the issue depended completely on the point recognized by everyone as the basic principle, that art was "a following of nature." One of the speakers argued that the prize should go to sculpture because it came closer to reality as a result of its three dimensions. But later it was agreed that a painting is able to express nature much more completely, since it does not only reproduce forms but also colors, lights and shadows, perspective, and so forth. With this naïve theory of realism Castiglione had in mind the art of Raphael and Michelangelo. One could hardly argue that with it he expressed what we consider as the Renaissance element in their art.

It is well known that it was precisely in the art form where the principle of imitation is least at home, namely, in music, that the theory and the need for imitating the natural were pursued most industriously. In the history of music the concepts of art and craftsmanship are even more closely related than elsewhere. From the fourteenth until deep in the sixteenth century the preferred musical forms were those intended as imitations of natural sounds: the noises of the hunt, the din of the market place, the fury of the battle. It is hard to see what this attempt at musical naturalism could have to do with the spirit of the Renaissance. It is quite something else when Thomas More praises the church music of *Utopia:*

> But in one thing doubtless they go exceeding far beyond us. For all their music, both that they play upon instruments, and that they sing with man's voice, doth so resemble and express natural affections; the sound and tune is so applied and made agreeable to the thing; that whether it be a prayer, or else a ditty of gladness, of patience, of trouble, of mourning, or of anger, the fashion of the melody doth so represent the meaning of the thing, that it doth wonderfully move, stir, pierce, and enflame the hearers' minds.[15]

Here, too, realism was an ideal, but with an intent that was quite different from the naïve urge to deceptive imitation: a realism that was directed toward the meaning of things, and that could abolish the antithesis between the Scholastic concept of realism and the modern aesthetic one. Behind More's plain and beautiful words one can, if one likes, hear Mozart and Beethoven, the entire music of the eternal Utopia that is the true land of music.

We shall see below that another great master was in remarkable agreement with More in his conception of true realism.

So far, we seem to have determined that there is a certain conjunction of realism and Renaissance. From around 1400 on, artists and thinkers became more and more aware of realism in art as a problem and a task. Uccello wrestled with perspective. Masaccio found a method of expressing truth to nature that surpassed and surmounted the style of Giotto. Dutch painting achieved a level of realistic depiction of matter which has not been matched before or since. In literature realism stayed much more in the background. It is at all times more concerned with things than with forms, and was obstructed by the fact that, though the new classicism did on the one hand reinforce the urge toward direct observation, on the other hand—and to a much greater extent—the rhetorical element in language forced its way to the fore. The language of Joinville or Villani was, in the final analysis, more realistic than that of Machiavelli, however realistic the thought of the latter may have been.

In short, the only conclusion that seems justified at this juncture is that the various expressions of literary and visual realism that manifested themselves here and there from the thirteenth century on were simultaneities that display no links either to one another or to a general principle to be called the Renaissance. There is a general and gradual increase in the urge toward and the skill in realistic expression. But if a cultural phenomenon is best characterized by its acme, then it is easy for us to pass judgment on the relationship between realism and Renaissance. The attempt to reproduce natural things directly, in their individuality, reached its culmination earlier than the intellectual movement that is called the Renaissance. No one has demonstrated this more clearly and satisfactorily than Heinrich Wölfflin. It is the fifteenth century that is naturalistic; the sixteenth century is no longer so. The *quattrocento* and the Flemish painters are united by their painstaking observation, unbridled elaborateness, and scrupulous detail. In it all they are naïve, and youthfully archaic. The *cinquecento,* in which the spirit of the Renaissance culminated, triumphed over realism—and had to triumph over it to achieve what are most intrinsic to it: noble form, grand style, epic and dramatic gesture, perfect harmony.

In Michelangelo's mind this transformation and rejection took place in full, passionate consciousness. He considered it, so it is said, a humiliation to art to depict something earthly in its specific limitation unless it was of supreme beauty. Leonardo's titanic reverence for nature gave birth to the bizarre naturalism of his painting as only one offshoot of a spirit that as a whole was far beyond scrupulous realism. His realism, says Séailles, is in actuality the most amazing faith in the spirit.

One might say that realism was for the Renaissance a

preparation, a transitional stage, not a final result or an aim. Dürer embodied the transition, both in his art and in what he had to say about his ideal of art. According to Melanchthon,[16] Dürer toward the end of his life described his evolution as an artist as follows: In his youth he had liked to make gaily colored and multiform portrayals and to sketch misshapen, bizarre figures. At a more mature age, however, he began to observe nature and to imitate her original countenance as faithfully as possible, and he discovered that that simplicity was the highest adornment of art, though at the same time he learned how difficult it was not to deviate from nature.

At first sight this seems to be nothing more or less than an unambiguous confession of sheer naturalism, and that appears to be confirmed in more than one place in Dürer's own writings:

> But life in nature allows the truth of these things to be perceived. Therefore observe it industriously, conform to it, and do not deviate from it thinking that you know how to find it better by yourself, for then you are misled. For truly art is in nature; whoever can distill it therefrom has it. . . . Therefore never imagine that you could or should create something better than God has given His created nature power to effect. For your ability is powerless in the face of God's creation.

And elsewhere: "For if it is against nature, then it is evil. . . ."[17]

It hardly needs to be said that Dürer did indeed repeatedly show himself in his work to be one of the sheerest naturalists the history of art can point to. This is especially true of his drawings: one has only to recall the turfs of sod, the bouquet of violets, the wing of the dead roller, the hare. No one else, before the modern French painters, produced a landscape or a panorama of a town such as Dürer's, devoid of any stylization, arrangement, or transformation. But all this has to do with sketches and exercises, and not with Dürer's highest, consciously artistic efforts.

A doubt arises when one questions whether Dürer's major work confirms his own interpretation of his evolution as he described it to Melanchthon. If indeed there was a turning away from the fantastic and the bizarre to a simple imitation of nature, then his later works should exhibit the highest degree of direct naturalism, and the earlier ones should betray a certain deficiency in accurate observation of nature. But a comparison of his last work, the apostles and evangelists, with works from his youth, such as the portrait of his father, reveals rather the reverse. In the youthful work one can see the painstaking realism, the accurate delineation of details he himself recommended, "without omitting the smallest wrinklets and veins. . . ." The apostles, on the other hand, manifest a realism that is at the same time restricted, deepened, and exalted. We suddenly feel that though in the portrait of his father realism seems synonymous with naturalism, for the apostles and evangelists the designation realism still applies, but not that of naturalism.

Did Dürer have a wrong view of his own evolution, or did Melanchthon misunderstand him and record his words wrongly? Perhaps not. Dürer had sought not only nature, but at the same time, in it, beauty. "What beauty is I do not know, although it depends on many things." It is embodied in nature, and at the same time points beyond nature. Man cannot comprehend absolute beauty. "For I believe there is no man alive who could fathom the highly beautiful purpose of the tiniest living creature."

What actually happened was that Dürer had gradually recognized with a growing awareness that all the accidental, elaborate, curious, and unimportant details that had intrigued him in his younger years were needless and disturbing, and that he rejected them to pursue heroic simplicity, absolute repose, and immediate significance. And it was this that he called "the original countenance of nature" in his conversation with Melanchthon.

In this transition from multiplicity to unity Dürer had undergone in himself the great transformation of his day, the transformation that marks him as a representative of the Renaissance and makes him essentially akin to Raphael and Michelangelo. The essence of the Renaissance lies in the triumph over naïve naturalism, and it is the failure to understand this that has led to the mistaken incorporation of Jan van Eyck in the Renaissance. If a division has to be made, then it is more suitable to consider the Italian *quattrocento* as still basically medieval, precisely because of its realism.

Strict realism develops in the nonessential, the accessory, and it is in the long run only in that that it can maintain itself. Great art is always art with a purpose and a meaning that binds and determines its form of expression. It is rooted in a cult[18] or a liturgy, and as a result is monumental or hieratic. Such art, linked to a style of life, is always constrained to triumph over realism. Only when a large portion of art has lost or seems to have lost every connection with a cult can realism develop without hindrance as a form of art. That is what happened *after* the Renaissance. After the Renaissance there was a new and lengthy culmination in the line of realism, particularly in Dutch art.

This is perhaps the place to refer for a moment to the most absolute naturalist there has ever been, Bernard Palissy. He would seem difficult to isolate from the Renaissance, considering the age he lived in (1510-1589) and the milieu he worked for: French court circles. He was a ceramist, a garden architect, and a writer. He flew in the face of every principle of ceramics with his plates, on which lizards, leaves, and insects are set in *haut-relief* without any formal order or decorative stylization. Unfortunately nothing has been preserved of his large-scale creations (except the theory underlying them), in which he gave rein to the same utter naturalism. The rustic grottoes Palissy designed (and in part executed) for the queen, the Constable de Montmorency, and many others, we only know from his remarkable writings.[19] The direct imitation of nature, he believes, is worth more than all the rules of architecture. In his grottoes real trees were used as columns; the walls were completely enameled in merging colors, and so highly polished that the lizards and lobsters could see their own reflections.

It would seem to me that Palissy's naturalism should not be looked upon as the expression of an artistic principle of the Renaissance so much as of an intellectual current which, however much it may have stemmed from the spirit of the Renaissance, was in essence not its artistic aspect. Palissy's place is among those minds who enthusiastically hunted and grubbed in nature to discover its secrets, and thus prepared the way for a positivistic natural science. He, too, had a share in that: Bacon learned from him.[20] It is the sphere of the adventurous, semimystical, alchemistic search in which technical tracts still called *magia naturalis*[21] arose; the sphere in which Georgius Agricola, the greatest technologist of the sixteenth century, who populated his mines with demons, lived and worked; the sphere that produced Geronimo Cardano, Paracelsus, Guillaume Postel, and Jean Bodin, and also Vesalius and Rembert Dodoens. It was in the same spirit that Leonardo composed his peculiar fantasies of animal forms, conducted his experiments, and made inventions. But as an artist Leonardo possessed and gave so much more: he was universal and a genius; Palissy was a talent with his limitations. Basically a scientist, he sacrificed art to naturalism.[22]

The line of realism is always more difficult to trace in literature than in the pictorial arts. Literary realism in the sense of an accurate and detailed description of a fragment of reality is the exception, and as a literary phenomenon is usually only a passing fashion. Realism in literature is intrinsically a much more relative concept than is realism in a visible image, for the idea is always intermingled in linguistic expression, and forces choice, interpretation, restriction. A consistent aesthetic realism in language would amount to an applied nominalism. But language can no more live in a radically nominalistic world than man himself. Hence the very nature of our thinking and speaking always draws descriptive realism back to the stage of evocative or emphatic realism.

At the height of the Renaissance the same thing happened to literature as befell the visual arts: the inclination toward realism triumphed and resolved itself in the principle that was the spirit of the Renaissance itself, that of harmony. What Raphael was in painting, Ariosto was in literature. Whoever desires to express the fullness of the Renaissance in names has enough in these two.

Ariosto was a poet of sheer imagination, and at the same time one of absolute precision. He expresses everything with basic words. He does not obscure, he does not work with nuances. He is not suggestive or allusive. Everything appears so clear in him, so direct, as pure and brightly colored as a summer sky. Seemingly there is no place for an application of a concept of literary realism. And yet there is a consciously realistic element in Ariosto, quite apart from the fact that his extremely realistic use of language might itself be given that appellation. Beneath the fantastic image one can repeatedly trace a careful endeavor to depict reality accurately. For all its illusion, Ariosto's topography is quite specific and real. On tracing the routes that the poet has his heroes (Astolfo, for instance) travel, one is amazed to find that they can sometimes be traced in detail on a map. He describes Paris, where he had never been, as if he were gazing at the town plan:[23]

> Siede Parigi in una gran pianura,
> Nell' ombilico a Francia, anzi nel core:
> Gli passa la riviera entro le mura,
> E corre, ed esce in altre parte fuore;
> Ma fa un' isola prima, e v'assicura
> Della città una parte, e la migliore:
> L'altre due (ch'in tre parti è la gran terra)
> Di fuor la fossa, e dentro il fiume serra.•

It has already been mentioned that for a long time almost the only admiration early art-criticism was able to express for a painting was that it was a successful approximation of reality. This is also the point of view of the contemporaries of Ariosto and Tasso regarding literature. They agree with the priest in *Don Quixote* who preferred *Tirante el Blanco* above all the other chivalric romances because "in it Knights do eat and drink, and sleep, and die in their beds naturally, and make their testaments before their death: with many other things, which all other books of this subject do want." [24]

The sixteenth century censured inaccuracies and improbabilities in Ariosto and Tasso: Angelica was too candid, Armida too passionate, Rinaldo too weak, Orlando too gentle. Even Galileo, who attacked Tasso out of admiration for Ariosto, criticized the latter on the grounds that Erminia could not have seen the persons she described from the given distance, and that it was unnatural for all Christians to say the same thing at the same time.

• Paris is seated in a pleasant plain, / Ev'n in the navel, rather in the heart / Of France; the river cuts the same in twaine / Making an Island of the better part, / The rest that doth in greatness more contain, / A ditch and wall doth from the plain depart.

The serenity of the Renaissance was not realism, for the reality that it refined and elevated to a style was confused. But instead of being elevated into a style, aesthetic realism can be intensified and become hyperrealism. In the search for the most striking expression of reality exaggeration is unavoidable. The expression on the human countenance becomes a grimace. Actually this step had already been taken, not only by the great Dutch painters of the fifteenth century, but even earlier by Giotto. Hieronymus Bosch merely converted exaggeration into a conscious artistic method. In the hands of the great masters such hyperrealism quickly led to the most grandiose, fantastic art: Matthias Grünewald and Pieter Brueghel. In literature the form was that of Rabelais.

Abel Lefranc, Rabelais's most recent editor, has entitled a part of his Introduction "The Realism of Rabelais." It begins as follows: "One of the most certain results of recent research on Rabelais has undoubtedly been to demonstrate that Rabelais was the greatest and most adroit of the realists, that is to say, the writer who sought, loved, and represented truth, or better still, life, with unequaled passion, continuity, and force." [25] That is a statement in no uncertain terms. Nor is Gustave Lanson's opinion any different: "Never has a purer, more powerful, more triumphant realism been seen. . . . He is and remains the source of all realism, by himself greater than all the currents that branched off after him." [26]

Since no one could want to isolate Rabelais from the complex phenomenon we call the Renaissance, there would here seem to be a link between the Renaissance and realism to give us pause—unless it might appear that what Lefranc and Lanson mean by realism is not quite the same as the concept we have here gradually attempted to delineate.

Lefranc detects Rabelais's realism in his fervent interest in all the affairs of his day: government, politics, discoveries, issues of the moment, religious questions, learned controversies, and so forth. He finds it in the accuracy of Rabelais's anatomy, in the precise use of shipping terms in the story of the storm. And also in the absolute accuracy and precision of expression and perfection of imagery; the looseness of the dialogue; the "infinite curiosity" revealed in the accumulation of words and images; the catalogues of games, foodstuffs, crafts, apparel, kitchen activities, and so forth. And above all he demonstrates

Rabelais's realism in the fact that the whole design of the biography of Gargantua is drawn from Rabelais's own family and local history. Gargantua's youth takes place in the environment of Chinon, and the estate of Grandgousier is La Devinière, where Antoine Rabelais, the author's father, lived. The war between Grandgousier's shepherds and the cake-bakers of King Picrochole corresponds to a legal dispute between Antoine Rabelais and a certain Gaucher de Sainte-Marthe.

It all seems to be perfect realism, and at the same time High Renaissance. In a flood of luscious, effervescent, thunderous words the whole reality of life seems to spin past us in a constant stream. As far as the matter, the content, and the objects are concerned, it can be called realism. But can one say that this is realism in its intent and its form, in the sense of a need to depict reality accurately? Rabelais's treatment of the "Picrocholine War" is fundamentally quite the opposite. His starting point is a certain reality, but he deliberately transforms that reality into an exuberant fantasy and a quasi-heroic form. And this is what he does everywhere. He distorts everything into the extravagant, he toys with reality, he warps its proportions with a childish pleasure, he inflates it to a gigantic, comic phantasmagoria.

Also in Rabelais's case, then, there was a triumph over realism, and here, too, a triumph by the Renaissance. That is to say, by a spirit that longs to return to the mythical, the elementary, the dithyrambic, the Heraclean—a spirit that can no longer be expressed in allegories of the Church or of the *Roman de la rose*. As long as the medieval spirit predominated, such needs had found expression in simple realistic forms, spontaneous and naïve. With the Renaissance the form became heroic. In his heroic fantasy Rabelais is closely akin to Ariosto, despite the opposition of chaos to cosmos separating the two.

The heroic fantasy also links Rabelais and Ariosto to a genius greater than them both: Michelangelo. Ariosto and Rabelais mark the two poles of the Renaissance—the harmony, the serenity and sonority, the happy clarity of the one, opposed to the turbulent, turbid, seething, fermenting chaos of the other (which, after Paracelsus, was to lead to a new science, and which foreshadowed Cervantes, Ben Jonson, and Rembrandt). Michelangelo in his art bridged the abyss

separating Rabelais and Ariosto; the opposition between restless, probing hyperrealism and the eternal serenity of the
grand, harmonic style was resolved in him. But he lacked
the laughter.

When one attempts to penetrate to the very essence of the
Renaissance it becomes clear that the criterion of realism
is not especially important in understanding it. Realism ac-
companies the great renewal of Western culture for a time
during its rise, and then suddenly has disappeared from view
and seems to have become of little importance. In other ages
aesthetic realism may appear repeatedly as a protest, a reaction against excessive stylization of thought and image, but
for the Renaissance it was more a growing-pain. The Middle
Ages had always been naïvely realistic, in so far as their
technique of expression made it possible. The Renaissance
does not draw any sharp line in the history of realistic composition. In general the attempt to reproduce the forms of
reality accurately—which, strictly speaking, ought rather to
be called plastic nominalism—indicates only the gradual rise
of a technical mastery. It springs up as a wild growth in the
garden of art. From the point of view of the Scholastic concept of realism it only touches the appearance of things. But
the essence of things, expressed in the idea, constantly needs
to be fathomed anew, and for that it is constantly necessary
first to penetrate to a clear view of the given reality. Max
Scheler[27] speaks of the new nominalisms that human civilization has a need for every now and then. Wisdom and
scholarship see themselves faced anew from time to time by
the recognition that the world is not actually like that, not
the way words and concepts present it to us. In the same way
art, to remain alive, constantly has to make the return to
nature we call realism in the ordinary sense.

Once such a realism has developed it usually dissolves
again quickly, after having given new life to precisely the
tendencies it seemed in opposition to. A new symbolism, a
new ideography, typology, or style frequently derives its
strength from the firmness in which it is rooted in a preceding
realism. This is true of the Renaissance, and is true as well
of baroque, neoclassicism, and romanticism.

IN COMMEMORATION OF ERASMUS •

Some time after Erasmus had taken up residence in Basel
there came the suggestion from Zurich that he should settle
there and acquire citizenship of the town. He declined the
suggestion with the argument that he preferred to be a
citizen of the whole world, not of one single town. Zurich
remained alien to him, however lively his intellectual contact
with Zwingli may at times have been. Basel became the town
to be forever linked with his memory. The day before yesterday we stood beside his tomb here at Basel. Surrounding us
were the same objects on which his eyes had dwelt in the
twilight of his old age. Basel has chosen to commemorate his
death almost on the day of his birth, which falls the day after
tomorrow. It is as though the intention was to sum up the
memory of the whole of his life in this one hour. That life
was polarized between the distant Holland of his childhood
and his youth and the industrious Basel of his most productive activity and his death. Paris, England, Italy, and Louvain
constituted important chapters in his life, but Holland and
Basel gave it its definitive form. The flowing silver ribbon of
the Rhine links Basel and Holland, and the life of Erasmus

• *"Erasmus-Gedenkrede,"* an address given at the Basel cathedral
on October 24, 1936. First published in *Parerga,* edited by Werner
Kaegi (Amsterdam and Basel, 1939), 65-84. Translation from the
German text in *Verzamelde werken,* VI, 204-19.

of Rotterdam once flowed similarly between its source and its end. Erasmus may belong to the whole world, but he belongs in a more intimate sense to Holland and to Switzerland.

When Erasmus was living at Basel he could not have dreamt that shortly these two countries, his original homeland and his chosen refuge, were to occupy similar places in the European political scene. True, the Swiss Confederation had already established itself as a new, separate political entity. Basel was not merely Germania to Erasmus; he called it Helvetia. The coming independence of the Netherlands, however, still lay hidden in the womb of time. But nevertheless, his homeland, too, was not simply Germania to him. He spoke of the Netherlands as *patria,* but he hardly had a separate name for that "fatherland." Brabantia came nearest to it, and even Burgundia could serve as a collective name. That half a century after his death his Batavian homeland was to establish a counterpart to the Swiss Confederation as the United Provinces—two free republics that were to make such a characteristic imprint on the political world of the seventeenth century—that is something Erasmus could have had no notion of.

In this hour here in Basel, just as earlier in Rotterdam, the thought of the similarity in the fate of our two countries and of the seasoned friendship that has united them throughout the years has added an element of solemn emotion to our joint celebration of Erasmus's memory. The Swiss and the Dutch have commemorated the anniversary of Erasmus's death together, united by spiritual bonds: bonds that have found their symbolic expression here in Basel in the fact that a Dutchman has been awarded the honor of being allowed to remember Erasmus in the city where Froben printed him and Holbein painted him, where his dearest friends surrounded and protected him. I have gladly and gratefully accepted this high honor as a symbol of the deep sense of unity and like-mindedness between your country and mine.

What is it that has lent such a deeply serious note to this year's celebrations dedicated to Erasmus's memory? The answer is not difficult. The fact is that the memory of Erasmus pains us. The world of today is in many respects so violently and so harshly opposed to the spirit of Erasmus that we, in our ardent need for a redeeming word, for a saving idea, have had to look to him once more. Twelve years ago I voiced the opinion that Erasmus had had his day. His influence had long since permeated our culture. Last year one of your fellow townsmen, Professor Werner Kaegi, to whom, thanks to Erasmus, I am bound in warm friendship, wrote with reference to this opinion of mine: "It appears that the course of the world has in the meantime done everything possible to lend Erasmus new topicality. His countenance has a more modern appearance in the world today than it had around 1923, as if he had something to say again, as if the irony of his words would sound as bitter and biting as ever." So it is. Erasmus is admonishing us once again, and urgently. Does he really still have something new to say, then, something that we have not understood before? That is hardly what it amounts to. They are the old words, but they have acquired a new sound.

I do not intend to have Erasmus speak for himself here in a series of quotations. To quote Erasmus verbatim takes up a great amount of time. He simply does not write in maxims. All that was best in him, his noble, if naïve, disapproval of violence, discord, and perfidy; the biting comedy of his serious satire; his ripe insight into the art of right living; the muted tone of his plain piety—all that comes through only in the gentle flow of his Latin disquisitions. Quotation in translation divests it of all its charm. Let us therefore rather attempt to expound a certain dilemma that Erasmus poses for us. In the figure of Erasmus as it forms a part of our spiritual heritage each specific detail seems outdated and only to be appreciated historically. And yet the sum total, the figure as such, emanates a strong influence even today. The world cannot forget him. He is still standing there, beckoning and admonishing. What is the reason for this evident contrast? I shall try to illustrate the contrast, and perhaps provide the key to it, by means of rapid survey of Erasmus's attitudes in religious, political, social, and economic affairs, concluding with his attitudes toward nature, learning, and art.

I have just said that the specific aspects of Erasmus are all outdated. The world no longer reads and enjoys him. Consequently it is impossible to consider his figure altogether in the classical category. That mind is classical whose creation —whether poetry, philosophy, or art—in its details still moves and captivates posterity directly, strengthening or irritating as do Aeschylus, Dante, Rembrandt, Pascal. Not Erasmus. Could it, then, perhaps be the image of Erasmus as a human being which attracts and consoles us? Not that either. The image of his personality looming up from every page of his writings is always essentially the same, for all its splendid many-sidedness. Yet on being confronted with that personality most of us are capable of managing a greater degree of admiration and recognition than the mere smile of understanding with which Erasmus himself looked upon the world. There is always a small Erasmus in the way of the great Erasmus we would like to honor. He always reveals his weak sides so guilelessly that as a matter of convenience one is inclined to take him at his word, judging him solely on the basis of his weaknesses. But that would be wrong. There is a deeper sense in the Greek inscription on Dürer's portrait of Erasmus: his writings provide a better portrait. It is not the person but the mind that exerts an attraction on us. His person lacked precisely those qualities that are now once more valued most highly. There was nothing chivalric in Erasmus. Every tendency toward the heroic was alien to him.

But in any case, he had the courage not to play the hero. And other sorts of courage as well, such as the refreshing bravery not to wait until a work was complete in every minute detail, but to publish it as soon as the first draft was ready. Though physically he may have been timid, he never hesitated to expose his mental character to criticism and insinuation. True, he lacked the calm strength to scorn such criticism and insinuation with resignation. His everlasting self-justification regarding even the most trifling points makes his later letters an endless apologetic litany. But there are sometimes striking sounds in the apologia. Among all mortals, he asks, should Erasmus alone be infallible? Mistakes can be found even in Augustine and Jerome. On another occasion he says that consistency is not always to say the same thing, but always to aim at the same thing. And a last example, this one in a resigned tone: posterity will, he hopes, pass a fairer judgment. He will continue to be himself to the last day of his life. And in essence he did remain so.

However, the false notes that keep us from admitting Erasmus unconditionally into the pantheon of human greatness are to be found not only in his personality. His intellectual attitude also disillusions us time and again. This applies above all to his religious ideas, which I should like to treat only very briefly. For people of our time, of whatever faith, it is often difficult to do justice to Erasmus's piety. To our feelings he stops somewhere halfway in his faith. We do not deplore his dropping the shrill, whining tone of late medieval piety in favor of the calm, penetrating style of his *Enchiridion militis christiani* [*Manual of the Christian Knight*]. But we *are* troubled all the more frequently by the frivolous lightness of his humanistic style when he writes about things sacred. To Beatus Rhenanus he sends "a choice flower culled from the very green fields of Divine Literature." [1] It is hard for us to accept piety with such a strong aesthetic tinge as serious. It is neither Luther's accent, nor Calvin's, nor Saint Theresa's. Erasmus's religious sentiments, it seems to us, more often moved in a middling sphere of poetic learning than cried toward heaven out of the deep. Erasmus's voice hardly ever has the sound of coming *de profundis*.

If his piety seems too flaccid or too shallow to us, his theology seems too vacillating and too vague. He had abandoned the rigid logic of Scholasticism. He placed little value on definitions. As a consequence he had no desire to advance toward a profound and clearly defined philosophical foundation of his beliefs, and the direct, mystical basis of his theological thinking was also weak. He was just as little a rationalist. His beliefs were rooted in deep ethical needs. That ethical basis gave such a social coloring to his attitude in the great religious controversy of his time that he valued concord on earth above all else. He reproached Luther for attaching no value to the *consensus populi christiani*. Theological disputations he found odious, and void of any apparent utility. He did not shy from leaving fundamental religious issues unsettled. Sacred truth cannot bear subtle definitions. "The whole controversy," he wrote in 1527 to Sir Thomas More, "is much more a dispute about words than one about things." [2] It was but little service to piety for one to attempt to penetrate further than was seemly into the cave of the unfathomable mystery.

In the *Praise of Folly* Stultitia somewhere comments offhand: *Adumbrata quidem omnia, sed haec fabula non aliter agitur* ["And all this is done under a certain veil or shadow, which taken away once, the play can no more be played"].[3] This is a profound phrase, one that to a certain extent reflects Erasmus's whole religious attitude. Everything is merely suggested, sketched in outline, but that is the only way the play can be played.

Many would accept Erasmus's general lack of philosophical precision more readily if it were counter-balanced by a higher degree of precision in his opinions on practical life. But that is not the case. His opinions of the things of the world are quite decided, it is true, but by no means exact. His pronouncedly moralistic attitude prompts in him a consistent but nonetheless stereotyped judgment. Such a point of view can hardly be called a sound and considered realism.

Erasmus lived in a world of books. That world was populated by a vast host of classical personalities and a small but select number of exalted Christian figures. In his intellectual world these latter constituted the highest authority. Only a very few of them were truly guiding forces for Erasmus. Besides the Saviour himself and Saint Paul there were, actually, only the early Fathers of the Church. The words of the Old Testament prophets found but little echo, and those of the Psalmist solely in long-winded paraphrases. Later theology hardly played a role in the structure of Erasmus's conceptual world. Below this supreme level of the Christian element that world swarmed with classical authorities, writers and historical figures alike. They made up a sort of vast but little-differentiated landed nobility that voiced its opinion on everything as it pleased.

Erasmus's mind left this imaginary world of the past only unwillingly and hesitantly. He shaded his eyes against the bright light of the present with the spectacles of his Christian and pagan past. Though he was the very embodiment of the triumph of the printed book, he looked upon the swelling stream of new books and the freedom of the emerging book-trade with aversion. Such overproduction seemed to him extremely harmful to learning. Because of saturation in itself, and also because the abundance of new writings would keep the capricious human from reading the classics, although it was impossible to produce anything better than those classics. At best the new writers might occasionally discover something that had eluded the ancient authors. If true learning was to go on being neglected in this way, the authority of imperial counselors, councils of the Church, schools, lawyers, and theologians would come to nought and a barbaric military tyranny like that of the Turks would set in.

Thus spoke the man who was imprisoned in his world of books as in an enchanted garden. He could and would not go outside its bounds, but nonetheless he had the desire to look at what was outside. There he saw a world that did not fit his ideal image at all. He shied away from that rough-and-tumble reality. He could not muster an understanding and interest in things beyond the sphere of his biblical-classical moralism. He could not get a grasp on this world. In the current of his times he discerned only a shrill and alarming crudeness and unreasonableness that upset and offended him, and saw hardly ever, if at all, the new and fruitful elements that were emerging and struggling painfully to the fore.

Around 1517 Erasmus did devote himself temporarily to the pleasant idea that *bonae literae,* cultivated and sustained by the concord of ruling princes, were about to usher in an era of happiness, culture, and peace. But that mood of his soon passed. Thenceforward his view of the near future was just as gloomy as that of a medieval cleric had ever been. Time and again he complained that the world was groaning in the throes of an amazing transformation of all things, that the affairs of man were tending toward Scythian barbarism and utter corruption of the liberal arts. The political world seemed to Erasmus to be on its way toward a rapid decline that would lead to the tyranny of a few. For the moment the tyranny would have to be endured, lest it give way to anarchy.

Is this despondent and despairing Erasmus the man whose spirit has remained for us a treasured possession? Definitely not. Are there, alongside this general political pessimism, practical, concrete recommendations for the amelioration of political life? It is doubtful. His constructive opinions on the state and statecraft hardly go beyond the sphere of pious desires. Erasmus believed his whole life long that good intentions on the part of princes would suffice to assure world peace and prosperity. It would be such an easy thing for them to devote themselves to works of peace instead of constantly warring upon each other for the sake of supposed rights or out of sheer cupidity. In itself *monarchia,* that is to say, world dominion, would be the best form of rule on earth. But that was unattainable and impractical—and also unnecessary, if only there could be concord among the Christian princes.

In this connection Erasmus, in a letter to the dukes of Saxony dating from 1517, went beyond mere lamentation to concrete ideas about reforms:

> If it were possible to introduce renovations without violent intervention, it would in my opinion be of particular service to the general well-being of the Christian world if by means of special conventions the boundaries of the dominions of every ruler were to be regulated for the general weal, which boundaries, once established, could not be restricted or enlarged either by bonds of marriage or by treaties, while simultaneously the old legal titles should be abolished which each ruler is wont to produce according to circumstances whenever he desires war. If it might be protested that in such a way the rulers would be deprived of a right incumbent on them, it should better be considered whether it were just that for the sake of such a right, which a ruler might actually possess or perhaps only contrive, the Christian world should be endlessly shaken by outrageous and patricidal feats of arms. . . .[4]

Here, again, there is a sudden flash of a political ideal for the future: the ideal of peace between nations organized on a permanent basis. The utterance may be called naïve, utopian, illusory; we may be reminded that now, after four centuries more of increasingly destructive conflict, the so-called Christian world has shown itself more incapable than ever of achieving such an ideal. Yet Erasmus poses here the ideal that mankind cannot and may not let go if it is not to perish in the bottomless swamp of its secular iniquity. Here, all at once, is the Erasmus whose lasting worth we celebrate. *Saecularum furiosum . . .* you are still right, Erasmus. In 1520 he wrote to Willibald Pirkheimer: "Everywhere I see the affairs of man so corrupted I believe that in no age has so much been permitted to impudence, stupidity, and crime." [5]

It is easy to denounce proclaimers of the lofty principles of a just and rational organization of society as utopians. Nearly always that will gain the approval of the masses. But if the question is raised which minds have proved more indispensable to the progress of humanity, such dreamers or the men of military action—Plato or Alexander—then only a convinced historical determinist will choose the latter, for Plato and Christ could also be termed utopians. And among history's indispensable figures a modest place should also be reserved for Erasmus.

True, the contradiction we postulated earlier immediately rears its head once more: in practically every detail Erasmus is antiquated. That appears the moment one turns from his ideas on war and peace to those on administration and economics. The confident superiority of his judgment in matters of state is only too often based not on real knowledge of affairs, but on ignorance. He was an utter stranger to practical life. He did not know how the world works or what was necessary to govern a country. His views on statecraft and economic life were radical in their simplicity. Almost the only word he did not begrudge trade was *sordidissima,* extremely sordid. Taxation and officialdom he considered from the point of view of the troubled *petit bourgeois.* Problems of unemployment were nonexistent for him: whoever was healthy and contented with little did not have to go begging. He scoffed at the study of law as *a veris literis alienissima,* quite alien to true learning. He thought it ridiculous that a person should have a reputation for being clever because he knew what was happening in the world, what the market situation was like, and what the plans of the rulers were.

All that is no more than the cheap wisdom of a mind that has taken refuge from life amidst books, a flight from the world without any true ascetic significance, touched up with a veneer of stoicism. This is not the field where one should look for the great Erasmus. In the neighboring field, however, we find him again, as soon as purely social questions are raised. In order to perceive the significance of Erasmus's ideas on education and social hygiene one should read his *Christiani matrimonii institutio* [*On Christian Marriage*].

This aspect of his nature, his love for uncorrupted. naturalness in the conduct of life, leads us to one of the main points in this survey: Erasmus's relation to nature in general. Did he share without reserve his friend Thomas More's intense and frank sense of the blessing of a life lived according to nature? Did the rich flowering of the Renaissance also find expression in him? The answer cannot be given in a single word.

For an understanding of great minds it is of importance

not only to know what works they created but also what works they intended to create but left undone, and why. Erasmus has left us an incidental piece of evidence which in the present context deserves our attention. In a letter to Johannes Botz-heim dated January 30, 1523, Erasmus lists his works, and remarks after having mentioned the *Encomium moriae:* "At the time we had a series of three declamations in mind: the praise of folly, of nature, and of grace, but the peevishness of certain people led me to renounce the idea." [6] One asks oneself in vain what form this Praise of Nature may have had in Erasmus's mind. There must have been something daring about it; why should he otherwise have abandoned his intention because of the criticism to be expected? The Praise of Nature as the central panel of a triptych between the unique *Praise of Folly* on one side and a Praise of Grace on the other: we can vaguely divine the highest intellectual achievement of an Erasmus unknown to us. Folly, nature, and grace as a trinity of ascending potential: is it not as if we here have lost a most intimate credo of the Renaissance? In the *Praise of Folly* itself Erasmus somewhat anticipated the two following themes, but what more he was planning to say about them is lost to us.

Only disconnected and informal utterances here and there inform us of Erasmus's ideas on nature. Considering his classical point of view, and likewise his simple ethical attitude, he had to come close to making approval of uncorrupted naturalness a guide for living. The person who admires the Renaissance without sufficient historical training always runs the risk of taking all too seriously the catch phrase of natural freedom which he hears resounding in that period. In the *Fais ce que vouldras* ["Do what thou wilt"], the rule of life in the abbey Thélème in Rabelais's fantasy of *Gargantua,* and in the *Virtutem definiunt secundum naturam vivere* ["They define virtue to be a life ordered according to nature"] of More's *Utopia,* he detects too easily a license for a modern immorality. Erasmus took care that his appreciation of the natural always remained definitely subordinated to the supremacy of the divine commandments.

Erasmus's relations to nature can be learned above all from the *Colloquies.* He indulged in a lush and joyful description of nature in the *"Convivium religiosum"* ("The Religious Feast"), the first full-length dialogue by means of which he gave a larger context and a more elevated meaning to the *Familiarum colloquiorum formulae* in 1522. The fruits, the dishes, the crockery of the feast, everything is served up for us as in a painting by Pieter Aertsen. The garden pavilion with its ingenious wall-paintings and inscriptions is described affectionately in simple images. The friends enjoy their frugal meal outside to the accompaniment of pious conversation. Eusebius says:

> But in the meantime, while we plentifully feed our minds, let not our companions be forgot. Who are those? [asks Theophilus] Our bodies, are not they the companions of our souls? for I had rather call them so, than instruments, or houses, or sepulchers.[7]

In another colloquy, "The Pilgrimage for Religion's Sake," the natural splendor of the colors of precious stones, each of which seems to reflect the image of an object of nature, is opposed to the absurd miracles wrought by the images of saints. Menedemus remarks:

> I wonder that Nature hath so much leisure, as to sport her self in this manner in the imitation of all things. . . . There is no part of nature . . . which she . . . hath not expressed in precious stones. . . .

The answer comes:

> She hath a mind to exercise the curiosity of man's wit, and even in this manner drive us away from idleness; and yet as if we had nothing to put away the time, we dote upon fools, on dice, and upon Jugglers' tricks.[8]

Here, then, are the first suggestions of that admiration of the magnificence and opulence of nature which was to yield such ripe fruits to life, the arts, and learning. But this appeal of nature is still merely termed *curiositas*.

In "The Epicure" Erasmus returns once more to the beauty and appreciation of nature. There he says:

> What can be a more stately show than the contemplation of this world? Those men whom God loveth take far more

pleasure from that than others do. For indeed while these
do carefully view this admirable work, they are troubled
in their mind, because they understand not the causes of
many things. In some things also, as it were some *Momuses,*
they murmur at the workman, and oftentimes call *Nature*
a *Stepmother* in stead of a Mother: which reproach, 'tis
true, striketh at Nature in word, but in very deed it recoils
upon him who created Nature, if there be any Nature at
all. But a pious man looks upon the works of the Lord and
his Father with a great pleasure of mind, with religious
and sincere eyes, much wondering at every thing, finding
fault with nothing, but giving thanks for all things. . . .[9]

The appreciation of nature reflected in these utterances
is basically still the same as the medieval attitude, though
there may also be a Platonic touch in it. Erasmus found in
the joyful observation of nature nothing more than the praiseworthy satisfaction of a pious curiosity. He did not feel the
need that prompted Leonardo da Vinci or Paracelsus to bore
and probe into such mysteries, and in fact considered it
wicked. In the golden age, Stultitia says, the people

were more religious, and godly, than with an ungodly
curiosity to ensearch the secrets of Nature, the quantity of
the stars, their courses, or influences, or the hidden causes
of things, supposing it against gods' forbode, that they
being mortal and earthly men, should struggle to know
beyond their degrees. Much less that ever such madness
came in their brains, as once to think upon the inquiry of
things set above the stars.[10]

It is hardly to be doubted that Stultitia here voices Erasmus's
grave conviction. Later, in one breath with her rejection of
the philosophers, the Scholastics whom Erasmus so utterly
despised, Stultitia says:

But (lord) how sweetly do they rave in their own opinion:
when constantly they affirm there be worlds innumerable?
Or when they take upon them to measure the sun, the
moon, the planets and their compasses, as it were by inch-
meal, or drawn with a line: Or when they expound the
causes of thunder, of winds, of eclipses, and such other
inexplicable things, nothing doubting, as if they had crept
into nature's bosom, or were of counsel with the gods.

And yet doth nature loudly laugh them to scorn, with all their conjectures. . . .[11]

It is evident enough from these quotations that Erasmus not only had no share in the development of natural science but also that he had just as little notion of its coming. If in the *Ratio seu methodus* he advised a knowledge of natural objects based on direct observation, it was, properly speaking, merely for the purpose of a more accurate interpretation of the Holy Scriptures. Although he observed and noted down with interest curious phenomena of animal and plant life, such as the monkey that protected the rabbits against the weasel, and the aloewood that looked so light and yet would not float in wine, for him the classical authors remained the basis for knowledge of nature. *Mundum docet Plinius:* the teacher about the world is Pliny. He even believed in many an animal fable Pliny had rejected, and quietly added the *monophthalmi,* who have but one eye, and the *skiopodes,* who protect themselves with their one broad foot against the sun, to the list of possible variants of the human species.

In the *Colloquies* he gives two specimens of scholarly discussion on natural phenomena. The "Friendship" treats of the question of affection and enmity in the animal world, and the "Problems" of heavy and light objects. In both cases the discussion is carried on entirely in the manner of a logical disquisition. Erasmus failed to detect the birth pains of a new spirit in this field.

Argument from silence is always a hazardous affair, but vis-à-vis Erasmus its validity can hardly be maintained at all in two respects: he scarcely mentions the discovery of the world which was taking place in his day, and just as rarely refers to the magnificent developments in the art of his time. Once, quite by accident, he comes to mention that in his age unknown lands were being discovered whose bounds no one had so far been able to explore, though it was certain that the countries were immeasurably large. The fact serves him only as an argument that there had not yet ever been a true world dominion. When in the dedication of his edition of Saint John Chrysostom to the king of Portugal he praises the Portuguese rule of the seas, which had made the voyage to the Indies as secure as that on any other sea whatsoever, he adds: "If only the monopolies of certain persons do not corrupt this blessing. For, as I hear, though import has become so much easier, yet prices are climbing, especially sugar becoming more expensive in price and at the same time worse in quality. Perhaps the king could remedy this." Needless to say, this trade-policy note parenthetical to Chrysostom caused irritation in Portugal.

It is constantly stressed that Erasmus showed little understanding of or interest in the art of his time. It is a cause for surprise that, for all his aesthetic talents, this man who in his youth had tried his hand at painting had nothing to say on the magnificent flowering of the arts in the Italy of the early *cinquecento*. It is even more striking that his unconditional veneration of antiquity hardly ever has to do with ancient works of art. To reproach him of a lack of sensibilities on the basis of this silence would, however, mean a misunderstanding of the true facts of the case. Erasmus happened to be looking for something other than art, and in his day it was not yet the custom to indulge in dithyrambs of artistic appreciation if the theme did not require it.

To be sure, an examination of his infrequent statements containing an aesthetic opinion would reveal him to be the same in this field as he was in general: a mind of limited resilience, in things aesthetic filled by that same taste for the plain, simple, and delicate which he displayed in his whole personality and thinking. Here are two examples of such aesthetic judgments. In the morning one should rove around in the garden, and in the evening go out to the river, for at sunset the view there is at its finest. And he already knows that the altar adds to the charm of a painting.

In his youth Erasmus had received musical instruction from no less a master than Jakob Obrecht. But so far as I know he wrote nothing that reveals a deep understanding of musical beauty. Music was to him above all an ephemeral and fugitive thing. Like so many people before him, he feared a lascivious influence from music, especially from folk songs and dance tunes. He did not want to admit the new art-music into the church service. His appreciation of the fine arts, then, remained completely subordinate to his moralistic disposition: biblical scenes such as those of Bath-sheba and Susanna ought not to be portrayed; all the money spent on memorial monuments might better be given to the poor.

Viewed from this angle Erasmus appears to us much more

like a medieval cleric in bourgeois surroundings than a main-
stay of the great general renascence of his time. This picture
is in sharp contrast to our conception of the Renaissance.
However, we should be reminded again and again that the
people of the sixteenth century should not be measured by
our conception of the Renaissance; rather the contrary: our
conception of the Renaissance should be measured by the
people of the sixteenth century.

Erasmus was fully aware that the spiritual process of his
time was a renascence. *Renascuntur bonae literae, resipiscit
mundus, reflorescit politior literatura* ["Learning is reborn, the
world is returning to good sense, polite literature is flowering
once more"]. Such expressions recur frequently in Erasmus's
writings. The accent falls disproportionately on literary aspects. But the Renaissance quality of his personality does not
lie solely in this intellectual credo. He shares in all the most
exalted qualities that together constitute for us the definition
of the term Renaissance: the noble proportion, the clarity,
the simple dignity, the high seriousness, the deep longing for
an eternal harmony in all things.

For all that, what he lacks to give his creations a supreme
shape is passion and the vigor to form. He continually produces marvels of literary expression, but always piecemeal,
as patchwork. He lacks repose and readiness to omit non-
essentials. He lacks—and here the deficiency goes beyond the
bounds of the merely aesthetic—the great forms of verbal
expression. His mind is neither epic, nor lyrical, nor dramatic.
It is all too easy to mention for each of these categories the
name of another great contemporary and to conclude that
Erasmus does not measure up to him.

Erasmus would retort: Did I intend to, or want to? He
once said quite clearly how he preferred to be appreciated.
He did not aspire to being admired and venerated. It sufficed
him to be loved as a frail Christian.

The scholar who occupies himself with Erasmus's writings
is constantly struck by shortcomings that keep him from
giving the great man of Rotterdam a place among the very
greatest. He, in turn, passes on to his readers or his hearers
a sort of censure of Erasmus or irritation at him. But afterward a feeling sometimes steals over him that he has done

Erasmus an injustice. At such a moment it will be a good thing for him to remember that in our days a noble mind and a fervently good man whose lifework has made him the mediator, as it were, between Erasmus and the present—I am referring to Percy Stafford Allen—never doubted Erasmus's true and genuine greatness, though he knew Erasmus's weaknesses better than anyone else. We should attempt to understand Erasmus the way Allen understood him.

We should like to transport a living Erasmus across the years to our day. We might ask ourselves what Erasmus, the man he was, would have made of our difficult times, what he would have said to them. It is an idle question. One can only reply that he would have deplored the folly and malice of the world at least as vociferously as in his own day. Erasmus was aware of the insufficiency of all things earthly and the imperfection of every human being. He was prepared to abide them both in as far as the Creator himself had fixed those limitations. He refused, however, to put up with the world and with man in a more imperfect form than they could and should have. He posited the obligation toward the better with a determination no later age could surpass.

True, he viewed the possibility of betterment too simply. He thought that in order to recognize the better and distinguish the true a simple decision of the intellect was sufficient. The only thing one had to do was to separate the essence from the appearance. In the colloquy "Of Things, and Names," he says: "But if a man be a reasonable creature, how far is this from reason, that in the profits rather than goods of the body, and in outward things, which fortune giveth, and taketh away when she listeth, we rather choose the thing than the name; in the true goods of the mind, we make more account of the name than of the thing." [12] That is a question the world can still put to itself.

We are aware that the problems of our day are no more solved by such a simple ethical admonition than those of Erasmus's day were. But if something of Erasmus's simplicity and clarity in ethical and rational judgments were to return, that in itself would be a great gain for the world of today. Mingled in the commemoration of the year of Erasmus's death there is for countless people throughout the world a feeling of revulsion at the falsehood and the folly, the crudity and the malice that seem to be more abundant than ever in the world. We are still in need of Erasmus. It is not for all of us to plunge into his works. That remains to the few who still form a stately and truly international community. But all of us are in need of Erasmus as a symbol. In the final analysis the best proof of his imperishable greatness is the fact that his historical personality did acquire the weight of a symbol, that it remains before the eyes of the world, admonishing and warning. His is one among the minds that are indispensable to us.

The hour in world history which we are passing through is once more the hour of Erasmus. His voice is calling in the distance, faintly amid the din of a giddy world. But this voice, the call of humanity, sounds loudly and firmly in the heart of all those who cannot despair that truth and goodness will prevail.

GROTIUS AND HIS TIME •

Every Dutch child obtains his earliest notions of history from the seventeenth century. The golden age of the Netherlands provides the morning meal for his mind. His sense of the past is nourished on Prince William and Jan De Witt, Ruyter and Tromp. It all seems to him as clear and simple as the red, white, and blue of the flag. He understands the period and loves it.

Later comes Rembrandt, with a host of his fellows. They are fitted into the child's picture, illuminating and elevating it. The poets present themselves: Jakob Cats finds his place, and Gerbrand Bredero, too. But Joost van den Vondel? A first doubt arises whether everything in the seventeenth century is so easy to understand after all. Vondel's glorious magnificence seems alien to the simplicity and calm of Jan van Goyen. And as the young Dutchman approaches the seventeenth century from more and more angles, he becomes increasingly aware how incomplete his view of it as a child had

• "Hugo de Groot en zijn eeuw," a memorial address given at the Hague Folk University for the Society for the League of Nations and Peace on June 16, 1925, on the opening of a Grotius exhibition. First published in De Gids, LXXXIX, X (October 1925), 1-16. Translation from the Dutch text in Verzamelde werken, II, 389-403.

327

been. He discovers that Rubens and Van Dyck offer more help than Rembrandt in understanding Vondel. And what if he were to speak of the age of Vondel, Sweelinck, and Van Campen, instead of the age of Rembrandt? What a different tone, what a different color, what a different visage!—formal beauty, strict construction, taut harmony.

> *Van Campen, dien die eer voor eeuwich toe sal hooren*
> *Van 't blinde Nederlands mis-bouwende gesicht,*
> *De vuyle Gotsche schel te hebben afgelicht.*•

The lines are Constantijn Huygens's. For him, then, all that preceded Van Campen was Gothic malformation. That is to say, Lieven de Key, Hendrik de Keyser, everything we call the Dutch Renaissance? But then our Dutchman has not yet understood Huygens's mind. No, and when he reflects, not Rembrandt's either.

There is perhaps no century so hard to understand as the seventeenth, and much of everything that to the young Dutchman had seemed familiar in the period—the lushness, the suppleness, the naturalness—was a wild growth; a tree blossoming near the fence in the garden of European civilization, a tree the gardener and most of the strollers passed by without noticing.

The seventeenth century is the young hero of the Renaissance ripened into manhood, restrained by faith and his own conscience, still obsessed by the pathos of beautiful form, but no longer exuberant and wild. Inspiration now compels toward the creation of succinct and strict forms, of order, unity, and regularity. There is no other century in which the ideal has weighed so heavily on reality, in which life has reflected such an image of earthly perfection in the mirror of the spirit. It is the age of the dramatic view of life. The thought expressed in Vondel's motto on the Amsterdam Theater is also to be found in Walter Raleigh and in Francis Bacon. Displaying, playing, portraying—who has ever done it as well as Louis XIV!

It is the age of cold passion. In the sixteenth century some-

---

• Van Campen, whose everlasting honor it shall be / To have removed the filthy Gothic scales / From the blind Netherlands' malforming face.

times the trumpet sounds, sometimes the violin. In the eighteenth violins alternate with the flute. The seventeenth century has the resonance of an organ.

This by way of introduction. Enter Grotius. We have known him since our childhood: the child prodigy, the Latin poet, the jurisconsult, the hope of the Netherlands, the Arminian, the prisoner of Loevesteyn, Maria van Reigersberg's husband, the exile, the writer, the ambassador. Perhaps in this case the point of view of our childhood does not need to be changed in its fundamental outlines, but only filled out somewhat. Joseph Scaliger saw clearly when he predicted in the youth "a cautious statesman, an excellent jurist, a moral gentleman. But Janus Dousa saw even more clearly when, on the arrival of the eleven-year-old boy at Leiden University, he compared him to Erasmus in a Latin ode. Grotius's intellectual kinship with Erasmus is of very great importance for an understanding of his personality. It is, in fact, not solely an intellectual kinship but also an influence and an example. Grotius himself felt the relationship profoundly. It may be recalled that, when in his attempt to return to Holland he arrived at Rotterdam in October 1631, the first thing he did was to go to see the bronze statue of Erasmus which had replaced the older stone statue in 1622. In the bitterness of exile, Grotius (with a great deal more nostalgia for Holland than Erasmus ever had felt) attempted to console himself for Dutch ingratitude and lack of appreciation with the thought that Holland had also failed to appreciate Erasmus. Or he would comment that a theological grievance thrown up at him by Cloppenburg had also been charged to Erasmus.[1]

There is also a certain kinship in character between the two. Grotius was no more a born martyr than Erasmus; his most vigorous deeds were inspired by his wife. If only Erasmus could have had a Maria van Reigersberg at his side! It is no mere chance that the nineteenth-century historian Robert Fruin is rather too severe in his judgment of both Erasmus and Grotius. Their weaknesses were to some extent of the same sort, but Fruin did not fully understand their characters because he did not fully appreciate their minds. Fruin's own mind, however deep and broad it may have been, was in the last analysis little open to the enthusiasm of the Renaissance and humanism. In considering Erasmus and Grotius, he did not see their view of the world, and in both cases it was in a certain sense the grandeur of their world-view and the purity of their spirit that exalted them as men.

Grotius's thought, like Erasmus's, is permeated in every fiber with the essence of antiquity, and at the same time, like Erasmus's, shot through with the luster of a broad and mild Christianity. Every concept, every thought, is immediately linked to an image, a word, a motif from antiquity. Antiquity in the very broadest sense: the Church Fathers of the first centuries alongside the pagan poets, philosophers, and historians. Grotius, like Erasmus, avails himself of that resounding trove of silver and gold with inimitable ease. For us, with our indispensable reference books, the capacity and the alertness of the humanist memory has become almost inconceivable, and only the knowledge that the sphere in which everything took place for them was restricted leaves us any self-confidence. How indefatigable the seventeenth-century brain was, both in registering and in rendering. No length of disquisition frightened the writer or the reader, the speaker or the listener; Grotius is just as copious as Erasmus. His Latin is just as muscular, and almost as clear and plastic. But there is no sparkling wit, no bitter irony, to spice that vigorous prose. It is Erasmus's spirit, but without Erasmus's chuckle.

In this respect Grotius seems to us almost the antithesis of Erasmus, and the very model of what one might almost call naïve seriousness. Perhaps our picture of him is a bit too grave. It would be of interest to make a closer study of the aesthetic side of his personality. One would have to consider his Latin poetry, and even his Dutch. Grotius wrote more than ten thousand lines of verse in Latin, and almost as many in Dutch, without being a poet. Such a thing was possible in Latin. The writing of Latin verse, as it was practiced by the humanists, was one of the most remarkable occupations of the human spirit known to cultural history. It was a pastime, but what a majestic one.

Grotius made no claim to being a great poet. "At my time of life," he writes to his brother Willem in 1615 (he was then no more than thirty-two), "the making of verses is no longer appropriate—and not even the very best of them was forgivable." In his religious verse, he goes on, he had wanted to show himself more a Christian than a poet, and in his patriotic verse more a good citizen. He is apologetic that in the latter he had extolled the Dutch point of view rather too triumphantly and abused the enemy rather too bitterly. And he excuses his epithalamia: we were young.

But allow me to quote a few examples of aesthetic nicety from that Latin poetry. I have chosen them from the *Epigrammata*. In the prolix seventeenth century it is lengthiness that kills and succinctness that quickens. In that age of the endless disquisition the epigram flourished. Succinctness quickens— that, and reality. In imitation of Martial, Grotius devoted a hundred distichs to all sorts of household articles: the bootjack, the bedpan, the snuffer, the game of goose, and what not. He gives to the whole the title *Instrumentum domesticum*. It is like an elegant pendant to the Dutch still life. Here is poetic symbolism:

PYXIS ARENARIA
Pulveris aurati pluvia sit sparsa papyrus:
Rescribet Danaë sollicitata, Veni.●

Here is a portrayal achieved with a rhythmic effect:

SOLEAE FERRATAE
Quae Batavûm miratur hyems sola ferrea cernis.
His per aquas nec aquas ire nec ire licet.●●

Who would have thought it?: Grotius sketching a skater as well as Avercamp or Jan van de Velde. And here is a humorous turn:

SCIATHERAS
Dant medios soles contractae gnomonis umbrae,
At mihi pro tali gnomone venter erit.●●●

● "Sandbox": The paper rained with yellow-golden sand: / Answer the question of Danaë, do.
●● "Skates": Behold the iron sole that Holland's winter sees; / Going on it is not going, water is water not.
●●● "Sundial": The shortened shadow of the dial announces noon: / For me my stomach can announce it well enough.

Learned poetry sometimes has unexpected results: it saved the life of Grotius's son Cornelis. When he and his brother Dirk were on their way to serve the king of Sweden, they were attacked in the night by their rapacious manservant, who shot and killed the sleeping Dirk. Cornelis was busy writing a Latin verse; he grabbed his pistol and wounded the murderer.

Though Grotius lacks the sparkle of Erasmus's wit and humor, in another sense his mind would seem to be superior to that of his predecessor. Erasmus, for all the sharpness and clarity of his amazing intelligence, was primarily a co-ordinator. He places his countless examples, his inexhaustible arguments, alongside one another, he summons up endless processions gaily revelling like Rabelais's adventures or sedately striding like Dürer's triumphs. That is the High Renaissance; its form of expression is line and movement.

Grotius subordinates; he measures, he designs, he constructs. That is the seventeenth century. Erasmus spreads light wherever he goes, Grotius creates order wherever he stands. When Erasmus wrote his *Enchiridion militis christiani* [*Manual of the Christian Knight*], he called it an art of piety, *ars pietatis*. Grotius in the Introduction to *De iure belli ac pacis* declared his desire to give jurisprudence the form of an art. To that extent the two humanists run parallel. But in developing the idea, what a difference! The *Enchiridion* is an effusion, a flowing stream of argumentation. The three books of the law of war and peace are an edifice.

I do not want to speak here of the significance of the work that gives occasion for this commemoration. Enough others have done that better than I could do it. I should, however, like to consider for a moment the construction, the form, of that work. Grotius, as he himself said, drew his lines as a geometrician draws figures. The basic concepts are sharp and well defined, they are succinct and simple, hewn stones for the builder. Constantly throughout the work the ancient authorities and references stand ready to lend support. How well he is able to arrange them: what balance and regularity. The function of the classical motif is comparable to that which it has in the architecture of the period, but it is perhaps even more essential, less exclusively decorative. If Grotius constantly worked with examples from antiquity in order to give advice to his own day, it was not solely diplomatic caution that led him to do so, but also sheer aesthetic preference. The ancient as it were represented everything that came later or was still to come, in a sense that did not differ a great deal from that of the relationship between the Old and the New Testaments. The presence of the classical example more or less neutralized the particularities of more recent events in a general unity. The image of history served as a substitute for immediate reality. In honor of Sweden Grotius wrote the *Historia Gotthorum, Vandalorum et Langobardorum,* for the Goths were Sweden's prefiguration and their renown was Sweden's. In his early years, in order to honor the Netherlands, he had written *Parallelon rerumpublicarum,* a comparison of the Athenian, the Roman, and the Batavian commonwealths. The example of antiquity tended to simplify political theory; the concept of the state was reduced to the tangibility of those age-old forms, and indeed the convergence of the classical state and the West European was perhaps never greater than in the seventeenth century, when states came closer to those of antiquity than in the Middle Ages with regard to the principle of nationality, and closer than in recent times with regard to their self-sufficiency.

Considered as a work of art, *De iure belli ac pacis* is very closely allied to the Amsterdam Town Hall. If there is any basis for dividing the seventeenth century into two aspects, as I have done in my introductory remarks, it does not have to be asked on which side Grotius stands. He does not belong with Bredero, Van Goyen, and Jan Steen, but with Vondel, Sweelinck, and Van Campen, with polyphony and classicism, with strict form and the august ideal.

More than one writer has viewed the exalted eulogies of the dedication to Louis XIII prefacing *De iure belli ac pacis* as sheer flattery and favor-currying. According to Grotius the young king, who had as yet done nothing remarkable, was in the suffrage of mankind already honored for his merits with the name "the Just." Certainly a more illustrious sobriquet than those of the Roman commanders—Africanus or Numidicus, or the Philopator and Philadelphus of the Ptolemies. Thus the dedication begins, to climb higher and higher in ever more loudly reverberating praise. But one must read those sonorous phrases with Rubens and Sweelinck in mind, that is to say in the light of the seventeenth-century ideal and its form of expression. This dedication is built up like a polyphonic chorus, with the word *iustus* constantly being taken over more resoundingly by voice after voice. Louis is just in everything he does, but more than that: for the purity of his virtue he should also be called "Holy," like his ancestors Charlemagne and Louis IX. He is the "Prince of Peace" who does not covet other kingdoms and does not invade the right of any others by his arms. The rules of war, which one now looks for in books, may hereafter be taken from Louis's actions, as from a most perfect example: "The God of Peace, the God of Justice, O Just and peaceable King, Crown your Majesty (nearest to His) as with all other happiness, so with this also, the procuring of a Just and Universal Peace."

Did Grotius mean all this? Very definitely. Such was the thought of the seventeenth century. It wanted to believe, it desired, with an infinitely strong desire, that the noblest and the most beautiful, in the form dictated by the poetry of antiquity, might be the truth. Anyone who cannot feel to some extent the high tensile force of that ideal cannot understand the age. What remains of most of the art of the seventeenth century but the dry husk if one judges its contents and tendencies with a present-day sense of reality? What for example is to be made of the eulogies of Grotius himself?

De Zon des Lants wert dus van Mierevelts penseel
Geschildert, toen ze gaf haar schijnsel op 't panneel,
Doch niet gelijck ze straelt op 't heerlijkste in onze oogen,
Maar met een dunne wolk van sterflijkheit betogen.
Om duytsch te spreken, dit 's de Fenix Huig de Groot,
Wiens wijze Majesteit beschijn den wereldkloot.
Wie vraagt nu wat Cefis of Delfos eertijts zeide?
Een Delftsch orakel melt meer wijsheit dan die beide.●

Thus Vondel wrote. And these are Daniel Heinsius's lines beneath the portrait of the thirty-one-year-old Grotius:

● The Country's Sun was thus portrayed by Mierevelt's / Brush as it shed its rays upon the paneling, / Though not the way it shines its brightest in our eyes, / But veiled within a thin cloud of mortality. / To speak plain Dutch, it is the Phoenix Grotius, / Whose sapient Majesty illumes the ball of earth. / Who queries now what once Cephis or Delphi said? / One oracle of Delft speaks wiser than they both.

Depositum coeli, quod jure Batavia mater
Horret et haud credit se peperisse sibi,
Talem oculis, talem ore tulit se maximus Hugo.
Instar crede hominis, caetera crede Dei.●

The seventeenth century viewed the world through the glory of antiquity, and in full sun. Its optimism was of a different sort from that of the eighteenth century—it was more of an intoxication. It went less into details, had less to do with the individual person; it was more general, more vague, more poetic, and above all, more formal. It finds expression in Grotius's expectations of Louis XIII and his reverence for Gustavus Adolphus, but above all, seriously and steadfastly, in his letters and his writings, and in his firm hopes for peace and the reunification of the Church.

Grotius believed he could see the dawn of that happy day already breaking. So many great, learned, and pious men of both parties—he writes to his father on May 12, 1640 [2]—are beginning to realize how wrong it was, here (that is to say, on the side of the Catholics) not to make up for the obvious shortcomings, and there (on the side of the reformers) to create new doctrines and heap bitter abuse on the old ones, though they lacked nothing but a good interpreter. He is less and less despairing, he says elsewhere, of a Christian peace. He has spoken to people of his own age who believe they will live to experience it in France. Cardinal Richelieu, he thinks, is of the opinion that the reunification will succeed.[3]

In what form did Grotius imagine such a peace by means of reunification? Certainly to a large extent as a movement toward the Catholic Church. We shall not here attempt to solve the question, much discussed in his own day, of how far he had moved toward the bosom of the Mother Church. But this much is certain: in his whole intellectual attitude he was closely akin to the large host of prominent converts of his day. Here, too, there is a parallel to be traced with Vondel. He regrets, as Erasmus had regretted, that it had been attempted to cure the evils of the Church by separations and schisms.[4] For him, as for Erasmus, the true reformation

● A pledge of heaven's with which Holland, his mother, rightly / Is perplexed, hardly believing she has borne him— / So appeared the supreme Hugo. / Consider the exterior human, but the rest divine.

would have meant nothing more than restoration, a return to the old, pure Church of the first centuries. The traditions of the Church had a very high value for him. Respect for the *consensus*, the general agreement of the thinkers of all ages, and for history, both of which served him as guiding principles in *De iure belli ac pacis*, lent to his ecclesiastical viewpoint a degree of catholicity which could not help seeming suspicious to many Protestants.[5]

In all this he built on the foundation of his Arminian youth. He declared gratefully that he had received the germ of his later efforts for unity from his father.[6] If I am not mistaken, there is a misconception among many Dutch laymen regarding the nature of seventeenth-century Remonstrantism. Misled by the identical name of the present-day denomination, and perhaps also set on the trail by the term Libertines, which the Calvinists used to fix suspicion on their opponents, one easily imagines the Arminians as liberal, freethinking, modern. They were, indeed, more tolerant and less dogmatic in viewpoint than the Calvinists. But that is not enough to define the real nature of their movement.

One realizes the positive character of the group most clearly on recalling that in England "Arminians" became the term with which the Puritans abused the High-Churchmen. William Laud, the archbishop of Canterbury, the soul of Charles I's ecclesiastical policy, the hardened persecutor of the Puritans, the partisan of Strafford, was the Arminian par excellence. And, indeed, there is considerable kinship and close contact between Dutch Remonstrantism and the Anglican High Church. No one exemplifies that relationship more clearly than Hugo Grotius.

While Calvinist and Anabaptist views took strong root among broad levels of the English people, everything that was viable of aristocratic, conservative, and humanistic ideas found a refuge and new scope for development in the sturdy edifice of the State Church. There a learned and cultured clergy worked out a new theology in the same spirit of respect for the Church Fathers and for the old forms, the sacraments and rituals, which had seemed to Erasmus in his later years as the guarantee of a pure and true Church. The spirit of the Counter Reformation, with its stern sense of uniformity and conformity and its holy awe for the powers that were (above all for the episcopate and the monarchy), and the spirit of baroque, with its passion for splendor and decorum, had found an excellent receptacle in the Church of England alongside the renovated Catholicism of Rome and the rigidified Lutheranism of the German courts.

Now, all these things were Grotius's ecclesiastical ideal: the old unity, with its noble forms, preserved in the new meaning. In England he saw his wish achieved: the return to the old, pure Church. "I am surprised," he writes in 1615, "that anyone can deny that people in England have more respect for the authority of the old Church than in France." [7] In 1638, at the time when Laud and his fellows had already applied their system with an intolerance alien to Grotius's leanings, he wrote: "In England you can see how well the extermination of harmful doctrines have advanced, above all by reason of the fact that the persons who have there taken this holy work upon themselves have not intermingled anything new, anything of themselves, but have focused their gaze on *better ages*." [8]

Grotius, as he himself declares, had long revered the embodiment of aristocratic and despotic Anglicanism, Archbishop Laud. In that same year, 1638, after the great conflict with the Calvinists in Scotland (which was eventually to drag King Charles to his destruction) had already begun, Grotius prayed for Laud that the blindness of those Scots might be healed, *Scotorum skotoma*.[9] The young Reigersberg, traveling in England, did not fail to visit Laud.[10] In his misery Grotius compared the archbishop's sufferings for a good cause with those of Erasmus, Cassander, and Melanchthon.[11] Laud, for his part, referred to Grotius in the most praising terms.[12]

Fruin scored Grotius's inclination for Laud against him as a mistake. But the young Fruin of 1858 was still too naïvely protestant-liberal to understand the vast current of the seventeenth century which held Laud and Grotius together, and Laud, for all his hardness, deserves better than Fruin's characterization: "the narrow-minded man with nothing to plead for him except his unhappy end. . . ." [13]

Nonetheless there is truth in Fruin's judgment of Grotius: "He had no eye for his time." His gaze was focused on an ideal that was the reflected image of an imaginary past. The obsession of antiquity obstructed his view. The flaw in his

great spirit was his one-sidedness. Only half of the Dutch
golden age is embodied in him, and the half he lacks seems
to us the more vital half. Everything with any direct connections to peasant and bourgeois life was alien to him. The
learned Grotius did not fit into Holland's everyday business,
its energetic struggle for prosperity, its jokes and rude pleasures. Equally alien to him was the stream of Renaissance
romanticism that inspired Hooft's love poetry. He lacked both
a firm footing in reality and a radiant warmth of the emotions.
He knew only the formal side of the culture of his day. Hooft,
Huygens, and Vondel knew both sides.

Grotius's one contact with vigorous, healthy life was Maria
van Reigersberg. Maria represents that other aspect of the age:
everything that is direct and warm-blooded—the side of Jan
Steen and Pieter de Hooch, if I may draw an auxiliary line. In
the life of this courageous and natural woman—as it unfolds
for us in the pure, happy conjugal love of the initial years,
then to be submerged in grievous callousness in the face of a
hard lot and family cares—there is more true tragedy than in
that of her great husband, the illustrious exile. Also in her case
Fruin, a bachelor, was too severe. When she hardens and sours
until she can write the bitter words, "I am growing almost
insensitive, as I always live in one equal grief," does the deepest cause not lie in the fact that Grotius, the intellectual, had
failed to return what she had given: a total love? Even in
the first charming letter of 1613—when she wrote to him in
England: "Monsieur T. was here and left a book for you,
but I'll not send it you, so that you will come home sooner"
—even there the motif of her lifelong sorrow can actually
already be traced. Her robust soul and her great heart helped
her to retain joy and courage for a long time. Few stories
tell of bravery and strong nerves as striking as those in the
well-known tale of the escape from Loevestein. When she
had closed the chest-lid over her beloved she kissed the cold
iron of the lock. No hardness of later years can wipe out
that touch.

While cares tarnished Maria's happiness, rancor at Holland's
ingratitude continued to gnaw at Grotius's soul. This one
great sorrow dominated his mind constantly, however much
consolation he found in his books and his hopeful struggle.
Complaints about ingratitude and lack of recognition became his life's refrain: "No plant anywhere in the world

flourishes as easily as ungrateful people." "The Dutch commonwealth is such that no one who is at all wise should have anything to do with it, for he will injure either himself or the country." "Love for my ungrateful fatherland bars every way to happiness for me." [14] Fate was extremely harsh to Grotius when it withheld even the presence of kin from his solitary deathbed at Rostock.

Hugo Grotius died forsaken at the moment when his life (he was then sixty-two) was about to take a new turn. Relieved of a task that had not contented him, the Swedish embassy at the French court, he was in search of a place to pass the years of his old age. He had not lived to behold the ecclesiastical and political peace which were his hope and his consolation, yet in any case he did not die disillusioned.

What would a longer life have brought him? Given three years more, and in 1648 he would have experienced the great treaties of peace: at Münster and at Osnabrück tranquillity and concord were restored to most of Europe, and the independence of the Netherlands was illustriously confirmed. In the Holy Roman Empire there came, if not the unification of the Church, then in any case a mutual recognition of both persuasions on the basis of equality. The peace treaties were calculated to provide a basis for future international law, with guarantees of the common defense of justice against violation, completely in accord with Grotius's views.

Given ten years more, and in 1655 he would have seen the power that he had served for years as ambassador begin, under a new king, Charles X Gustavus, the most aggressive war the *De iure belli ac pacis* could have condemned. Poland, North Germany, and Denmark were in flames. Grotius's fatherland, now guided by persons to whose politics the name of the former prison Loevestein was ominously linked, threw the weight of Holland's sea power into the scale against Sweden—to defend its privileges, true, but also to restore a just peace.

If Grotius had lived to be eighty-four or eighty-five, he would have beheld the rise of that other Louis, the son of his "Prince of Peace," as the Sun King. And Louis XIV, who in 1667 used a legal ruse as an excuse to attack the Spanish Netherlands in full peace, a trial stroke for his later *réunions*

—this Louis was to inhale with full confidence the incense of the dedication to his father as the Prince of Justice. Only in Louis XIV did the ideal of the baroque era which Grotius served—with its tremendous tension, its majestic illusion, and the hollow lie behind them—come to full life.

But the advocate of the law of war and peace would not only have seen Louvois and his monarch in action, but also, once more, Jan De Witt. The Triple Alliance arose: a league of those states not immediately involved in the injustice called halt to the king of France. The grand pensionary was confident that he laid the foundation for a durable European tribunal of states, and that it only would be necessary to supplement and develop the Triple Alliance with the admission of the emperor, the imperial princes, and the Swiss confederates. But the poor man's alliance was weak and unstable. It was not only that French statecraft and French gold was able to detach first England, then Sweden. De Witt's work, considered as an application of Grotius's concept, was fundamentally unsound, for the Triple Alliance had not based itself on law, but had merely sought to compromise at the cost of the wronged party, Spain. And it had not been prepared to give support to an appeal to law by the force of arms if necessary.

Grant Grotius ninety years, and he. would have been alive in 1672: the most disgraceful aggressive war of them all; the humiliating fall of the political system of the anti-Orangeists in Holland; and the atrocity of August 20, the murder of their leaders, the brothers De Witt, in comparison to which Olden Barneveldt's execution in 1619 pales, not as more forgivable, but merely as less animal. But Grotius would also have experienced the rise of a man who from then on devoted his life to preventing the conquest of Europe by a single military monarchy. William III, hard, stiff, limited, without a great deal of culture, but with an iron aim and an unyielding toughness and perseverance, seems in many respects Grotius's antipode. Nonetheless, there is a similarity in objective, and despite everything, in fate. Together they are among the "great defeated." But triumph came to William III in his own life—in so far as there is such a thing as real triumph in affairs of state. What he achieved was a highly defective, unstable system of balance of power, attained and maintained with streams of blood. Nonetheless, this system with which Europe entered the eighteenth century meant progress, and it deterred a general war several times before warfare broke out anew in 1740. Was it something of Grotius's spirit that became reality in William III? We should be pleased to believe it.

One more prospect: 1685, two years after Grotius's first centenary. In the France that he so glorified, where he had expected the first fruits of his efforts for Christian reconciliation, the unity of the Church was indeed restored—by the revocation of the Edict of Nantes. This was the embodiment that history was able to give to the vision. Thus the ideal allowed itself to be realized.

But is this a thought with which to take leave of Grotius —the clearest proof of the inadequacy of his noble illusion? His century, the seventeenth, was drawing to a close. But not his time. That would last longer than a hundred years. His hopeful expectation of a coming peace had been troubled now and then by the doubt whether it might not be for a later age that he was working. "Yet, if it is not granted us to enjoy the sight of that blessing, even so it is our task to plant the trees which may be of value for another age." [15] It is the illusion of a *pax christiana* which he envisioned. We, of a later generation, would prefer to apply that *serere arbores alteri forte saeculo profuturas* to peace among nations.

The effects of a book can never be measured. Hugo Grotius molded the law of nations. His ordering mind gave to the world the vision of a just community of states. The world went on its cruel way, but it never forgot that vision completely. A copy of *De iure belli ac pacis* lay in Gustavus Adolphus's tent at Lützen. The name of Grotius cropped up again and again, and ever louder as time passed by. Even if it were nothing more than a symbol that the unanimous witness of the civilized world now honors in him, he would not have lived and written in vain.

NOTES

THE TASK OF CULTURAL HISTORY

I

[1] Unless it is explicitly mentioned that the word is used in another sense, "realist" ought always to be used in contrast to "nominalist." That Scholastic antithesis is still of major importance and everyday value for our thinking and our idiom. I am repeatedly surprised how frequently I come across the word "nominalist" in contemporary scholarly literature.

[2] Mainly as a result of the activities of the Historical Association and its periodical *History*.

II

[1] Reference may be made to Erich Rothacker, *Logik und Systematik der Geisteswissenschaften* (*Handbuch der Philosophie;* Munich and Berlin, 1927); Theodor Litt, *Wissenschaft, Bildung, Weltanschauung* (Leipzig and Berlin, 1928); and, in a less direct connection, also Hans Freyer, *Theorie des objektiven Geistes,* second edition (Leipzig and Berlin, 1928). Recently a new vindication of the sole supremacy of the methods of the exact sciences was attempted by Wilhelm Ostwald, *"Grundsätz-liches zur Geschichte der Technik,"* *Zeitschrift des Vereines deutscher Ingenieure,* CXXIII (1929), 1-8.

343

[2] Cf. Litt, op. cit., 13; Karl Joël, *"Die Überwindung des 19. Jahrhunderts im Denken der Gegenwart,"* Kantstudien: Philosophische Zeitschrift, XXXII (1927), 475-518.

[3] Rothacker, op. cit., 80 ff.

[4] Ibid., 85 ff.

[5] Cf., e.g., Henri Sée's use of the term in his *"L'idée d'évolution en histoire,"* Revue philosophique, LII (1926), 161.

[6] Wilhelm Bauer, *Einführung in das Studium der Geschichte,* second edition (Tübingen, 1928), 150.

[7] Leibnitz, *Accessiones historicae* two volumes (Hanover, 1698, 1700), quoted in Revue de synthèse historique, New Series, XLIX (1929), 266.

[8] This should not be compared to the death of the biological individual, but to the catastrophic extermination of a whole species, which even in nature is a historical and not a biological phenomenon. The historical elements in biology are indicated in Litt, op. cit., 32 f.

[9] On the role of political and other noneconomic factors in the formation of general economic systems see Otto Hintze, *"Der moderne Kapitalismus als historisches Individuum,"* Historische Zeitschrift, CXXXIX (1929), 457-509, especially 466, 476, 479.

III

[1] Cf. what follows with Litt, op. cit., especially 4, 19, and Eduard Spranger, *"Die Kulturzyklentheorie und das Problem des Kulturverfalls,"* Sitzungsberichte der Preussischen Akademie der Wissenschaften, Philosophisch-historische Klass, CXLVI (1926), li (reprinted in Geisteskultur: Monatshefte der Comeniusgesellschaft für Geisteskultur und Volksbildung, XXXVII [1929], 65-90).

[2] André Jolles's theory of the simple literary forms has pointed my way here.

[3] Alexis de Tocqueville, *La démocratie en Amérique,* two volumes (1835), Book Three, 113, 115 [quoted from *Democracy in America,* two volumes (New York, 1948), II, 69-70].

[4] Ernest Seillière, *Le mal romantique: Essai sur l'impérialisme irrationel* (Paris, 1908); *Les mystiques du néo-romantisme: evolution contemporaine de l'appétit mystique* (Paris, 1911); *Le péril mystique dans l'inspiration des démocraties contemporaines* (Paris, 1918); *Les origines romanesques de la morale et de la politique romantiques* (Paris, 1920).

[5] To my pleasure I see that H. Temperley, in his "Foreign Historical Novels," *Historical Association Leaflet,* LXXVI (1929), shares my distaste for this sort of overwritten history, though in

my opinion he exaggerates the value of the genuine historical novel for the understanding of history.

[6] Rothacker, op. cit., 166.

[7] Ernst Troeltsch, review of Oswald Spengler, *Der Untergang des Abendlandes: Umrisse einer Morphologie der Geschichte*, two volumes (Munich, 1918), in *Historische Zeitschrift*, CXX (1919), 281-91, quotation on p. 290.

IV

[1] Heinrich Ricket, *Kulturwissenschaft und Naturwissenschaft* (Tübingen, 1894), 39.

[2] Wilhem Windelband, *Geschichte und Naturwissenschaft* (Strasbourg, 1894), 31.

[3] Friedrich Meinecke, review of G. P. Gooch, *History and Historians in the Nineteenth Century* (London, 1913), in *Historische Zeitschrift*, CXII (1914), 150-4, quotation on p. 153.

[4] Litt, op. cit., 97 f.

[5] Ibid., 21, 22.

[6] Karl Joël, *"Der säkuläre Rhythmus der Geschichte,"* *Jahrbuch für Soziologie*, I (1925), 159, 146.

[7] Rothacker, op. cit., 82.

[8] Spranger, loc. cit., xlvii.

[9] Cf. W. B. Kristensen, *"De goddelijke bedrieger,"* *Mededeelingen der Koninklijke Akademie van Wetenschappen, Afdeeling Letterkunde*, LXVI, Series B, No. 3 (1928); Fritz Blanke, *Der verborgene Gott bei Luther* (Berlin, 1928).

[10] I believe that grammarians still tend to use the word "morphology" exclusively in the more outward sense.

[11] See the sensitive treatment of this point in Rochus von Liliencron, *"Die Insassen des vierten Dante'schen Sünderkreises,"* *Zeitschrift für vergleichende Litteraturgeschichte und Renaissance-Litteratur*, New Series, III (1890), 24-45. Cf. Fritz Kern, *Dante* (Kämpfer, *Grosses Menschentum aller Zeiten*, I [Berlin, 1923]); Paul Piur, *Petrarcas Buch ohne Namen und die päbstliche Kurie* (Halle, 1925), 35 f., and the literature quoted there.

V

[1] Daniel 7:3-28, 2:31-46.

[2] Matthew 1:17.

[3] Alfons Dopsch summarized his views in his *"Vom Altertum zum Mittelalter: Das Kontinuitätsproblem,"* *Archiv für Kulturgeschichte*, XVI (1926), 159-82.

Henri Pirenne, *Mohammed and Charlemagne* (New York, 1957).

[5] Ferdinand Lot, *La fin du monde antique et le début du moyen-âge* (Paris, 1927).

[6] Karl Heussi, *Altertum, Mittelalter, Neuzeit in der Kirchengeschichte: Ein Beitrag zum Problem der historischen Periodisierung* (Tübingen, 1921).

[7] Ernst Troeltsch, *Der Historismus und seine Probleme: Gesammelte Schriften*, III (Tübingen, 1922).

[8] Georg von Below, *Über historische Periodisierungen. Mit einer Beigabe: Wesen und Ausbreitung der Romantik* (Berlin, 1925).

[9] See the review of ibid. by Paul Joachimsen, *Historische Zeitschrift*, CXXXIV (1926), 369-73, especially 372.

[10] Hans Spangenberg, *"Die Perioden der Weltgeschichte," Historische Zeitschrift*, CXXVII (1923), 1-49.

[11] *Revue de synthèse historique*, XLI (1926) and following issues.

[12] See also his *"Moyen-âge et temps modernes: Une nouvelle défense des divisions traditionelles de l'histoire," Revue de synthèse historique*, XLII (1927), 69-82 (occasioned by Von Below, op. cit.).

[13] Henri Sée, *"La division de l'histoire en périodes: A propos d'un ouvrage récent," Revue de synthèse historique*, XLI (1926), 61-7, especially 65, 66.

[14] Cf. Spranger's very important study op. cit., xxxv.

[15] Ottokar Lorenz, *Die Geschichtswissenschaft in ihren Hauptrichtungen und Aufgaben*, two volumes (Berlin, 1886), I, 279; II, 1891. On other similar points of view cf. Ernest Bernheim, *Lehrbuch der historischen Methode und der Geschichtsphilosophie*, fifth edition (Leipzig, 1908), 81 f.; Bauer, op. cit., III.

[16] Walter Vogel, *"Über den Rhythmus im geschichtlichen Leben des abendländischen Europa," Historische Zeitschrift*, CXXIX (1924), 1-68; Karl Joël, op. cit.

[17] Wilhelm Pinder, *Das Problem der Generation in der Kunstgeschichte Europas*, second enlarged edition (Berlin, 1928). Cf. also Alfred Lorenz, *Abendländische Musikgeschichte im Rhythmus der Generationen* (Berlin, 1928).

[18] Pinder, op. cit., 20 f., takes these difficulties into account, but explains them away. Essential objections against the generations theory similar to mine are developed by Lucien Febvre, *Bulletin du centre international de synthèse*, No. 7 (June 1929).

HISTORICAL IDEALS OF LIFE

[1] Philippe de Commines, *Mémoires*, ed. B. de Mandrot; two volumes (Paris 1901-3), I, 390 [*The History of Comines*, trans. Thomas Danett (London, 1897), 325]: "Covetous he was of glory, which was the chief cause that made him move so many wars. For he desired to imitate those ancient Princes, whose fame continueth till this present." Philippe Wielant, *Recueil des antiquités de Flandre*, ed. J. J. De Smet (Brussels, 1865), IV, 56: "He had grown rough and hard in many ways, and delighted only in romantic histories and the feats of Julius Caesar, Pompey, Hannibal, Alexander the Great, and many other great and high men, whom he wished to follow and imitate." Cf. Olivier de la Marche, *Mémoires*, eds. Henri Beaune and J. d'Arbaumont; four volumes (Paris, 1883-8), II, 334.

[2] The agrarian laws of 1906 and 1910 have largely broken with this system.

[3] De la Marche, op. cit., I, 145.

[4] According to Ed. Meyer only the golden age is based on a folk myth, and the silver and following ages are independent discoveries of Hesiod's: *Genethliakon Carl Robert zum 8. März 1910* (Berlin, 1910), 174. This theory is, of course, not completely disproved by the fact that the Indians also had a system of four periods; the Indian series bore more of a speculative than a mythical character. Cf. Rudolph Roth, *Der Mythus von den fünf Menschen geschlechtern bei Hesiod und die indische Lehre von den vier Weltaltern* (Tübingen, 1860).

[5] Tacitus, *Annales*, III, 26; Posidonius, in Seneca, *Epistolae*, 90; Dionysius of Halicarnassus, *Archaeologia*, I, 36; cf. E. Graf, *Ad aureae aetatis fabulam symbola* (*Leipziger Studien zur classischen Philologie*, VIII [Leipzig, 1885]), 43 ff.

[6] Cf. H. Oldenberg, *Die Religion des Veda* (Stuttgart, 1894), 532 ff.; E. Rohde, *Psyche: Seelencult und Unsterblichkeitsglaube der Griechen* (Freiburg im Breisgau, 1894), 98 f.; Ed. Meyer, op. cit., 173. Later the character of Yama was further modified into that of the lord of the underworld.

[7] Atharva-Veda, XVIII, 3:13.

[8] First sermon on the Feast of Saint Peter and Saint Paul, Saint Bernard of Clairvaux, *Opera*, eds. René Massuet and Texier (Paris, 1719), I, 995; cf. Epistle 238, ibid., I, 235 [Samuel J. Eales, *The Life and Works of Saint Bernard, Abbot of Clairvaux*, three volumes (London, 1889), II, 702], to Pope Eugene: "Who will grant me to see before I die, the Church of God as in the days

of old when the Apostles let down their nets for a draught, not of silver and gold, but of souls?" (cf. I, 734; II, 785, 828).

[9] *Paradiso*, XI, 64 ff.: "A thousand and a hundred years and more / She, robbed of her first husband, unrenowned, / Unwooed, till he came, scorn of all men bore." [*The Divine Comedy*, trans. Laurence Binyon, in *The Portable Dante*, ed. Paolo Milano (New York, 1947), 423].

[10] Thomas Aquinas sums up all the fruits of evangelical poverty in the *Expositio in Isaiam prophetam* (Antwerp, 1621), XIII, 40: "Poverty entails many things: first, remission of sins . . . , secondly, retention of virtues . . . , thirdly, quietude of heart . . . , fourthly, fulfillment of desire . . . , fifthly, sharing in divine sweetness . . . , sixthly, exaltation . . . , seventhly, inheritance of heaven."

[11] "How happy in his low Degree, / How rich, in humble Poverty is he, / Who leads a quiet Country Life . . ." Horace, Epode 2 [trans. John Dryden in *The Odes and Satyrs of Horace* (London, 1730), 133]. Cf. Propertius, III, 25-46; Calpurnius, *Bucolica*, I, 44.

[12] Ernst Dümmler, *Poetae latini aevi carolini, Monumenta Germaniae historica;* Poetae Series (Berlin, 1881), I, 269, 360, 384.

[13] "*Recollection des merveilles advenues en notre temps,*" in Georges Chastellain, *Œuvres*, ed. J. B. H. C. Kervyn de Lettenhove; eight volumes (Brussels, 1863-6), VII, 200.

[14] Links with sacral usages are also not lacking in the bucolic and the golden-age myth.

[15] "*Le livre des faits du bon chevalier messer Jacques de Lalaing,*" in Chastellain, op. cit., VIII, 254. On the authorship of the work cf. Georges Doutrepont, *La littérature française à la cour des ducs de Bourgogne* (Paris, 1909), 99, 483.

[16] It does not seem to me to be desirable to follow Ed. Wechssler, *Das Kulturproblem des Minnesangs: Studien zur Vorgeschichte der Renaissance* (Halle, 1909), in considering the courtly ideal of life as something separate from the chivalric ideal; in my opinion the first was merely a specialization and refinement of the second.

[17] Regarding the custom see, e.g., Enguerrand de Monstrelet, *La Chronique . . . 1400-1444*, ed. L. Douet d'Arcq; six volumes (Paris 1857-62), IV, 65; Thomas Basin, *De rebus gestis Caroli VII et Ludovici XI historiarum libri XII*, ed. J. Quicherat; four volumes (Paris, 1855-9), III, 57.

[18] Jean Froissart, *Chroniques*, eds. Siméon Luce and G. Raynaud; eleven volumes (Paris 1869-99), IV, 69; ibid., ed. J. B. H. C. Kervyn de Lettenhove; twenty-nine volumes (Brussels, 1867-77), V, 291, 514.

[19] *Chronique de Berne* (A. Molinier, *Les sources de l'histoire de France, des origines aux guerres d'Italie*, six volumes [Paris, 1901-6], No. 3103; in Froissart, *Chroniques* [Kervyn edition], II, 531):

"After several excuses he vowed that he would serve the one from whom he would have most benefit, saying that he would be like a cock that turns with the wind; that therefore he would hold with him from whom he received the greatest largesse. At these words the bystanding English began to laugh." Compare the words put into the same Beaumont's mouth by the poet of *Le vœu du héron, Société des Bibliophiles de Mons,* No. 8 (Mons, 1839), p. 17, vv. 354-71. It is of no importance what historical basis the tale may have had. At the "vow of the pheasant" at Lille in 1454 a nobleman swore "that if he did not obtain the favors of his lady before the crusade he would marry the first lady or damsel in the possession of twenty thousand gold pieces [he met] upon his return from the Near East. . . .": Doutrepont, op. cit., 111. For a caricature tournament see Jean Molinet, *Chronique,* ed. J. A. Buchon; five volumes (Paris, 1827-8), III, 16.

[20] Wilibald Schrötter, *Ovid und die Troubadours* (Halle, 1908); Karl Heyl, *Die Theorie der Minne in den ältesten Minneromanen Frankreichs* (Marburg, 1911); Edm. Faral, *Recherches sur les sources latines des contes et romans courtois du moyen-âge* (Paris, 1913).

[21] On the significance of the Christian element in the Renaissance see, e.g., Konrad Burdach, *"Sinn und Ursprung der Worte Renaissance und Reformation,"* in his *Reformation, Renaissance, Humanismus: Zwei Abhandlungen über die Grundlage moderner Bildung und Sprachkunst* (Berlin, 1918), 13-96, especially 26 ff.; Ernst Walser, *"Christentum und Antike in der Auffassung der italienischen Früh-renaissance," Archiv für Kulturgeschichte,* XI (1913), 273-88.

[22] Even Froissart had an utterly Renaissance outlook on the chivalric obligations: see his *Chroniques,* eds. Luce and Raynaud; I, 3, 4; IV, 112. Chastellain says: "Honor invites every noble nature; to love everything that is noble is of its essence.": *"Le dit de vérité,"* in Chastellain, op. cit., VI, 221.

[23] Dietrich Schäfer, *Weltgeschichte der Neuzeit* (Berlin, 1907), I, 7.

[24] From a notice in *Historische Zeitschrift,* CV (1910), 456, of an article by Ed. Heyck, *"Die Nachdauer Bismarcks," Konservative Monatsschrift* (April 1910). The need to bring the new culture that the German feels he is helping to build into a relationship with the Germanic heroic age is not restricted to the monumental arts and national poetry. This may be clarified by a few examples. In L. Schmidt's strictly matter-of-fact and scholarly *Geschichte der deutschen Stämme bis zum Ausgange der Völkerwanderung,* six parts (Berlin, 1910-18), the non-German reader is struck by the extent to which the author gives vent to his modern national feelings in his account of Arminius' deeds (II, Part Two, 105 ff.).

Arminius was "one of the greatest heroes of our nation," to whom Germany must be eternally grateful, "the first definite embodiment of the national idea," a person of "innate genius," "the brilliant figure of the ruler of the Cherusci." Modern concepts are projected into the relations between the Romans and the Cherusci: "Actually the struggle was not won in open battle, but by a cunning surprise attack. But the Germans repaid the Romans, who had preceded them in perfidy and in violation of the law of nations, in their own coin" (p. 116).

Karl Lamprecht, in *Der Kaiser: Versuch einer Charakteristik* (Berlin, 1913), emphasizes the (outward) parallels between the high culture of a people and the *Urzeit*, the "prehistoric period," of the same people—for example, the democratic spirit of the twentieth century and that of the German heroic age (ibid., 7). He detects in Wilhelm II powerful "remnants of a prehistoric inclination" revealing themselves in the emperor's "ancestor cult," his concept of God, and his view on the loyalty of his subjects (ibid., 6, 40, 42, 47).

The "prehistoric" attitudes are extremely closely related to a firm belief "in the special calling and talent of the German people in world history" (ibid., 99), which was recently proclaimed with such surprising clarity by Eucken. This thought can degenerate from a purely intellectual domination of the world by German culture (as expressed by the emperor, see ibid., 99) to an undisguised imperialism: "Germany and a good share of the world for the Germans, who . . . are proceeding . . . from geographical nationalism to a racial belief in the life and the personality of our nation. . . .": F. Siebert, *Der deutsche Gedanke in der Welt: Deutsch-akademische Schriften, herausgegeben von der H. von Treitschke-Stiftung*, III (1912). This thought is developed in a remarkable way in the writings of Arthur Bonus: *Deutscher Glaube: Träumereien an der Einsamkeit* (Heilbronn, 1897); *Zur Germanisierung des Christentums*, revised essays dating from 1895 to 1901 (Jena, 1911), constituting the first volume of *Zur religiösen Krisis;* and *Vom neuen Mythos: Eine Prognose*, Volume Four of the same work (Jena, 1911). Taking an untempered national prepossession as his starting point, Bonus strove initially for a restoration of the worship of Woden as a sort of vassal of Christ (*Deutscher Glaube, passim*). "The religious evolution of the future is the conscious return to the medieval beginnings: the re-Germanization of Christianity. . . ." The German nation has "demonstrated [its] extreme suitability to take over the heritage of Israel. . . ." There is "hardly a beginning of an understanding of the deeper meaning of Christianity" among the Latin and Slavic nations (*Zur Germanisierung*, 12, 14, 15—an essay originally dating from 1895). Gradually his views have become more refined and less restricted. He now ridicules the modern Woden worshippers. The Icelandic sagas and the German heroic age can only provide a background mood; one senses that that world was "more genuinely and sternly German," one can even regret the fact that such highly promising seeds of a Germanic religion did not develop, but Iceland cannot give us a religion (*Zur Germanisierung*, 105-11—an essay dating from 1901). There remains a need for a religious mood in which "an unbending will to the power and authority of the soul" predominates "as the most inward and highest pride and defiance" (ibid., 66); "the old Germanic conception of religion as a source of strength in place of a refuge for the ailing" (ibid., 42); "religion does not consist of dreams, but of courage and action" (ibid., 34); the vital German question is "How can I rule the world?" (ibid., 16, 34). In *Vom neuen Mythos* the nationalist content of these ideas is restricted and refined further (pp. 40 ff.). In the preface to *Zur Germanisierung* the writer warns the reader not "to give a trivial interpretation" to the title, and one would indeed do this thinker an injustice by imagining him as merely an intellectual imperialist and race-theorist.

The war has given many of these attitudes a crude and material turn. It is strange that a theologian such as Deissmann now seriously takes up a notion with which the radical Bonus had toyed in his first period (*Deutscher Glaube*, 85, 216), and for Christmas of 1914 praises the Old Saxon Heliand, Jesus as a military hero, as "the deepest and truest impression that the German spirit ever received of Christ. . . .": *"Heliands Weihnacht," Illustrierte Zeitung*, No. 3728 (December 10, 1914). One should, of course, not overestimate the significance of war homiletics and war poetry. The world will later wish to deny an enormous mass of printed matter dated 1914 (and how much later?).

PATRIOTISM AND NATIONALISM IN EUROPEAN HISTORY

I: *To the End of the Middle Ages*

[1] *Iliad*, V, 213.

[2] II Maccabees 8:21, cf. 14:18.

[3] Augustine, *De civitate Dei*, Book Four, Chapter 15 [trans. John Healey, Augustine, *The City of God*, ed. R. V. G. Tasker; two volumes (London, 1957), I, 125].

⁴ Cf. Heinrich Finke, *Weltimperialismus und nationale Regungen im späteren Mittelalter* (Freiburg im Breisgau, 1916).

⁵ See Albrecht Werminghoff, *Geschichte der Kirchenverfassung Deutschlands im Mittelalter* (Hanover, 1905), I, 151.

⁶ See Halvdan Kort, "A Specific Sense of the Word *Patria* in Norse and Norman Latin," *Archivum latinitatis medii aevi* (*Bulletin Du Cange*), II (1925-6), 93-6; Francesco Arnaldi, "*Ancora sul significato di* Patria," ibid., III (1926-7), 30-1; C. Johnson, "*Patria*," ibid., III (1926-7), 87; Luis Nicolau d'Olwer, "*Notes lexicographiques, I: Patrie*," ibid., III (1926-7), 145-7; Harriet Pratt Lattin, "*Patria*," ibid., VII (1932), 43-4. Cf. *Les annales de Flodoard publiées d'après les sources*, ed. Ph. Lauer (Paris, 1906), 17, where the editor reads more in the word than it contains.

⁷ *Cronica fratris Salimbene de Adam ordinis minorum*, ed. Oswald Holder-Egger; *Monumenta Germaniae historica*, Scriptorum Series, XXXII (Hanover and Leipzig, 1913), 534.

⁸ Suger of Saint-Denis, *Vie de Louis le Gros, suivie de l'histoire du roi Louis VII*, ed. Auguste Molinier (Paris, 1887), 26-30.

⁹ John of Salisbury, *Opera omnia*, ed. J. A. Giles; five volumes (Oxford, 1848), I (*Epistolae*), 63 f. [quoted from eds. W. J. Millor and H. E. Butler, *The Letters of John of Salisbury, I: The Early Letters* (1153-61); (London, 1955), 206-7].

¹⁰ *Van den derden Edewaert*, ed. Jan Frans Willems; *Belgisch Museum der Nederduitsche taal- en letterkunde en der geschiedenis des vaderlands*, IV [1840], 298-367, ll. 1585-7.

¹¹ *Purgatorio*, XXX, 133 ff. [quoted from *The Divine Comedy*, trans. Laurence Binyon, in *The Portable Dante*, ed. Paolo Milano (New York, 1947), 348].

¹² Louise L. Loomis, "Nationality at the Council of Constance," *American Historical Review*, XLIV (1938-9), 508-27.

II: *From the Renaissance to the Napoleonic Era*

¹ The point of view in Robert Michels, "*Zur historischen Analyse des Patriotismus*," *Archiv für Sozialwissenschaft und Sozialpolitik*, XXXVI (1913), 14-43, 394-449, see p. 15.

² A point of view recently stated in C. W. van der Pot, "*De plaats van het koningschap in ons hedendaagsche staatsrecht*," *Mededeelingen der Koninklijke Nederlandsche Akademie van Wetenschappen, Afdeeling Letterkunde*, New Series, II, No. 10 (1939), 321-66, see p. 360: ". . . the sense of nationality, like the concept nation itself a product of the nineteenth century . . ."

³ The reference in Paul-Emile Littré, *Dictionnaire de la langue frar̄aise, ꞏ̇at the word patrie is to be found in Jean Chartier's Histoire de Charles VII* (1477) is based on an error, just as is

the statement that Joan of Arc used it in her hearings, or that it is to be found in the report on the session of the Estates-General at Tours in 1484; see François-Alphonse Aulard, *"Patrie, patriotisme avant 1789," La révolution française*, LXVIII (1915), 193 ff. In English neither the Latin word nor its Germanic translation has been adopted, for a glance in the Oxford Dictionary is sufficient to show that "fatherland" is hardly a current word.

⁴ See my contribution *"Erasmus über Vaterland und Nationen,"* in the *Gedenkschrift zum 400. Todestage des Erasmus von Rotterdam* (Basel, 1936), 34-49 [*Verzamelde werken*, VI, 252-67].

⁵ Literally, *alba sum amussis:* Erasmus, *Opus epistolarum*, eds. P. S. Allen et al.; twelve volumes (Oxford and London, 1906-58), VII, No. 1840; cf. *Adagia*, in Erasmus, *Opera omnia*, ten volumes (Leiden, 1703-6), II, 215 (No. 488).

⁶ Thomas More, *Utopia*, eds. Victor Michels and Theobald Ziegler (Berlin, 1895), 30.

⁷ See my article mentioned in note 4 above.

⁸ The title *archidux* was not adopted at any one specific moment, but gradually came into use at the end of the Middle Ages; it also occurred earlier for other princes now and then, especially for the dukes of Lotharingia-Brabant.

⁹ Cf. Aulard, op. cit., 207.

¹⁰ Cf. my article mentioned in note 4 above, p. 48.

¹¹ *Journal des débats*, No. 221, XXI, 416.

III: *The Nineteenth Century*

¹ Werner Kaegi, *"Der Typus des Kleinstaates im europäischen Denken," Neue Schweizer Rundschau*, New Series, VI (1937-8), 257-71, 345-61, 414-31.

² *Dictionnaire philosophique*, under *"Patrie,"* Section III.

³ Jacob Grimm, *Kleinere Schriften*, ed. Gustav Hinrichs; four volumes (Berlin, 1881-7), I, 1-25.

⁴ Ibid., VI, 411-18.

⁵ A letter dated November 15, 1830, in *Briefwechsel der Brüder Grimm mit Karl Lachmann*, ed. Albrecht Leitzmann; two volumes (Jena, 1927).

⁶ "I still feel passionately attached to all the intrinsic qualities of my *Heimat*": *Kleinere Schriften*, I, 27 (*"Über meine Entlassung"*).

⁷ Robert Michels, op. cit.: Robert Michels, *Der Patriotismus: Prolegomena zu seiner soziologischen Analyse* (Munich, 1929); Robert Michels, *Prolegomena sul patriottismo* (Florence, 1932); *"La nationalité et l'histoire,"* papers by H. Koht, L. Eisenmann,

M. Handelsman, H. Oncken, H. Steinacker, and T. Walek-Czernecki for the International Historical Congress held at Oslo in 1928, published in the *Bulletin of the International Committee of Historical Sciences*, II (Paris, 1929).

JOHN OF SALISBURY: A PRE-GOTHIC MIND

[1] "*Über die Verknüpfung des Poetischen mit dem Theologischen bei Alanus de Insulis*," *Mededeelingen der Koninklijke Akademie van Wetenschappen, Afdeeling Letterkunde*, LXXIV, Series B, No. 6 (1932), 89-198 (*Verzamelde werken*, IV, 3-84). [The study of Abelard, written later, appears in this book.]

[2] Two volumes (Oxford, 1909). [Joseph B. Pike has translated Books I-III and parts of Books VII-VIII under the title *Frivolities of Courtiers and Footprints of Philosophers* . . . (Minneapolis, 1938), and John Dickinson Books IV-VI and parts of Books VII and VIII under the title *The Statesman's Book of John of Salisbury* (New York, 1927).]

[3] (Oxford, 1929) [translated by Daniel D. McGarry under the title *The Metalogicon of John of Salisbury: A Twelfth-Century Defense of the Verbal and Logical Arts of the Trivium* (Berkeley, 1955)].

[4] Clement C. J. Webb, *John of Salisbury* (London, 1932).

[5] Carl Schaarschmidt, *Johannes Saresberiensis nach Leben und Studien, Schriften und Philosophie* (Leipzig, 1862), 9, rightly concluded this from vv. 137-42 of the *Entheticus* (in Salisbury's *Opera omnia* [ed. J. A. Giles; five volumes (Oxford, 1848)], V, 243), reading the comma there *before* the word "*Normannus.*"

[6] It should be distinguished from the "*Entheticus*" that serves as a verse introduction to the *Policraticus*. It is not completely certain what the author meant by the title.

[7] It was published by Wilhelm Arndt as an anonymous continuation of Sigebert of Gembloux in the *Monumenta Germaniae historica*, Scriptorum Series, XX (Hanover, 1868), 515-45. Reginald Lane Poole has brought out a new edition: *Ioannis Saresberiensis historiae pontificalis quae supersunt* (Oxford, 1927). [Marjorie Chibnall has now produced a translation (with facing Latin text) in the Medieval Texts Series: *John of Salisbury's Memoirs of the Papal Court* (London, 1956).]

[8] For the letters one still has to resort to the unsatisfactory text in the first two volumes of Giles's edition of the *Opera omnia*, reprinted in Jacques-Paul Migne, *Patrologiae cursus completus, series latina*, 221 volumes (Paris, 1844-64), CXCIX. The chronol-

ogy of the early letters has been determined critically by Reginald Lane Poole, "The Early Correspondence of John of Salisbury," *Proceedings of the British Academy,* XI (1924-5), reprinted in Poole, *Studies in Chronology and History* (Oxford, 1934). [The letters are now being published in translation with facing Latin text in the Medieval Texts Series under the title *The Letters of John of Salisbury.* To date only Volume One: *The Early Letters (1153-61),* eds. W. J. Millor and H. E. Butler and revised by C. N. L. Brooke, has appeared (London, 1955).]

[9] Epistle 97 (1157) (Giles, I, 144) [quoted from Millor and Butler's translation, I, 52].

[10] Epistle 274 (1168) (Giles, II, 182).

[11] Epistle 190 (1166) (Giles, I, 334); cf. Epistle 193 (1166) (Giles, II, 18).

[12] Epistle 277 (1168) (Giles, II, 186).

[13] Epistle 194 (1166) (Giles, II, 18).

[14] Epistle 155 (1166) (Giles, I, 246); cf. Epistle 156 (1166) (Giles, I, 248): *condicio mea non modo mihi tolerabilis est sed iucunda* ["my condition is not only tolerable for me, but even pleasant"].

[15] Epistle 169 (1166) (Giles, I, 268).

[16] *Metalogicon,* Prologue and Book IV, Chapter 42 (Webb edition, 3, 218).

[17] Epistles 175 (1166) and 296 (1170) (Giles, I, 282, II, 235).

[18] Epistle 323 (1176) (Giles, II, 291), a congratulatory message from King Louis VII on his appointment.

[19] Epistles 325-7 (1176) (Giles, II, 293 ff.).

[20] Given by the tanners' guild of Chartres.

[21] *Œuvres complètes de Suger de Saint Denis,* ed. A. Lecoy de la Marche (Paris, 1867), 380-90.

[22] *Bibliotheca Cluniacensis,* eds. Martin Marrier and André Quercetanus (Brussels, 1915), 589.

[23] Pierre of Poitou in the panegyric in ibid., 510.

[24] Epistle 234 (1168) (Giles, II, 100), probably to Baldwin, canon of Exeter and later archbishop of Canterbury; cf. Schaarschmidt, op. cit., 267, and Webb, *John of Salisbury,* 153. What was meant by the knight's girdle is not clear.

[25] Epistle 145 (1166) (Giles, I, 227). On Saint Drausius see Bollandus, *Acta sanctorum martyrum* (Antwerp, 1668), I, 404.

[26] *Policraticus,* Book VI, Chapters 1-19.

[27] Epistle 275 (1168) (Giles, II, 183); cf. ibid., I, 253; II, 59, and especially Epistle 300 (1170) (ibid., II, 246).

[28] Migne, *Patrologia,* CLXXVI, column 1011.

[29] *Œuvres,* 283, 316, 317.

[30] Abelard, *Opera,* ed. Victor Cousin; two volumes (Paris, 1849, 1859), I, 716.

[81] Epistle 85 (*circa* 1157) (Giles, I, 118) [quoted from Millor and Butler's translation, I, 57]; cf. Epistle 283 (Giles, II, 193).

Peter of Celle liked to jest about beer and wine in his letters to John (Migne, *Patrologia*, CCII, columns 573a, 574d (Epistles 123 and 125), and repeatedly refers to John's harmless jokes: "your witticisms are without teeth, your jokes without meanness." Epistle 69 (column 515a); cf. Epistle 73 (column 519d) and 124 (column 573b).

[82] Epistle 138 (Giles, I, 195-6).

[83] When John refers to the end of the world he does so calmly and without threatening emphasis: Epistle 144 (Giles, I, 220). Such a mood does not by any means exclude complaints about the depravity and misfortune of his age, see *Policraticus*, Book VI, Chapter 16, and Book VIII, Chapter 16; *Metalogicon*, Book IV, Chapter 42.

[84] *Entheticus*, vv. 461-8 (Giles, V, 253).

[85] *Policraticus*, Book III, Chapter 1 [quoted from Pike's translation, 202].

[86] Reginald Lane Poole, "John, called of Salisbury," in *Dictionary of National Biography*, XXIX (London, 1892), 439-46, see p. 445.

[87] *Metalogicon*, Prologue (Webb edition, 4) [quoted from McGarry's translation, 216]. The word *forte* ("perhaps") seems to me to occur frequently in his work. On John's philosophy see also Webb, *John of Salisbury*, 51 ff., 75 ff., 85 ff.

[88] *Metalogicon*, Book II, Chapter 10 (Webb edition, 82).

[89] *Policraticus* (Webb edition), I, 234.

[40] II Cor. 3:17; cf. John's *Vita sancti Thomae Cantuariensis archiepiscopi et martyris* (in Giles, V, 366).

[41] After Psalms 51:5, 118:46.

[42] *Historia pontificalis* (Poole edition), 16-41.

[43] Ibid., 18.

[44] *Policraticus*, Book VII, Prologue (Webb edition, II, 93) [quoted from Pike's translation, 216]. Cf. *Metalogicon*, Prologue (Webb edition, 3-4), where not only feelings of inferiority toward the ancients are to be heard but also confidence in the worth of the contemporary. See also *Metalogicon*, Book III, Chapter 4 (Webb, 136), for the feelings of Abelard, and Abelard, *Opera* (Cousin edition), I, 326.

[45] *Metalogicon*, Book III, Chapter 4 (Webb, 136) [quoted from McGarry's translation, 167]. Ecclesiastical art presents this motif in a different sense, by depicting the apostles on the shoulders of the prophets. There is a similar theme in Buddhist art, with the *bodhisattvas* on the shoulders of the *dhyanibuddhas*.

[46] Abelard, *Opera*, I, 225.

[47] Like Anselm's *Monologion* and *Proslogion*, Bernardus Silves-

tris's *Megacosmus et Microcosmus,* William of Conches's *Dragmaticon;* cf. Webb in the Introduction to his edition of *Policraticus,* xlviii, and in *John of Salisbury,* 22.

⁴⁸ *Metalogicon,* Book I, Chapter 12.

⁴⁹ Ibid., Book IV, Chapter 2.

⁵⁰ Epistles 149, 169, 230 (Giles, I, 238, 268; II, 95). Cf. Webb, *John of Salisbury,* 156.

⁵¹ It is nowhere more refined and more typically English than in the letter congratulating Sigillo on his appointment as archdeacon (Epistle 166, Giles, I, 260). Cf. Webb, *John of Salisbury,* 154.

⁵² *Policraticus,* Book III, Chapter 4 (Webb, I, 179).

⁵³ Epistle 14 (Giles, I, 16) [quoted from Millor and Butler's translation, I, 74].

⁵⁴ E.g., Epistles 48 and 54 (Giles, I, 49, 56).

⁵⁵ *Historia pontificalis* (Poole edition), 81; *Monumenta Germaniae historica,* Scriptorum Series, XX, 542 [quoted from Chibnall's translation, 79-80].

⁵⁶ *Policraticus,* Book V, Chapter 16 (Webb, I, 350).

⁵⁷ Ibid., Book I, Chapter 4.

⁵⁸ *Metalogicon,* Prologue (Webb, 1).

⁵⁹ Ibid., Book I, Chapter 1 (Webb, 6, 7) [quoted from McGarry's translation, 10].

⁶⁰ *Policraticus,* Book VIII, Chapter 9 (Webb, II, 280).

⁶¹ Ibid., Book IV, Chapter 1 (Webb, I, 235).

⁶² Ibid., Book IV, Chapters 2 and 3 (Webb, I, 238, 239).

⁶³ Ibid., Book IV, Chapter 3.

⁶⁴ Ibid., Book III, Chapters 1 and 15; VIII, Chapters 17 and 20.

⁶⁵ *Entheticus,* v. 1297 (Giles, V, 280), cf. vv. 1341, 1412, 1435.

⁶⁶ *Policraticus,* Book VIII, Chapter 17.

⁶⁷ Ibid., Book V, Chapter 16.

⁶⁸ See above, p. 169.

⁶⁹ John borrowed this part of his title from the work of Flavian so entitled. Cf. *Policraticus,* Book II, Chapter 26 (Webb, I, 141).

⁷⁰ "*Entheticus*" (part of *Policraticus:* Webb, I, 5).

⁷¹ *Entheticus,* v. 1467 (Giles, V, 286).

⁷² *Policraticus,* Books I-IV, VI-VIII, *passim.*

⁷³ Ibid., Book III, Chapter 3 (Webb, I, 177).

⁷⁴ Ibid., Book I, Chapter 4 (Webb, I, 34).

⁷⁵ *Metalogicon,* Prologue (Webb, 1).

⁷⁶ *Vita sancti Thomae* (Giles, V, 363).

⁷⁷ Thomas's worldly pomp is painted in detail, and with undeniable pleasure, by one of his biographers, William Fitzstephen, in *Materials for the History of Thomas Becket, Archbishop of Canterbury,* ed. J. Craigie Robertson; Rolls Series; seven volumes (1875-85), III (1877), 20-33.

[78] *Entheticus*, vv. 1435-40 (Giles, V, 285): *Tristior haec cernit iuris defensor et artem, / Qua ferat auxilium consiliumque, parat. / Ut furor illorum mitescat, dissimulare / Multa solet, simulat, quod sit et ipse furenes; / Omnibus omnia fit, specie tenus induit hostem, / Ut paribus studiis discat amare Deum* ["The defender of the law sees these things in a sadder way, / And prepares the art that is to bring help and counsel. / In order that these people's frenzy may be calmed, / He is used to hide many things, and pretends he too is frenzied; / He becomes all things to all men, he puts on his opponent's appearance, / That by such efforts he may learn to love God"].

[79] *Vita sancti Thomae* (Giles, V, 361).

[80] Ibid.

[81] *Policraticus*, Book VIII, Chapter 24 (Webb, II, 423-5).

[82] *Entheticus*, vv. 875, 887-900 (Giles, V, 266-7).

[83] *Policraticus*, Book III, Chapter 8 (Webb, I, 190).

[84] Ibid., Book III, Chapter 7.

[85] Ibid., Book I, Chapter 6; Book VI, Chapter 16; Book VIII, Chapter 6 (Webb, I, 41; II, 41, 259). I have not been able to find any definite confirmation for my suspicion that *stulticinia* is a specific term derived from the poetry of the troubadours. My colleague C. de Boer called my attention to the phrase *Chanso eu le fola* in *Rambaut d'Orange*, cf. *Romani*, LVI (1930), 510 (v. 1150).

[86] *Metalogicon*, Prologue (Webb, 2) [McGarry's translation, 4].

[87] Ibid., lines 15-18 (Webb, 4). Cf. also *Policraticus*, Book IV, Chapter 4 (Webb, I, 245), and especially Book VIII, Chapter 24 (Webb, II, 425).

[88] Walter Map took over the title *De nugis curialium*, but his assorted collection of anecdotes and tales does not at all reflect John of Salisbury's attitude, although Map begins with a brief elaboration of the theme of antipathy to court life. Walter Map was through and through a *histrio,* a court *jongleur* of a lesser caliber, and probably borrowed his title from his greater countryman partly out of irony and partly by way of advertisement. Somewhat closer to John's point of view is the work of Nigel Wireker, *"Contra curiales et officiales clericos"* (ed. Thomas Wright in *The Anglo-Latin Satirical Poets and Epigrammatists of the Twelfth Century*, two volumes [London, 1871], I, 146), which is, however, directed in particular against ecclesiastics who were pro-court. In the context of my observations a striking light falls on the fact, constantly mentioned in the history of literature, that one of Thomas à Becket's murderers, hence one of the *bestiae curiae,* was Hugh de Morville, who (in as far as his identity can be ascertained) imported the *Lancelot* into Austria when he was there as a hostage for Richard Lion-Hearted. My assumptions regarding

the attitude of John of Salisbury toward courtly culture should be compared to what I had to say regarding Alain de Lille's court relations: see my *"Über die Verknüpfung des Poetischen mit dem Theologischen bei Alanus de Insulis,"* 65-82 [in *Verzamelde werken,* IV, 51-64]. The antithesis courtier-philosopher, with the wordplay Gnatho-Plato, was already to be found in the *Dragmaticon philosophiae* of William of Conches: *Gnathonis est non Platonis, hodie amari* (published under the title *Dialogus de substantiis physicis, a Wilhelmo Aneponymo philosopho* [Strasbourg, 1567], 157).

[89] Webb (*John of Salisbury,* 26) calls the first book of the *Policraticus* "a good illustration of the medieval Puritanism familiar enough to students of the period. . . ." The persistency of an orientation in thought that may be called "puritan" in the English (and Anglo-Latin) literature of the late Middle Ages is well epitomized in the final sentence of W. F. Schirmer's *Der englische Frühhumanismus* (Leipzig, 1931): "Humanism withdraws, and there is Puritanism." (p. 181).

ABELARD

[1] *"Über die Verknüpfung des Poetischen mit dem Theologischen bei Alanus de Insulis,"* *Mededeelingen der Koninklijke Akademie van Wetenschappen, Afdeeling Letterkunde,* LXXIV, Series B, No. 6 (1932), 89-198 [*Verzamelde werken,* IV, 3-84].

[2] *"Een praegothieke geest: Johannes van Salisbury,"* *Handelingen van het Nederlandsche Philologen-Congres,* XV (1934), 27-43, and *Tijdschrift voor geschiedenis,* XLVIII (1933), 225-44 [*Verzamelde werken,* IV, 85-103; translated in this volume as "John of Salisbury: A Pre-Gothic Mind"].

[3] Jacques-Paul Migne, *Patrologiae cursus completus, series latina,* 221 volumes (Paris, 1844-64), CLXXV, xiv.

[4] In John of Salisbury, *Opera omnia,* ed. J. A. Giles; five volumes (Oxford, 1848), I, 189.

[5] From two epitaphs attributed to Peter the Venerable, the abbot of Cluny, in Abelard, *Opera,* ed. Victor Cousin, two volumes (Paris, 1849, 1859), I, 717.

[6] *"Metamorphosis Goliae episcopi,"* in Thomas Wright, *The Latin Poems Commonly Attributed to Walter Mapes* (London, 1841), 29, where the third line is printed incorrectly. Bernhard Geyer, *Peter Abaelards philosophische Schriften, Beiträge zur Philosophie des Mittelalters,* XXI; two volumes (Münster, 1919, 1933), I, v, n. 1, corrected the reading, but wrongly amended

opobalsamum to *ope balsamum*. The form Abaielardus is also to be found in John of Salisbury's *Entheticus*, line 57 (in Volume Five of Giles's edition), and in his *Historia pontificalis*, ed. Reginald Lane Poole (Oxford, 1927), 17, 64; also in *Monumenta Germaniae historica*, Scriptorum Series, XX (Hanover, 1868), 522. Other alternative forms are Abagelardus, Bagelardus, Balaardus, Baelardus, Abailardus, Abaleardus, Baialardus, Baiolardus, Balalardus, Balardus, Bagardus, Baiargadus: see *Monumenta Germaniae historica*, Scriptorum Series, XI (Hanover, 1854), 261 ff.; Lodovico Antonio Muratori, *Rerum italicarum scriptores ab anno 500 ad 1500*, 28 volumes (Milan, 1723-51), V, 576; Geyer, op. cit., I, 505; Paul Ruf and Martin Grabmann, *"Ein neuaufgefundenes Bruchstück der Apologia Abaelards," Sitzungsberichte der Bayerischen Akademie der Wissenschaften, Philologisch-Historische Klasse*, Part Five (Munich, 1930), 30; Michele Amari, *Storia dei Musulmani di Sicilia*, three volumes (Florence, 1854-72), III, 62; *Monumenta Germaniae historica*, Legum Series, IV (Hanover, 1868), 319, 575. The earliest persons known to have borne the name are the jurist Bagelardus, in the first half of the eleventh century (see ibid.) and Abagelardus, the son of Count Hunfred and nephew of Robert Guiscard (*Monumenta Germaniae historica*, Scriptorum Series, XI, loc. cit.; Muratori, op. cit.). The strange form resists every attempt at explanation. A contemporary of Abelard was the Salerno astrologist Petrus Baialardus (died 1149), who is sometimes confused with him: see Francesco Novati, *L'influsso del pensiero latino sopra la civiltà italiana del medio evo*, second edition (Milan, 1899), 244. As late as the fifteenth century the first person to write on children's diseases, Paolo Bagellardi, bore the name as a family name.

[7] Abelard, *Opera*, I, 29: *Terra quippe barbara et terrae lingua mihi incognita erat* ["Verily, the land was barbaric and the language of the land unknown to me"].

[8] See Richard of Poitou's chronicle, in Martin Bouquet *et al.*, *Recueil des historiens des Gaules et de la France*, 24 volumes (Paris, 1738-1904), XII, 415. J. G. Sikes, *Peter Abailard* (Cambridge, 1932), 6, believes that we have a description of Abelard in the words *Erat enim albus quidem et decorus aspectu, sed exilis corpulentiae et staturae non sublimis* ["For he was pale, however, and of a dignified countenance, but had a thin body and was not very tall"] in the anonymous *Vita Gosvini* (on the occasion of the dispute Goswin risks with Abelard). However, it is clear from the context that the description is of Goswin and not of Abelard, since the former is compared to David and the latter with Goliath. See Bouquet, op. cit., XIV, 443, and also Abelard, *Opera* (Cousin edition), I, 43. Abelard was called "the new Goliath" by Bernard of Clairvaux himself.

⁹ Ibid., II, 801.

¹⁰ See his own description of his grief and rage when the Council of Soissons forced him to burn his book and read the Athanasian Creed aloud: ibid., I, 22.

¹¹ In his last letter to Héloïse, ibid., I, 680.

¹² Ibid., I, 27.

¹³ Ibid., I, 11, 76.

¹⁴ An echo of his love for Héloïse is supposedly found in his *Planctus*, David's lament for Jonathan: ibid., I, 338; cf. also Helen Waddell, *The Wandering Scholars* (London, 1927), 196.

¹⁵ B. Schmeidler, *"Der Briefwechsel zwischen Abälard und Heloise eine Fälschung?" Archiv für Kulturgeschichte*, XI (1914), 1-31. The main argument is the similarity in turns of phrase in their letters. Sikes rightly says that this similarity is "hardly good evidence; Héloise had been educated by Abailard, and she would naturally have wished to model her Latin on his": op. cit., 269. Schmeidler's thesis was recently launched again by Mlle Charlotte Charrier: see the note on her doctoral dissertation *"Héloïse dans l'histoire et dans la légende"* (Paris, 1933), in *Annales de l'Université de Paris*, X (1935), 68-71.

¹⁶ Abelard, *Opera*, I, 77, 90.

¹⁷ Hugh of St. Victor, *Didascalia*, in Migne, *Patrologia*, CLXXVI, 771.

¹⁸ *Over de grenzen van spel en ernst in de cultuur* (Haarlem, 1933) [*Verzamelde werken*, V, 3-25; the more elaborated form became *Homo Ludens: A Study of the Play-Element in Culture* (London, 1949)].

¹⁹ L. Tosti, *Storia di Abelardo e dei suoi tempi* (Naples, 1851) had already referred to him as a "knight of dialectic."

²⁰ Abelard, *Opera*, I, 4.

²¹ Ibid., I, 6.

²² *Magistrum Petrum dicens disputatorem non esse sed cavillatorem, et plus vices agere joculatoris quam doctoris, Vita Gosvini*, in Bouquet, op. cit., XIV, 442.

²³ Hugh of St. Victor, *Didascalia*, in Migne, *Patrologia*, CLXXVI, 773d.

²⁴ Ibid., 803.

²⁵ Abelard, *Opera*, II, 3, I, 7, 9, 19.

²⁶ Ibid., I, 5; John of Salisbury, *Metalogicon*, Book I, Chapter 3; *Policraticus*, Book V, Chapter 15.

²⁷ Hugh of St. Victor, *De vanitate mundi*, in Migne, *Patrologia*, CLXXVI, 709, cf. 773d, 774d. Professor Snouck Hurgronje tells me that all these traits of the scholastic match are also to be found in quite congruent forms in the history of Moslem theology.

²⁸ *Nil quippe voces in substantia rerum faciunt, sed tantum de eis intellectum excitant. Officium itaque earum, ad quod institutae sunt,*

significare est, hoc est intellectum constituere. . . . ["For words do not operate in the substance of things, but evoke as much as is understood by means of them. And so their task, for which they are instituted, is to signify, that is to say, to establish understanding. . . ."]: *Logica ingredientibus,* in Geyer, op. cit., I, 309, line 19. *Oportuit igitur universalia inveniri, ut facerent quod singula facere non poterant.* . . . ["And it is therefore necessary to invent universals to do what the individuals could not do. . . ."]: *Glossulae super porphyrium,* in ibid., II, 532, line 16.

[29] *Sic et non,* eds. Ernst Ludwig Theodor Henke and Georg Stephan Lindenkohl (Marburg, 1851), 14, lines 9-10.

[30] Ibid., 17.

[31] Jean Cottiaux, *"La conception de la théologie chez Abélard,"* *Revue d'histoire ecclésiastique,* XXVIII (1932), 247-95, 533-51, 788-828.

[32] Ruf and Grabmann, op. cit., 15; cf. Cottiaux, op. cit., 791, n. 5.

[33] Ibid., 254.

[34] *In epistolam ad Romanos,* in Abelard, *Opera,* II, 152, 356.

[35] *Apologia, seu confessio fidei,* in ibid., II, 722.

[36] *"Epistolae,"* in ibid., I, 235.

[37] Ibid., I, 590.

[38] Ibid., I, 298-306.

[39] Ibid., I, 104, 121, 236, 351.

[40] Etienne Gilson, *La philosophie au moyen-âge,* two volumes (Paris, 1922), I, 91, 88.

[41] Cf. the ending of the *"Metamorphosis Goliae,"* in Wright, op. cit., 29-30.

[42] Abelard, *Opera,* II, 771-86. The warning that the reader should not take the work seriously, which undoubtedly dates from after Berengar's retraction, is to be found in his letter to the bishop of Mende (ibid., II, 788): *Nolui esse patronus capitulorum objectorum Abaelardo, quia etsi sanum saperent, non sane sonabant* ["I do not want to be the patron of the chapters which object to Abelard, for although they know about sensible things, they do not sound sensible"].

[43] Ibid., II, 776. Present-day criticism is in agreement that the accusations against Abelard were exaggerated, and that Bernard's handling of the case was not above suspicion. Cf. Ruf and Grabmann, op. cit., 36 ff.; Sikes, op. cit., 231; Cottiaux, op. cit., 826 ff.

[44] Abelard, *Opera,* I, 3: *Sicut natura terrae vel generis animo levis, ita et ingenio extiti ad litterateriam disciplinam facilis* ["As I am by nature light of heart with regard to the world and the species, so I have also proved to be of a mind easily inclined toward scholarly studies"].

[45] See, e.g., ibid., I, 421, 407, 539, 623, 638, 688, 697; II, 719; *Sic et non,* 4, 6, 7, 15, etc.

BERNARD SHAW'S SAINT

I: *The Play and Its Performance*

[1] I am, of course, not thinking of Joan in *Henry VI.*

[2] February 1925.

II: *The Figure of Joan of Arc*

[1] Salomon Reinach attempts to take away the point of the answer, arguing that Joan cannot have meant such an impertinence, but he does not convince me. *"Observations sur le texte du procès de condamnation de Jeanne d'Arc,"* *Revue Historique,* CXLVIII (1925), 200-23, see p. 208.

[2] According to Catherine de la Rochelle's testimony in Jules Quicherat, *Procès de condamnation et réhabilitation de Jeanne d'Arc, dite la Pucelle,* five volumes (Paris, 1841-9), I, 295, and in Pierre Champion, *Procès de condamnation de Jeanne d'Arc,* two volumes (Paris, 1921), I, 244, Joan spoke of her two advisers as "the counselors of the spring," but the testimony is unreliable.

[3] As Shaw also mentions, Joan was definitely not a shepherdess, and stressed the fact, though she had helped to care for the livestock. But the age could not conceive of a maid from the country as anything but a shepherdess, and the onus of the characterization I leave to Dunois.

III: *The Opinion of Her Age*

[1] G. Lefèvre Pontalis, *"La panique anglaise en mai 1429,"* *Le Moyen Age,* VII (1894), 81-95.

[2] See note 3 to Part II of this essay.

[3] In between is a brief summary of a letter dated June 4.

[4] Giustiniani was anticipating events: Joan was not yet in Rouen.

[5] The *Kirchenlexikon,* V, 1707, mistakenly states that this tract has not been published. It is the seventh piece in *Tractatus consultatorii venerandi magistri Henrici de Gorychum* (Cologne, 1503); the Royal Library at The Hague possesses a copy of this rare work.

[6] Extant only in extract.

THE PROBLEM OF THE RENAISSANCE

I

[1] The history of the concept Renaissance has been studied almost exclusively by German scholars. Although I have attempted to pose the problem somewhat more broadly in this essay, mention should be made of several of the studies from which I have profited in what follows: Walter Goetz, *"Mittelalter und Renaissance,"* *Historische Zeitschrift,* XCVII (1907), 30-54; Karl Brandi, *Das Werden der Renaissance* (Göttingen, 1908); Konrad Burdach, *"Sinn and Ursprung der Worte Renaissance und Reformation"* and *"Über den Ursprung des Humanismus,"* in his *Reformation, Renaissance, Humanismus: Zwei Abhandlungen über die Grundlage moderner Bildung und Sprachkunst* (Berlin, 1918); Ernst Troeltsch, *"Renaissance und Reformation,"* *Historische Zeitschrift,* CX (1913), 519-36; Werner Weisbach, *"Renaissance als Stilbegriff: Dem Andenken Jacob Burckhardts,"* *Historische Zeitschrift,* CXX (1920), 250-80; Karl Borinski, *"Die Weltwiedergeburtsidee in den neueren Zeiten, I: Der Streit um die Renaissance und die Entstehungsgeschichte der historischen Beziehungsbegriffe Renaissance und Mittelalter,"* *Sitzungsberichte der Bayerischen Akademie der Wissenschaften, Philosophisch-Philologische und Historische Klasse,* (Munich, 1919).

[2] François Rabelais, *Gargantua et Pantagruel,* Book I, Chapter 9.

[3] Plutarch, *Les vies des hommes illustres* (Paris, 1578), fol. a iiii.

[4] Erasmus, *Adagia,* ed. Nicolas Chesneau (Paris, 1571). On Erasmus's own use of the terms *bonae literae* and *renascentia,* see my *Erasmus of Rotterdam* [(London, 1952), 103 f., 137 f.].

[5] Lorenzo Valla, *Elegantiae linguae latinae,* in his *Opera* (Basel, 1543).

[6] Just as the men of letters of the fifteenth century derived *humanista* from the classic Latin *humanitas* (in the sense of civilization), so German historians in the nineteenth century in turn abstracted "humanism" as an indication for the intellectual movement.

[7] Machiavelli, *Opere,* eleven volumes (Milan, 1805-11), X, 294 [quoted from Peter Whitehorne's translation, *The Arte of Warre,* in *Machiavelli* (London, 1905), I, 231-2].

[8] Giorgio Vasari, *Le vite de' piu eccellenti pittori, scultori e architettori,* ed. Karl Frey (Munich, 1911), I, 5 (dedication to

Duke Cosimo, 1550) [quoted from Giorgio Vasari, *The Lives of the Most Eminent Painters, Sculptors and Architects,* trans. Mrs. Jonathan Foster (London, 1800), I, 1].

[9] Vasari, op. cit., I, 216 (*"Proemio"*) [quoted from Vasari, *The Lives,* I, lviii].

[10] Ibid., I, 175-217 (*"Proemio"*); 402 (*"Vita di Cimabue"*) [quoted from Vasari, *The Lives*].

[11] Ibid., I, 168-9 (*"Proemio"*).

[12] Giovanni Boccaccio, *Decamerone,* VI, 5; Woldemar von Seidlitz, *Leonardo da Vinci: Der Wendepunkt der Renaissance,* two volumes (Berlin, 1909), I, 381; Erasmus, *Opus epistolarum,* ed. P. S. Allen *et al.;* twelve volumes (Oxford and London, 1906-58), I, 108; Ernst Heidrich, *Albrecht Dürers schriftlicher Nachlass* (Berlin, 1910), 223, 250.

[13] Pierre Bayle, *Dictionnaire historique et critique,* fifth edition; four volumes (Amsterdam, 1740), IV, 315.

[14] As is done in Borinski, op. cit., 90.

[15] Voltaire, *Œuvres complètes,* ed. Antoine-Augustin Renouard; sixty-six volumes (Paris, 1819-23), XIV, 349 [quoted from Voltaire, *An Essay on Universal History* (Dublin, 1759), II, 160].

[16] Voltaire, *Œuvres,* XIV, 355 [quoted from Voltaire, *Essay,* II, 162, 163, 166].

[17] Voltaire, *Œuvres,* XV, 99 [quoted from Voltaire, *Essay,* III, 44].

[18] Voltaire, *Œuvres,* XVII, 187 [quoted from Voltaire, *The Age of Lewis XIV* (London, 1753), I, 1].

[19] Johann Wolfgang von Goethe, *Werke,* 143 volumes (Weimar, 1887-1920), XXXII, 36 (July 22, 1787) [quoted from *Goethe's Travels in Italy,* trans. A. J. Morrison and C. Nisbet (London, 1892), 385].

[20] Goethe, *Werke,* XXXII, 207.

[21] Johann Wolfgang von Goethe, *Tagebücher,* I, 305 (October 19, 1786).

[22] Goethe, *Werke,* XXXII, 67-8 [quoted from *Goethe's Travels*].

[23] Goetz, op. cit., 46.

[24] Jules Michelet, *Histoire de France au XVI ième siècle: Renaissance* (*Histoire de France,* VII), (Paris, 1855), 14-15 (*"Introduction"*).

[25] See Goetz, op. cit., 40.

[26] After the second edition Burckhardt delegated the task of revising his book and bringing it up to date to Ludwig Geiger, and though pleased by the work's success, Burckhardt refused to be consulted about it or to correct proofs. Little by little the book changed so much in character and expanded so much in size as a result of Geiger's digressions and revisions that Burckhardt's own work could hardly be recognized in it. It has now been republished

in the original version, thus being given the stamp of the classic that is its due.

[27] Jacob Burckhardt, *Die Kultur der Renaissance in Italien: Ein Versuch*, thirteenth edition; ed. Walter Goetz (Leipzig, 1922), I, 142 [quoted from Jacob Burckhardt, *The Civilization of the Renaissance in Italy*, trans. S. G. C. Middlemore (New York, 1958), I, 143].

[28] Ibid., I, 185 [quoted from Burckhardt, *The Civilization*, I, 175].

[29] Ibid., II [quoted from Burckhardt, *The Civilization*, II, 516].

[30] Ibid., I, 142 [quoted from Burckhardt, *The Civilization*, I, 143].

[31] Emile Gebhart, *Les origines de la Renaissance en Italie* (Paris, 1879), 51.

[32] Ibid., vii.

[33] Emile Gebhart, "La Renaissance italienne et la philosophie de l'histoire," *Revue des deux mondes*, LXXII (1885), 342-79, later included in his *Etudes méridionales: La Renaissance italienne et la philosophie de l'histoire* (Paris, 1887).

[34] Michelet, op. cit., 142, 16 ff., 69.

[35] Henry Thode, *Franz von Assisi und die Anfänge der Kunst der Renaissance in Italien*, second edition (Berlin, 1904), 61.

[36] Carl Neumann, "Byzantinische Kultur und Renaissance," *Historische Zeitschrift*, XCI (1903), 215-32.

II

[1] Ernst Troeltsch, *Die Bedentung des Protestantismus für die Entstehung der modernen Welt* (Munich, 1911) [*Protestantism and Progress*, trans. W. Montgomery (London, 1912)].

[2] According to Troeltsch, in a conversation I had the privilege of having with him in April 1919.

[3] Troeltsch, too, admitted this in passing; see Troeltsch, op. cit., 7; "Renaissance und Reformation," op. cit., 534.

[4] Jacob Burckhardt, *Weltgeschichtliche Betrachtungen* (Stuttgart, 1905), 158 [quoted from Jacob Burckhardt, *Force and Freedom: Reflections on History* (New York, 1955), 134].

[5] *Inferno*, X; *Paradiso*, X.

[6] Ernst Walser, "Christentum und Antike in der Auffassung der italienischen Früh-renaissance," *Archiv für Kulturgeschichte*, XI (1913), 273-88.

[7] Psalms 103:1, 4, 5, 104:30, 51:12 (Vulgate 102, 103, 50); Ezek. 11:19, 36:25; Isa. 43:19.

[8] John 3:3; Matt. 19:28; Rev. 21:1; Rom. 6:4; Eph. 4:22; Col. 3:10; I Pet. 1:23; II Cor. 4:16; Rom. 12:2; etc.

[9] John 1:16.

[10] [Quoted from *Virgil: The Pastoral Poems*, trans. E. V. Rieu (Harmondsworth, 1949), 41.]

¹¹ *Purgatorio,* XVI, 106 [quoted from *The Divine Comedy,* translated by Laurence Binyon, in *The Portable Dante,* ed. Paolo Milano (New York, 1947), 270].

¹² Paul Wernle, *Die Renaissance des Christentums im 16. Jahrhundert* (Tübingen, 1914), 1, 38.

¹³ Erasmus, *Opus epistolarum,* II, 527 (No. 566) [quoted from *The Epistles of Erasmus from His Earliest Letters to His Fifty-First Year Arranged in Order of Time,* trans. Francis Morgan Nichols; three volumes (London, 1901-17), II, 522].

¹⁴ I am thinking of the studies of Alfons Dopsch on economic developments in the Carolingian period and of Henri Pirenne on the early forms of capitalism.

¹⁵ Several of these lines are indicated in the studies by Troeltsch mentioned above.

RENAISSANCE AND REALISM

¹ I shall here leave out of consideration the relationship of the term in this sense to the Scholastic concept "realism." For convenience's sake, when I use the words "realism" and "realistic" in the medieval sense I shall say so explicitly.

² Cf. A. de Buck, *Het typische en het individueele bij de Egyptenaren* (Leiden, 1929).

³ After Julius Wellhausen, *Muhammed in Medina, das ist Vakidi's Kitab al-Maghazi in vergürzter deutscher Wiedergabe* (Berlin, 1882).

⁴ [E. R. Edison, translator, *Egil's Saga* (Cambridge, 1930), 111.]

⁵ Cf. Max Dvořák, "*Idealismus und Naturalismus in der gotischen Skulptur und Malerei,*" *Historische Zeitschrift,* CXIX (1919), 1-62, 185-246.

⁶ Cf. on this and the following my "*Het probleem der Renaissance*" [*Verzamelde werken,* IV, 231-75; translated in this volume as "The Problem of the Renaissance"].

⁷ *Herfsttij der Middeleeuwen* (Haarlem, 1919), 418 ff. [*The Waning of the Middle Ages: A Study of the Forms of Life, Thought and Art in France and the Netherlands in the XIVth and XVth Centuries* (New York, 1954), 284 ff.]

⁸ Georges Chastellain, *Œuvres,* ed. J. B. H. C. Kervyn de Lettenhove; eight volumes (Brussels, 1863-6), VII, 219-21. [Cf. J. Huizinga, "*La physionomie morale de Philippe le Bon,*" *Verzamelde werken,* II, 222 ff.]

⁹ *Inferno,* XI, 97 ff. [quoted from *The Divine Comedy,* trans. Laurence Binyon, in *The Portable Dante,* ed. Paolo Milano (New York, 1947), 60].

[10] Thomas Aquinas, *Summa theologiae,* Part One, Question 1, Article 9.

[11] *Purgatorio,* X, 31 ff.; XII, 64 ff. On Dante cf. Wolfgang Seiferth, *"Zur Kunstlehre Dantes," Archiv für Kulturgeschichte,* XVII (1927), 194-225; XVIII (1928), 148-67.

[12] *Decamerone,* VI, 5 [quoted from Edward Hutton's translation, *The Decameron* (London, 1909), III, 121-2].

[13] Giovanni Villani, *Croniche dell' origine di Firenze,* XI, 12.

[14] Baldassare Castiglione, *Libro del cortegiano* (Venice, 1528), I, 90.

[15] In order to remove the ambiguities and inaccuracies unavoidable in translation, I shall quote the Latin: *Verum una in re haud dubie longo nos intervallo praecellunt: quod omnis eorum musica, sive quae personatur organis, sive quam voce modulantur humana, ita naturales adfectus imitatur et exprimit, ita sonus accommodatur ad rem, seu deprecantis oratio sit seu laeta, placabilis, turbida, lugubris, irata, ita rei sensum quendam melodiae forma repraesenta, ut animos auditorum mirum in modum adficiat, penetrat, incendat:* Thomas Morus, *Utopia,* eds. Victor Michels and Theobald Ziegler (Berlin, 1895), 110. [The English is quoted from Raphe Robynson's translation *The Utopia of Sir Thomas More,* ed. J. H. Lupton (Oxford, 1895), 295-6.]

[16] Joannes Manlius, *Locorum communium collectanea . . . , tum ex lectionibus D. Philippi Melanchthonis tum ex aliorum doctissimorum virorum relationibus excerpta* (Basel, 1562), 212.

[17] Ernst Heidrich, *Dürers schriftlicher Nachlass* (Berlin, 1910), 270, 273, 277, 281, 282.

[18] This continues to be true even when the cult becomes worldly instead of transcendental.

[19] Bernard Palissy, *Œuvres complètes,* ed. Paul-Antoine Cap (Paris, 1844).

[20] Cf. Thomas Clifford Allbutt in *Proceedings of the British Academy,* VI (1913-14), and see O. Auriac, *"Bernard Palissy et la science positive," La grande revue,* CXXVII (1928), 113-32.

[21] Cf. Werner Sombart, *"Die Technik im Zeitalter des Frühkapitalismus," Archiv für Sozialwissenschaft und Sozialpolitik,* XXXIV (1912), 721-60, see 726.

[22] Dürer delighted in a similar immediate naturalism in designing a triumphal column for the repression of the Peasants' Revolt, and a tombstone for a drunkard (the sketches, "made as a joke," are to be found among his works). The pedestal of Victoria is surrounded by livestock, and the column is built up out of all kinds of agricultural equipment. But what was satire for Dürer became a life-aim for Palissy.

[23] *Orlando furioso,* XIV, 104 [quoted from John Harington's translation (London, 1591), XIV, 92 ff.].

²⁴ *Don Quixote,* I, 6 [quoted from Thomas Shelton's translation, *The History of Don Quixote of the Mancha* (London, 1896), I, 60-1].
²⁵ *Œuvres complètes de François Rabelais,* ed. Abel Lefranc; four volumes (Paris, 1912-22), I, l.
²⁶ Gustave Lanson, *Histoire de la littérature française,* fourteenth edition (Paris, 1918), 258 ff.
²⁷ Max Scheler, *Die Wissensformen und die Gesellschaft: Probleme einer Soziologie des Wissens,* I (Leipzig, 1926), 109, 117.

IN COMMEMORATION OF ERASMUS

¹ [Desiderius Erasmus, *Opus epistolarum,* ed. Percy Stafford Allen; twelve volumes (Oxford, 1906-58), II, 61 (No. 327). Quoted from trans. Francis Morgan Nicholas, *The Epistles of Erasmus from His Earliest Letters to His Fifty-first Year Arranged in Order of Time;* three volumes (London, 1901-17), II, 195 (No. 320). The words "very green" have been added for the *vernatissimis* of the original Latin.]
² [Erasmus, *Opus epistolarum,* VII, 7 (No. 1804).]
³ [Quoted from Desiderius Erasmus, *The Praise of Folie,* trans. Sir Thomas Chaloner (reprinted London, 1901), 22.]
⁴ [Erasmus, *Opus epistolarum,* II, 586 (No. 586).]
⁵ [Ibid., IV, 337 (No. 1139).]
⁶ [Ibid., I, 19 (No. 1).]
⁷ [Quoted from Desiderius Erasmus, *The Colloquies or Familiar Discourses* (London, 1671), 103.]
⁸ [Ibid., 319.]
⁹ [Ibid., 536.]
¹⁰ [Erasmus, *The Praise of Folie,* 27.]
¹¹ [Ibid., 49-50.]
¹² [Erasmus, *Colloquies,* 400.]

GROTIUS AND HIS TIME

¹ Grotius, *Epistolae* (Amsterdam, 1687), Nos. 1168, 1742.
² Ibid., Appendix, No. 496.
³ Ibid., Nos. 474, 610, 530.
⁴ Ibid., Appendix, No. 610.
⁵ See K. Krogh Tonning, *Hugo Grotius und die religiösen*

Bewegungen im Protestantismus seiner Zeit (Cologne, 1904); H. C.
Rogge, *"Hugo de Groot's denkbeelden over de hereeniging der
kerken," Teyler's Theologisch Tijdschrift,* II (1904).

⁶ Grotius, *Epistolae,* Appendix, No. 496.
⁷ Ibid., No. 62 (p. 21). He is, of course, referring to the
Protestant Church in France.
⁸ Ibid., No. 966 (p. 434).
⁹ Ibid., No. 1074.
¹⁰ Ibid., Appendix, No. 382.
¹¹ Ibid., Appendix, No. 530.
¹² Caspar Brandt and Adriaan van Cattenburgh, *Historie van het
leven des heeren Huig de Groot* (Dordrecht, 1727), Part One, 447;
Part Two, 59.
¹³ Robert Fruin, *Verspreide geschriften,* IV, 91.
¹⁴ Grotius, *Epistolae,* No. 1168; Appendix, Nos. 573, 133.
¹⁵ Ibid., Appendix, No. 474 (December 3, 1639).

INDEX

371

Library of Congress Cataloging in Publication Data

Huizinga, Johan, 1872-1945.
  Men and ideas.

  Translated from texts in Verzamelde werken (1948-53)
  Reprint. Originally published: New York: Meridian
Books, 1959.
  Includes index.
  1. History--Addresses, essays, lectures. I. Title.
D7.H8213 1984   909   84-42546
ISBN 0-691-05422-3
ISBN 0-691-00802-7 (pbk.)